Sovereign of the Market

American Beginnings, 1500–1900
A Series Edited by Edward Gray, Stephen Mihm, and Mark Peterson
Also in the series:

National Duties: Custom Houses and the Making of the American State
by Gautham Rao

Liberty Power: Antislavery Third Parties and the Transformation of American Politics
by Corey M. Brooks

The Making of Tocqueville's America: Law and Association in the Early United States
by Kevin Butterfield

Planters, Merchants, and Slaves: Plantation Societies in British America, 1650–1820
by Trevor Burnard

Riotous Flesh: Women, Physiology, and the Solitary Vice in Nineteenth-Century America
by April R. Haynes

Holy Nation: The Transatlantic Quaker Ministry in an Age of Revolution
by Sarah Crabtree

A Hercules in the Cradle: War, Money, and the American State, 1783–1867
by Max M. Edling

Frontier Seaport: Detroit's Transformation into an Atlantic Entrepôt
by Catherine Cangany

Beyond Redemption: Race, Violence, and the American South after the Civil War
by Carole Emberton

The Republic Afloat: Law, Honor, and Citizenship in Maritime America
by Matthew Taylor Raffety

Conceived in Doubt: Religion and Politics in the New American Nation
by Amanda Porterfield

Sovereign of the Market

The Money Question in Early America

JEFFREY SKLANSKY

The University of Chicago Press
Chicago and London

The University of Chicago Press, Chicago 60637
The University of Chicago Press, Ltd., London

Published 2017
Printed in the United States of America

26 25 24 23 22 21 20 19 18 17   1 2 3 4 5

ISBN-13: 978-0-226-48033-6 (cloth)
ISBN-13: 978-0-226-48047-3 (e-book)
DOI: 10.7208/chicago/9780226480473.001.0001

Library of Congress Cataloging-in-Publication Data

Names: Sklansky, Jeffrey, author.
Title: Sovereign of the market : the money question in early America / Jeffrey Sklansky.
Other titles: American beginnings, 1500–1900.
Description: Chicago ; London : The University of Chicago Press, 2017. | Series: American beginnings, 1500–1900
Identifiers: LCCN 2017000465 | ISBN 9780226480336 (cloth : alk. paper) | ISBN 9780226480473 (e-book)
Subjects: LCSH: Money—United States. | Currency question—United States. | Banks and banking—United States.
Classification: LCC HG501 .S553 2017 | DDC 332.4/9730903—dc23
LC record available at https://lccn.loc.gov/2017000465

♾ This paper meets the requirements of ANSI/NISO Z39.48–1992 (Permanence of Paper).

For Helen

Contents

Introduction

The Elusive Sovereign

In 1621, a new kind of fictional memoir appeared in London, recounting the travels of an English coin. Its author was a Thames River ferry boat driver named John Taylor, a prolific essayist and poet who styled himself a plebeian counterpart to the celebrated seafaring explorers of his day. The adventure and fortune described in accounts like Sir Richard Hawkins's *Voyage into the South Sea* (1622) took darker shape in Taylor's long poem, *A Shilling; or, The Trauailes of Twelue-Pence*, the first of hundreds of imaginary autobiographies of traveling coins and commodities published in seventeenth- and eighteenth-century England. Like Taylor himself and other itinerant watermen, the narrator of his story is "tossed too and fro" among people of "all degrees and trades," "shifting of Masters, more often then the Serveants do." The "world's greatest traveler" is increasingly wanted everywhere, but like the growing numbers of the wandering poor, it is nowhere at rest. Presiding over the dispossession of rural laborers and the enclosure of common lands, the coin laments:

> I am of that great power, and high command,
> In joyning house to house, and land to land:
> That where one hath a dwelling to abide,
> One hundred knowes not where their heads to hide:
> And as one may three hundred Tenants have,
> Five hundred knowes not where to have a grave.[1]

Like the famous cover of Thomas Hobbes's *Leviathan* (1651), Taylor's frontispiece depicts a new kind of ruler, an "artificial person" created by a social contract (figure I.1). But in place of the multitude of subjects that make up the body politic of Hobbes's giant monarch, the little king on the shilling is torn between two competing claimants, a fur-gowned moneylender and a set of tools of manual labor. The silver sovereign rides a snail toward the laborer's shovel, flail, and oar while a falcon's wings pull it in the opposite direction toward the lender's staff and money-bag. Taylor explains:

> Which Emblem truly to the world implies,
> That Money to the Mizers Coffers flies.
> Whilst unto those that paines and labour take,
> It doth a creeping, sleeping dull pace make.

As the coin confides, "If I did serve a poore man but one day, I five yeare (for it) with the rich would stay."[2]

This book is about the long class struggle over the rise of money as not only the means of payment, but also the means of rule. The conflict over currency that Taylor prefigured began in England in the early 1620s, crossed the Atlantic with the founding of the Massachusetts Bay Colony later that decade, and critically shaped American class relations until the first decades of the twentieth century. Through a series of intellectual biographies, this book explores why the creation and organization of money became a searing political question for early Americans, ranging far beyond market relations, and how the terms and poles of public debate were transformed over the course of capitalist development.

Taylor's *Shilling* appeared at a decisive moment of economic depression and political unrest. A steep decline in the European market for English textiles triggered a devastating wave of unemployment and poverty beginning in 1620, prompting the king's advisors in the Privy Council to warn two years later of the consequences when manufacturers "dismiss their workfolks, who, being many in number and most of them of the poorer sort, are in such cases likely by their clamours to disturb the quiet and government of those parts wherein they live." In 1625, the philosopher and jurist Francis Bacon likewise observed that if "poverty and broken estate in the better sort be joined with a want and necessity in the mean people, the danger is imminent and great: for the rebellions of the belly are the worst," advising policy makers "to remove, by all means possible, that material cause of sedition of which we spake, which is, want and poverty in the estate: to which purpose serveth the opening and well-balancing of trade; the cherishing of manufactures; the banishing of idleness." While the causes of the imbalance of foreign trade and the depression of domestic industry were hotly debated, one essential means of restoring prosperity was widely agreed on: England's expanding commercial economy demanded more money. The crisis of the 1620s sparked the rise

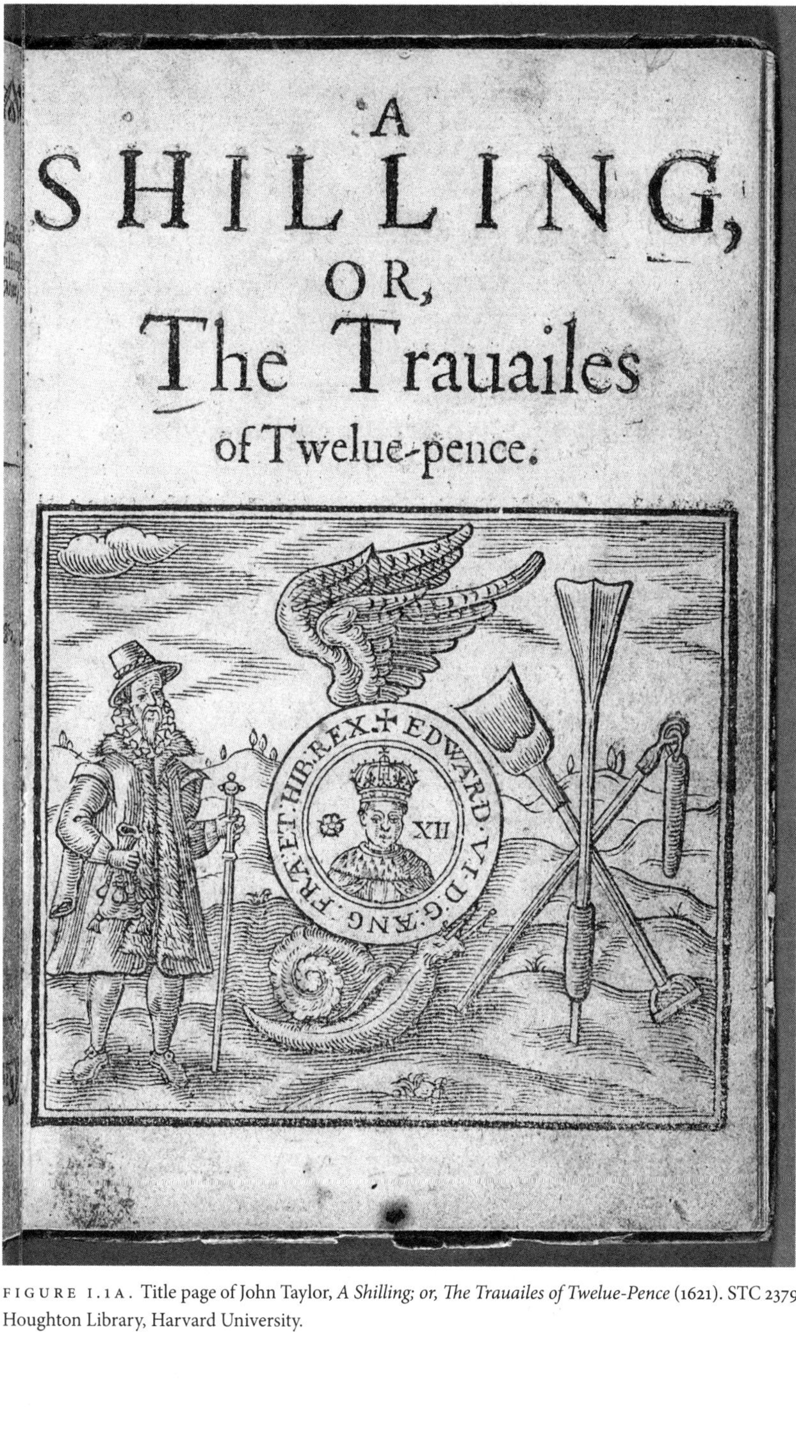

A
SHILLING,
OR,
The Trauailes
of Twelue-pence.

FIGURE 1.1A. Title page of John Taylor, *A Shilling; or, The Trauailes of Twelue-Pence* (1621). STC 23793. Houghton Library, Harvard University.

FIGURE I.1B. Title page of Thomas Hobbes, *Leviathan; or, The Matter, Forme, and Power of a Commonwealth Ecclesiastical and Civil*, engraving by Abraham Bosse (London: Andrew Crooke, 1651). Photo courtesy of the Newberry Library, Ruggles 171.

of a new discourse that came to be called "political economy," centered on the monetary means of exchange as key instruments of governance in an emerging market society. The controversy spawned a culture of currency extending from the elite circles of the Privy Council and Francis Bacon down to popular writers like John Taylor.[3]

More than a century later, Adam Smith disparaged the "mercantile system" of his preclassical predecessors as the narrow dogma of monarchs, misers, and merchants premised on the commonplace notion "that wealth consists in money, or in gold and silver."[4] But earlier writers on political economy had not strived to stockpile precious metal as treasure. They had aimed to *mobilize* it as currency, envisioning the growth of market exchange as the motor of modern agriculture and industry, and seeking a freely flowing money supply as its fuel. "Money is like muck, not good except it be spread," as Bacon wrote in 1625, with farmers as much as merchants in mind. The physiologist William Harvey's 1628 treatise on the circulatory system of the human body informed what became the dominant metaphor for money as the lifeblood of the body politic, or, as Hobbes wrote in *Leviathan*, "the Sanguification of the Common-wealth," "Nourishing (as it passeth) every part thereof." Inspired by Bacon, Harvey, Hobbes, and the Prussian educational and agricultural reformer Samuel Hartlib, who moved to England in 1628, new monetary theories arose at the center of the seventeenth-century revolution in English politics, science, and religion. Fundamental debates about the nature, form, and function of money remained inseparably bound up with wide-ranging disputes about value and power long after Adam Smith, as we will see.[5]

Nor were early modern conceptions of money restricted to gold and silver specie. Rising demands for means of payment spurred experiments with new kinds of paper IOUs that could circulate from hand to hand without being limited by the supply of the precious metals. Long-distance merchants had developed "bills of exchange" as a means of paying debts in one country with credits in another, avoiding the need to ship coins along with goods. Over the course of the seventeenth century, these personal bills became widely used for domestic commerce in England as well. More critically, common-law courts came to treat such "inland bills" as freely transferable by endorsement from one merchant to another. Detached from the original transactions in which they arose, the bills circulated as a general means of payment in commercial circles. At the same time, merchants and landlords increasingly deposited their coins with London goldsmiths in exchange for promissory notes that became transferable by endorsement much like bills of exchange. More importantly, goldsmiths became borrowers rather than merely custodians of the cash deposited with them, in a development that marked the emergence of the business of banking in England, as in Holland and Italy earlier. They gained the right to lend their funds out at interest, not by transferring the actual coins from their vaults, but by issuing so-called cash notes or crediting customers' accounts, redeemable in coin on demand. By lending more in paper than they kept on hand in coin, these nascent bankers were not simply conveying funds from savers to borrowers or substituting paper for precious metal. They were actually creating an expanding currency of circulating notes and drafts on deposits backed by fractional specie reserves, taking on what had long been an exclusive prerogative of the sovereign. The government itself came to depend on the services of financial intermediaries for the means of borrowing from bondholders and paying public servants and suppliers, establishing the Bank of England for this purpose in 1694.[6]

It is often presumed that paper money took the place of "hard money" based on the value of gold, silver, or some other material commodity. In fact, however, paper money and the hard metallic standard arose together, as twin offspring of the union of bank and state. Even as English authorities sponsored the rise of commercial banking, they implemented a related series of reforms designed to tether the money supply more tightly to the market value of the bullion on which it was legally based. They introduced milled-edged coins to prevent clipping, rescinded prohibitions on exports of precious metals to subject the coinage to world markets, abolished minting taxes and fees for converting bullion into coin, decreed a fixed legal ratio between the monetary standards of silver and gold, and called in and reminted the entire English coinage in order to match its metallic content to its face value.[7] The high and relatively stable exchange value of gold and silver was supposed to secure the growing volume of circulating debts, guaranteeing the claims of creditors on both the government and the market economy.

Like the mercantile system of which it was part, however, the financial revolution did not strictly serve the interests of the central state and its wealthy creditors. It rather formed a new terrain of social struggle over the coin of the realm.[8] The innovations in English banking prompted divergent developments across the Atlantic in Massachusetts Bay, where the 1690s witnessed the creation of the first government-issued paper currency outside of the Chinese empire. Controlled by elected assemblies instead of commercial bankers, the "bills of credit" authorized by Massachusetts and by other British American colonies in the following decades made money a means of self-rule. Initially introduced as a temporary expedient to pay soldiers and suppliers, the bills soon became the main form of colonial currency. They were redeemable not in exchange for specie on demand but in payment of taxes, and they were often designated legal tender for the payment of private debts.

The radical experiment set off a sixty-year war of pamphlets and periodicals, pitting big Atlantic merchants and their colonial agents, who favored the British system for domestic as well as transatlantic commerce, against inland farmers and traders demanding local control of the means of local exchange. As Michael Warner has written, the spread of printers and presses in the early eighteenth century made possible the wide circulation of both paper money and publications, calling into being the new kind of public sphere embodied in provincial legislatures that coalesced around the currency issue. Popular politics emerged with what Americans came to call the "money question," conceived as a constitutional question of self-government.[9]

What should serve as the standard of value and the means of payment, who should control its creation and circulation, and according to what principles?[10] For more than two hundred years, the money question shaped American political thought. "In no other country in the history of the world has the subject of money and banking given rise to such long-sustained, deep-rooted, widespread, acrimonious, publicly debated and eagerly reported controversy as in America," writes the Welsh economist Glyn Davies.[11] This book explores why the mode of producing money became the subject of prolonged social conflict, how the stakes of struggle changed from the late seventeenth to the early twentieth century, and why the money question eventually moved from the center to the margins of American political discourse, like the "labor question" with which it rose and fell.

At its heart, the money question concerned the nature of the peculiar power that governed the expanding domain of market relations. Its early exponents identified that elusive sovereign with the new forms of currency and credit invested in commercial and agricultural enterprise, which they called "capital."[12] In eighteenth-century England, merchants, moneylenders, tax collectors, and the demands of wealthy households for gold and silver plate soaked up most of the contracted supply of coin, leaving laboring people with little access to the means of paying rising taxes, prices, and rents.[13] "What one notices about it first of all is the importance of money," E. P. Thompson writes of the period, when large profits stemmed from financial speculation and from cornering agricultural staples such as grains and meat, and when repeated riots and other extralegal resistance arose in response to the artificial scarcity of food and money. In Boston as in London, class figured less as a preexisting collectivity than as a set of formative campaigns, battles over new forms of exploitation that drew new lines of social solidarity prior to the rise of a large propertyless workforce. In the American colonies, however, the broader distribution of land and representation in provincial legislatures enabled family farmers and artisans to ally with middling traders and aspiring gentry in laying claim to the legal machinery for authorizing and issuing money itself. While the marketplace rather than the workplace became the main arena of labor struggle in preindustrial England, the money question formed the crucible of class conflict in early America.[14]

The British Parliament constrained colonial legislatures' authority to issue paper money in the 1750s and 1760s, but rising American resistance to taxation without representation was linked to popular opposition to the tyranny of creditors who controlled the silver currency in which taxes had to be paid.[15] In the aftermath of the Revolution, struggling farmers defended their lands and livelihoods in the face of foreclosure and debtors' prison, demanding paper currency and legal-tender laws. The U.S. Constitution prohibited state governments from emitting money or "mak[ing] any thing but gold and silver coin a tender in payment of debts," while leaving the federal government's authority to create paper currency subject to judicial debate for nearly a century. Yet even as the new nation came to follow the British model of commercial banking and the specie standard, movements of farmers and workers long continued to challenge monopoly control over currency and credit.[16] "In England the triumph of Ricardo's monied class was complete or nearly so," writes John Kenneth Galbraith. "In the United States, however, it was subject to the sharpest of challenges. In one form or another, this challenge was to dominate American politics for the first century and a half of the Republic."[17]

Amid a chronic shortage of coin in the early republic, primary responsibility for the money supply fell to hundreds of state-chartered banks. The banks issued thousands of varieties of notes, creating a hodgepodge of competing currencies loosely regulated by the First and Second Banks of the United States, which were successively chartered by Congress. In the second main phase of the money question, the "bank war" of the 1820s and 1830s shaped the advent of modern political parties and class politics. The currency conflict fostered a nascent labor movement in the seaboard cities in reaction to the skyrocketing prices of basic necessities, while a national commercial and financial elite arose in defense of the national bank. The defeat of the Second Bank of the United States left the nation without a central monetary authority until the Civil War. Then the cash-strapped federal government created the first national paper currency of Treasury notes or "greenbacks" along with the National Banking System, which issued its own notes, while a prohibitive federal tax drove the state banknotes out of circulation. In the final phase of the money question, southern and western farmers mounted the largest movement in American history for a popularly controlled currency backed by the prodigious output of farms and factories. Responding to the challenge, business leaders and bankers mobilized on behalf of the international gold standard and a currency system tied to the new corporate structure of industry and investment, leading to the establishment of the Federal Reserve and the eclipse of monetary theory and policy as central subjects of popular politics. The management of the nation's money supply became thereafter the more or less exclusive province of professional economists and bankers, commonly regarded as "a highly technocratic, mostly apolitical form of government intervention in the economy," as Paul Krugman has written.[18]

This book comprises three parts, respectively devoted to the conflicts over these distinctive monetary regimes. While previous scholars have produced separate literatures on these pivotal periods in the life of the money question, the purpose of my work is to trace its trajectory across the long epoch that historians have charted as the transition to capitalism in America. By following the issue from its origins in an agrarian economy in which money served most households largely as a means of buying land and imported goods, paying taxes, and settling accounts, to an industrial economy in which money became the main reward of work and means of wealth, to a corporate economy in which money formed the primary basis of property and savings and the general measure of progress and prosperity, I aim to explain the centrality of the extended struggle over the constitution of modern money to capitalist development.[19]

Earlier social historians typically treated money as a sign rather than a source of the transformation of class relations, which were supposed to be determined by the mode of producing wealth, not the means of exchanging it. Much recent work defines itself against this conventional distinction between a "real economy" of goods and services and a superstructure of monetary claims and credits. Amid the proliferation of financial instruments and institutions and the transfer of profits and power from manufacturing to banking since the 1970s, finance has become the dominant form of capital in the pages of history as well as on the front page. Promoting the English financial revolution to a foundational role comparable to that of the Industrial Revolution in the preceding generation of scholarship, pathbreaking studies contend that "capitalism is founded on the social mechanism whereby private debts are 'monetized' in the banking system," or on the invention of "a new repertoire of material value, a particular kind of currency" produced for private profit in early modern England.[20] Sweeping surveys of world economic history find the financial roots of modern capitalism much earlier, in the medieval union of monarchs and merchants or the ancient bond between debt and servitude.[21] The history of American capitalism has likewise taken a financial turn, indicated in the capacious titles of recent studies—*Republic of Debtors*, *Debtor Nation*, *A Nation of Counterfeiters*, *A Nation of Deadbeats*, *One Nation under Debt*—and in a wave of revisionist scholarship on the "financialization of American slavery."[22]

While the new history of finance has illuminated other axes of power and resistance—between empires and colonies, merchants and planters, bankers and counterfeiters, speculators and gamblers—it has tended to eclipse class struggles between wealthy elites and common people.[23] Recent scholars have found older models of class conflict, broadly shaped by Marxist theory, incapable of comprehending not only the financialization of the past few decades, but the origins of modern money in the seventeenth and eighteenth centuries. To a large extent, Karl Marx shared with Adam Smith and other classical economic writers a conjectural history of the emergence of modern money as an outgrowth of the inexorable progress of the division of labor and the expansion of commerce rather than the result of a revolution in government and banking. Because the perceived inadequacies of that master narrative of monetary development have called into question the explanatory power of the "class concept" itself, it is worth pausing to consider the limits of the traditional teleology.[24]

The first step in the classical genealogy of money and markets was the transition from the direct barter of goods to the circulation of commodities mediated by a "money commodity," most commonly gold or silver, for which all others exchanged. Money was purportedly born in the market as a representative of the exchange value that commodities derived from the labor power required for their production, which rendered them "qualitatively equal and quantitatively comparable," as Marx wrote.[25] But the growth of commerce eventually elevated money from a means of exchange among those who produced commodities into an independent power over the producers.[26] The alienation of labor from the exchange value of its products reached its apotheosis with the rise of world trade, ushering in the second stage in the imagined evolution of the market economy: the dual "transformation of money into capital" and of labor power into a commodity itself.[27] Money metamorphosed into capital when it became the ends rather than the means of market relations, as the exchange value embodied in money added to itself the "surplus value" that came from commodifying the very basis of value in "objectified human labour."[28] The ultimate expression of the autonomy of capital was the movement from "real money" based on a material commodity to "credit money," the purest symbol of abstract exchange value. Together, the ascendance of paid labor and paper money marked the coming-of-age of capitalist relations, the climax of the bildungsroman begun in barter.[29]

This canonical account of the proletarianization of labor and the financialization of money has been profoundly challenged by a range of new work. On the one hand, historians have discredited the presumption that the coming of capitalism signaled the demise of age-old forms of bound labor and the rise of a propertyless and legally free working class compelled solely by the demands of the job market and the wage contract. Scholars have demonstrated instead the broad panoply of labor relations that flourished under capitalist dictates, variously combining elements of extra-economic compulsion and contractual freedom, from unpaid housework to debt peonage and chattel slavery.[30] On the other hand, historians have joined anthropologists and sociologists in finding modern monetary relations to be as divergent as the forms of capitalist labor. Objective, quantitative calculations of pecuniary value appear enduringly entwined with subjective, qualitative assessments of moral, spiritual, and social values conveyed along with money and merchandise in market transactions.[31] "Commerce does not homogenize," as one historian has written. "The infamous cash nexus is not impersonal or anonymous in most of its manifestations."[32] The deeper problem with the stock story of the genesis of money from barter to bills, however, lay in its mystification of the original and ongoing basis of money in class power—the authority of ruling classes to exact tributes, tolls, and taxes and determine the means of discharging those debts.[33] In attributing the emergence of modern money to the development of markets and trade, and in treating money as a reflection of the exchange value of commodities determined by their social relations of production, the narrative of commercialization slighted the social relations of production of money itself and the class relations they constituted.[34]

This book builds on recent work that considers money as a creature of law and culture as much as commerce, but it highlights more basically the ways in which the monetary order was the outcome of protracted class conflict. As eighteenth- and nineteenth-century Americans across the political spectrum insisted, recurrent battles over bills and banks manifested an underlying struggle between cash-poor households and moneyed men, between producers and patricians, indeed between "labor" and "capital" as those terms were commonly used. The pervasive class rhetoric reflected the recognition that the mode of issuing money played a central part in determining the structural positions within which people increasingly depended on buying and selling, lending and borrowing, and earning and saving. Long after most Americans became accustomed to being paid for their labors and paying for their subsistence, they persisted in treating the mode and means of payment as an urgent political question rather than a foregone conclusion. And long after the monetary system came to be generally accepted except in times of crisis, it was shaped by the intense contest from which it had emerged.

Like labor struggles, conflicts over currency and credit were experienced on multiple levels, from the country store and the county courthouse to Westminster and Washington, and from diaries and account books to sermons, political tracts, and economic treatises. For the subjects of a recent history of common laborers in the early republic, "class struggle was trying to meet the rent and scavenging for firewood to stay warm during winter," and something similar might be said of many Americans for whom the most pressing question about money was how they could get it, not how it was created to begin with.[35] Yet much as popular protests against food prices were not merely "rebellions of the belly," as Francis Bacon suggested in the seventeenth century, currency campaigns were not simply spurred by the desire for more money, or what the twentieth-century economist Joseph Schumpeter derisively called "the servant girl's economics."[36] Early Americans could not take for granted what money was and where it came from, for many things served as money, and money meant many things. Before it became an established form of property and wealth with a settled set of functions as a measure, medium, and store of value, money appeared as a complex, often confounding social relationship, and the terms of that relationship were as sharply contested as the kind and quantity of the money supply. As much as it was a sought-after resource, money was also a fiercely fought-over ideal, like "the market" as a model of social relations more broadly. The class struggle over the production and distribution of the means of payment amounted to more than a clash of "economic interests" as we understand them in monetary terms today. It was a conflict over the conception of those monetary terms themselves. With that in mind, this book approaches its topic from the perspective of intellectual history, examining early Americans' conflicting efforts to make tangible the intangible, personal the impersonal, and visible the invisible hand that ruled the growing market realm.[37]

Each of the book's three parts takes as its thematic focus a multifaceted problem of political and economic power with which the money question came to be identified, each delineating a different dimension of the emergence of the market economy as an ostensibly self-regulating system. The book thus considers the money question in turn as a question of *circulation* raised by the advent of paper money in the colonial era, a question of *representation* related to the development of commercial banking between the Revolution and the Civil War, and a question of *association* tied to the rise of big business in the late nineteenth century. More concretely, each part consists of intellectual biographies of two influential monetary reformers who took up opposite sides of the issue and jointly defined the changing parameters of public discourse in successive eras: the Puritan minister John Wise and the Boston physician William Douglass; the Jacksonian journalist William

Leggett and the central banker Nicholas Biddle; and the agrarian organizer Charles Macune and the financial adviser Charles Conant. A small group of key figures cannot stand in for a whole society, and the money question surely looked different in other places and times than colonial New England, the antebellum Middle Atlantic, and the upcountry South and metropolitan Northeast in the Gilded Age and Progressive Era. The views of most Americans were not directly informed by the works of my main subjects. But these select writers and reformers expressed with extraordinary force, clarity, and scope what was ideologically at stake in the money question for many of their contemporaries. By following their eclectic careers, the paired essays in each part of the book pursue the connections between the money question and other aspects of early American culture including natural law and natural history, melodramatic literature and neoclassical architecture, and Christian fellowship and fiduciary trust.

Part I explores the religious and scientific roots of popular political economy in debates over the rise of paper money in colonial New England. What united the two sides of the currency question was as important as what divided them in staking out a new terrain of class struggle. Both sides supported the growth of the market economy, guided by a strong state. Both sides favored the expansion of the British Empire, coupled with the increasing power and wealth of the American colonies. What fundamentally divided them was the question of who should control the means of market exchange that both sides regarded as the new means of rule.

Chapter 1 focuses on the life and work of the Congregational minister John Wise, the most forceful proponent of paper money in his day, and an eloquent advocate for his community of family farmers and shopkeepers in Ipswich, Massachusetts. The son of an indentured servant, Wise first gained renown for leading a tax revolt in the 1680s, inspiring grassroots resistance to a major effort to concentrate power and property in the hands of the Crown and its courtiers at the expense of communities like Ipswich. He next led the opposition to a movement to consolidate authority over the Congregational churches of Massachusetts in regional councils of eminent clergymen, which likewise threatened to take power over the central political and social institution in the province away from local congregations. By the time he took up the cause of paper money in the 1720s, Wise had developed a contentious political theory in support of the autonomy of communities of smallholders. He introduced into American discourse the theory of natural law, drawn from elite European sources, which took on a newly egalitarian character in his popular polemics. Bringing the ideal of a higher law than that of kings and clerics to bear on the money question, Wise called for townships and provincial assemblies to create their own currency as a free public resource instead of a costly commodity, supporting local farms and crafts instead of moneylenders and import-export merchants.

Wise's communitarian conception of the natural laws of trade met its keenest opponent in the Boston physician William Douglass, the "oracle of the anti-paper party," whose closely related ideas about medicine, natural history, and money form the subject of chapter 2.[38] A member of the network of Scottish expatriates who played key roles in administering the British colonies, Douglass similarly came to the currency question at the end of a controversial career in other arenas, passionately identified with the colonial aspirations of large landowners and merchant capitalists. He made his reputation as the leading opponent of smallpox inoculation and folk medicine provided by ministers, midwives, and unlicensed healers. But he made his fortune by lending money and speculating in real estate, while becoming a noted naturalist and political polemicist in the 1730s and 1740s. The keynotes of his work were his linked theories of contagion, classification, and credit, in which Douglass strived to establish the authority of cosmopolitan elites such as university-trained physicians and transatlantic traders over freehold farmers and provincial pastors. From his understanding of the human "œconomy of spirits" and the broader "œconomy of nature," he drew the contours of his critique of paper money. Escalating issues of colonial currency, he argued, substituted an artificial medium contrived by indigent and insolvent debtors for the natural silver specie of responsible merchants and creditors. For Douglass as for Wise, the battle for control of the currency had more to do with class power than with prices or profits. Both sides sought to marshal the combined power of the state and the market on behalf of their competing class visions of economic development.

Rising prices incited the second awakening of the money question in the Jacksonian era, and falling profits framed the climactic crusade over the gold standard in the aptly named Gilded Age, but class power remained the underlying issue throughout. Born with the new nation, commercial banks took charge of the expanding money supply that fueled the agricultural and industrial development of the early nineteenth century. By the bank war of the 1820s and 1830s, paper money meant banknotes redeemable in gold or silver coin instead of public bills of credit spent into circulation or loaned out at low interest by elected legislatures.

Democratic resistance to the "money power" found its strongest voice among urban artisans and journeymen protesting the soaring cost of food and fuel and the depreciating currency in which they were paid, which they attributed to feverish financial speculation. Chapter 3 considers the work of the New York City newspaper editor William Leggett, the intellectual leader of the local labor movement and most fervent critic of the new banking system. Shaped by Leggett's previous career as an author of poetry, short stories, and literary criticism, his philosophy of "plaindealing" was steeped in the logic of melodrama, calling for faithful representation in business and government as in art and literature. His celebrated editorials portrayed an epic struggle between honest industry and fraudulent finance, railing against the alliance of government with state-chartered corporations that commandeered the infrastructure of market exchange, most importantly the banks that monopolized the money supply. In demanding the "separation of Bank and State," Leggett exalted an opposing ideal of a truly free market that his colonial predecessors would hardly have recognized, but that influenced his successors in the fight for democratic finance.

The nation's chief banker, Nicholas Biddle, was equally attuned to the question of representation at the core of the bank war. Like Leggett, the powerful president of the Bank of the United States turned to literary and artistic sources for models of monetary representation, as chapter 4 shows. As editor of the preeminent literary journal and a prominent literary nationalist, as an elegant essayist and travel writer, and especially as the foremost authority and sponsor of the Greek Revival in American architecture, he fostered a culture of beauty that literally changed the face of finance. By making the pillared portico of the Greek temple the blueprint for banks across the country, Biddle bolstered bankers' new role as financial sovereigns of a commercial republic, presiding over the market economy like ancient statesmen and sages. The neoclassical form was more than a facade. In his policies as bank president and in his widely followed speeches, reports, and letters to editors and congressional leaders, Biddle promoted the very autonomy of the "money power" that critics like Leggett assailed. He directed the national bank's twenty-five branches from New York to New Orleans to embrace their authority as independent guardians, answerable neither to elected officials nor to business owners, regulating economic activity with Olympian disinterest and devotion. Though Biddle's bank fell victim to Jacksonian opposition, his vision of central bankers' right to rule reemerged in the third act of the money question at the turn of the twentieth century.

As the nation's biggest business corporation and the largest agency of the federal government before the Civil War, the national bank was a harbinger of the dual rise of corporate capitalism and the nation-state in the postbellum era. The renewed partnership of private profit and public authority proved as controversial as the royal marriage of mercantilism and monarchy had been. Once again, the struggle centered on a conflict of currencies. In the late nineteenth as in the early eighteenth century, both sides lay claim to the state as the agent of their opposing agendas. Much as the promoters of colonial bills of credit had fought the purveyors of British sterling, the battles of the 1860s and 1870s pitted "producing-class" partisans of the greenbacks against creditor-class investors in National Banking System notes. In the 1890s, "free silver" Populists contended against "sound money" supporters of the gold standard, as farmers and financiers sought to make money the raw material for rival associations of cooperative labor and corporate capital.

Chapter 5 concerns the principal economic theorist of the agrarian movement, Charles Macune, who organized the most systematic alternative to the banking system since the colonial era. The roots of Macune's challenge to "the power of money to oppress" lay in his experience as a newspaper editor and physician in the Texas hill country, where he witnessed the rise of a system of debt peonage for white yeoman farmers and black sharecroppers that replaced slavery as the basis for cotton cultivation. The chapter follows his intellectual development through a series of frustrated efforts to combat the dependence of upcountry farmers on the scarce cash and credit supplied by local merchants and eastern investors. Beginning as a booster of laissez-faire and white supremacy, Macune emerged from the class war in Texas in the mid-1880s with a broader perspective. As leader of the Farmers' Alliance, he directed an unprecedented campaign to organize all farmers—landowners and tenants, white and black, northern and southern—into large-scale marketing and credit cooperatives designed to end their reliance on merchants and lenders. The commercial failure of cooperation prompted him to take a more radical turn, calling for the transformation not just of agriculture, but of the whole industrial order, and the creation not only of new modes of marketing, but of a new national system of currency and credit controlled by the "producers" themselves. Macune's "subtreasury plan" was defeated along with his vision of a fellowship of finance, but the demands for easier access to cash and publicly provided, low-interest loans resulted in major reforms in the Progressive Era.

Big capitalists no less than small cultivators sought to combine in order to control the mass markets they required to maintain profits in the age of mass production. They too came to regard reform of currency and banking as the basis of their audacious class agenda. Among the most influential architects of the new national and international monetary order was the financial journalist Charles Conant, a scion of the Boston Brahmin class that William Douglass had helped to bring into being, and the subject of chapter 6. Much as Douglass had expounded the ideology of the British empire of credit and commerce in the eighteenth-century Atlantic, united by silver,

Conant championed a new American empire of industry and investment in the Caribbean and across the Pacific, united by a colonial adaptation of the international gold standard that he designed. Much like Macune's program of popular finance, Conant's dedication to financial imperialism arose from his understanding of the novel challenges of "overproduction" and surplus savings facing wealthy investors in the late nineteenth century. As the most important American theorist of capitalist crisis, he came to see the inelasticity of the nation's money supply and the barriers to foreign investment in silver-standard countries as critical causes of industrial depression. More basic than his espousal of monetary reform, however, was Conant's call for the emancipation of capital from both popular politics and particular enterprises through the management of savings and investment by professional bankers and trust fund managers. He and like-minded custodians of capital transformed the centuries-old legal tradition of trusteeship into a fiduciary model of class and colonial relations, identifying the pursuit of profit with the public interest. In counterpoint to the agrarian agenda for democratizing finance, Conant contended for the means of production of money to be operated by a financial ruling class acting as trustees for a society of beneficiaries.

After the Federal Reserve Act of 1913 and amid the decline of agrarian radicalism in the early twentieth century, the political structure of money and banking became increasingly off-limits to public debate. Popular demands came to focus on more enlightened management and broader access to financial resources rather than democratic control over them. If we can no longer imagine our lives without the money and credit that banks control, however, we might still learn from those who could. As the literary theorist Raymond Williams has written, "Everywhere in the nineteenth century we see men running for cover from the consequences of their own beliefs. In our own century, they do not even have to run; the temporary covers have become solid settlements."[39] The value of reconsidering such long-running struggles lies in reopening the vital questions they raised about the lasting social order they brought into being. History often recalls the competing answers on offer at particular moments more clearly than the shared questions that divided early Americans across the whole period when the basic structure of market society was still unsettled. But while their responses were inevitably limited by their historical circumstances, the deeper questions they posed about the sovereignty of the market remain as relevant as ever.

PART ONE

Paper Money and the Problem of Circulation in the Colonial Era

1

John Wise and the Natural Law of Commerce

In September 1687, six men from Ipswich, Massachusetts, were summoned before the royal governor and his council in Boston to face charges of sedition. The previous month, they had led their town in refusing to pay a property tax imposed without the consent of their representatives in the colonial assembly, which royal officials had recently dissolved. Other towns in coastal Essex County had soon followed the lead of the Ipswich "insurrectioners." According to the indictment, the defendants had conspired to convince other colonists "that they were not oblidged to obey or observe the Laws or Acts made by his said Excellency Sir Edmund Andros," who had been appointed by King James II to impose royal rule on the recalcitrant colonies of New England. Yet in defying the governor's edicts, the town had professed its loyalty to a higher body of English law, "the laws of the land, by which it is enacted that no taxes shall be levied on the subjects without the consent of an assembly, chosen by the freeholders for assessing of the same." Among the accused, the leading advocate of this appeal was a Puritan pastor named John Wise (1652–1725) whom the council singled out for censure, noting that he had "excite[d] and stirr[ed] up the people" by insisting that the tax warrant was "not legall, and to obey and comply with the same were to lose the liberty of freeborne English men."[1]

Convicted of "high misdemeanors," the young minister and his co-conspirators were sentenced to twenty-one days in jail, fined, barred from public office, and, in Wise's case, temporarily prohibited from preaching. Yet after the overthrow of James II less than two years later, it was Governor Andros who was ousted from office, arrested, indicted by a colonial council, and sent back to England for trial. In the wake of what the victors dubbed the Glorious Revolution, Wise returned to Boston as one of two representatives from Ipswich who helped to reorganize the Massachusetts legislature in May 1689, inaugurating an era of closer coordination between New England's provincial leaders and metropolitan authorities in England.[2]

In the first two decades of the eighteenth century, Wise brought his expansive vision of the rule of law to the defense of local self-government in the New England churches, rallying the popular opposition to efforts by some of his fellow clerics to transfer authority from individual congregations to ecclesiastical councils or associations. His two acclaimed books on the "churches quarrel" constructed a capacious framework for congregational as well as colonial autonomy based on the early modern theory of natural law, earning his reputation among subsequent scholars as the most powerful polemicist in the colonies.[3] Wise's most pathbreaking contribution, however, came several years later in the 1720s, when he brought the legal perspective that he had developed in the context of conflicts over the traditional authority of monarchs and ministers to bear on a new set of struggles over the rising power of merchants and moneylenders. In one of the first American works on political economy, he applied the general model of scientific "laws of motion" formulated in Isaac Newton's *Principia* in 1687, the year of Wise's trial for sedition, to the accelerating movements of currency, credit, and commodities in the British Atlantic.[4] In this and several other essays at the end of his career, he became the most eloquent early exponent of the colonies' pioneering experiment with paper money.

The closely linked controversies in which Wise engaged concerned the three main dimensions of a transatlantic revolution in political, religious, and commercial affairs. The Glorious Revolution formed the foundry of capitalist empire as well as of Wise's career. It marked the decisive defeat of royal absolutism in England and the ascendance of a parliamentary coalition of commercial gentry, Puritan clergy, and colonial merchants and planters that had first come together in founding the Massachusetts Bay Company in the late 1620s, on the eve of the English Civil War, and that emerged triumphant with the ouster of James II and the arrival of William and Mary on the throne.[5] In the late 1680s, New England formed the western frontier of the reformed empire, the front lines of its aggressive pursuit of military conquest, settler colonialism, and commercial expansion.[6] But having led the earlier resistance to royal rule, Massachusetts was also where the new union of Crown and capital met its sharpest challenge in Wise's lifetime.[7] His popular polemics reveal how an understanding of natural law born of the battles over civil and church polity set the stakes of struggle over governance of the emerging market society. Much as that jurisprudential ideal inspired the Puritan slogan, "fighting the king to defend the King," it enabled early critics like Wise to oppose the rising rule of moneyed men and transatlantic traders in the name of the natural law of currency and commerce.[8]

The scarcity of money posed a formative political challenge throughout mainland British America. Britain banned the export of English coin to its colonies and prohibited them from establishing their own mints, aside from an abortive effort in mid-seventeenth-century Massachusetts. The value of colonial imports from England persistently exceeded that of what the colonies sent home in return, especially in New England. So the money that the colonies accrued from trading with the West Indies and Europe tended to flow back across the Atlantic instead of remaining in America. They drew most of their bullion and specie from Spanish America, aided by colonial laws conferring an artificially high "proclamation value" on Spanish coins. But British authorities increasingly restricted commerce with the Spanish colonies and outlawed the overvaluing of Spanish specie. Wampum, acquired through trade with native peoples, served as currency in some colonies, while others designated local commodities such as tobacco as legal tender in place of precious metal. But the most important innovation by far was colonial legislatures' emission of paper currency, which circulated as a general means of exchange for ordinary transactions for the first time in the Western world. By the mid-eighteenth century, every British colony in continental North America had created its own paper money. But the practice arose first, most enduringly, and most controversially in New England.[9]

A reconsideration of Wise's work as a pastor and political theorist, tracing his path through the tax revolt and the churches' quarrel before culminating in the currency crusade, can illuminate the ways in which the rise of the money question manifested a profound conflict over the spiritual and social ends as well as the financial means of market relations. The first struggle over paper money in colonial America did not pit liberal, cosmopolitan exponents of widening market development and financial innovation against backward-looking, provincial defenders of traditional, communal norms. To the contrary, both proponents and opponents of colonial paper money avidly embraced the growth of commerce and the creation of a new kind of partnership between finance and statecraft, predicated on a shared understanding of the circulation of money and goods as the basis of prosperity and progress. What separated the two sides were their opposing visions of who should control the media of market transactions, in whose interests, and according to what rules, founded on conflicting conceptions of the natural laws of currency and trade, based in turn on rival notions of natural law more generally. To understand the far-reaching cultural resonance of the money question in early America, we must carefully consider the broader set of issues that framed it.

"A Good God and a Good King": The Common Law of the English Empire

The town seal of Ipswich proclaims, "The Birthplace of American Independence, 1687." It commemorates the insurrection of Wise and his compatriots as the opening act of the American Revolution completed a century later, rather than the climax of the English Revolution begun sixty years earlier. So too, Wise's polemics on church government, republished at the beginning of the Revolutionary War and again at the start of the American Civil War, inspired subsequent hagiographies of him as the "first great American democrat," connecting the creation of the Puritan commonwealth to the founding of the new republic.[10] His late work on the natural and beneficent laws of market relations has lent itself to a related narrative of the development of classical political economy, crystallized in Adam Smith's *Wealth of Nations* in 1776, the same year as the Declaration of Independence.[11] Perry Miller calls him "the first American Populist," the founding figure in the literary tradition that exalts "the farmer, the agrarian, the 'native' American" as opposed to "the miseries of artificial Europe."[12] Wise thus occupies a pivotal place in a common creation myth in which democratic politics and liberal economics are twinborn of the long Anglo-American resistance to taxation without representation.[13]

This dual genealogy is aptly called "Whiggish" for its association with the English Whig party that arose in the 1680s, with which Wise has been rightly identified.[14] But it casts Wise and his town in a chronicle of the ideological origins of independence, for colonists, Christians, and commercial farmers and traders alike, that they scarcely would have recognized. His was an ideal not of individual or collective independence, but of integration into a closely knit constitutional empire, congregational church, and commercial commonwealth. It was a vision of autonomy for the new imperial, ecclesiastical, and economic order as a whole, conceived as a self-regulating system. Wise applied the corporate concept of natural law, which had long served to sanction the caste and class hierarchies of medieval Europe, to the flux and fluidity of the British Atlantic. He imagined the laws of motion of modern market society, picturing how sovereignty itself might no longer emanate from a central authority, but rather circulate along with money, merchandise, and migrants. Neither a democrat, a populist, nor an economic individualist, he envisioned a political, religious, and economic empire in which power was broadly diffused among colonies, congregations, and communities of credit, governed by a higher law that protected the people from the dual dangers of despotism and antinomian individualism.

Wise was a product of the great migration of the early seventeenth century, when English people took to the road and the sea in unprecedented numbers seeking land and livelihood.[15] Most who crossed the Atlantic came to America as unfree laborers like his father, Joseph Wise, an indentured servant for a physician in the town of Roxbury named George Alcock who had arrived in the founding company of migrants to Massachusetts Bay in 1630.[16] Alcock would have heard or read John Winthrop's famous address to the first fleet, propounding the difference between the harsh "Law of Nature" and the merciful "Law of Grace" that was to govern charitable relations between rich and poor, which provided a point of departure for Wise's later work on the natural laws of money and trade.[17] Evidently Alcock heeded Winthrop's words, as the Roxbury church recorded that he "left a good savor behind him, the poor of the church much bewailing his loss" when he died in 1640.[18] To Wise's father, he bequeathed freedom from the remainder of his bond of service along with a "young heifer" and possibly a plot of land. The elder Wise apparently set up shop as a butcher and malt miller and married a minister's daughter from a neighboring town, with whom he raised ten or more children. The fifth of these was John Wise, born in the summer of 1652.

Wise was educated at the Roxbury Free School and the Roxbury church. At the latter, his teacher was the famed Puritan preacher and "apostle to the Indians," John Eliot, from whom he likely gained his zeal for religious crusade and imperial conquest. Eliot was the author of a utopian tract, *The Christian Commonwealth* (1659), calling for the civil polity to be based on the model of elected government given by God to the Hebrew people—a work banned by the colony for its radical republicanism in the years before the Glorious Revolution, and perhaps a model for Wise's own writings on self-government in church and state.[19] At seventeen, Wise entered Harvard in preparation for the ministry, where his father paid the tuition partly in malt from his mill. Apparently the first son of an indentured servant to attend the college, Wise retained a scornful sense of his social distance from more privileged members of the colonial clergy. Later in life, he associated their higher status with the scarcity of currency to pay for college before the advent of paper money in the 1690s, as well as with subsequent efforts by Cotton Mather and other members of the Bay Colony's clerical elite to elevate the ministry above the laity formally and institutionally.[20]

With his comparatively limited means, Wise participated in what historians have described as a "rural Enlightenment," through which metropolitan literature and learning came to circulate widely in the colonial countryside. Long-distance networks of trade and print created the conditions for a kind of transatlantic intellectual exchange deeply rooted in remote, place-bound communities.[21] Second-generation Congregational pastors like Wise experienced and articulated such "cosmopolitan rootedness" most acutely. While their calling remained anchored in their local congregations, they found themselves increasingly compelled to move several times in search of a permanent pulpit and to secure their support with written contracts.[22] Their clerical careers depended on a combination of regional mobility and communal stability that shaped Wise's evolving views of the empire, the church, and the market economy.

While Wise's intellectual allegiances spanned the Atlantic and the Mediterranean, he traveled in a provincial orbit that also framed his understanding of circulation. After graduating from Harvard in 1673, he was called to minister to a new congregation on Long Island Sound in Branford, Connecticut, where he preached for nearly four years in a primitive meetinghouse. He served as an army chaplain in King Philip's War, as part of a disastrous expedition against the Narragansetts, then briefly took an appointment in Hatfield, Massachusetts, a town largely destroyed in the war. These sobering experiences informed his later writings on money as the means of military preparedness, the lack of which had left the early colonies vulnerable to attack.[23] In 1680 he moved a third time, accepting a call from Chebacco Parish (now Essex, Massachusetts) on the southern outskirts of Ipswich.

Like his first two pulpits, the newly gathered congregation on the Chebacco River was the product of the pervasive contention dividing New England parishes, having just broken off from its parent church in Ipswich.[24] Wise took from these internecine struggles a political outlook that stayed with him through the tax revolt, the churches' quarrel, and the currency campaign. Like those later conflicts, the Chebacco schism actually stemmed from a desire for deeper participation in the Congregational church, as the spread of settlement made it increasingly difficult for outliers to attend services five or six miles from their homes. When authorities in Ipswich refused to permit them to form their own congregation, Chebacco residents recorded that "some women, without the knowledge of their husbands, and with the advice of some men, went to other towns, and got help, and raised the house, that we intended for a meeting-house, if we could get liberty." In a rehearsal for the resistance to the Andros regime several years later, three women and two men were arrested, tried, and convicted for contempt before being allowed to go forward in founding the church. Wise presided over the dedication of the plain oak-framed meetinghouse that they had clandestinely built. Roughly forty families provided their new pastor with a starting salary of sixty pounds per year—twenty pounds in money and forty pounds in corn, malt, and pork—along with wood, hay, a parsonage house and barn, and ten acres of farmland near the river. It was enough to afford a modest but comfortable living for Wise, his new wife, and their growing family, with relatively little reliance on cash.[25]

Chebacco had been settled by the children of the founding generation in Ipswich, whom a contemporary observer described as "men of good ranke and quality, many of them having the yearly revenue of large lands in England before they came to this wildernesse."[26] Wise's second- and third-generation parishioners were mainly middling sorts, the better-off living in two-story clapboard houses with steep roofs and glass windows, others in simple log cabins. Few owned land, livestock, or other property worth more than a hundred pounds, and few acquired much more over the course of their lives. Their gardens grew corn, rye, and vegetables for home consumption. The surrounding marshlands were devoted to pasturing cows, hogs, and horses for local use as well, allowing time for most residents to practice a trade such as milling, tanning, smithing, or carpentry in addition to stock-raising. The only significant commercial produce from Chebacco was a surplus of hay and sheep sold to neighboring communities. The population of the parish nearly doubled while Wise was there, prospering for much of the period as part of a growing regional economy centered on Boston and the staple-growing bottomlands of the Connecticut River valley. He and his neighbors depended increasingly on the provincial paper currency issued exclusively for the domestic market, while they engaged only peripherally in transatlantic trade on the basis of specie.[27]

In August 1683, the Chebacco church was formally organized and Wise ordained as its pastor, tying his fortunes to those of the community he would serve for more than forty years. Less than a year later, those fortunes were jeopardized when the Court of the King's Bench in England declared the original charter of Massachusetts Bay invalid, calling into question the legal basis of every township, church, and property title the colony had authorized. The ruling was part of a sweeping effort to centralize authority in the Crown and its courtiers on both sides of the Atlantic, including vacating the corporate charters of dozens of towns and counties in England and regranting huge tracts of land in the colonies to royal retainers. In New England, a haven for the Crown's fiercest critics since the English Civil War, James II ordered the revocation of all nonroyal property rights and the enforcement of long-dormant land grants to loyalists of the Stuart monarchy, claims that encompassed every town lot, farm, and pasture in Ipswich and far beyond. Abolishing elected assemblies and townships, royal officials conglomerated the colonies of New England, New York, and East and West Jersey into a single new Dominion of New England, the name itself indicating that they were now the king's property rather than semiautonomous provinces.[28]

At stake in the colonial struggle of the 1680s was not American independence, but two rival visions of an increasingly integrated English empire, both predicated on the extension of English law. They were closely related to what Elizabeth Mensch calls the competing "voluntarist" and "hierarchical" conceptions of property rights in the British American colonies, based on "title by occupancy versus title by grant from the crown."[29] On the one hand, the Crown pursued its goal of consolidating power through the courts, suing the colonies and municipalities under writs of *quo warranto* ("by what warrant"), which challenged their authority as extralegal outposts that had violated the terms of their charters (or whose charters were illegitimate in the first place) and forfeited their right to self-rule. Along these lines, royal magistrates sought to bring the colonial courts, which had long served as pillars of Puritan communalism and informal, lay resolution of disputes in Massachusetts, into much closer conformity with the formal writs, pleas, and procedures of English common law, removing the appointment of judges and juries from local control.[30] At the same time, monarchist designs depended on developing the king's independent sources of revenue to fund imperial wars without relying on Parliament, particularly tariffs and customs duties and nonparliamentary taxes on property and consumption.[31] Doing so put the Crown increasingly at odds with commercial gentry and colonial merchants (as well as Puritans opposed to centralization in the church or the state), especially in New England. In Massachusetts, repeated violations of the Navigation Acts regulating transatlantic trade prompted the annulment of the colony's charter in 1684, and grassroots resistance to taxation without representation provoked the prosecution of Wise and his townsmen three years later.[32]

On the other hand, the rising American resistance to Stuart absolutism staked its own claim on the growth of the imperial state and its colonial apparatus. Ironically, the tax that sparked the Essex County uprising in 1687 had been levied originally by the colonial assembly, the Massachusetts General Court. But anticipating the dissolution of the charter, the legislature had repealed its previous taxes as of 1684. When Governor Andros reinstated the country rate of a penny per pound on all real and personal property in 1687, small farmers protested what they deemed the overvaluing of livestock, which burdened regionally oriented stock-raising communities like Ipswich more than staple-growing regions serving overseas markets.[33] But the legal justification for disobeying the decree lay in the constitutional principle that taxes could not be imposed without the "common consent" of those taxed, or rather of their representatives. Enshrined in the Magna Carta in 1215 and reaffirmed in the Petition of Right passed by Parliament in 1628, that basic precept of English common law had inspired the establishment of an elected assembly for Massachusetts in the first place, in the wake of an earlier controversy over taxation without representation.[34] The provincial opposition to royal rule was predicated on the claim that the protections of English law extended fully to its colonial subjects.

Wise invoked that fundamental principle in a celebrated speech calling for resistance to Andros's edict in August 1687, telling his townsmen, "we had a good God, and a good King, and should do well to stand to our Priviledges." Such faith in a higher law both secular and sacred formed the refrain of his account of the subsequent trial of the Ipswich six, written on behalf of the town. "Note the evidence in the case as to the substance of it, was that we too boldly endeavoured to perswade our selves we were English men, and under priviledges," Wise wrote shortly after the overthrow of Andros. He decried the violation of the defendants' common-law rights of due process and *habeas corpus*, and their conviction by a rigged jury of "Strangers and Forreigners, gathered up (as we suppose) to serve the present turn." The defense rested, as he recalled, on "the Magna Charta of England, and the Statute Laws that secure the subjects' properties and estates, &c. To which was replied by one of the judges, the rest by silence assenting, that we must not think the laws of England follow us to the ends of the earth, or whither we went. And the same person . . . declared in open Council upon examination of said Wise, Mr. Wise you have no more priviledges left you than not to be sold for slaves, and no man in Council contradicted."[35] The specter of slavery was more than metaphorical for the son of an indentured servant living in a region with a small but growing population of African slaves, particularly when related rulings by royal courts threatened to turn dispossessed settlers into tenants if not serfs, obliged to pay quasi-feudal quitrents to absentee aristocrats, as occurred in the Middle Atlantic and Chesapeake colonies.[36] Hence Wise's urgent insistence that the fundamental "laws of the land" did indeed follow English subjects across the sea, even when their rulers tried to leave those laws behind.

The rule of law that Wise espoused in the tax revolt was no less committed to the expansion of the empire and the strengthening of the state than the ultraroyal absolutism of his opponents. The liberties he claimed for the colonists were distinctive privileges of English freemen such as due process and the consent of the governed, collectively rather than individually exercised through the agency of formal legislative, judicial, and administrative institutions: the township, the assembly, the militia, the county court, the jury of one's peers. Such liberties were founded on the seventeenth- and eighteenth-century construction of what Mary Sarah Bilder calls "the transatlantic constitution," which united colonial and metropolitan authorities in shared obeisance to the common law.[37] Indeed, the language of Wise and his neighbors' protest marked a broader departure from the general disregard for the forms and procedures of English jurisprudence among the founding generation of Puritan settlers, in favor of an emphatic embrace of English law along with English empire as the foundation for colonial liberties after the 1680s.[38] In the common-law confederation that he envisioned, and in the Whig version of empire that emerged victorious in the Glorious Revolution, greater Britain (including English America) joined with greater Germany (including the Netherlands) in an escalating Protestant struggle against Catholicism and absolutism at home and abroad.[39]

As New England formed the western front of King William's War against the French empire under Louis XIV, Wise enlisted in the crusade of "black coats and redcoats."[40] He was chosen as one of three chaplains for the second ill-fated military campaign of his career, joining twenty-five hundred soldiers and sailors in an unsuccessful assault on Quebec, the capital of New France, in the late summer and fall of 1690. In a sign of his new renown, he wrote a narrative of the expedition for Increase Mather, the leading clergyman and de facto leader of New England after the fall of Andros, when Mather was in London negotiating a new charter for Massachusetts.[41] Wise's account embraced the fighting spirit and impassioned devotion to a collective endeavor that he found in the army while decrying the "cowardice" of its commander, echoing his earlier indictment of Andros and his council for betraying the laws of the land. He derided in particular the commander's abdication of authority and inability to mobilize the troops under his faltering command. "Saith he I cannot rule them," Wise reported. "Whilst we were with God in the way of duty God was with us. But when we desert[ed] our dutie and business we were sent about by God and our countrey[;] God follow[ed] us with crosses and confusion," he wrote, anticipating his later observations of the chaos that ensued when leaders failed to uphold the higher laws of the Congregational church and the market economy.[42]

Despite its failure on the battlefield, the expedition inaugurated a new era in colonial politics, in which Wise took a leading part. For it was to pay restive troops returning home empty-handed from Quebec that Massachusetts issued the first government-issued paper currency in the Western world, £40,000 in short-term "bills of credit" backed by the province's promise to accept them in payment of future taxes. Larger, longer-term emissions of such bills soon followed in Massachusetts and elsewhere in British America, in a colonial counterpart to the English financial revolution of the 1690s, creating an alternative monetary system governed by provincial assemblies instead of metropolitan bankers.[43] In eighteenth-century New England, struggles over taxation and representation became bound up for the first time with contests for control of the currency in which taxes had to be paid. But the understanding of law that defined the terms of debate was most rigorously developed in contemporary conflicts within the Puritan church, with Wise once again at the center of the struggle.

"The Whole Soul Is in the Whole Body": The Divine Law of the Congregational Church

Five years after the Ipswich revolt, Essex County was rocked by another set of trials, convened by a special court in the town of Salem in 1692. Among those convicted of witchcraft were two former members of Wise's church in Chebacco, a tavern-keeper and his wife named John and Elizabeth Proctor.[44] As in the earlier trial for sedition, the defendants' purported actions were less significant than the disloyalty they demonstrated in their supposed subversion of lawful authority and allegiance to Satan instead. Yet in rising to the defense, Wise once again invoked a higher law that the court rather than the convicts betrayed.

Along with thirteen other ministers, Wise signed a preface to Increase Mather's rigorous critique, calling the prosecution's reliance on "spectral evidence"—eyewitness accounts of crimes committed by apparitions of the accused—"bold usurpations upon [the] spotless soveraignty" of the Almighty.[45] A separate petition on the Proctors' behalf signed by Wise and thirty-one of his congregants explained that God "sometimes may permit Sathan to personate dissemble and thereby abuse innocents and such as in the fear of God defie the Devill and all his works." Much as the Salem court sought to protect the Puritans' godly community against its wayward members, the Chebacco church's appeal decried individuals' susceptibility to deceit and subversion, which could taint the testimony of the victims of witchcraft no less than that of its alleged perpetrators. "What God may have left them to we cannot go into [for] Gods pavilions [are] cloathed with cloudes of darkness round about," Wise and his parishioners wrote, resting their call for clemency on the strength of communal institutions and norms. "His breading hath been amongst us and was of religious parents in our place[,]" the petition said of John Proctor, "and by reason of relations and properties within our towne [he] hath had constant intercourse with us." It concluded, "we never had the least knowledge of such a nefarious wickedness in our said neighbours since they have been within our acquaintance. . . . As to what we have ever seen or heard of them upon our consciences we judge them innocent of the crime objected."[46] Disregarding the petition, the court convicted both defendants of witchcraft. John Proctor was hanged, while Elizabeth Proctor was eventually granted a reprieve by the governor. But Wise and his congregants' defense of the accused signaled an abiding allegiance to a higher law, transcending the vagaries of individual conscience as well as the arbitrary authority of civil and ecclesiastical elites.

The witch trials reflected a crisis of authority in the Congregational church and the New England township between the downfall of the Andros regime and the granting of a new charter for Massachusetts in 1691.[47] In linking the weakness of individuals to the danger of despotism, the Chebacco petition expressed a common conception of the crisis and of the broader basis of lawful authority it jeopardized. That popular understanding received its fullest formulation in Wise's widely followed writings on the churches' quarrel, a conflict over clerical authority that began to emerge almost as soon as the new charter was sealed. As the literary scholar Vernon Parrington observed nearly a century ago, "What [Jonathan] Edwards did later for the doctrinal side of Congregationalism, John Wise did for the institutional. His exposition of the Congregational principle was so luminous and convincing that it soon became authoritative."[48]

Modern, progressive claims on the legacy of the New England Puritans have been deeply impressed by the spiritual individualism of Jonathan Edwards and his intellectual descendants, especially Ralph Waldo Emerson and William James, with their iconoclastic insistence on the priority of personal faith over institutional practice. Wise's work, however, reveals a profound Puritan commitment to law and government as well as grace, inhering in neither individual parishioners nor pastors, but in the cohesive congregations for which their church was named. "Arminian" popery went hand in hand with "antinomian" anarchy for Wise, threatening the autonomy of the congregation from above and below. As property supplanted piety as the basis of political rights, and as paper currency took the place of common land as the basis of commonwealth, Wise's congregational ideal shaped an enduring model of the fundamental laws that governed the market economy as well as the church and the state.

To see how the churches' quarrel formed the crucible of Wise's leading part in the emergence of the currency question, we will review, first, the extraordinary autonomy of the local congregation in the early generations of Puritan New England, manifested particularly in congregational control over membership in the "gathered church" as well as suffrage in town and colonial politics. Second, we will turn to the challenges to that communal authority arising by the late seventeenth century both within Congregationalism and from outside its ranks, seen in demands for easier access to the privileges of church membership and greater political rights for non-Congregationalists. Third, we will see how the controversy over the collective power of the congregation came to a head in a set of fiercely fought proposals for transferring authority over major decisions to regional ecclesiastical associations dominated by leading ministers. Fourth, we will examine Wise's pivotal defense of the congregational ideal, as opposed to both greater liberty for individual parishioners and greater authority for the clergy, in an argument based first on the English common law as theorized by contemporary jurists led by Edward Coke and then on the more universal concept of "natural law" theorized by the German philosopher Samuel Pufendorf. Finally, we will consider how the vision of natural law that Wise drew from the ecclesiastical struggle propelled his advocacy of paper money in the final years of his career.

For most of the seventeenth century, the church and the civil polity in Massachusetts were largely coextensive, and both were tightly controlled by the membership of local congregations. To vote in elections for town selectmen and representatives to the General Court, you had to be a member of the Congregational church. To become a member of the church, you had to be examined by the congregation and testify to your personal conversion, your experience of grace—a high bar to entry, jealously guarded by the membership, and the basis of the "gathered church" of "visible saints," with its rigorous discipline of members' behavior and religiosity by lay leaders and pastors. Both the test of grace and the bond between church membership and political rights provoked rising calls for greater inclusiveness and less restrictive policing of members' lives. In practice, such demands for liberalization meant more leeway for individual members, but also, surprising as it may seem, more power for ministers and magistrates, bolstering both individual license and clerical authority at the expense of the collective autonomy of the congregation and its elected elders.[49]

Outside the Puritan church, a growing minority of non-Congregationalists, particularly Anglicans, pressed for the franchise and political power, aided between the Restoration and the Glorious Revolution by the Crown. In 1664, the General Court loosened the qualifications for suffrage to include all persons "orthodox in religion and not vicious in their lives," provided that non-Congregationalists possessed a minimum of taxable property. In 1691, the new charter entirely abolished ecclesiastical qualifications for voting, granted freedom of worship to all Protestants including Presbyterians and Anglicans, and replaced the church restriction with a property requirement for all voters. At the same time, reforms granting greater "toleration" for non-Congregationalists went along with fragmentary efforts to introduce the episcopal polity and practices of the Church of England in Massachusetts—swearing oaths as a means of consecrating contracts, recognizing only Anglican marriages, making saints' days official holidays, flying flags bearing the Cross of Saint George—even as royalists cracked down on nonconformist preachers and printers in England. For Congregationalists like Wise who came of age politically in the struggle of the 1680s, religious liberalism was closely associated with royalism, representing a twofold challenge to the power of the congregation over church and state.[50]

Inside the Congregational church, meanwhile, a similarly double-edged movement toward both easier access to membership and heightened authority of clergy threatened the self-governing capacity of the congregation. A growing number of second-generation New England Puritans chafed at the requirement of professing their experience of grace. Their demands for inclusion resulted in what orthodox opponents dubbed the "Halfway Covenant" of 1662, allowing the children of dutiful but "unregenerate" parishioners to be baptized into church fellowship, though not admitted to "full communion" and voting rights. In the frontier parish of Northampton, Massachusetts, the Reverend Solomon Stoddard and his followers dispensed entirely with the test of grace. They granted full communion and membership to anyone who subscribed to the congregation's covenant and agreed to abide by its precepts, setting a precedent soon followed by others, including the elite founders of the Brattle Street Church in Cambridge, Massachusetts, in the shadow of Harvard. These deeply contested movements away from the close regulatory authority and godly discipline of the early church arose along with a series of reforms augmenting the power of clergy. Leading ministers increasingly emphasized their distinctive educational and professional training, by contrast to the conversion experiences of lay congregants, as sanction for rising clerical authority. They moved to transfer the basis of ordination from election by local congregations, as in Chebacco, to a "laying-on of hands" by other ministers, as in the Brattle Street Church. They claimed the authority to deliver sacraments in so-called bereaved churches lacking permanent pastors, based on their membership in the clerical guild rather than their selection by congregants. They declined to call elections for lay elders, who traditionally shared church governance and discipline of members with ministers.[51]

Most importantly, beginning in 1690 and continuing for the next two decades, prominent Puritan ministers formed clerical associations or synods seeking to take charge of the examination and appointment of pastors and of key decisions regarding membership, liturgy, and practice. In 1704–5, leaders of this "presbyterian" faction drafted a set of proposals calling for the establishment of ministerial associations on a firmer footing. More controversially, they also sought to create "standing councils" of ministers and lay leaders that would issue binding decisions on contentious questions arising in particular congregations, with ministers exercising the decisive voice. The bitter quarrel surrounding these proposals—rejected in principle if not practice in Massachusetts, Rhode Island, and New Hampshire, but legally enacted in Connecticut's "Saybrook Platform" of 1708—brought Wise to the forefront of grassroots resistance once again. The conflict formed the context in which he authored his foundational works, *The Churches Quarrel Espoused* (1710) and *A Vindication of the Government of New-England Churches* (1717).[52] We turn now to examine Wise's critical contributions to the ecclesiastical controversy, in which he embraced English common law and then universal natural law as the basis of the congregation's collective authority, in adamant opposition to the Proposals of 1705.

Cotton Mather, Increase Mather's son, once noted of Ipswich, "Here was a renowned church, consisting mostly of such illuminated Christians, that their pastors, in the exercise of their ministry, might, in the language of Jerome, perceive that they had not disciples so much as judges."[53] Unlike his father, Cotton Mather was a leading proponent of the "presbyterian" proposals. But his reference to Wise's parishioners as "judges" reflected the shared jurisprudential framework of the conflict, in which both sides based their positions on an elaborate analogy between the laws of the Congregational church and those of the English empire. "That Government which sensibly Clogs tyranny, and Preserves the Subject free from Slavery . . . is the only Government in the *State* to advance mens temporal Happiness," and so too "such a Constitution in Church Government is also the only way to advance grace and mans Eternal Happiness," Wise wrote, much as his boyhood teacher John Eliot had based his *Christian Commonwealth* on the shared principles of ecclesiastical and civil government. Dedicating his work to the fraternity or "honourable brethren" of the New England churches, Wise recalled his earlier "Service of my Country" and its "Sacred Liberties," urging his lay readers likewise to "Stand in the Defence of, and Maintain your *Church Liberties*." He resolved "That you will put such an Estimation and value on your Church Liberties as the English do on their Civil," lest the laity come to be ruled as in other countries "with a Hook in their Nose (like wild Cattle in a string) by the mercy and pleasure of their Drivers," with no more share in their government "than the Horses in the Royal Stables."[54] But unlike earlier New England divines who had distanced themselves from the corruption of English government and the Anglican Church, Wise coupled his exposition of the Congregational way to an effusive identification with the reformed empire born of the 1680s. He professed his fealty to "our wise and Protestant Princess," Queen Anne, praying "that she may live to see all the *Protestant Churches* thro' her vast Empire, more vertuous and more united."[55] The means of resisting clerical tyranny in the era of William and Mary lay not in separation from English decadence and despotism, but in closer identification of the congregation with the legal structures of the reformed English empire.

Much as Wise had predicated his opposition to royal absolutism on a strident identification with the rights of English subjects dating from the Magna Carta, so he founded his case against the clerical proposals on the "Political Charter of these Churches." In the words of the Cambridge Platform of 1648, which Wise called "this Spear or necessary weapon, in the defence of your Gospel Liberties," "there is no greater church than a *Congregation*, which may ordinarily meet in one place." The basic principle was reaffirmed in the Synod of 1662, stating, "Every church, or particular congregation of visible saints . . . hath received from the Lord Jesus full power and authority, ecclesiastical within itself to administer all the ordinances of Christ, and is not under any other ecclesiastical jurisdiction whatsoever."[56] By this "Form of Government," according to Wise, the Congregational churches were "distinguished from most of the Reformed churches in the World, more than by their Grace." The Proposals of 1705 thus threatened, as he saw it, the fundamental constitution of New England Puritanism, the underlying law by which the church lived. Implicitly comparing the proposals to the annulment of the Massachusetts charter twenty years earlier, Wise inquired of their authors, "*Who gives them Letters of Attorney, or Commission to Sue these Churches (by a* Quo Warranto*) out of Possession of Their Government?*" As in the 1680s, Wise demanded due process for the dispossessed, or "at the least a Grand Sessions, a Jury, and Liberty to make Plea in their own Defence."[57]

Once again, the lawful "liberties" he championed were not the rights of individuals. They rather inhered in the lay fraternity of each congregation as a "Gospel Combination, and Collectively Considered." The principal liberty of the brethren—what Wise called "the *One Thing* in the *Essence of our churches, . . . their peculiar Infranchizement and Birth-Right*"—was the corporate capacity to discipline their members, often with a stronger hand than liberalizing clergy, for whom strict orthodoxy in matters of faith increasingly conflicted with efforts to broaden the membership. "Government is the greatest Blessing in the World, of a Worldly Nature," Wise wrote, noting that "a churlish Tyranny, is better than an insolent Anarchy, where men are without Law, and all *hail Fellows*, not well, but badly met."[58]

As in his report on the military expedition to Quebec and his appeal in the witchcraft trials, Wise identified the caprice of individual judgment with the danger of deviltry and despotism. "It is the duty of all Publick Officers, to Minister according to the Plain Rules of the Publick State, and not by their own Phancy or Wills," Wise wrote, for "if such Powers which belong to the inside of mens being, *viz.* their Hearts, Phansies, Notions, Judgments Imaginations or Consciences . . . are to be the Rule of Churches, then Pastors and Ruling Officers have (in their degree) as absolute a Dominion over the churches, as the great *Turk* has over his Bashaws, and other Vassals."[59] This conventional identification of absolutism with "arbitrary rule," in which the only law was the will of the ruler or "arbitrator" and the willingness of the ruled, ran throughout Wise's work on the churches' quarrel, epitomizing the orientalist alternative against which he defined his own vision of English law.[60] "*English men hate an Arbitrary Power (Politically Considered) as they hate the Devil,*" he wrote, decrying tyrants who "Aggrandize themselves in the servile state of the Subjects, by setting up their own *separate Will*, for the great Standard of government," and denouncing in the same terms ministers who "abdicate their Office, by changing the Acts of a limited Trust, bounded by precept, into what is meerly arbitrary." Under the clerical proposals, according to Wise, a ministerial elite assumed the arbitrary power to dictate policy and adjudicate disputes, power that was rightly vested in the full fraternity of the gathered churches themselves. Christ had chosen for his church "that Government as should least Expose his People to Hazard, either from the fraud, or Arbitrary measures of particular men." Those clergy who sought to usurp the powers vested in their congregations appeared akin to the "Arbitrary Princes of the Earth (such as the great *Czar*, or *Ottoman Monarch*) who have no other Rule to govern by, but their own Will." "They have Out-King'd all Kings on Earth whose Prerogatives are Bounded, and their Kingdoms Governed by Law," Wise wrote. ". . . *They have Out-Bishop't all the Bishops of* Great-Britain, while they themselves have acted with such Lawless Liberty. . . . *They have Out-Pop't the Pope himself*, who is Head of an Hierarchy, supported by certain Laws, Acts and Ordinances."[61]

Wise's central charge against the proposals was thus lawlessness, evidenced both by the extralegal manner in which they were put forward and by their replacement of the constitutional principles of the Congregational church with an unruly abyss, a world at once anarchic and despotic in which leading clergy would be governed by no higher law than themselves. "Where is that Lawful Authority?" Wise demanded, contending that the main property of the proposals was their utter "disorder," supplanting the "Beautiful Structure" of the Cambridge Platform with "a Chaos."[62] The tyranny of the "Turk" appeared the inevitable accompaniment of societal "chaos," the political equivalent of the primordial void that natural philosophers such as Hobbes, Newton, and Bacon counterposed to cosmic order. For in an anarchic world where individuals obeyed no greater authority than themselves, despotic rule would take the place of higher law.

Wise figuratively prosecuted the perpetrators of the "Criminal Proposals" in the name of the higher law that they would annul: a transcendent, impersonal authority that he defined first as common law, then as natural law, and which finally formed the model for his conception of what Adam Smith would call the "invisible hand." He urged that "Zeal and Conscience, those two Solicitors for the Crown, will at this Grand Court of *Oyer* and *Terminer* Implead and Prosecute them as Traytors to the Prince of Peace, and Felons to these Churches, Christ's Loyal Subjects." In drawing up what he called "the Indictment, upon which these Proposals are to pass, and abide a Tryal," Wise patterned his work explicitly on the famed English jurist Edward Coke's prosecution of Walter Raleigh for treason in 1603.[63] But his repeated citations of the preeminent seventeenth-century legal theorist reveal a deeper debt, rooted in Coke's adaptation of the medieval maxim that the prerogatives of rulers were limited by a fundamental law beyond their command, which monarchs, legislators, and judges "disclosed" or "declared" but did not create and could not disobey.

Coke articulated that axiom most famously in his decision as chief justice of the Court of Common Pleas in *Bonham's Case* (1610), holding that "in many cases, the common law will controul acts of parliament, and sometimes adjudge them to be utterly void," and as the lead author of the Petition of Right (1628), contending that kings likewise could not legally enact taxes without parliamentary approval, suspend *habeas corpus*, or otherwise trample on the liberties of English subjects enshrined in the Magna Carta. At the core of the conception that Wise drew from Coke was the understanding that the common law did not ultimately derive from either the command of the sovereign or the consent of his subjects. It arose instead from the unwritten, "immemorial" constitution of the English people, never explicitly enacted but ever evolving along with social norms and needs, as it had been elucidated over the centuries by judges and jurists, much as ministers drew out but did not decree divine law.

Contrary to contemporary "command theories" of law associated with the lineage of Hobbes and Locke, Coke's common law rested not on the "natural reason" of the king or the people, individually or collectively, but on the "artificial reason" of custom, precedent, and experience, crystallized by the courts. "And therefore if all the reason that is dispersed into so many several heads were united into one, yet could he not make such a law as the law of England is; because by many successions of ages it hath been fined and refined by an infinite number of grave and learned men," as Coke wrote in his classic *Commentary upon Littleton* (1628). ". . . No man out of his own private reason ought to be wiser than the law, which is the perfection of reason."[64] It was this notion of a transcendent common law that Wise brought to bear on church government (and later the market economy), contrasting the "chaos" of both individual license and "arbitrary rule" to the fundamental law given voice by the corporate congregation, much as the common law found its social expression in the English bench and bar.

In his second treatment of the subject, *A Vindication of the Government of New-England Churches*, Wise moved beyond the common law to ground his political theory in a more universal conception of "natural law," which he enduringly introduced into American public discourse.[65] His main source shifted from Coke to the German jurist and philosopher Samuel Pufendorf, particularly Pufendorf's classic work, *De Jure Naturae et Gentium* (1672), or *On the Duty of Man and Citizen According to Natural Law*, which was widely adopted as a basis for moral philosophy in England, Scotland, the Netherlands, and France during Wise's lifetime.[66] Descended from the canon of Greco-Roman and Scholastic sources, natural law enjoyed a rebirth in the wake of the Protestant Reformation, particularly in the work of Pufendorf and his Dutch predecessor, Hugo Grotius. It offered a versatile philosophical foundation for new forms of decentralized civil and ecclesiastical authority in the absence of any pan-European power such as the Vatican or the Holy Roman Empire, amid the rise of independent nation-states and the proliferation of confessional and territorial conflicts in the century after the end of the Thirty Years' War in 1648. In Pufendorf's work, the field of natural law defined a novel subject of inquiry: the social realm, governed by the universal laws of human nature and society, making possible a new "science of morals."[67] Emerging along with mercantilist writings on trade, the philosophy of natural law played a foundational part in classical political economy.[68]

Pufendorf came from the Lutheran clerical estate in rural Saxony, at the opposite end of the "Protestant International" from Wise's New England. This transnational realm of natural law encompassed the German states, the Netherlands, and Britain after the French revocation of the Edict of Nantes in 1685 and the ascension of the Dutch William of Orange to the English throne four years later, sharply dividing Catholic from Protestant Europe.[69] Like Coke's common law, Pufendorf's natural law derived from a feudal heritage within which roles and responsibilities were defined collectively rather than individually. In contrast to subsequent theorists of "natural rights" and contractual transactions among rights-bearing individuals, Pufendorf founded social relations on bundles of complementary privileges and duties that he called "offices," through which people obeyed the predetermined mandates of natural law. Sovereigns and subjects alike were the agents but not the authors of the offices they occupied, much as Coke and his common-law inheritors envisioned contractual relations as predefined statuses that individuals voluntarily entered into but did not determine or design, like monarchy, marriage, and mastery. Society was bound together by the dictates of what Pufendorf termed "sociability," not individual self-interest, in the corporate model of natural law that Wise applied to the problems of church government and market relations.[70] Wise followed Pufendorf in articulating a communal conception of natural law quite at odds with the way in which natural law has long been invoked by American jurists and legal scholars across the political spectrum, who have generally conceived of natural law as a protection for individual rights such as due process, freedom of contract, private property, and the "right of privacy" against the depredations of state and federal laws.

While Wise took as his subject "Man in a state of Natural Being, as a Free-Born Subject under the Crown of Heaven, and owing Homage to none but God himself," he quickly explained that the distinguishing feature of human nature was man's subjection to the "Law of Nature," "wherein by a Law Immutable, Instampt upon his Frame, God has provided a Rule for Men in all their Actions," and the "General Rule of Government." To discern and obey this providential law through the exercise of "right reason" was the "Original Liberty" with which all individuals were endowed. "*They alone live as they Will, who have Learnt what they ought to Will,*" Wise wrote, invoking Plutarch along with Pufendorf. Inscribed on men's hearts like Scripture, the law of nature drew them together under what Wise, following Pufendorf, called "the Principles of Sociableness," which decreed "that Man is not so Wedded to his own Interest, but that he can make the Common good the mark of his Aim: And hence he becomes Capacitated to enter into a Civil State."[71]

The agent of natural law was thus not each individual, but "the People" acting as "one Man," "the Will of a Community," "a Compound Moral Person, whose Will . . . is the Will of all; to the end it may Use, and Apply the strength and riches of Private Persons towards maintaining the Common Peace, Security, and Well-being of all." "The People or Fraternity under the Gospel, are the first Subject of Power," Wise wrote. He described this corporate person in the familiar organic terms of the medieval church, in which society itself was figured as an immortal creature. "The Sovereign Power is the Soul infused, giving Life and Motion to the whole Body," he wrote, and while "Subordinate Officers are the Joynts by which the Body moves," "the Happiness of the People, is the End of its Being." His model was the early "Primitive Churches" of the first centuries after Jesus, which he said shared a congregational polity governed by all of its members, without a clerical ruling class. The epistles of Paul, Wise reminded his readers, were addressed to "the Body of the Brotherhood . . . with little or no Notice at all taken of the Ministry therein." So too, the gathered congregation was the soul and sovereign of the Puritan church, which ministers and elected officers rather served than led. "For that the Church is Superiour to its Officers; and not the Officers to the Church," Wise wrote, recalling Pufendorf's conception of individuals and their "offices" as organs of natural law.[72]

In a pivotal theoretical move, Wise developed this traditional organic analogy into a model of power flowing naturally throughout the body politic. The "*Principles* of the *English* Government," he wrote, "are like the *Vena Cava*, or great Arteries in Nature, which Circulate the Blood and Spirits thro' the Imperial Body."[73] He elaborated, quoting Thomas Aquinas: "If we take a Survey of the whole Land, we shall find Religion placed in the Body Politick, as the Soul in the Body Natural. *Nam est Tota Anima, in Toto corpore, et Tota in Qualibet parte*; That is, the whole Soul is in the whole Body, and whole in every Part. . . . So Religion is placed and exercised in its Principles, Vertues and Governments, Through the Families of the Country, so many Families so many little Sanctuaries."[74]

"The whole Soul is in the whole Body": Wise, via Pufendorf, transformed this Scholastic ideal into an early modern vision of healthy circulation, describing the natural laws of motion that governed the English empire, the Congregational church, and the increasingly commercial society over which they presided. Indeed, commercial and organic metaphors were closely entwined in Wise's writing on the churches' quarrel, both predicated on an emerging conception of lawful circulation as the natural basis of a well-governed society.

The chief impediment to such circulation was what Wise repeatedly referred to as monopoly (from above) or piracy (from below)—the dual dangers of absolutism and anarchy, conceived in circulatory terms. "Therefore these *Proposals* being Apprehended as Sea Rovers, and Indicted upon the *Statute of Pyracy*," he wrote of the clerical platform of 1705, ". . . they can no ways in Justice escape, but must pass under the Sentence, and endure the Pains of Death, for they are taken Fighting without Commission."[75] Piracy was a real presence in coastal New England in Wise's lifetime, particularly during the war years between 1689 and 1713, threatening the colonists' sea trade. According to local lore, Wise once publicly prayed "for some of his neighbors then held captive by pirates, that if there were no other way of release, they might rise and slay their captors. On that same day they arose and, killing the pirates, effected their escape."[76] More broadly, piracy represented an important dimension of the rising British Empire, as the English government, in keeping with the emerging ideology of free trade, sought to define piracy as an illegitimate violation of freedom of the seas. Piracy thus formed an illicit counterpoint to evolving norms of commercial capitalism.[77]

Wise's references to monopoly point to the connections he repeatedly drew between ecclesiastical and commercial affairs—as when he compared the "differing treasuries" of "immortal souls" and "outward fortunes," or when he warned that it was far worse to despoil men of their Christ-given authority in church governance than "to plunder men of their Estate & Wealth." A church, he wrote, was essentially a "Charter-party to manage a Trade for Heaven."[78] "To Monopolize (in the Great Articles of Trade) some very rich Species, and of such use for the good of Kingdomes, that they must needs perish without it, or be greatly Injured by excessive Sales, is accounted by good Common-wealths Men intolerable," Wise argued in deploring the attempt to establish a clerical guild with monopoly control over the pool of eligible candidates for ministerial appointments.[79]

Such cross-currents of religious and economic discourse were everywhere to be found in early New England, as Jennifer Baker, Mark Peterson, Mark Valeri, and other scholars have recently shown. The language of commerce and finance saturated contemporary sermons and religious tracts by the turn of the eighteenth century, as latter-day Puritans increasingly identified the development of the market economy with the health and prosperity of the Christian commonwealth.[80] So too, debates over political economy were heavily influenced by religious concerns, spiritualizing monetary relations, as Wise's writings on the currency question in the 1720s exemplify.

"The Common Fountain": The Natural Law of Currency and Commerce

In February 1721, an anonymous advertisement appeared in the *Boston Gazette*, accusing the "Worldly Wise" author of a new manifesto for paper money of shirking his debts. "From Twenty Years long experience he has not been able to pay Interest for Money borrowed of Private People," the notice said of "Amicus Patriæ," John Wise's pseudonym, "and of Twelve Hundred & Fifty Pounds (of his Miracle working Paper Money) borrowed of the Government by himself and two Sons, he has yet paid but 250 l. of it in again; 'tis therefore that he declares, and will insist on it, as the best way to enrich his Country, to make Paper Bills enough for every body to take what they please."[81] Once again at the center of a major political conflict, Wise found himself the target of another public attack on his personal finances a few weeks later. This time, his unnamed critic published in the *Gazette* a recent letter from the Chebacco minister to the local Court of Quarter-Sessions concerning a salary dispute between Wise and his congregation. Noting that his seventy-pound annual salary was "but a poor business to maintain a Family Sick & Well, [and] That to diminish, or any ways weaken it must needs stand under the head of Oppression," Wise protested his church's failure to pay him in coin or its "full Equivalent." In what the publicist evidently deemed damning hypocrisy coming from the popular champion of congregational autonomy and paper currency, Wise petitioned the court to instruct his congregants "that Bills are not Money, nor must they be so understood, and also that they must pay me in the proper Specie, . . . or otherwise if they pay in Bills, then to do it to my Satisfaction."[82] Wise probably had debts to creditors in Britain that had to be paid back in specie or in bills of exchange that were expensive to purchase in Massachusetts since the colony's agricultural staples were not in high demand abroad.

Never one to shy from controversy, the sixty-nine-year-old pastor swiftly fired back in print. Wise took out his own newspaper advertisement proclaiming that his dual dedication to "the Settlement and true Practice of their [the Puritans'] Church Order; And the Erecting, or Settling a Fund with a Lasting Paper Medium of Trade," flowed alike from his love for his "People and Province," and that his petition for more money from the church fully accorded with his call for more currency from the colonial government.[83] He wrote a caustic pamphlet satirizing his opponents as "Gentlemen hoarders" who sought to force their neighbors into "unsolvable Penury and Vassalage, for want of a Plentiful Medium." He appended to the pamphlet an open letter to his son, explaining that he had mortgaged an estate worth £2,000 against a loan of £1,000 from the public land bank, that he had "solved our former Money Obligations" with the benefit of the "Auspicious and Prosperous Bills," and that his income from the family farm would soon enable him to pay back what he had borrowed. His advocacy of further emissions of paper currency was intended, he wrote, to extend the same opportunity to other cash-strapped farmers and to the colony as a whole, "that all Men in their Affairs, may be as Prosperous as I have been," or "that our Country may Universally Flourish."[84]

The previous year, in a brief essay titled *The Freeholder's Address to the Honourable House of Representatives*, Wise had endorsed a stepped-up public program of low-interest loans secured by land, with the interest payable in crops rather than cash. In the same legal language that he had earlier employed in defense of the congregational brethren and the colonial assembly, he had pleaded "on behalf of our poor condemned Bills . . . that they may have a fair and legal Tryal," noting that the paper currency had "brought some" (such as himself) "from nothing, to the Enjoyment of plentiful Estates" and fostered the prosperity of the province as a whole.[85] By 1721, however, New England was entering an era of peacetime economic stagnation, as war-borne demand for shipping and shipbuilding dropped off, agricultural productivity declined, and Boston lost its position as the preeminent entrepôt for British imports and American exports. A worsening balance of trade drained specie from colonial merchants to their creditors abroad, while farmers struggled with deepening debt and difficulty finding markets for their shrinking surplus. When bills of exchange on London became prohibitively expensive in New England, colonial merchants and debtors shipped specie itself across the Atlantic.[86]

The return of hard times prompted Wise's turn from extolling the constitutional laws of the church and the state to expounding those of currency and commerce. He shifted conversely from denouncing the arbitrary rule of princes and priests to decrying what he or a faithful ally called "the tyranny of the Usurers and Misers, whose desires . . . are regulated by no other rules, than the length of their own Consciences." A pamphlet entitled *A Letter to An Eminent Clergy-Man in the Massachusetts Bay* (1721), apparently written by either Wise or a close associate, blamed the colony's "woefull Circumstances" on the tightfistedness of "the most Screwing Misers who are for no Bank at all, but the Clam bank," who sought to extort their poorer neighbors in a time of scarcity, when "Every Man's Hand is against his Brother." The riotous pursuit of self-interest was creating the conditions for the rapacious rule of "your Rich, (who are commonly, tho falsly, call'd Great,) Men" in the growing market economy, much as an unruly veneration of individual faith above divine law ironically opened the way for autocracy in the church. Such selfishness violated what the author of the *Letter* considered the fundamental law that economic no less than ecclesiastical and political power must naturally circulate through the body of the commonwealth, by means of a collectively created and controlled medium of exchange. "It seems the want, as well as the love of Money, is in some sense the root of all evil," he wrote, "for the scarcity of it is undoubtedly the great Source, from whence all your Miseries and Calamities; the divisions and sub-Divisions you are run into, proceed."[87]

Where had Wise learned these economic principles? Though he only turned his full attention to the province's mercantile and monetary affairs late in life, the currency question loomed behind his earlier activism. Commercial banking, which emerged in England in the mid-seventeenth century, made its first abortive appearance in New England in the tumultuous 1680s. At the same time that Wise and his neighbors were defending the autonomy of the colonial assemblies under the aegis of English common law, merchants and ministers were experimenting with the creation of a locally issued paper currency as a means of increasing integration into the English empire of trade while fostering regional economic development. Wise surely would have read the proposals for two short-lived banking schemes authored by his fellow Congregationalist minister in nearby Newbury, John Woodbridge, and by the merchant John Blackwell, which lay the groundwork for his own foray into finance several decades later. Both proposed the creation of a company that would issue loans backed by land or commodities to subscribers in the form of paper notes, which would serve in place of coins or personal IOUs as a local currency. As Blackwell explained:

> A considerable number of persons, some of each Trade, calling & condition . . . agree voluntarily to receive as ready moneys, of and from each other and any Persons in their ordinary dealings, Bank-bills of Credit, signed by severall persons of good Repute joyned together in a Partnership; Given forth on Lands of good title mortgaged; and staple unperishable goods & merchandizes Deposited in fitting places to be appoynted by them for that purpose, . . . which said Bills, in a kinde of Circulation, through their experimented usefullnes, become diffused by mutuall consent, passe from One hand to another, and so have (at least) equall advantages with the Current moneys of the Countrey, to all who become satisfied to be of this Society or agreement, & that shall deale with them.[88]

Inspired by like-minded authors in England, Woodbridge and Blackwell contended that such a semiautonomous community of credit and commerce, in control of its own currency, would make market transactions more fluid, transparent, and equitable. Without such a communal monetary medium, they argued, buying and selling were reduced to the level of barter, pitting individuals and classes against each other while rendering everyone reliant on the dictates of moneyed men instead of the providential principles of the nascent field of political economy. "Merchants, and Shop-keepers, undersell one another; and pitifully help themselves, by beating down Craftsmen: who again, through necessity, underwork others of their occupation; or slight over their work; adulterate Manufacture, and hasten poverty on all," Woodbridge wrote, providing a precedent for Wise's later laments over the general immiseration resulting from the absence of an adequate medium of exchange. "Nor can ever Trade be ballanced, or the advantage of *Fairs* be enjoyed, where Money is wanting." With a communal currency, by contrast, "no *Buyer* will be bound to one person, or Market; nor purchase Credit at the Grantor's price; nor be necessitated to become Servant to the Lender."[89]

Blackwell agreed, writing of his own plan for a plentiful paper currency, "It will not be in the power of any, by extortion and oppression, to make a Prey of the Necessitous."[90]

As Woodbridge and Blackwell envisioned it, a paper currency unmoored from scarce specie would ebb and flow naturally with the tides of trade. Unlike gold and silver coins that were "covetously hoarded up; & so, like dung in a heap, unprofitable," according to Woodbridge, bank bills would circulate productively among households, trades, classes, and sectors. Farmers and craftsmen would find easy credit and ready customers, and merchants would plow their profits into developing domestic agriculture and manufacturing instead of siphoning them off to fill the coffers of creditors whose "Stocks lye dead."[91] A freely flowing currency would foster a virtuous cycle of commerce and a harmony of interests among farmers, manufacturers, and merchants. Such circulation "Increases & quickens Merchandizing and trade," "promotes shipping and navigation," "increases the Kings duties, & consequently his Revenues," and "imployes the poore," Blackwell contended. "The trade and wealth of this Countrey is established upon it's owne Foundation, & upon a medium or Balance arising within it selfe, viz[t], The Lands and Products of this Countrey," he wrote, "and not upon the Importation of Gold or silver or the Scareceity or plenty of them, or of any thing else from Forreigne Nations, which may be with-held, Prohibited or Enhansed, at their pleasures."[92]

Along with contemporaries in England, Woodbridge and Blackwell were conceptualizing something like what came to be called "the economy" or "the market" as a self-regulating system akin to a natural organism or environment.[93] The origins of that distinctively modern domain lay in important part in mercantilist designs for the North Atlantic as an arena of centripetal commercial circulation, such as the ambitious agenda mapped out by the English writer Richard Hakluyt (the younger) in the late sixteenth century, in which the colonies were to supply raw materials and staple crops to the metropole while consuming its finished products and employing its swelling population of propertyless migrant laborers. The economic architects of the empire conceived of "a sealed, self-contained commercial system [that] would coordinate the getting and spending of producers and consumers throughout the Atlantic world," as Nuala Zahedieh has written.[94]

English authorities drew the boundaries of that transatlantic economy in the Navigation Acts of the 1650s, 1660s, and 1670s, restricting trade between Europe and the American colonies to English ships and English ports. At its heart, they located a new kind of sovereign based on the joint rule of the Crown and commercial classes in Parliament, through which the reformed central state acquired a permanent basis of revenue and credit to pay for imperial wars, which in turn paved the way for further commerce and colonization. The lifeblood of this system lay in the rapid ascendance in the second half of the seventeenth century of legally transferable (assignable and negotiable) paper IOUs—bills of exchange, promissory notes, exchequer orders, and banknotes, controlled by bankers and their merchant-capitalist investors, redeemable on demand in silver specie.

Each aspect of the emerging order was distinctively refracted in New England. The mercantilist construction of an Anglo-American trade zone was mirrored in colonial merchants' designs for a regional market economy with its own infrastructure of currency and credit in the 1680s, though they transposed the center of the system from London to Boston and its periphery from the Atlantic to the American interior. The rise of commercial banking and paper money in England was echoed in the innovation of colonial bills of credit in the 1690s, but the provincial currency was controlled by elected legislatures instead of bankers and wealthy investors, and it was backed by public fiat rather than private funds. The structure of the currency issues varied widely between colonies and over time. Most colonial paper money was introduced into circulation when provincial legislatures authorized it to be printed and paid out to soldiers and suppliers during wartime, designating it legal tender for the payment of future taxes and public fees, like the first bills of credit issued by Massachusetts Bay in 1690 (figure 1.1). In peacetime, Massachusetts and other colonies pumped more paper money into their economies by lending it to individuals, with land serving as security for the loans. Unlike British banknotes, the colonial bills were not redeemable on demand in gold or silver, but they could be redeemed at a legally specified future date either in payment of taxes or in specie. Before the 1750s, none of the colonial bills were interest-bearing, but they were issued at a discount below their face value reflecting the time until they could be redeemed, transaction costs, and the risk of default. For this reason, the economist Farley Grubb likens the colonial bills of credit to "zero-coupon bonds" such as non-interest-bearing U.S. savings bonds today, with the difference that the colonial bills were freely transferable—and indeed, they were often decreed to be legal tender for the payment of private as well as public debts within their colonies of issue.[95]

The British union of Crown and capital found its American counterpart in the political and economic ascendance of a coherent community of New England merchants by the turn of the eighteenth century. However, the provincial society of self-styled "merchants" extended from big transatlantic traders

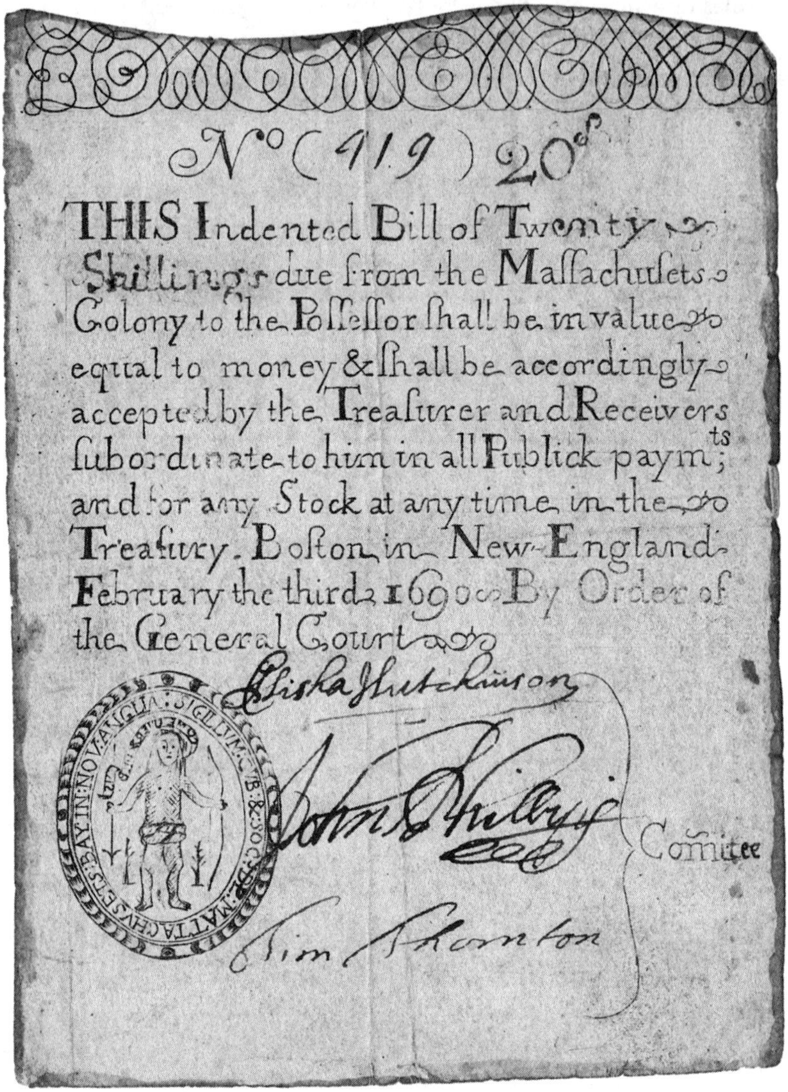

No (419) 20s

THIS Indented Bill of Twenty Shillings due from the Maſſachuſets Colony to the Poſſeſſor ſhall be in value equal to money & ſhall be accordingly accepted by the Treaſurer and Receivers ſubordinate to him in all Publick paym^ts; and for any Stock at any time in the Treaſury. Boſton in New-England February the third 1690 By Order of the General Court

Eliſha Hutchinſon
John Phillips
Tim Thornton
Comitee

FIGURE 1.1. Massachusetts Bay Colony twenty-shilling bill (altered), 1690. The original bill for two shillings, sixpence, has been altered by a counterfeiter. National Numismatic Collection, National Museum of American History, Smithsonian Institution.

to small shopkeepers and country peddlers closely tied to local farmers and fishermen. As Bernard Bailyn has observed, "In New England in the 1690s, as indeed throughout the eighteenth century, the occupation of trade, though it defined an area of common interests for the men engaged in it, did not delimit a stratum of society as it did in England. It was not so much a way of life as a way of making money; not a social condition but an economic activity."[96] Indeed, as mercantile pursuits came to dominate provincial politics, they formed a new terrain of class conflict rather than consensus, inspiring rival visions of commerce and of how to create and control the currency on which it depended.

Written forty years after the tax revolt of the 1680s, amid another colonial crisis, Wise's widely read tract *A Word of Comfort to a Melancholy Country* (1721) marked the culmination of his career and the coming-of-age of the currency question.[97] While paper money in New England attracted enthusiastic support from prosperous merchants and prominent land speculators, Wise represented the smallholding rank and file of the currency cause. His starting point in approaching the issue was a supreme faith in the laws of trade. "Trade and traffick, is the Life of a CommonWealth," he wrote, quoting Coke.[98] The conception of a flourishing commonwealth that Wise took from the English jurist, however, was predicated not on the free play of individual interests, but on the strength of the state, at once the cause and consequence of commercial activity in a symbiotic cycle. Wise excerpted Coke's explanation of how a lively trade sustained the prosperity of farmers, whose ranks supplied soldiers for the defense of the kingdom, whose power made possible the growth of commerce. "For that the Body's of Husbandmen being more strong, and able, and patient of Cold, Heat and Hunger, than of any other Men," in Coke's words, "they therefore make the Best Souldiers." Coke's was a fertile vision of the profits of trade irrigating agricultural production, which supported the state, which promoted trade in turn.[99]

Wise learned from Coke the larger lesson that the lawful circulation of money and commodities could effectively regulate social relations more broadly, sustaining harmonious class relations, provided that commerce itself was equitably and sufficiently facilitated by the supply of currency and credit. In a market economy, if paper bills "bring things nearer to the Rule of Equity; and Adjust matters in Commerce so fairly, that all Men may live and thrive, upon their Labour and Profits; this is to bring the Bills to such a Level as the Money ought to be at in a country of Trade, and Religion, where Men should love their Neighbours as themselves," Wise wrote. The growth of colonial agriculture and industry would enable New England to sell more of its surplus abroad, lowering the cost of bills of exchange on London, thus easing colonists' debts to creditors across the Atlantic as well as to those closer to home.

> And this may be further supported by the Judicious Opinion of Sir Edward Coke in his Tenure by Rents (and indeed in some sense all our Lands are

> Rent Tenure-Lands; as we owe and must pay for them an Annual Income to Church and State) Therefore (according to Sir Edward) If Trade and Commerce be maintained, so that our Native Commodities, and Produce of our Country, which are Rich, Necessary, and costly Things; without which we cannot possibly subsist; If these be holden up at a good Rate; and be kept salable at such a Value, that the Labourer and Farmer may make a clear Profit by them, then may Tenants do their Duty to their Landlords the better; and they themselves live like Men.[100]

In a society in which even self-employed farmers and landowners needed to turn a profit from their property in order to be able to pay monetary tithes and taxes, commerce was king. And just as English monarchs must obey as well as uphold the common law, so the market must follow a higher law as well. A popularly controlled paper currency expanding in step with the volume of market transactions for which it was called into use would afford tenants and smallholders ready access to the cash required to fulfill their rising obligations to landlords, creditors, and tax-collectors, preventing their becoming beholden to the arbitrary dictates of moneyed elites.

The "Merchandize of any Country, Wisely, and vigorously managed, this is the king of business, for increasing the Wealth, the civil Strength and Temporal glory of a People," Wise wrote. Pointing to the Bay Colony's abundance of natural harbors and promontories, he continued, "what a Capacity, may this Place be brought to, by Commerce and Merchandize, in a few Ages more, unless they are Mortifyed, and Slain for want of a Suitable Medium, to support their Trade?"[101] The medium of exchange was crucial, Wise argued, because it made possible the particular *mode* of exchange that supported a prosperous commonwealth—namely, the expanding circulation of money and goods, emancipating society from the lawlessness of direct exchange or barter. Here Wise participated in the emerging discourse of commercial empire that distinguished "civilized" commodity exchange from the "primitive" exchange of fetishized goods and honor-laden gifts, which were inherently tied to particular persons and things, lacking the abstraction of exchange value from both labor and use-value that underwrote a modern market economy.[102] A primitive barter economy, as Wise conventionally described it, was one ruled by the natural scarcity of resources and the animal needs for food and shelter, rather than the distinctively human capacity for "right reason" and productive labor governed by natural law. Barter, he wrote, "is fitter for such a People who (to indulge themselves in great Idleness & Sloath,) Dwell in the Clefts of the Valleys, in Caves of the Earth, and in the Rocks, and digg *Juniper Roots* for their Meat, or can Live upon *Acorns*: But it is not at all agreeable with a Wise and Busling People, that would spend their Life, to the height of Religion, and right Reason."[103] Circulation fostered a self-sustaining cycle of expanding wants, not limited needs, in which growing consumption fueled investment, employment, and economic growth. Wise thus rejected arguments for the colonists to scale back their consumption of imported manufactured goods so as to improve their balance of trade through thrift rather than spending. "If we will Live upon Ground-Nuts and Clams, and Cloath our Backs with the Exuviæ, or Pelts of Wild Beasts, we may then lower our Expences a great Pace," he wrote, ". . . but if we intend to Live in any Garb, or Port, as becomes a People of Religion, Civility, Trade and Industry, then we must still supply our selves from the Great Fountain [of commerce]."[104]

Lack of adequate currency threatened to drag New England backward toward a subsistence, barter-based economy. "Without a *Medium*," Wise warned, "all things will Jumble, Run Retrograde, and Tumble into Caos," sapping ambition and sowing despair, "Cut[ting] the Throat of all Endeavours."[105] For what motivated men toward productive labor was the prospect of profit and advancement, spurred by free-flowing credit and currency and the rising demand for the produce of farms and shops that they made possible. Wise spoke in part from personal experience, having borrowed against his small estate through the public loan office. From his own success he drew a broad moral. "It is too hard a Fate for Men of good Conduct to spend their Days in Rolling the Stone of Sisyphus: But that by their frugality and Painful Improvement of the Means of their Subsistence, they ought to make a clear Gain, as being most agreeable with the Law of God and Nature," he wrote.[106]

The circulation of credit and currency, in Wise's view, crucially transformed relations between buyers and sellers and between lenders and borrowers. Direct bilateral exchanges of commodities he identified with personal and class exploitation. Aside from the unlikely event in which both parties to such transactions were equally in need of what the other had to offer, he reasoned, "he that has least necessity will over-reach the other, by imposing the Price of both; and always to his own Advantage and the others Detriment; which is not any ways just or equal."[107] According to Wise, the transferability of debt and its converse, the ready circulation of paper money, emancipated debtors from servitude to their creditors, and it freed sellers from exploitation by buyers. Both developments redounded to the benefit of small farmers and traders.

Wise came now to the cornerstone of his argument for paper currency. Because gold and silver coin were precious commodities in themselves, they were liable to be hoarded or to be exported by those with payments to make abroad when the price of exchange made it cheaper to send coin than to buy bills of exchange. This meant that metallic money naturally tended to be withdrawn from circulation. Indeed, Wise laid it down as a rule that "The more Cost and Intrinsick Worth a Medium carries with it, or the more Valuable it is in it self, the less useful it will be in supporting an Universal Trade and Commerce."[108] To the extent that New England came to depend on coin for its currency, circulation tended to grind to a halt. "And its well if more then one Third of our Supply and present Stock is not stopt by this means, like Stagnate Waters, in Pits and Mud-holes," Wise wrote.[109]

Due to its liability to becoming increasingly scarce, a metallic medium recreated the conditions of exploitation that Wise associated with a more primitive economy based on bilateral exchange rather than multilateral circulation of credit and currency. The "Money Medium"—that is, specie—"has been the Means of Our Oppression" instead of a ready means of exchange, Wise wrote. It lent itself to the oppression of farmers by the middlemen on whom they relied as both creditors and customers. "*The Money Medium inclines Men more to Extortion, Dissembling, and other Moral Evils in Trade, then One which has no Intrinsick Value in it.* They are the Moneyed-Men that higle and stand high upon their Terms; and usually undervalue every Commodity exposed to Sale."[110] So too, the scarcity of specie led to usurious interest rates, encouraging creditors to save or to lend their money at high interest instead of investing it productively in industry or trade. "The allowing of [high] Interest interposes instead of Moneys circulating, and the Debts remain obstructed, swelling and breaking out in the ruin of many," so that "the course of Money is turned to the spoiling of Trade," instead of supporting commerce.[111]

By contrast to hard money, paper bills of credit such as those issued by Massachusetts and the other colonies were only valuable when they circulated. Such non-interest-bearing bills tended to be exchanged rather than saved, and they remained within the colony instead of going abroad. Paper money thus exemplified for Wise the way that the "Common Fountain" should always "move and Circulate, like the Main Ocean." Just as the ocean supplied "the Earth with Showers; with Rivers, and smaller streams, for the satisfying the Thirst, and nourishment of every living Thing," he contended, so a plentiful medium would nourish industry and commerce.[112] Indeed, the continuous movement of paper money made it peculiarly fertile, he argued—inverting the traditional view of money as "barren," dating to Aristotle. Paper bills had built up new shops and wharves in the seaboard cities, cleared new farms and pastures in the country, and dotted the colony with churches and schools. They had primed demand for local furs, grains, fruit, fish, cattle, lumber, and ships. They had drawn immigrants, fostered growing families, and promoted the settlement of new towns. Wise thus envisioned a perpetual commercial cycle—commodities sold for cash, which was invested in land

and labor, which produced more commodities—joining commerce to agriculture and industry in a way that reflected the novel seventeenth-century alliance of English and American merchants, farmers, planters, manufacturers, and shopkeepers, which took power on both sides of the Atlantic after the Glorious Revolution. He praised the union of "Landed Men, & Great Merchants, who (tho' worth many Thousands) keep the main of the Personal Estate, *stirring* in a way of Trade," or those "*Amphibious* beings, who live in both Elements, Land and water"—that is, agriculture and commerce.[113]

"These bills are of a very impregnating Nature, they will beget and bring forth whatsoever you shall please to fancy," Wise wrote, identifying the generative capacity of paper money with natural reproduction in an innovative manner associated with contemporary English writers such as Daniel Defoe.[114] Most notably, paper money appeared to Wise to bring forth wealth by sheer force of public confidence and collective willpower. Its productive and reproductive powers rested on no material resources, but rather on public esteem, confidence, and reputation. "Gentlemen! You must do by your Bills, as all Wise Men do by their Wives; Make the best of them," he exhorted his readers, invoking marriage as the model of a relation originating in contract but sustained by sentiment. ". . . Therefore you must set them high in your Estimation, and be no ways Prodigal of their Reputation. . . . Such a temper of Mind will for ever, not only secure the Currency of our Bills; but will most certainly keep up their Value equal with [metallic] Money."[115]

More particularly, the value of the paper currency depended, in Wise's view, on the willingness of leading merchants and landowners to accept it on a par with coin. Their vital support would enable the bills to support a growing market in turn. Their disapproval of paper currency, on the other hand, would bring it down along with the regional economy as a whole. Wise therefore looked to create a powerful partnership between the legislatures that issued the provincial bills, in which family farmers were represented alongside lawyers and merchants, and local shopkeepers, retailers, and traders who identified their interests principally with the development of the domestic market rather than transatlantic commerce. "Merchants & Farmers, are the Grand Pillars of the Flourishing State of this Common Wealth," he wrote, "so being joyned together are the Atlas which bears up the great Globe of our Temporal Business."[116] In this sense, Wise was conceptualizing the marriage of sovereignty and capital that lay at the heart of the financial revolution in both England and America. But he envisioned it in broadly egalitarian, popular terms. While he styled himself "a freeholder," he addressed his writing primarily to the merchants of Boston, whom he deemed to be at once "principal Steers-Men in the common Affairs of temporal Interest and Profit" and "Great Agents, and Factors for your Country."[117] As trustees of the commonwealth, given responsibility in particular for the paper currency on which economic prosperity depended, "landed men and great merchants . . . must needs act in such a sphere in some proportion like the Government it self; as being now become Publick Benefactors." They would become, Wise hoped, "masters of the market," governing in such a way so that all men's property, liberty, and opportunity for prosperity would be secured.

Wise's vision of a new kind of joint rule by merchants and farmers, city and country, capitalists and legislative representatives of smallholders, gained added significance during the 1720s, at the end of his life. Economic stagnation combined with spiraling inflation, with dire consequences for laboring people in the towns and others on fixed incomes that did not rise apace with the price of goods. Many observers were quick to blame the depreciation of the paper currency for the hard times. Paper bills depreciated especially sharply relative to specie; an ounce of silver cost twelve shillings, four pence in 1720, but twenty shillings ten years later.[118] In Wise's view, however, the rising cost of living resulted not from too much paper currency in circulation, but from too little. The inadequate supply of currency, he contended, held down wages, encouraged usurious interest rates, and allowed for forestalling and engrossing of food and fuel, encouraging dealers to corner supplies of basic necessities in order to inflate their prices. The remedy that Wise recommended lay partly in issuing more paper currency, not less, and using it to employ people on public works. It lay also in a stronger hand at the helm of the market, regulating the prices of essential goods instead of leaving it "to the Will of every Cut-Throat, to raise the Price." Once prices were limited to a just level for "the principal Commodities of our own Produce," Wise argued, "other things would easily and naturally submit to an equal value in the course of Trade, and if once the great Swells of advancing Prices were laid aside . . . then Men would know their Business without huckling and bartering."[119]

"Treasure in Earthen Vessels": Wise's Contested Legacy

When John Wise died in 1725, his son-in-law, the Reverend John White, delivered the funeral sermon at the Chebacco church. Taking as his text a line from 2 Corinthians, "For we have this Treasure in Earthen Vessels," White suggested that ministers like Wise could be seen as the "earthen vessels" in which the ultimate "treasure" of the Gospel was conveyed. The comparison between spiritual and material wealth was familiar to New England Puritans from countless sermons, and White drew a traditional moral, emphasizing what distinguished faith from the commerce in commodities that increasingly dominated daily life. The immeasurable and invariable truth of the Gospel was literally priceless, cherished solely for its "Intrinsick Virtue and Value" rather than its social esteem. Indeed, it was all the more precious because its value was hidden from view. Its grace could not be obtained in return for any amount of work or will, but solely as the "free gift" of God. In other words, "The Gospel is a *Market*, where the Spiritually Necessitous may buy all that he needs, and all *without money, and without price*," as White told Wise's parishioners.[120] Wise himself, however, had found more redeeming value in money and markets than was suggested by White's eulogy. White recalled Wise's defense of the "Liberties and Priviledges" of colonies and congregations but neglected his final fight for paper currency. Like many Puritan ministers and merchants by the end of his life, Wise sanctified the natural laws of the market economy much as he did those of civil and ecclesiastical government.

Wise and his compatriots in 1687 did not seek greater separation from England, but rather closer integration into the expanding empire, under the agency of local leaders and the auspices of English law. Twenty years later, he and his Congregational allies did not desire a less powerful, more permissive church, but rather tighter communal control over an increasingly far-flung following, governed by frontier congregations in accord with the principles of natural law. In the last years of his life, Wise and the partisans of paper money did not aim to defend a local agrarian economy against the encroachment of long-distance mercantile and monetary relations. They embraced the commercial and financial revolution and strove to marshal it on behalf of small farmers, shopkeepers, and country pastors like themselves through a strong state exercising democratic control over a regional, locally governed market economy through the creation and regulation of currency and credit. Wise's work on the currency question was founded on a bedrock commitment to the political and economic autonomy of self-employed householders like himself, which he aimed to advance by placing regulatory authority over the means of exchange and the prices of essential goods in the hands of local legislatures. He was thus a pioneering theorist of republican finance, through which popular control over currency and credit would secure broad-based access to the means of production. That egalitarian ideal endured long after the demise of the colonial monetary regime in which it first emerged.

2

William Douglass and the Natural History of Credit

The conflict over public finance in New England arose along with an equally searing controversy over public health. In the spring of 1721, just when John Wise was joining the rising debate over paper money, smallpox arrived in Boston by ship from the West Indies. The most dreaded disease in the North American colonies had struck eight times in the previous century, but the latest outbreak elicited a novel response. A group of Congregational ministers led by Cotton Mather were inspired by recent reports on the experimental practice of deliberately infecting people with smallpox in order to give them a mild case of the disease that would immunize them against a more deadly attack. The inoculation of several hundred Bostonians amid the devastating epidemic of 1721–22 sparked furious resistance, particularly from a few physicians led by an aristocratic recent arrival from Scotland, William Douglass (1691–1752). Championing the exclusive prerogatives of "doctors of medicine" with scientific training, Douglass accused the ministers of violating the providential authority of nature itself. "The Determination of this as a *Case of Conscience*, I refer to Divines," he wrote, "how the trusting more the extra groundless *Machinations of Men* than to our Preserver the ordinary course of Nature, may be consistent with that Devotion and Subjection we owe to the *allwise Providence* of GOD Almighty."[1]

Douglass's faith in the "ordinary course of Nature" and its sanction for new forms of power and privilege formed the abiding principle of his subsequent career as a leading American physician, natural historian, and political polemicist. It shaped his pathbreaking studies of epidemic disease and advocacy of colonial medical reform, his prodigious collection of botanical specimens and copious reporting of meteorological, geological, and astronomical phenomena, his landmark historical and geographical surveys of British North

America, and his final role as the foremost critic of paper money in provincial New England. Through his writings on the related problems of contagion, classification, and credit in the colonial world, Douglass articulated an influential vision of healthy and unhealthy circulation in the physiological "œconomy of spirits," the biological "œconomy of nature," and the political economy of currency alike.

"Buying the Smallpox": Commerce and Contagion in Colonial Medicine

Douglass was born in Gifford, Scotland, the second son of a small landowner or "laird" who served as the financial agent for a politically prominent nobleman, the Marquess of Tweeddale.[2] He was a scion of the rising class of landlords, merchants, and academics that directed the transformation of the Scottish lowlands from feudal villages into large commercial farms in the eighteenth century, especially in the rich southeastern region from which he came.[3] His older brother, who became a surgeon, inherited the family estate. So Douglass joined the growing ranks of Scottish expatriates who found their calling as teachers, ministers, merchants, overseers, officers, and physicians in the British Empire following the Act of Union between England and Scotland in 1707, when he was sixteen. He entered a migrant gentry for whom university degrees served as titles to a new kind of portable patrimony, staking their status within the widening networks of commercial and intellectual exchange around the Continent and across the Atlantic. This was the professional circuit, neither metropolitan nor provincial but cosmopolitan, that shaped Douglass's perspective on an emerging market society charted by the early modern discourses of medicine, natural history, and political economy, to which he critically contributed.[4]

Those three closely connected fields found a shared philosophical framework in the concept of circulation, which received its classic exposition in the founder of modern physiology William Harvey's 1628 treatise, *De Motu Cordis et Sanguinis*, "On the Motion of the Heart and the Blood." Circulation was to the seventeenth and eighteenth centuries what evolution was to the nineteenth and twentieth, a widely shared explanatory paradigm for a broad range of natural and social phenomena. From bodily fluids, contagious diseases, celestial bodies, oceanic currents, and electrical charges to colonists and commodities, handwritten letters and printed publications, and currency and credit instruments, the paradigm of circular movement within a self-enclosed system provided the pattern for many of the "laws of motion" found to govern both nature and society in the early modern British Atlantic. "But of all the modern discoveries, wit and industry have made in the œconomy of human nature, the noblest is that of the circulation of the blood," wrote Joseph Glanvill, spokesperson for the Royal Society of London for Improving Natural Knowledge.[5] Circulation, writes Joyce Chaplin, represented "the first example of an idea within the modern sciences becoming a metaphor or even model for the human world."[6]

Douglass's formal understanding of circulation arose from his training as a physician. At Edinburgh University, he learned from the renowned Scottish anatomist Archibald Pitcairne, founder of the British school of "hydraulic iatromechanism." Pitcairne's philosophy was based on the increasingly conventional premise that "life consists in the circulation of the blood produced by motion of the heart and arteries," as he wrote. He conceived the human or animal body as a machinery of "Canals of diverse kinds, conveying different sorts of Fluids," much as William Harvey had modeled his depiction of the cardiovascular system on hydraulic engineering. Pitcairne described disease as "the circulatory Motion of the Blood too much increased or diminished," and he further proposed that health depended on "the Secretions being duly made from the Blood" according to the laws of Newtonian mechanics. "For the Circulation of the Blood is not more necessary for the Preservation of Life, than its perpetual Supplies of the Secretion of abundance of Fluids, and its Disposal of them into different Parts; and the Causes of most diseases are to be look'd for in the Disorder of this Secretion," Pitcairne wrote, articulating the hydraulic physiology that informed much of Douglass's theory and practice.[7] Douglass continued his studies at the University of Leiden in Holland, under the tutelage of the preeminent Dutch botanist, physicist, and physician Herman Boerhaave, then trained in Paris and Flanders before returning to the Netherlands at the University of Utrecht. There he wrote his doctoral dissertation entitled *Animalium Hydraulisin*, on circulation as the essence of animal life, as if reflecting his peripatetic graduate career.[8]

After a brief sojourn in the mercantile hub of Bristol, England, Douglass migrated to its American counterpart in Boston, where he set up a thriving practice as the sole physician with a university medical degree. Joining a generation of Scottish "medical missionaries" to the colonies, he arrived in a region with no schools or hospitals where aspiring physicians could receive specialized training in anatomy and physiology as they could abroad. Most colonial practitioners learned their trade through a more general apprenticeship in the healing arts. The primary professional healers were clergymen who ministered to both body and soul, along with locally trained midwives and self-taught "empirics." A faithful if irreverent Anglican, Douglass moved to the head of a small group of local physicians contesting the popular power of the Congregational church over the "body natural" as well as the "body politic," possibly influenced by Pitcairne's Jacobite disdain for the Presbyterian establishment in Scotland.[9] The anti-inoculation campaign that he soon came to lead represented "the most outspoken, the most snarling, wave of antiministerial sentiment New England had yet witnessed," according to Perry Miller.[10] "To be more or less *Book learned*, is not a sufficient Qualification for a *Physician*," Douglass wrote in 1722. ". . . A very eminent modern Physician says, That many *Gentlemen* of universal reading, and *old Women* by long Nursing, know as much of Physick as to kill themselves and Neighbours when sick, by the preposterous indiscreet Use of some noted Medicines."[11]

Beyond Boston and Salem, the ill and the injured generally depended on exchanges of carefully accounted care-giving among neighbors and relatives, though the wandering poor and the very sick were forced to turn to poor relief or hired help, as Ben Mutschler has shown. In the same way, most New Englanders relied when possible on informal accounts of "social credit," along with paper currency controlled by townships and assemblies, in reckoning their exchanges of other goods and services within their communities. Douglass aimed to supplant this communal market in care and credit based on local relations of trust with a cosmopolitan market in medicine and money based on the imperial connections of university-educated physicians and transatlantic merchants.[12] When colonial critics called him an "abject" "stranger" or exile from abroad, he tellingly retorted, "Our Governours and other King's Officers from home, are they to be branded with the Appellation STRANGER?"[13]

Douglass sought to reproduce the institutional structure of guilds, medical schools, and medical societies that had developed in Britain along with the hierarchy of royally licensed physicians, apothecaries, and surgeons. He campaigned unsuccessfully for the regulation of local practitioners by a board of doctors, and he tried but failed to endow a chair of medicine at Harvard and launch a medical journal. He briefly established the first professional medical society in the colonies, paralleling the Anglicizing efforts of colonial lawyers and merchants with close ties to their counterparts in London. Medicine, like money, was not rightly the province of provincial authorities, according to Douglass. It required an active membership in the transnational society of physicians, with their uniquely wide knowledge of human nature and the natural order.[14]

Nature as Douglass and his colleagues conceived it was resistant to the universal rules and regimens peddled by parochial healers who mistook local peculiarities for general principles. Authoritative understanding of health and illness could only emerge inductively from wide-ranging experience and communication among scientifically trained observers. Not all of his European-trained peers agreed; the Scots-born Maryland physician Alexander Hamilton derided Douglass as a member of "the clynicall class of physitians, [which] crys up empiricism, and practices upon grounds which neither he himself nor any body for him can reduce to so much as a semblance of reason."[15] But for Douglass and his Boston disciples, studies of the epidemic diseases that were seen to spread with the extension of trade routes must be cautiously reported in the kind of case-by-case narratives of divergent symptoms, stages, and remedies that he provided in his accounts of a variety of colonial distempers. He focused on observable characteristics and practical results while eschewing theoretical speculation and generalization. "*Observations* reduced to Method and Analogy from thence is all we know or can learn in any Distemper," he wrote in his aptly titled *Practical Essay Concerning the Small Pox* (1730).[16] As he explained in his 1736 "practical history" of scarlet fever, considered by medical historians "the first—and the best—description of the disease in English," a "Speculation that is a novelle might have been composed sooner, but not a real History, for as among Naturalists, many repeated observations and experiments are requisite to form established truths or conclusions; so it ought certainly to be in the practice of Medicine."[17] In their exhaustive attention to the diversity of forms with which common illnesses presented themselves in different individual and environmental "constitutions," such chronicles of the course of epidemics testified to what Douglass called the physician's distinctive "genius" for diagnosing diseases. Disavowing "zealously bigoted" faith in particular therapies, he insisted on the disparate evidence of trial and error, or what he called "the Experience of the *juvantia and ledentia*," as the sole reliable means "to prevent, alleviate, or remove the various disturbing *Symptoms*" of diseases in different countries and conditions, if not to cure or eradicate them once and for all.[18]

"There are so many inequalities" among patients, Douglass wrote, "as not to admit of any fixed rules."[19] Medical expertise relied instead on the enlightened practitioner's "circumspection"—literally, the ability to "look around" the particular conditions or "circumstances" bearing on each case in order to form a general conception of the underlying ailment, or the singular perspective gained from reviewing multiple superficially dissimilar incidents of the same basic malady, which only physicians could truly discern. Their exclusive stock in trade, as Douglass described it, derived not just from their intensive education, but from their extensive circulation, much as Atlantic merchants traded on their ability to distill the commensurable exchange value from a multitude of colonial commodities. Hence the facility with which Douglass identified medical with mercantile pursuits. He referred to Boston in a letter to a friend as "no better than a factory [a colonial trading post] as to my interest, for here we have a great trade and many Strangers with whom my business chiefly consists." He noted in another letter that he had not yet had time "to reduce my loose observations to any distinct method fit for communication, finding it more natural to begin by reducing my small-pox accounts into bills and notes for the improvement of my purse."[20]

Douglass's financial and clinical accounts of the smallpox epidemic that launched his American career signaled a new departure in the centuries-old association between commerce and contagious disease. Beginning with the spread of the Black Death along the Silk Road from Asia in the fourteenth century, European authorities had commonly attributed the rise of pestilence to the growth of long-distance trade and the expanding sphere of activity of urban merchants, while describing the plague in biblical terms as divine punishment for commercial corruption.[21] They had responded with systematic efforts to restrict the movements of persons and goods. They had quarantined merchant ships in ports, excluded travelers suspected of carrying contagion from country towns, and confined infected individuals in boarded-up houses or in segregated hospitals. Thus the Massachusetts General Court had passed "An Act for the Better Preventing of the Spreading of Infectious Sicknesses" in 1699 and constructed a pesthouse on Spectacle Island in Boston Harbor in 1717, the year after Douglass's arrival.[22] Like similar efforts to confine market transactions to designated times and places and to impose strict limits on foreign exchange, however, measures to contain contagion had emerged alongside a host of regulations designed to sanitize rather than segregate commercial activity. Targeting the rising refuse of so-called noxious or nuisance trades such as those of tanners, brewers, and butchers, sanitary laws were based on the theory that infection arose not from market exchange per se but from its by-products of sewage and squalor. Traders and their wares were not the problem, but rather the "corruption" of commodities due to inadequate provisions for their expanding trade.[23]

On the eve of the smallpox epidemic of 1721–22, the growing belief that illness stemmed from the corruption *of* commerce rather than from commerce itself found expression in two parallel commentaries in the *Boston News-Letter*, the first continuously published newspaper in British North America. The first, more metaphorical consideration of contagion came in response to the collapse of the South Sea Bubble in 1720. An essay reprinted from a London monthly called the *Political State of Great Britain* decried the "Pestilential Phrenzy" that had "seize[d] the Dealers in all Kinds of Stocks" and thence contaminated the market economy more broadly. "The Public Stocks, and the large Premiums, Divert Mens Thoughts from entering upon the Principal Business of Navigation and Commerce," the anonymous author wrote, counterposing the "Mysterious Springs, and artful Machines" of financial chicanery to the "Arts, and Sciences, and Trade, the Main Springs that uphold a Kingdom, or a State, like the Great Axis of the Globe, which keeps the earth in a continued regular Motion." Once the feverish "Traffick . . . in scraps of Paper" had broken, a healthy trade could resume, "our Manufactures set to work, the Poor every way imployed, Tradesmen and Artificers find Business, and Money circulate in every Country, City and Town."[24]

This portrayal of speculation as a sickness of circulation appeared in tandem with an extended excerpt in the Boston paper from the English physician Richard Mead's *Short Discourse Concerning Pestilential Contagion* (1720). Mead's work was occasioned by the last great European outbreak of the plague, which arrived in Marseilles, France, the same year that the South Sea Bubble burst. Invoking classical conceptions derived from Hippocrates and Galen, he found the source of infection in the *lack* of circulation that created "miasmas" of stagnant water, fetid soil, and foul air, which he associated chiefly with hot, tropical countries where the climate was relatively constant and "the Winds (the use of which is by Motion, to purify the Air) do not shift and change so often as they do in Northern Climates." Drawing on the hydraulic physiology that Mead, like Douglass, had learned from Pitcairne, he explained that "Malignant Fevers, especially Pestilential Ones" created a "Fermentation" in those afflicted, causing them to "throw off a great Quantity of active Particles upon the several Glands of the Body, particularly upon those of the Mouth and Skin, from which the Secretions are naturally the most constant and large." In still water and putrid air, the "Infectious Matter" secreted by sick and dead bodies grew "much more active and powerful, and likewise more durable and lasting." It lodged in "Goods of a loose and soft Texture" such as cotton, silk, linen, and wool, "which being packed up, and carried into other countries, let out, when opened the imprisoned seeds of Contagion." In this way, previously endemic diseases came to be conveyed over long distances by infected sailors, soldiers, clothes, and commodities. While Mead endorsed measures to quarantine contagious ships and prevent the "Clandestine Importing of Goods," he cautioned that efforts to isolate or separate the sick often reproduced in European cities the miasmatic environment that bred infection in Asia and the Near East. "For nothing approaches so near to the first Original of Contagion, as Air pent up, loaded with Damps, and corrupted with the Filthiness, that proceeds from Animal Bodies," he noted—and these were precisely the conditions created by confining sick people in their houses or in overcrowded hospitals, prisons, and poorhouses. The modern means of preventing the spread of disease, according to Mead, was not segregation but integration, especially ensuring the flow of clean water and fresh air through congested districts.[25]

If the circulation of people and products bore the "seeds of contagion," it also carried the remedy. Nothing so starkly conveyed this lesson to contemporaries as the spread of smallpox, the great scourge of the early modern Atlantic as the plague had been of the late medieval Mediterranean, and nowhere was it illustrated more brutally than Boston. For the saving grace of smallpox was that it conferred immunity on those who survived it. In places where it became a more or less constant presence, like England and its Caribbean colonies, the vast majority of victims were children young enough not to have been previously exposed. The New England provinces, however, were distant enough from their trading partners and sufficiently effective in quarantining ships and travelers so that smallpox virtually vanished for extended periods, only to strike with greater ferocity a population left vulnerable by its lack of exposure, much as native peoples were repeatedly decimated by the European disease.[26]

Nearly twenty years since the last case had been reported in Boston, a man suffering from smallpox disembarked from a British warship leading a fleet of merchant vessels from the West Indies in 1721. The ensuing epidemic, which afflicted more than half of the town's ten thousand residents and claimed 844 lives, occasioned the first extensive test of the emerging theory that contagion itself could offer the best means of prevention when properly managed.[27] Just as the concept of contagion developed within early modern medicine out of the preventive measures long taken by magistrates and town dwellers, so the idea of inoculation arose in the early eighteenth century from a spate of published accounts of the folk practice of purposely acquiring a low-level infection. The custom reportedly dated back many centuries in Asia, Africa, and rural communities in various parts of Europe. Commonly called "buying the smallpox," it was typically described as a purchase of immunity, as when families paid a small sum for a few pustules from someone with smallpox, or when slave traders reportedly infected their female chattel to see if they survived without being unduly disfigured and therefore would "bear a good price," as Douglass wrote in his own account. By April 1721, when smallpox reappeared in Boston, the practice of injecting infected pus into a healthy person was attracting growing interest among medical writers across the Atlantic. They called it "inoculation" or "variolation," from the Latin for smallpox, *variola*. That same month, the first recorded inoculation was reported in England on the daughter of the British ambassador to Turkey, whose wife, Lady Mary Wortley Montagu, had witnessed the practice in Constantinople. Within a year, there were several more trials, including the inoculation of two daughters of Princess Caroline.[28]

In New England, however, such attempts to marshal the means of contagion were undertaken by local town and church leaders instead of the likes of the royal family and the Royal Society. Therein lay the main problem as Douglass saw it with colonial experiments in preventive medicine as in paper money. It was Cotton Mather, having read the recent reports from the Near East, who joined with several other ministers in promoting inoculation from the outset of the epidemic in Boston. Douglass, meanwhile, swiftly expanded his competing medical practice to serve the sudden demand. "By lucky-chance my first [smallpox] patient was an intricate case and her recovery gained me some credit so that at present my hands are full," he wrote to his fellow physician and former Edinburgh classmate Cadwallader Colden in July 1721, noting that he had assumed a "large share" of the burgeoning market.[29] In allying with other medical men to form what they dubbed the Society of Physicians Anti-Inoculators, his immediate aim was "to maintain the Practitioners in their *Rights and Privileges*" against provincial pastors who "exceeded their Bounds, and wrote practically on a *medical* Subject," as Douglass contended in an open letter to a London "M.D. & F.R.S." (Fellow of the Royal Society) published as a pamphlet in 1722. Ministers, he wrote, "should cease pretending to *Physick*, there being Practitioners sufficient in Number and Qualifications to supply the Place."[30]

Broader principles were at stake in Douglass's early opposition to "unbounded inoculation," as he explained in two longer treatises based on his experience with smallpox in 1721–22. Recklessly administered by unqualified "quacks," inoculation upset the natural rhythms of both urban commerce and human health, he argued, reflecting the circulatory logic of the essays on public finance and public hygiene in the *Boston News-Letter*. He denounced his opponents for "*propagating the Infection* in the most Publick Trading Place of the Town," in a manner "*of pernicious consequence* to populous and trading Towns by spreading Infection and damping their Trade." He dedicated his *Dissertation Concerning Inoculation* (1730) to the royal customs collector in Boston, "the Darling of all fair Traders."[31] Yet even in the midst of the epidemic, Douglass privately acknowledged that smallpox "seems to be somewhat more favourable received by inoculation than received in the natural way." By 1730, he was comparing inoculation to earlier examples of popular nostrums that were initially "opposed by the generality of the Faculty" but eventually "proved to be the best of Medicines." "How mean or rash soever the beginning of the Practice of Inoculating the Small Pox may have been," he wrote, ". . . nevertheless if in the Event by repeated experiments it prove useful, it ought to be embraced."[32] The point was that unlearned practitioners were often the first to stumble upon effective treatments, but it took higher expertise to extrapolate reliable remedies from the welter of anecdotal evidence and irregular procedure.

What enabled physicians to transform "buying the smallpox" and "unbounded inoculation" into scientifically proven practice was their understanding of the fundamental physiological processes of health and disease, based on the theory of circulation. Thus Douglass recognized in various symptoms of smallpox—sweating, swelling, and salivating, along with hemorrhages, discharges, and diarrhea—the signs of an essentially "colliquative" disorder, or in other words, of an "inflammatory fever" characterized by "melting and dissolving." From this diagnosis of the disease Douglass drew his approach to its treatment, which relied on fostering the body's self-healing systems of circulation and secretion to fight off the infection. He warned against both "hot" and "cold" regimens, observing that "hot medicines" known as "alexipharmicks" tended to fuel the fever, while "*Coolers so retard* the Circulation, that there may arise a Sort of Ferment from Stagnation." He advised instead that "the Patient ought to be kept in a moderate natural Temper," and that "the more *perspirable* the Body (I do not mean Sweating, which is a Colliquation) the better." Do not confine patients in cramped, stuffy rooms behind blanketed windows and drawn bed curtains, he cautioned, "for the *Spring* of the inspired *Air* is the continued cause of the *Circulation* in our bodies." He condemned the indiscriminate use of bloodletting, emetics, cathartics, and other forced evacuations, which "disturb[ed] the course of nature" and patients' peace of mind. "*Avoid Grief, Study, intense Thinking, and the like*," he advised those ailing, for "they hinder Perspiration, and all other Tendencies to the Surface or *ad. extra.* of the Body." The best prevention lay in maintaining a robust diet while avoiding gluttony and inebriety, "which are Violence done to Nature." "When the Vessels are impregnated with rich Food, and generous Liquor, . . . we are less liable to receive the Injuries of the circumambient Air, as in catching cold, Epidemical contagious Distempers, *&c.*," Douglass wrote. "Thus the Poor suffer most in Times of a Plague," he added, suggesting that his medical model of the "œconomy of spirits" reflected a broader philosophical conception of "economy" in nature and society, informing a new, naturalistic view of class relations.[33] He found the frame for that economic understanding in the emerging field of natural history, with its comprehensive taxonomies of the animal, vegetable, and mineral "kingdoms" as well as the expanding dominion of merchants and moneyed men.

Œconomia Naturae: Class and Classification in Natural History

Though the systematic study of plants and animals had ancient origins, natural history first emerged as a distinct discipline in sixteenth-century Europe, devoted to the discovery and description of a growing multitude of natural species in the age of exploration. Its institutional foundation was laid in seventeenth-century England, with the first formal organizations of botanists and apothecaries seeking to catalog and categorize the herbs, oils, salts, spirits, and other "simples" from which medicines were made.[34] Physicians became the masters of the new discipline, distinguished by their specialized training in "physic" (from the Greek for "nature") based on systematic study of specimens from botanical gardens, herbaria, and "cabinets of curiosities" as opposed to the common knowledge derived from animal husbandry and horticulture. "'The word Physician . . . is plainly and fully rendered by the word *Naturalist*, (that is) one well vers'd in the full extent of Nature, and Natural things," as a contemporary English physician explained.[35]

What made medicine and natural history together "the 'big science' of the early modern period," as Harold Cook has written, was the broader project of identifying, measuring, mapping, counting, collecting, and classifying the panoply of animal, vegetable, and mineral resources to which European empires laid claim in Asia, Africa, and the Americas. Anglo-American naturalists played more than a peripheral part in the development of the natural and social sciences as well as the closely related exploration and exploitation of the colonies. Knowledge and power did not simply emanate from England in the expansive domain that natural history charted. Surveys, studies, and specimens rather circulated around the British Atlantic along with authority and expertise.[36]

Douglass's far-flung community of naturalists cultivated a sensibility of connoisseurship and "curiosity" akin to that of antiquarians and art collectors. They prized peculiarities and outstanding features of individual natural objects while classifying them according to their externally observable characteristics such as foliage, flower, and fruit as well as their social utility, aesthetic appeal, or commercial value.[37] Much as the explanatory power of early modern medicine stemmed from its ability to assimilate the bewildering variability of health and illness in different people and places, so natural history staked its claim on its command of the enormous variety of natural species in the Atlantic world. While scientific medicine was based on studies of various diseases in specific settings, the new composite science of life more generally entailed "natural histories" of particular regions—narrative accounts comprising systematic surveys of native plants, animals, landforms, waterways, and climates, modeled on works such as Robert Plot's *Natural History of Oxford-Shire* (1677) and Robert Boyle's *General Heads for the Natural History of a Country* (1692).[38]

Douglass began compiling the material for such an encyclopedic study soon after arriving in Boston, drawing on his knowledge of the work of pioneering European naturalists including Joseph Pitton de Tournefort of France and John Ray, Hans Sloane, and Mark Catesby of Britain, among others.[39] He eventually collected more than one thousand botanical specimens, particularly plants of medicinal or commercial value. He created voluminous records of the winds and weather patterns, geological features and astronomical events, as well as the crops and manufactures, imports and exports, and tribes and treaties of his adopted country, while continually exchanging intelligence with correspondents elsewhere in the colonies and in London. "I have minutes of all these as they from time to time fall under my own observation, or from very good vouchers," he wrote to Cadwallader Colden in New York in 1721. "I expect from you returns of the same nature."[40]

The ultimate objective of such inquiries was to derive from the diverse data of natural history an empirical understanding of the natural *order* that governed the new world of science and empire. In the medical theory of circulation, naturalists found a new basis of structure and stability within the very multiplicity and fluidity they described, providing the paradigm through which they interpreted a wide range of physical, chemical, biological, and social circuits. William Harvey's model of the circulatory system set the pattern for reconceiving the basic processes of revolution and transformation and the "subtle fluids" of light, heat, magnetism, and especially electricity, a central subject of experimental science in eighteenth-century England and America.[41]

By the centennial of Harvey's work and the beginning of Douglass's, circulation appeared increasingly central to a new conception of the cosmos as a self-regulating system: the "œconomy of nature." Natural historians drew on the classical notion of an "œconomy," traditionally associated with the cohesive order of a well-governed household, to envision the whole of creation as a harmonious ecosystem enclosed by the hydrological cycle uniting the fertile earth with the sheltering sky. In the Swedish naturalist Carolus Linnaeus's taxonomic treatise, *Œconomia Naturae* (1749), the leading model of an "economy" in the age of the Physiocrats and Adam Smith, each species of plant, animal, and mineral was integrated with every other in an intricate series of cycles of nutrition, growth, and decay.[42] "Is there a system, an order, an economy of things, by which matter can preserve that perpetual agitation which seems essential to it, and yet maintain a constancy in the forms which it produces?" wrote the Scottish philosopher David Hume in the mid-eighteenth century. "There certainly is such an economy; for this is actually the case with the present world. The continual motion of matter, therefore, in less than infinite transpositions, must produce the economy or order."[43]

Such ideas formed the intellectual environment for Douglass's progression from medicine into natural history. "There are Philosophers who would say that Matter and Motion are inseparable, that there is a continued Flux and Circulation thro' the whole Globe of Earth and Seas, that change and pass into different Forms and Appointments, as they were primarily ordain'd by the Omnipotent," wrote a correspondent in 1744 in the Boston monthly, the *American Magazine and Historical Chronicle.* Considering in turn the "perpetual Revolution" of the blood in the body, the "perpetual Motion" of "Animal and Vegetable Life," and the "continual flow" of "inanimate Substances," the article concluded with a somber reminder that "Power and Wealth" were increasingly subject to a "short Circulation" as well.[44]

In several seminal works composed in the 1740s, Douglass articulated in his own fashion these corresponding conceptions of circulation in the human body, in natural bodies more generally, and in the body politic. He produced a popular provincial almanac and a model regional map, together drawing the temporal and spatial dimensions of colonial New England. He also authored a historical and geographical survey of the British settlements from Nova Scotia to Virginia since the fifteenth century, situating Anglo-American society within a grand astronomical and geological scheme. As they traced the patterns of "matter in motion" in the heavens, the earth, and the empire, Douglass's almanac, map, and history provided the natural framework for his writings on currency and commerce, moving from the challenge of classification to the problem of class in a world of mercurial fortunes.

The first of these works was an almanac fittingly entitled *Mercurius Nov-Anglicanus* (New England Mercury), published in 1743 under the pseudonym "William Nadir, Student in the Mathematicks and a Lover of his Country." Douglass's pen name suggested the parallel between the laws of the universe and the laws of New England that formed the main theme of the volume, grounded in the mathematical sciences of magnitude in general and astronomy in particular, which early modern writers understood as the study of "magnitudes in motion." An epigraph from *Hudibras*, Samuel Butler's seventeenth-century poetic satire of religious enthusiasm, announced

Douglass's aim of reducing natural history and human history to a common calculus:

> From the Stars—
> *Some calculate the hidden Fates*
> *Of Monkeys, Puppy Dogs and Cats:*
> *Some take a Measure of the Lives*
> *Of Fathers, Mothers, Husbands, Wives.*

So too, the list of contents on the title page, arrayed in two columns—on the left, the days of the week and the month along with the times of the rising and setting of the sun and the moon, of the tides, and of eclipses; on the right, the civil courts of Massachusetts, the monarchs of Europe and of England, and the festivals and fasts of the Church of England—neatly aligned the celestial order with the social order. The "remarkables" or historic events that Douglass listed for each day of the year likewise commemorated the coronations, proclamations, and discoveries of monarchs, nobles, and scientists along with historic fires, earthquakes, eclipses, comets, and storms.[45]

Between the months, Douglass inserted mathematical notes on various forms of matter and motion, demonstrating the regularity of the movement of sound, the daily rotation and yearly orbit of the earth, the distance between the sun and other stars, and other natural relations, while offering similar summations of industrial and mercantile activity. One such note described the recently opened silk mill at Derby, England, quantifying its commotion like a force of nature:

> *There are 26,586 Wheels. 97,746 Movements. 73,728 Yards of Silk wound every Time the Wheel goes round, which is three Times every Minute. 318,504,960 Yards of Silk in one Day and Night, and consequently 99,378,547,550 Yards of Silk in a Year. One Water Wheel communicates Motion to all the rest of the Wheels and Movements, of which any one may be stopped separately and independent on* [sic] *the rest. One* Fire Engine *conveys* Air *to every individual Part of the* Machine, *and one* Regulator *governs the whole Work.*

In Douglass's depiction of an industrial automaton seemingly operated by air and water rather than labor and capital, nature itself implicitly appeared as a cosmic perpetual-motion machine, regulated by the steady circulation of its gears.[46]

He concluded the volume with three lengthy tables, identifying the naturally ordained cycles of the almanac with the inexorable extension of English rule. A "Table of the Kings and Queens of England" listed royal births, deaths, and years of reign, from the ascension of William I following the Norman Conquest in 1066 to that of George II in 1727. A "Table of Latitudes" subjected the sprawling sphere of commerce and conquest from Acapulco to Rotterdam to a uniform geographical matrix. Here Douglass appended "An Explanation of *Old* and *New Style*" dates in an effort to reconcile the Julian calendar of Great Britain with the Gregorian calendar observed by other nations, affording a universal time frame to go with the globe-spanning grid. (Britain converted to the Gregorian calendar in 1752.) Finally and most strikingly, a "Table of Interest at Six per Cent," designed "so that it is fitted to the meanest Capacity," enabled lenders and borrowers to determine how much was owed on a given sum, from five shillings to one hundred pounds, after one, two, three, six, nine, and twelve months. Along with the lines of royalty and the latitudes of empire, the schedule of interest imposed its own mathematical rule on the British realm, rendering the accumulation of capital as automatic and impersonal as the spinning of Derby silk.[47]

At the same time that Douglass was creating his New England almanac, he was also completing a definitive map of the region. He set the standard for subsequent maps—particularly the British cartographer John Green's celebrated *Map of the Most Inhabited Part of New England* (1755), which was largely modeled on Douglass's work—and established the dominant graphic vision of the four northernmost colonies until after the American Revolution. Having long exchanged cartographic texts with his correspondents elsewhere in the British Atlantic, he was well read in the contemporary theory and practice of map-making, a vital dimension of imperial knowledge and power. When it was posthumously printed in London in 1755, his *Plan of the British Dominions of New England* marked a qualitative advance in size and scale over earlier efforts to define the region geographically (figure 2.1).[48]

As the geographer Matthew Edney has shown, Douglass deliberately depicted New England as a unified, "natural" territory, not merely an artifact of British rule, based on a carefully contrived presentation of the map itself as the product of direct, unmediated observation, much like his earlier medical treatises. Douglass styled the work not a symbolic "map" but an empirical "plan," "Composed from actual Surveys," meaning a large-scale compilation of numerous small-scale governmental surveys of townships, districts, and proprietary claims from the preceding half century. Indeed, he gave his "plan of New England" the extraordinary appearance of a single, high-resolution land survey of the entire region, as opposed to a conventional low-resolution map based on the latitudes and longitudes of key points within a large area, though he understood that smaller plans charted at different times and places could not simply be stitched together in this way without considerable arti-

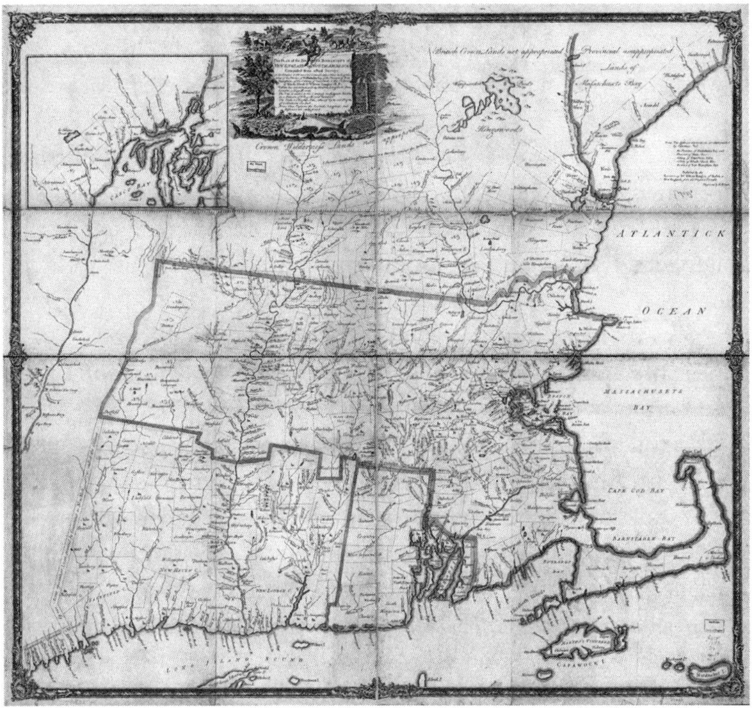

FIGURE 2.1. William Douglass, *Plan of the British Dominions of New England in North America*, engraved by R. W. Seale (London: Executors of the estate of William Douglass, 1755). Courtesy of the Library of Congress, G3720 1753 .D6.

fice.[49] Purposely spare in its use of symbols so that no legend was required to read it, the map appeared as a largely unadorned patchwork of parcels stretching from the vacant "lands not appropriated" of northern New England to the prime real estate along Massachusetts Bay and Long Island Sound. Originally intended for public display in the offices of township and district clerks, it presented less a transparent image of the region than an idealized vision in which property lines extended across the landscape with the stability and universality of Euclidean geometry, forming the natural basis of a cohesive colonial order.

In reality, the political and social terrain of New England was shaken violently in the years when Douglass was charting it from above and below. The resumption of imperial warfare in Europe set off a series of colonial conflicts in which Boston and its hinterland provided the bulk of the British soldiers, ships, and supplies, ending the long period of peace since Douglass's arrival in America. By Douglass's own estimate, nearly 20 percent of the able-bodied men of Massachusetts were killed in campaigns against Spanish bases in the

Caribbean and French outposts in Canada between 1739 and 1748, leaving behind a large number of impoverished widows and children and a critically weakened commercial economy. The ranks of recipients of public relief swelled, while the tax rolls dramatically declined as many became too poor to pay. Faced with skyrocketing expenses, the Massachusetts legislature increased poll and property taxes, which rose more than 40 percent per capita, while issuing an unprecedented volume of bills of credit to pay soldiers and suppliers, resulting in a drastic depreciation in the value of the paper currency.[50]

The poverty and social unrest of the 1740s prompted Douglass's efforts to classify the human subjects of empire as well as its natural objects, with money serving as the new basis of class distinctions. The creation of such a social taxonomy formed the underlying project of his survey of the history of British America and the implicit point of his writings on currency as well. Before discussing those works, however, a brief consideration of his own social status and his role as a founder of American philanthropy will illuminate his ideas about class and classification more generally.

Douglass expressed his sense of his class position in a letter requesting a tax abatement from the Boston town assessors in 1747, in which he enumerated his annual income from various sources—a noteworthy basis of argument in itself, since there was no income tax. He reported earnings from his medical practice the previous year totaling £500, considerably less than the £715 he had received from the tenants of his various rental properties and from those to whom he had loaned money at interest, and only half the value of the "outstanding debts" owed to him, which he estimated at £1,000.[51] "I contract the business of my Profession," he wrote candidly, "because considering long outstanding debts and bad pay, it is an affair of more labour than profit." As the petition indicated, much of Douglass's wealth lay in the substantial real estate he had acquired since the 1720s, including several houses and lots in Boston and Roxbury as well as lands in Middlesex, Worcester, and Hampshire Counties, later appraised at more than £3,000. His extensive acquisitions surely influenced his map of New England as a large-scale land survey.[52]

Unlike most early Americans, however, Douglass was interested in real estate mainly as a financial asset, as a means of generating rents and increasing the value of his estate rather than a means of production and support for a family and household. He invested in neither agriculture nor industry, and he never married. His primary residence in Boston, which he purchased in 1743, was the Green Dragon Tavern, a prominent example of the rising institution of the "public house" or "pub," which served as a sort of surrogate household for migrants, sojourners, and single men in late colonial New England. Cash formed the means of a new kind of kinship within commercial establishments such as his, affording access to room and board along with care and companionship, much as Douglass made his living as a physician selling services otherwise provided largely by family members and neighbors. Like the commodification of medicine that he helped to lead, the proliferation of taverns and inns represented a challenge to the role of local Congregational churches as overseers of such domestic services, as a rising chorus of lamentations by Puritan preachers attested.[53]

Douglass took a preeminent part in the emergence of another eighteenth-century alternative to the seventeenth-century commonwealth of households and churches. He was a longtime leader of the Scots Charitable Society in Boston, one of the first organizations of its kind in colonial America and a model for future philanthropies. It was founded in 1657 as a mutual-aid society of Scottish immigrants and prisoners of war transported to New England under Oliver Cromwell. The organization arose alongside but distinctly apart from the efforts of the Puritan establishment to promote its own charity schools, "societies for the suppression of disorder," and "young men's associations" ministering to a growing multitude of itinerant laborers and propertyless people in the countryside and port cities. The ecclesiastical organizations were designed to mobilize the increasing wealth of New England merchants under the aegis of an older religious ideal that received its classic statement in John Winthrop's "Modell of Christian Charity" (1630), updated for the new era in Cotton Mather's *Bonifacius* (1710). But Winthrop's original model of charity had been premised on a divinely ordained hierarchy of magistrates and subjects, masters and servants, heads of household and wives and children, "knitt more nearly together" in Christian love by paternal benevolence and grateful obedience. By contrast, Mather's later notion of "doing good" concerned the more fluid relations between the moneyed rich and the cash-poor in a nascent market society in which "liberality" served as an avowedly self-interested investment. In this changed context, discriminating donations to new "outdoor" institutions engaged in systematic, organized philanthropy demonstrated the gentility of the commercial classes and the subservience of the rising ranks of indigent sailors, soldiers, migrants, orphans, widows, and the seriously sick or disabled, for whom older forms of parish-, township-, and household-based relief proved increasingly inadequate.[54]

Taking its example from the Scottish Corporation of London, which was chartered in 1665 to assist "poor Natives of North-Britain, who are not entitled to any parochial Relief in England," the Scots Charitable Society in Boston was among the earliest organizations to take the "business of benevolence" out of the church and into the hands of merchants and shopkeepers themselves. Such commercial and philanthropic associations were modeled on the rise of the joint-stock corporation in England and inspired by the new discourse of political economy as much as by Christian piety. Douglass joined the society soon after arriving in America and became vice president in 1721. A few years later, Benjamin Franklin famously fled his apprenticeship at the *Boston Courant*, the organ of the anti-inoculation and anticlerical faction led by Douglass, and founded a mechanics' society in Philadelphia called the "Leather Apron Men," which is commonly considered the origin of American philanthropy.[55]

As vice president and later president, Douglass made the Scots Charitable Society more businesslike by diversifying its investments, instituting annual audits, and shoring up its finances. At the same time, he broadened the organization's mission to provide pensions for Scottish war veterans and regular assistance to the wandering poor, the elderly, the widowed, the orphaned, and the ill as well as recent immigrants. By the crisis of the 1740s, he had found in philanthropy an alternative to the family and household in more ways than one, endowing institutions that provided both social welfare services for the poor and cultural credentials for the rich, while preserving his estate in the absence of legal heirs.[56] "Having no family to provide for," as he wrote to the Boston assessors, he aimed to invest his savings "by dooing charities in my life time by donations and bounties."[57] His largest such endowment was a gift of thirty acres of land and £500 for the establishment and maintenance of a free school in the western Massachusetts town of New Sherburn in 1746, along with a promise of £50 per year for seven years to support the ministry there ("though quite a portion of these pledges was never received," according to a local historian), in exchange for renaming the town "Douglas" as his legacy.[58]

Douglass's *Summary, Historical and Political, Of the First Planting, Progressive Improvements, and Present State of the British Settlements in North America* (1747–52) brought the scientific perspective that he had developed in his previous work to bear on the growing concerns about class relations that guided his philanthropy. Originally issued as an irregular series of more than sixty pamphlets and subsequently collected as a two-volume set, it was soon acclaimed as the first comprehensive American history of the British colonies.[59] With its careful attention to provincial boundaries, topographical features, and cities and towns as well as its detailed chronicle of political and military events from the fifteenth century to the present, the work drew extensively on Douglass's experience in designing the almanac and the map. "Geography and chronology, are the two most considerable elements of History," he wrote.[60] Like his "practical histories" of contagious diseases, the

Summary was presented as a matter-of-fact synthesis of findings from first-hand observation, a study in "true *solid Philosophy* and *natural History*" as opposed to "pedantick *metaphysical Jargon*."[61] It was written in the rambling, "miscellaneous" style favored by contemporary naturalists, which Douglass deemed "more agreeable by its variety and turns, than a rigid dry connected account of things," and which was meant to demonstrate the author's patrician curiosity and discernment much as his composite portraits of disease displayed, as he put it, a refined "imagination" more often associated with "poets and painters."[62]

Its literary style reflected the central question of the *Summary*, which was how and where to draw new lines of class distinction and social authority at a moment of profound instability, as New Englanders found themselves on the front lines of Britain's escalating imperial conflict with France. "The FRENCH are the common Nusance and Disturbers of *Europe*," Douglass warned in the opening paragraphs, "and will in a short time become the same in *America*, if not mutilated at Home, and in *America* fenced off from us by Ditches and Walls." At the same time, he feared the consequences of the widening war for the fraying social fabric of the colonies themselves. A "small country" such as Britain must be careful "not to run upon Discoveries and Conquests, beyond what they can well improve and protect," he wrote, "because by overstretching, they weaken or break the Staple of their Constitution." The first essays of the *Summary* appeared on the heels of a massive attack by New England soldiers and sailors on the French fort of Louisburg in Nova Scotia in 1745, in which Douglass lamented the "loss of about 3,000 robust, labouring young men."[63] As Gary Nash has written of the Louisburg campaign, "the expedition had triumphed but in succeeding brought such human and financial devastation that the victory was lamented for years thereafter. The glory of bringing French Catholic power to its knees was slight comfort for hundreds of Boston families, for they had to reflect upon the victory in homes that were fatherless, husbandless, and dependent on charity for food and fuel."[64] Douglass's major concern was what the acute loss of men would mean for a colonial economy dependent on their labor. "It not only retards or stunts the growth of a colony, but in fact, minorates them, and pushes them backwards," he wrote of the military adventure. "This is the general complaint of the country; extravagant price of labour, and want of labourers."[65]

"Extravagant" was a keyword of Douglass's writings, appearing in his repeated criticisms of the "extravagant claims" of unqualified medical practitioners and his frequent denunciations of "idle and extravagant" debtors. In contemporary usage, it meant "straying" "out of bounds" or "roving beyond just limits," and was thus of a piece with his complaints about ministers "exceeding their bounds" and promoting "unbounded inoculation," and with his rigorous efforts in both the map and the *Summary* to draw clear property and province boundaries. The "extravagant price of labour" did not simply signify that the loss of manpower made labor excessively expensive for men like Douglass, who described himself as engaged in "an almost continued employ of tradesmen and labourers."[66] It suggested that the scarcity of labor blurred class lines much as quack medicine and debtor relief did, threatening the social position of prosperous merchants dependent on hired hands as well as the subsistence of poor widows and children dependent on charity.

In seeking to redraw the internal boundaries of colonial society along with its external borders, Douglass outlined a natural history of class relations based on currency and credit. Like the types and ranks of natural history more broadly, emergent eighteenth-century categories of race and class were expressly predicated on the empirical evidence of travel narratives and historical accounts, intended to reflect the flux of new social relations instead of the old fixed hierarchy of estates. Offering a materialist account that evidently influenced Adam Smith's conjectural history of commercial society in *The Wealth of Nations*, Douglass aimed to anatomize what he called the "political constitution" of the colonies, by which he meant not just their system of government but the class structure on which it rested.[67] "The Political Constitution, like the Human, is ticklish," he wrote. "There are but few who understand politick Health and Sickness."[68] Following contemporary political theorists such as Montesquieu and earlier James Harrington, Douglass contended that the health of the body politic depended on the maintenance of a "balanced constitution" in which monarchical, aristocratic, and democratic elements were harmoniously integrated. Leading European naturalists found analogs for such a class system among animals and plants, in the elaborate division of labor within ant and bee "colonies" and in Linnaeus's depiction of mosses, grasses, herbs, and trees as the peasantry, yeomanry, gentry, and nobility of the "polity of nature."[69]

Douglass began his own taxonomy of colonial peoples with the "Aboriginal Americans," whom he described in keeping with contemporary European conventions in almost entirely imaginary terms—a glaring exception to his general allegiance to empirical observation—as "the most barbarous and least polished People upon Earth," virtually devoid of agriculture or industry, government or culture. "Like the *wild Irish* they dread Labour more than Poverty," he wrote, in a nod to the proto-racial political arithmetic of William Petty and other architects of the commodification of land and labor in Ireland, though he allowed that "Many of our intermixed *Indians* are of good Use as Servants."[70] Among the English colonists, Douglass wrote that the first settlers included a handful of "ambitious adventurers" along with a much larger mass of criminals as well as "The Malcontents, the Unfortunate, the Necessitous," "the Disaffected and the Vicious." From these origins had arisen by Douglass's day "four Sorts of People": "1. *Masters* that is Planters and Merchants. 2. *White Servants*. 3. *Indian Servants*. 4. *Slaves* for Life, mostly *Negroes*."[71]

Conspicuously absent from this schema were the great majority of settlers who were neither servants nor masters, but small farmers or artisans and their families. Douglass regarded such petty proprietors as an essentially unnatural class whose outsized presence in the colonies upset the "balanced constitution" required for social stability and advancement. Lamenting the colonial practice of partible inheritance, he endorsed the laws in Britain for maintaining landed estates, like his father's in Scotland, in an argument worth careful consideration:

> Intestate real Estate divided among all the Children or Collaterals, and in the next Generation subdivided amongst their Children or Collaterals; will render a Colony for ever poor, because [such smallholders,] depending upon a small pittance of land, scarce sufficient to produce to [*sic*] the necessaries of life, and being under no absolute necessity of using further industry, they continue idle and miserable for life; whereas the younger children, if, instead of being freeholders, they become tenants[,] as a public good[,] they must be more industrious, and raise, besides a mere subsistence, a sufficient rent for the landlord, and acquire a habit of industry: some of their male children will become a nursery for the public land and sea service; as for the female children, their want of real estate will not disqualify them from being good breeders, but incite and oblige them to accept of husbands when they offer.[72]

The broad distribution of land and relative scarcity of labor nurtured the growth of a yeoman class engaged in subsistence farming, Douglass reasoned. Indivisible inheritance, by contrast, would consolidate property in the hands of large landowners and provide them with a ready supply of dispossessed tenants compelled to produce a surplus of staple crops in order to generate sufficient income to pay market rents. The concentration of landholding would also replenish the pool of willing soldiers, sailors, and mothers, bolstering the authority of commercial landlords and long-distance merchants over laboring men and women alike. While it was critical that those working the land be impelled to produce more than a "mere subsistence," it was equally vital that they not reap the surplus they sowed. For only by lowering the "extravagant price of labour" could "our merchants . . . afford in foreign markets to under-sell the merchants of other countries," Douglass contended.

"Besides," he continued, "let us suppose, their employers in generosity and beneficence to allow more wages than are merely sufficient to provide them the necessaries of life, perhaps, some few of them, may lay up this surplus, and, in a short time, aspire higher than this their mean labour, thus their labour is lost."[73]

If farming families earned enough from paid labor for some to become self-employed smallholders, their labor would be "lost" as surely as it was through partible inheritance; hence Douglass's call for the prohibition of "all combinations and agreements, between workmen concerning wages." The same logic informed his support for the establishment of three newly engineered industrial households in every colonial county: workhouses "to oblige and habituate idlers to some work," almshouses for those too aged, ill, or feeble for productive labor, and "orphan-houses" for children whose parents were dead or unable to provide for them, and who were "not to be brought up to idle learning (reading and writing excepted) but to trades and labour: generally these poor children may be bound to proper masters, as apprentices or servants."[74]

Douglass's proposals for altering the laws of inheritance and the system of poor relief were part of a broader blueprint for restructuring colonial politics and property relations in the image of the English "mixed government" of king and Parliament and the class triad of rent-seeking landlords, commercial tenant farmers, and hired laborers. Representing "the quintessence of Douglass's political philosophy," as John Bumsted has written, the "scheme for the better regulating these colonies" formed the thematic centerpiece of the *Summary*, which was largely devoted to demonstrating that the British colonies were naturally suited for such a sweeping set of reforms, much as his precedent-setting map imagined New England as a perfectly laid plan of properties and provinces.[75] Indeed, Douglass envisioned the American settlements themselves as interlocking units of a great colonial works, governed by a single sovereign "regulator" and powered by the carefully channeled circulation of labor throughout.

He proposed vacating all remaining proprietary and corporate colonial charters and reconstituting all the colonies as royal provinces, "*all Governments of the Colonies to be vested in the Crown*"; creating a uniform code of "general Laws for all the Plantations," to be drafted by a board of trade empowered to levy taxes and quitrents; paying the salaries of colonial governors from Westminster, rendering them independent of the provincial legislatures; granting a veto over the elected assemblies' laws to the royally appointed governors as well as to a council of the "hereditary Lords of large Manors . . . appointed by Royal Patents," that is, owners of estates of three thousand acres or more; and removing all civil power from the clergy, establishing instead a system for licensing ministers, assigning them to permanent pulpits, and treating itinerant preachers—like, Douglass hoped, unlicensed physicians—as "idle and disorderly Persons, Vagrants and Vagabonds." In justification of this last proposal, he noted that "vagrant enthusiasts" had distracted from their proper callings "poor deluded Tradesmen and Labourers (whose Time is their only Estate)," estimating that each of the touring evangelist George Whitefield's sermons in Boston had wasted roughly £1,000 in hours that might otherwise have been profitably employed.[76]

The reform he advocated most assiduously, however, concerned control over the circulation of money itself. In the *Summary* and in a series of extended essays on finance and trade in the 1730s and 1740s, Douglass became the leading critic of colonial paper currency in a period when the stock of outstanding bills nearly quintupled in New England.[77] Authorized by elected assemblies in which men of small means and growing debts exercised far more power than their counterparts across the Atlantic, paper money came to epitomize for Douglass the danger of commercial circulation spinning out of the control of monarchs, merchants, and moneylenders, much as the innovation of inoculation by clergymen and "quacks" had signified twenty years earlier.[78]

"The Great Wheel": Currency and Credit in Political Economy

Like many seventeenth- and eighteenth-century British writers, Douglass viewed money as the "lifeblood" of the market economy that they conceived on the model of the human body or the "œconomy of nature." Daniel Defoe's *The Complete English Tradesman* (1726) similarly depicted "the circulation of trade within ourselves, where all the several manufactures move in a just rotation from the several countries where they are made, to the city of London, as the blood in the body to the Heart."[79] Leading theorists of preclassical political economy including Hobbes, Petty, John Locke, and Nicholas Barbon trained in anatomy, physiology, and related fields, from which they drew the understanding of circulatory processes that they brought to their writings on commerce and currency. "In nature everything is intertwined," wrote the French physician and Physiocrat François Quesnay, "everything runs through circular courses which are interlaced with one another."[80]

For eighteenth-century economic writers, circulation represented the quintessentially modern conception of a self-regulating system in which power emanates from the mutual relations among constituent parts rather than from a supervening authority. Adam Smith's "invisible hand" of the market, ostensibly arising without deliberate design as the result of countless independent actions by a multitude of competing individuals, exemplified a general pattern taking shape within such varied fields as political theory, mental and moral philosophy, Newtonian mechanics, vitalist physiology, and natural theology.[81] Classical political economy in particular was predicated on the ideal of a market society in which fixed, coercive, and bilateral relations of dependence between sovereigns and subjects or masters and servants were giving way to fluid, contractual, and multilateral relations of interdependence among producers and consumers, bondholders and taxpayers, landlords and tenants, employers and employees—in other words, monetary relations mediated by new networks of impersonal credits and debts.

The political economy of credit and currency was never far from the surface of Douglass's *Summary*. He took every opportunity to inveigh against "depreciating Money-making Ass[emb]lies," which trampled on the exclusive "Prerogative of the Crown" (or rather of the king and his parliamentary allies among English commercial landlords, financiers, and colonial planters) and, along with other "Acts for the Relief of Debtors, hurt Creditors and the Credit of the Country very much."[82] He denounced the "fallacious and designed cheat of a plantation government public Paper Currency," anticipating by several decades a core argument of the Federalist Papers, in which paper money issued by the newly independent states demonstrated the need for constitutional reform to protect propertied interests from the "tyranny of the majority." "I have observed that all our Paper-money-making assemblies have been legislatures of debtors," Douglass wrote, "the representatives of people who from incongitancy, idleness, and profuseness, have been under a necessity of mortgaging their lands." Decrying "the vast incredible damages that personal estates have suffered in New England, by depreciation of denominations from the multiplying of a nominal Paper Currency," he estimated that whereas £100 in silver coin exchanged for £140 in colonial paper in 1711, by 1748 the same amount of specie exchanged for £1,000 in New England notes.[83]

Adam Smith emphatically agreed in 1776, drawing on the American example in explaining the vital importance of a stable means of payment and standard of value, or of what he called "the great wheel of circulation," "by means of which every individual in the society has his subsistence, conveniences, and amusements regularly distributed to him in their proper proportions."[84] Citing Douglass's critique of depreciated colonial paper, Smith wrote, "To oblige a creditor, therefore, to accept of this as full payment for a debt of a hundred pounds actually paid down in ready money was an act of such violent injustice as has scarce, perhaps, been attempted by the government of any other country which pretended to be free. It bears the evident marks of having originally been, what the honest and downright Doctor Douglas [*sic*] assures us it was, a scheme of fraudulent debtors to cheat their creditors."[85]

Douglass felt the sting of this scheme personally, not only because he earned a growing share of his income from lending money at interest, but because his medical practice depended on credit as well. "I have here practice amongst four sorts of People," he explained in a 1721 letter to Cadwallader Colden, classifying his patients according to their means of payment. "Some families pay me five pounds per annum each for advice sick or well, some few fee me as in Britain, but for the Native New-Englanders I am obliged to a keep a day book of my Consultations advice and Visits, and bring them a bill; others of the poorer sort I advise and visit without any expectation of fees."[86] The third and probably largest group—those whom Douglass billed after advising or treating them—roughly corresponded to the stratum of self-employed but cash-poor households that troubled his taxonomy of colonial classes in the *Summary*. Their unpaid bills accounted for the "long and outstanding debts" of which he later complained to the tax assessors, rendering his occupation by then "an affair of more labour than profit."

As with his campaign against "unbounded inoculation" in the 1720s, however, Douglass's opposition to the deluge of paper money in the 1740s reflected more than his immediate self-interest. It manifested his understanding of the uncertain authority of New England's landlord and merchant elite, in a region where real property remained comparatively widely distributed and relatively few families yet paid rent, worked for wages, or relied primarily on the production and sale of staple crops. In such a society of smallholders, as John Brooke has pointed out, the main leverage that leading families possessed lay in their control of the cash and credit that those with little liquid wealth but increasing ambition required in order to buy and develop new land.[87] The latter class of enterprising debtors included a wide range of farmers, artisans, shopkeepers, and merchants serving local and regional markets. They formed the backbone of the "land bank" movement of the early 1740s in Boston and more than sixty counties and towns in eastern and central Massachusetts, spurred into action by heightened royal restrictions on provincial bills of credit and the prospect of a drastic contraction in the money supply. This latest financial venture aimed to provide credit and cash in the form of transferable notes to small farmers who mortgaged their property and deposited their surplus produce with a newly formed private bank, which would take responsibility for marketing the goods on the borrowers' behalf. The Land Bank of 1740 was vociferously opposed by the royal governor and his council, who blocked its charter and prohibited provincial officials from accepting its notes, and it was soon suppressed by Parliament. But the resulting controversy sparked a popular insurgency leading to a series of large new emissions of public bills of credit. Douglass was drawn into the greatest struggle over the money question in fifty years, the climax of the currency conflict in provincial New England.[88]

Douglass joined an emerging school of thought associated in the colonies with big transatlantic merchants and large landowners with investments at interest, and with close ties to the Board of Trade and the Crown. Such colonial critics of paper currency were profoundly influenced by British mercantilist writings on trade and by exponents of the metallic standard and the "intrinsic value" or "natural value" of money such as John Locke, who helped to formulate the ideological basis for the English financial revolution.[89] Their ranks in Massachusetts included Paul Dudley, attorney general for the colony in the first two decades of the eighteenth century and son of Joseph Dudley, one of the members of Edmund Andros's governing council that had tried John Wise; Thomas Hutchinson, later governor of Massachusetts in the years leading up to the Revolution; and the clergyman and Harvard divinity professor Edward Wigglesworth.

As early as 1714, when the currency question was first emerging in American political discourse, Paul Dudley argued that colonial issues of paper money violated the sovereign prerogatives of the Crown, illicitly establishing an "independent Government, which like a Fire in the Bowels, will Burn up and Consume the whole Body." While a true "Money-bank" must be founded on "the true or common Current Money of the country," namely, gold and silver coin, Dudley contended, one founded purely on fiat or common agreement would "Alter and Destroy the very Nature of Money." "So that instead of Answering all things, as it has always done, and ought to do, it will now Answer nothing, and be worse than every thing else," Dudley wrote. "For that which really makes the Value of Money, among other things, is its Rarity: So that upon the whole, the Remedy proposed by these Projectors, will be much worse than the Disease." The real reason for the scarcity of metallic money in the colonies lay in a bad balance of trade, to be redressed by restricting imports of British luxuries. Dudley echoed Douglass's rhetoric of "extravagance," bemoaning "the great Extravagance that People, and especially the Ordinary sort, are fallen into, far beyond their circumstances, in their Purchases, Buildings, Families, Expences, Apparel, and generally in their whole way of Living."[90] Other writers sounded this call for greater thrift in a more republican key, arguing that imports of costly luxuries like silk stockings, fine china, and rum were corrupting the body politic along with the domestic economy. They implored the colonists to be "more *Frugal*" and more "diligent and laborious to *raise, produce, make* as much as we can for our own support," instead of engaging in speculative schemes of improvement and expansion. "WE in the Country think," wrote an anonymous pamphleteer in 1719, "that *Plotting heads, Proud hearts*, and *Idle hands*, will never maintain a People; and that a close following the *Wheel* within doors, and the *Plough* without are much better and stronger Politicks."[91]

This was the tradition to which Douglass signally contributed in his main writings on the currency question: *An Essay Concerning Silver and Paper Currencies* (1738), *A Discourse Concerning the Currencies of the British Plantations in America* (1740), *A Letter to —— Merchant in London* (1741), and *A Second Letter to —— Merchant in London* (1741). Douglass did not oppose paper currency per se. He supported government issuance of bills of credit as a means of short-term finance in anticipation of future taxes, so long as such bills were retired reliably and quickly, were not declared legal tender for the payment of private debts, and did not become a general medium of exchange, inflating the money supply. His case against the large, inflationary issues of provincial bills came down to three main arguments. The first concerned his vision of the marriage of sovereignty and capital, or public authority and private investment. The second concerned his understanding of the nature and advantages of circulation, as opposed to direct exchange of commodities or barter. The third concerned his conception of the capitalist transformation of political and class relations, particularly those between creditors and debtors; more broadly, it concerned the relationship between popular sovereignty and commercial capitalism. In all three of these areas, Douglass shared with his opponents a common set of assumptions that set the stakes of struggle over currency and banking in early America.

Douglass began each of his major works on the currency question with a tribute to the union of sovereignty and capital entailed in the English financial revolution. Much as Wise sought to enlist merchants on behalf of provincial bills of credit, Douglass contended that the essence of the partnership between Crown and commerce lay in the rise of the hard-money silver standard. He wrote that the long history of rulers debasing the coinage had finally come to an end in Holland, France, and England over the past century and a half, as commerce had become increasingly central to statecraft and empire. Merchants had long favored silver and gold coin as a medium of trade. Only in modern times, however, had merchants become partners with monarchs, bringing an end to debasement of the currency. "The Credit of *Merchants* in the commercial World is become more sacred, than the Probity of *Ministers* in the civil Administration, and is a Check upon them," Douglass wrote.[92] Or, as he put it elsewhere, "A general Stop has been put to those notorious publick Frauds ever since Trade began to flourish; the civil Governments becoming more polite, found it their Interest in Affairs of a *Medium* of Trade, to be advised by the more knowing and experienced Traders."[93] The "most glorious" aspect of the Glorious Revolution, Douglass declared, had been the reminting of the English coinage in milled-edged coins that could not be shaved or clipped and that contained the full amount of silver matching their face value. The recoinage of the mid-1690s, combined with Master of the Mint Isaac Newton's declaring the intrinsic value of the silver coins of all countries with which England traded a few years later, founded the financial strength of the rising British Empire firmly on the silver standard. It safeguarded the interests of moneyed investors and large import-export merchants who joined hands with the reformed English state.[94]

Thereafter, every nation that engaged in international commerce had to base its own currency on the money standard agreed on by the transnational mercantile elite. "The universal trading Part of the World, as one tacit Confederacy have fallen into some *general Rules*, which by Custom of Merchants are become as Fundamental," Douglass wrote. "One of these is a *Silver Medium of Trade*, that all Contracts . . . are understood to be payable in this Medium, being always of the same fixed Value."[95] A trading nation like Britain might thenceforth authorize banks to issue notes that could circulate among merchants as a convenient substitute for coin, but such paper promises must be payable in silver. Indeed, as he explained, "*A Paper Credit* well founded and under good Regulations, and not larger than what the Silver Specie Currency will bear; has been found to be a very good Expedient in Business, and it leaves the *Silver Species* at more Liberty to be used as Merchandize, and for petty Occasions."[96] In order for the notes to be as good as the silver for which they could be redeemed—to trade with silver "at par" or at a premium—they had to bear interest, since a promise to pay in silver in the future was generally not worth as much as the silver itself immediately in hand. And the volume of notes in circulation must be constrained by the amount of silver in which they were redeemable in order to avoid depreciation. "*If Paper Credit exceeds a certain Proportion of the concomitant Silver Currency, its Effects are bad, and ruinous*; by its precarious Loss of Value," Douglass wrote.[97]

While the French, Dutch, and British governments had thus made inviolable the compact between the Crown and the commercial gentry, according to Douglass, they had foolishly allowed their American colonies to violate that sacred bond. The colonies had debased the currency and defrauded creditors by issuing paper not backed by silver on demand, but by future tax revenues—paper that should have been limited to short-term financing of government expenses, not long-term circulation as a medium of trade—and thereby saddled future generations with a mounting burden of debt. "As it is a natural Instinct in Animals to provide for Posterity, it must be deem'd very *unnatural and wicked* in us, instead of doing so, to contribute to their future Misery," Douglass wrote. ". . . So much paper as is current in a Province, *so much really is that Province in Debt*; for the *Funds* Part, the Publick is in Debt; for the *Loans* Part, private Persons are in Debt: It is a Contradiction to assert that a Country may *grow rich by* (Paper Money) *running in Debt*."[98] The colonies had made their bills of credit non-interest-bearing, which ensured that their market value would be less than their face value in silver. Worst of all, they had declared such depreciated paper legal tender for the payment of private debts. "To make a Bill or Note bearing no Interest, and not payable till after a dozen or score of Years, a legal Tender . . . in Payment of Debts, is the highest of *despotick* and arbitrary Government," Douglass wrote, in terms that strongly resembled Wise's countervailing critique of "despotism" and "arbitrary government" several decades earlier. "Our Paper Money Colonies have carried the Iniquity still further," he continued. "The Popular or *Democratick* Part of the Constitution are generally in Debt, and by their too great Weight or Influence in Elections, have made a depreciating Currency, a Tender for Contracts done many Years before; that is, *they impose upon the Creditor side in private Contracts*, which the most despotick Powers never assumed."[99]

By making their paper bills legal tender, the colonies not only irresponsibly piled up public debt and interfered with the sanctity of private contracts, according to Douglass. They also forced into circulation an unnatural medium of exchange instead of trusting in the natural medium that markets supplied and merchants preferred. Far better, he contended, to trust that "Trade will find its own *natural proper Medium*, viz. *Silver and Gold*."[100] The natural dynamics of international trade would automatically redress any imbalances if left to their own operations. Too little coin in a country would tend to reduce imports, improving the balance of trade, and hence drawing in specie from abroad. "It is therefore vain and inconsistent to make *Provincial* or Municipal Bills of Credit, for a Medium of general Trade," he wrote. "Merchants know how to find their own Tools or *Medium* of Trade, better than any Civil Administration can prescribe."[101] In this regard, Douglass drew explicitly on his understanding of the self-regulating "œconomy of nature," on his criticism of "heroic" medical therapeutics that proved more harmful than the maladies they were supposed to cure, and on his previous writings on matter in motion more generally. He likened the popular demand for more and more paper money to "Thirst in a *Dropsy*, which by endeavoring to satisfy with Drink, increases the Distemper."[102] And he likewise compared the self-sustaining inflationary cycle "to natural *oscillatory* Motions," observing that "when got to their Extent on the one Side," "they must return gradually and in the same Path to the other Side."[103]

The second argument that Douglass advanced against the colonial paper currency regime concerned what kind of currency would circulate most speedily and widely. Like Wise and other supporters of the provincial bills, he presumed that the main object of the means of payment was "to avoid the inconveniencies of barter." But whereas Wise maintained that metallic money naturally tended to be hoarded or exported, while paper money tended to remain in circulation, Douglass argued that "paper Currency in large Quantities does not answer this End; because of its Fluctuation, or rather progressive less Value; which obliges the Merchant at length to return to *Barter* again, as being safe and better."[104] While legal-tender provisions could compel colonial merchants and creditors to accept paper currency in payment of local debts, they could not make such currency circulate across the Atlantic. Nor could they force moneyed men to extend credit in the first place. A depreciating currency and the broader damage it did to the sanctity of debt contracts pressured lenders to collect debts more frequently and assiduously for fear of losing what they had lent. "*People chuse rather to hoard it up*, and wait for better Times, than put it out and not be able to recover it again, but after an unreasonable Length of Time and much Trouble," Douglass wrote, noting that "Money hoarded up, is the same as if not in being, as to Currency."[105]

As a result, a strict specie standard and short-term credit, by protecting the interests of creditors and encouraging them to lend, fostered a higher volume of transactions, making the available stock of currency go further by heightening its velocity of circulation. "Ready Money and short Credit, give a quick Circulation; the quicker the Circulation, the less Quantity of *Medium* is required to carry on the same Trade and Business: long Credit, and insensibility of Discredit, have the contrary Effect," Douglass wrote.[106] In this way, overissue of paper bills had the seemingly paradoxical result, in his view, of reducing the real money supply even as it increased the nominal supply. Like Wise, Douglass staked his argument in part on a case for priming the pump of investment and economic growth; but whereas Wise contended that easier, cheaper money would fuel this virtuous cycle, Douglass insisted that the way to foster economic growth was to protect the hard-money interests of wealthy creditors, trusting that they would lend more readily to industrial, agricultural, and commercial entrepreneurs in turn.

While the depreciation of colonial paper thus constricted economic growth in monetary terms, Douglass maintained that it fueled, in the short term, a kind of unreal, speculative boom. The two things went together: paper currency and "long credit" fostered extravagant spending, reckless expansion, and a false sense of prosperity, even as they diverted common people's energies from patient industry and productive labor into gambling pursuits and frivolous consumption, bringing in train an inevitable decline of fortunes over the long run. He thus explained both what he deemed the overtrading and overbuilding of the first two decades of the eighteenth century and the downturn and doldrums of the next thirty years. "*Long Credit* occasions the unthinking of all Conditions and Occupations, to involve themselves," Douglass wrote. "A Merchant over-trades himself, a Shopkeeper buys more Goods, and at a greater Advance than he can afterwards comply with; the Countryman buys and Mortgages Lands, to his final Ruin."[107]

His third and most fundamental argument concerned the ways in which the monetary system restructured political power and class relations. The reason for the colonies' wayward embrace of depreciated paper bills was plain to see for Douglass. It lay in the rising ranks and increasing power in provincial assemblies of that middling class of freeholders who were neither servants nor masters. "In many of our Plantations of late Years, by bad Management and Extravagancies, the Majority of the People are become *Debtors*, hence their Elected Representation in the Legislature have a great Chance to be generally of the Debtors Side," Douglass wrote, "or in other Words, the *Representatives* being generally Freeholders, and many of them *much in Debt*; by large Emissions their Lands rise in Denomination Value while their Debts become really less, and the Creditor is defrauded in Part of his Debt. Thus our Colonies have defrauded more in a few Years, than bad Administrations in *Europe* have formerly done in some Centuries."[108] Or, as he candidly explained in an open letter to a London merchant, "In *Great-Britain*, the Landed Interest consists generally of Gentlemen very rich, with valuable Rent-Rolls; Our *Freeholders* generally are labouring Men, who earn less, and fare worse, than many in Boston, and without any Rent-Rolls. The Debtor part of the Country (which is vastly the most numerous) are contriving to baulk their Creditors by reducing the Denominations of Money (by their huge and ill-secured Emissions) to a small or no Value; that they who have laudably acquired Fortunes by Industry and Frugality, may reap no Benefit thereof, but be upon a level with the Idle and Extravagant."[109]

The challenge that such freeholders posed to the power of private financiers in partnership with royal authorities began with paper money schemes, which challenged the exclusive control of wealthy elites over the supply of currency and credit. "In other Countries, the Opulent, the Honest, the Men of Credit, become Bankers," Douglass wrote. "Here the Indigent, the Debtors, the Fraudulent, set up for Bankers."[110] In a second open letter published the same year, he drew the inescapable conclusion: "When poor People can have present Money (tho' only nominal) on so easy Terms, . . . can it be supposed that they will be assiduous in Labour to increase our Produce and Manufacture? No, they will become *Idlers* and *Extravagant*."[111]

The ramifications of such an experiment with popular rule over the means of payment extended beyond labor relations. For the logic of paper money spent on public salaries and supplies or lent on landed security by an elected legislature encouraged the dangerous delusion "that *common Consent*, or the Humour of the Multitude, ought to be the *Ratio Ultima* in every thing and particularly in *Currencies*; whereas not only according to the Constitution of *Great-Britain*, but of all polite Governments, Money or Currencies are the *Prerogative* of the SOVEREIGNS, and have followed the universal Custom of Merchants, whereby *Silver* from its own natural Qualifications, could not avoid becoming the *universal Medium of Trade*."[112] The leveling spirit quickly expanded to encompass all manner of lax enforcement of contracts, "which seem[s] to encourage this *insensibility of Discredit* in Debtors," including "*too general Laws for the relief of insolvent Debtors*, whereby the Fraudulent, the Idle, and the Extravagant, when sent to Gaol are too soon, at too easy a Rate turned loose to follow the same Courses."[113] It spurred the "most destructive and wicked Principle," "that every *Landed Man* . . . has a *Right* to make *Money*."[114] It led inexorably toward riot, redistribution, and revolt.

Douglass feared in particular the rising power of what he tellingly called "the Mobility" or "mob," a contemporary English epithet for crowds of common people engaged in extralegal resistance to engrossment, extortion, and usury by commercial farmers, traders, and moneylenders.[115] "Our Province in a peculiar Manner . . . requires some more severe Acts against *Riots, Mobs*, and *Tumults*. The least Appearance of a *Mob* (so called from *Mobile Vulgus*) ought to be suppressed, even where their Intention in any particular Affair is of it self very good; because they become Nurseries for dangerous Tumults," he wrote in the *Summary*.[116] In the social context of the colonies, the category of "the mobility" took on a broader significance, referring to the masses of men effectively challenging the rule of wealthy merchants and landlords in the colonial legislatures. "By the *Vulgar and Populace*," Douglass wrote in his *Discourse Concerning Currencies*, "I always mean the unthinking Part of Mankind, who are not capable of consulting their own Interest; the *Mobility* who do not reason for themselves; but are tossed about with every Wind of designing ill Men."[117]

Douglass found the seed of the trouble in the notion that money, like politics, should be governed by majority rule. In this sense, what was ultimately at stake in the money question was nothing less than the relationship between the rule of capital and popular sovereignty. "If common Consent were to take Place, all the Effects in the Province would be equally divided amongst the People, because we are all born equal," Douglass explained. "After some Time the Idle and Extravagant becoming empty handed, while the Frugal and Industrious become rich, common Consent would divide again. Our depreciating Paper Currency by taking from time to Time, Part of the Estates of the Creditors in Favour of the Debtor has the same Tendency: Is this to encourage Industry? Who would labour in Produce and Manufacture to be thus stript of his Earnings?"[118] At bottom, his was a vision of medicine, natural history, and political economy rooted in a fixed order of society and nature, a great chain of being extending from the natural into the social realm. Yet the accelerating circulation of people, goods, and money, which offered new possibilities for colonial gentry and natural philosophers like Douglass, also posed new challenges of contagion and popular unrest.

Douglass lived to see the colonial campaign for the silver standard triumph over the supporters of paper currency. Boosted by a reimbursement of £180,000 in specie from Parliament for the costs that the Bay Colony had incurred in King George's War with France, the Massachusetts legislature called in much of its fiduciary paper currency and replaced it with paper certificates backed by coin in 1749, and after 1750 all debts and contracts were declared legally payable only in silver. A year before Douglass died, Parliament effectively put an end to the province's radical experiment with paper money begun in 1691, the year he was born. Responding to the demands of transatlantic merchants and creditors, the Currency Act of 1751 prohibited the provinces of Massachusetts, New Hampshire, Rhode Island, and Connecticut from issuing any paper currency except short-term notes redeemed within two years, and from designating any of their bills legal tender for the payment of private debts.[119] Nevertheless, the half-century trial in New England—"the longest and most bitter fight over economic policy in British North America prior to the Stamp Act Crisis," according to Elizabeth Dunn—created an enduring political constituency and intellectual rationale for popular control over an elastic supply of currency and credit.[120]

Both sides of the conflict over colonial money embraced the novel merger of finance and statecraft—whether in Boston or Westminster, on the basis of banknotes or bills of credit, backed by private assets or public faith. As they staked out a new terrain of class struggle, they rooted their competing claims in a shared understanding of the underlying laws of commerce on which the monetary superstructure was supposed to rest. The early modern concept of circulation, founded on the religious precepts of natural law and the scientific principles of natural history, formed the first framework for that long-lasting conflict. For Douglass, the unchecked authorization of paper currency upset the natural circulation of credit and commodities much as "unbounded inoculation" disrupted the "ordinary course of Nature" amid the perpetual motion of the British Atlantic.

PART TWO

Commercial Banking and the Problem of Representation in the Jacksonian Era

3

William Leggett and the Melodrama of the Market

Long after Americans won their political independence, they remained financially dependent on British credit to pay for an excess of imports over exports. After a brief revival of the practice of state legislatures issuing paper currency in the 1780s, the U.S. Constitution followed the British model in making gold and silver coin the sole legal tender, while states authorized commercial banks to lend out banknotes redeemable in specie on demand, which became the main means of payment in the new nation. In the spring of 1837, the flow of British credit suddenly slowed to a trickle, and the supply of specie dried up along with it. Falling prices for American cotton and failing harvests of American wheat prompted anxious English lenders to demand payment in hard cash from American borrowers, at the same time that a new law required specie for purchases of land from the federal government. As Americans raced to cash in their banknotes and deposits for gold or silver, banks quickly ran out of sufficient coin. In early May, the New York banks "suspended specie payments," and banks across the country soon closed their coffers as well. Within weeks, tens of thousands of New York City shopkeepers and workers were thrown out of business or out of work.[1]

Among them was the intellectual leader of the local labor movement, a firebrand newspaper editor named William Leggett (1801–39), who greeted the crash as a vindication of his widely followed crusade against the banking system. "Let the banks perish! Let the monopolists be swept from the board!" Leggett declared. "Let the whole brood of privileged money-changers give place to the hardy offsprings of commercial freedom, who ask for no protection but equal laws, and no exemption from the shocks of boundless competition." Three months later, with banks and businesses failing across the country, Leggett exulted that the worst panic in its fifty-year history had exposed the fraudulence of the financial regime:

> But it has so turned out that these bankers now stand before the world, by their own confession, as a crew of swindling pirates, who have been preying on the property of the community. They threw open their vaults, where they led the publick to believe that they had abundant resources of hidden treasure, and lo, not an ounce of silver or gold is there! They are bankrupt, they are broken, they are utterly worthless. They have made way with that (if indeed they ever had it) on which the confidence of the community was placed, and their promises now, instead of representing silver and gold, represent nothing but violated faith, and the folly of publick credulity in the honesty of soulless corporations which derive their very being from legislative corruption.[2]

Nothing inspires faith in a good god like bad times. Much as Christian evangelists sought divine deliverance from the ensuing depression, leading writers and reformers found solace in the new gospel of "the market."[3] None offered a more powerful portrayal of this rising sovereign than Leggett, who championed the benevolence of market forces with surpassing creativity and zeal through the boom and bust of the 1830s. Yet like many Jacksonians, Leggett found a nemesis for the market he revered in what was at once the most concrete and most abstract manifestation of its dominion: the rise of commercial banks and the paper currency they created. In the titanic conflict between the "natural economy" and the "money power," he and the many writers who followed his lead staged a political melodrama that animated public debate for a century and still speaks to us today.

The clash of what have come to be called Main Street and Wall Street arose in the political imagination as a means of making sense of the travails of men like Leggett himself, a blacksmith's son who struggled on the edge of failure and poverty throughout his career. Like many journalists in early industrial America, he shared the fortunes and fears of the struggling class of skilled artisans and small shop owners from which he came. Their fathers, like his, had formed the rank and file of the American Revolution, from whom they inherited a proud tradition of artisanal republicanism associated with patriot printers like Benjamin Franklin and Thomas Paine. With the extension of suffrage to men of little or no property in the 1820s, self-styled "mechanics and workingmen" participated directly in electoral politics for the first time. They founded the first labor parties and trade unions in New York, Philadelphia, and other eastern cities in the 1820s and 1830s, much like their British and French counterparts in these same years. They looked to Leggett as the most prominent among a host of Jacksonian editors who championed their cause.[4]

At the same time, master craftsmen faced unprecedented pressure to maximize output and minimize cost as merchant capitalists took control of their trades. Journeymen aspiring to become masters competed instead with children, convicts, and unskilled laborers for low-wage sweatshop work. So too, the partisan press of which Leggett was part vied with a new breed of profit-driven "penny dailies" for the growing ranks of working-class readers. What most urgently incited the self-styled "workingmen's movement" he came to lead, however, was a devastating rise in the cost of food, fuel, and housing in the seaboard cities. Prices for basic commodities like flour and coal skyrocketed along with rents in the mid-1830s, while employment grew frightfully insecure amid a frenzy of speculative development of city lots and western lands fueled by an explosion of new banks and bank lending. The bubble burst in the panic of 1837, bringing a violent end not only to the boom, but to the early republic of craft workshops and family farms. Leggett died amid the wreckage two years later, as broke as the banks.[5]

The nascent labor movement itself fell victim to the crisis of the household economy that had reared it. But it bequeathed to the class politics of the nineteenth century a set of lessons from the crash course in capitalism, which Leggett best expressed. In the rhetoric of the workingmen and their political progeny, the market ironically appeared as a bulwark of propertied independence against the onslaught of wage labor and finance capital.[6] An idealized vision of a simple market economy was twinborn with the fraudulent other against which it was defined, namely, money as the ruler over industry and commerce instead of the subservient medium of exchange, forming the ends rather than the means of the market economy. Like gambling, counterfeiting, prostitution, and addiction, the "money power" constituted a haunting mirror image of industrial capitalism in its youth. It provided both an enduring language for political opposition and a corresponding way of legitimating the always unrealized market ideal. The money power stood for what was oppressive, artificial, volatile, and corrupt in the new order. The market, by contrast, became exalted as inherently free, natural, stable, and true.

This chapter explores the melodrama of the market through the lens of Leggett's life and work. Though best known as an editor and labor leader, he began his career performing in plays and recitals, gained a reputation as an author of poetry, short stories, and literary criticism, and formed a close friendship with Edwin Forrest, the leading stage actor of the day.[7] He stood at the center of a revolution in literary, political, and economic forms, marked by the advent of the star system in theater, the western and the sea story, and the penny press, along with modern political parties and industrial works. His previous writing gave Leggett a repertoire of characters, plots, and themes that enabled him to find transcendent significance in the politics of corporations and currency. Yet his meteoric career also exemplifies how the social and economic crisis of the 1830s stretched the literary logic of Jacksonian political economy to its breaking point.

"The Mischief of Misrule": Commercial Banking and the Problem of Representation

At the crux of the contrast between the market and the money power lay a three-dimensional problem of political, financial, and literary representation. The most basic lesson the workingmen drew from their experience was that economic misfortune reflected political misrule. Ruinous inflation and unemployment resulted from the kind of predatory government that the American colonists had meant to overthrow at the time of the Revolution, a rapacious regulatory bureaucracy of licensers and inspectors that set up exclusive franchises charging extortionate prices. For the workingmen as for their forebears, misrule reflected in turn a grievous failure of political representation. As a committee of workingmen proclaimed in 1836, "Our greatest misfortune is that our interests have never been adequately represented in our publick councils."[8]

The financial turmoil thus signaled a crisis of democracy, a threat to workers' newly won political rights. It was not enough for them to vote if their elected leaders were corrupted by moneyed interests. As Edmund Morgan has argued, the rise of popular sovereignty meant the empowerment of the representatives themselves, who increasingly legislated in the name of "the people" as an imaginary whole, above and beyond the actual voters to whom they owed office. Representative government carried with it an intrinsic tension between the role of representatives as dutiful servants of their constituents and their status as rulers in their own right, exercising wide discretion while governing on behalf of a fictitious sovereign that they effectively called into being.[9] As Jeremy Bentham put it in a passage that Leggett ran above the masthead in each issue of his weekly newspaper, "The immediate cause of all the mischief of misrule is, that the men acting as the representatives of the people have a private and sinister interest, producing a constant sacrifice of the interest of the people."[10]

The immediate cause of such concern in the early United States lay in the partnership of business and government embodied in the profusion of publicly chartered corporations deputized to manage the machinery of market exchange, especially the means of transportation and the media of credit and currency.[11] Rising apprehension of breaches of trust by officials of banks and joint-stock companies drove the development of the modern law of embezzlement in the eighteenth and early nineteenth centuries on both sides of the Atlantic.[12] "The people of this great state fondly imagine that they govern themselves; but they do not!" Leggett wrote in 1834. "They are led about by the unseen but strong bands of chartered companies."[13]

The spread of commercial banking, which had not existed in colonial America, posed a special danger. Banks were ostensibly the representatives of the depositors and borrowers for whom they served as go-betweens. They were merchants of other people's money, occupying a central position in a burgeoning market economy dependent on the circulation of credit among strangers. Unlike other financial intermediaries, banks were legally authorized not only to convey funds from savers to spenders, but actually to create currency, which had long been the exclusive prerogative of government. So, in addition to representing the political authority bestowed on banks, the thousands of varieties of banknotes that they issued in the course of their lending represented the economic value of the widening panoply of commodities for sale, including labor and land. As the antebellum currency reformer Edward Kellogg observed, "Money is as much the representative of the property of the people, as the legislature are the representatives of their constituents."[14]

Seen in this light, the yawning gap between the money supplied by banks and the "real economy" of work and wealth it was supposed to serve manifested a distinctively modern betrayal of financial as well as political representation. It revealed the dual corruption of public servants by private interests and of markets by embezzling middlemen. "We are menaced by our old enemies, avarice and ambition, under a new name and form," Leggett warned, ". . . A CONCENTRATED MONEY POWER; a usurper in the disguise of a benefactor; an agent exercising privileges which his principal never possessed."[15] The flood of banknotes for which they blamed the soaring cost of living appeared to his followers as the ultimate servant turned master of the market economy. In what seemed an obscene paradox, the more bank money circulated, the higher the toll taken by the banking system in every transaction, and the less workers' paper earnings bought them. This understanding of exploitation spawned what became the overarching demand of the workingmen's movement, which Leggett called the "separation of Bank and State." In concrete terms, it meant an immediate halt to the chartering of new banks and a ban on the issue of small-denomination notes of five, ten, or twenty dollars, the only banknotes workers generally saw. It also called for "free banking"—the banking equivalent of a "general incorporation law"—which would end the practice of special legislative charters and make banks simply businesses like any others without special sponsorship by the state.[16]

At the same time, early Americans understood paper money as a form of *literary* representation, not unlike newspapers. This was the third dimension of the problem of representation in finance and government. The increasing detachment of paper IOUs from the networks of borrowers and lenders in which they originated, allowing bills and notes to circulate like cash, mirrored the growing autonomy of banks and other financial institutions, raising related questions of misrepresentation. More broadly, contemporary concerns about illusion and artifice in literature and oratory went hand in hand with apprehensions about political and economic corruption. What the philosopher Hanna Pitkin describes as the dual meanings of representation—"standing for," like a poem or play, and "acting for," like a lawyer or legislator—appeared closely linked in the new nation.[17] The leading role of Jacksonian editors like Leggett epitomized the widely presumed connection between literary and political representation.[18]

"Plaindealing" was Leggett's label for both his democratic philosophy and the polemical style in which he hammered it home, connoting a close conjunction of social and literary ideals that enabled him to articulate the lessons that many Americans took from the tumult of the 1830s. His rigorously republican approach to economic questions threw into stark relief the growing disjuncture between money and labor, or between market value and the people and things it was supposed to represent. Leggett's allegiance to faithful representation in business and government as in art and literature allowed him to pose the problem most vividly. Yet that core commitment could not provide an effective formula for rejoining what had been torn apart.

"A Monster Cherished among Us": Frankenstein's Creature in Jacksonian America

In a tribute to Leggett written shortly before he died, his close friend and colleague William Cullen Bryant traced the fervor of Leggett's political writings to his tour in the U.S. Navy, culminating in his court-martial in 1825. "The hatred which Mr. Leggett has shown to tyranny, in all its forms, was rendered the more intense by his having tasted its bitterness," Bryant wrote.[19] Indeed, Leggett's first battle was with his commanding officer, and the transcript of his trial reveals how poetry and politics came together in Leggett's life as they did in his death fourteen years later, apparently hastened by the lingering effects of an attack of yellow fever while in the navy.[20]

Leggett served aboard the *U.S.S. Cyane* as a midshipman, or junior officer—a rank that rendered him largely immune to the corporal and capital punishment meted out to common sailors, but subject to the absolute authority of senior officers. Though he did not serve "before the mast" like his younger contemporaries, Richard Henry Dana Jr. and Herman Melville, he learned from the quarterdeck how petty officers were torn between captain and crew in the shipboard class struggles that such writers chronicled. Leggett was evidently strong-willed and short-tempered, quick to sense an insult and repay it with interest, and given to reciting Romantic poetry and Shakespearean soliloquies for his shipmates as well as writing his own.[21]

In January 1825, Leggett was charged with abandoning his post one night at port on the Mediterranean island of Minorca to fight another junior officer. Confined to the ship's cockpit, he persisted in reciting what his captain deemed "seditious poetry." Forbidden to speak with his shipmates, he tried to stab himself with a dagger and penned an outraged letter to the commander of naval forces in the Mediterranean. "I feel oppressed with the importance of my cause," he wrote, ". . . I speak in the character of an insulted officer, I speak the language of an assured gentleman, I invoke your aid as an imprisoned freeman." Imprisoned while awaiting trial, he composed a lengthy defense studded with verses from Shakespeare. "I address you, not in the apologetic language of an offender, but in the indignant tone of an offended officer," he began. "An armed sentinel has been placed over me," he wrote, "with orders to prevent my speaking, or being spoken to, by any one! Denied the priveledge of intercourse with my fellows—my constitutional priveledge of speech—one of the dearest priveledges of Nature!" Identifying his case with the cause of other midshipmen subjected to similar mistreatment, he declared that the "boasted freedom of our institutions" was at stake. "I did not expect to find, Gentlemen, among those who have so nobly and effectually defended our country from foreign aggressions, a domestic tyranny, more hateful in its operation, and more baneful in its effects," he wrote. "But let the degrading treatment that I have experienced be tolerated and there is a monster cherished among us that, in its brutal progress, will trample on every honorable impulse, poison every noble aspiration, and extinguish every manly and dignified sentiment."[22] Unpersuaded, the court convicted Leggett on several counts and sentenced him to dishonorable discharge. He was reinstated on account of his five-month confinement pending trial, but he quit his commission in disgust.[23]

At twenty-four, Leggett was already demonstrating a rich appreciation of the power of language as an instrument of freedom and oppression and an impassioned identification with the characters and conventions of melodrama, the keynotes of his career. How had he acquired these literary tools, and what can they tell us about the vision of political economy that he later fashioned with them? In his dramatic depiction of the "monster cherished among us," he recounted an archetypal story of subversion of American liberty by those entrusted with its defense, which formed the master narrative for much of his later writing. Inherited from the Revolutionary Era, the rhetoric of conspiracy and corruption provided the conceptual vocabulary for his influential critique of the market revolution.[24]

His father had fought in the American Revolution, been taken prisoner by the British, and written a memoir of his captivity that may have influenced Leggett's anguished account of his own imprisonment before his court-martial.[25] He recalled in his trial defense his elderly father's parting words after he had joined the navy: "Forget not that you wear the livery of a free, and of a generous Republic, and cherish as dearer than life those principles for which your father fought!" But Abraham Leggett's fight for independence, like that of many veterans of the Revolution, had not ended with the war.[26] His fall from relative prosperity fit a pattern of downward mobility in the early republic that formed a recurrent theme in Leggett's writing as in that of other authors from the retreating ranks of urban mechanics and family farmers.[27]

Born into an old New York farming family with a substantial estate, Abraham Leggett had lost his own father as a boy and been sent to live with a succession of relatives and then as a blacksmith's apprentice. His service during the Revolution had earned him an officer's commission, but after the war he had pursued a series of ill-fated business ventures as a shopkeeper and dry goods merchant in New York, South Carolina, and Georgia. He had finally succeeded as a blacksmith in New York City, where William was born in 1801, one of nine children. The elder Leggett did well enough to send his son to Georgetown College at the age of fifteen, majoring in mathematics. But William had to return home after his first year when his father suffered a bout of financial setbacks, and he never completed college. Three years later, the panic of 1819 destroyed the business that Abraham Leggett had built over the previous two decades. Applying for a veteran's pension that July, he included a statement from a relative attesting that he "was formerly in affluent circumstances but hath now become insolvent, and all his property hath been seized by his creditors."[28]

In many ways, William Leggett made his father's lifelong struggle his own, defending what he saw as the embattled ideals of the American Revolution against the monstrous creature of capital that came of age at the same time as he did, in 1819. Across the Atlantic, Mary Shelley's *Frankenstein* (1818) enlivened a generation of social commentary on the violent legacy of the French Revolution in Europe and the mounting class war in England, which peaked in the infamous "Peterloo Massacre" of 1819.[29] In the United States that year, the collapse of a bank-fed bubble in land and agricultural staples triggered the first major financial crisis of the nineteenth century, inciting a grassroots insurgency against what Senator Thomas Hart Benton of Missouri dubbed "the money power." The panic inaugurated a twenty-year political struggle between the ascendant classes of organized labor and finance capital, a conflict marked by opposing Frankenstein-like fears of the mindless mob and the "monster bank," which Leggett did more than anyone to dramatize.[30]

To help support his family with his father out of work, the eighteen-year-old Leggett took to the stage, starring in several plays for the first time. Though he had no formal theatrical training, he probably had learned to perform from the cheap schoolbooks that appeared in virtually every home and school in the Northeast when he was growing up. These "readers and speakers" offered instruction in how to reproduce an author's thoughts and feelings through an elaborate system of facial expressions, vocal intonations, and bodily gestures, aiming to represent the meaning of each word fully and unambiguously. More than a means of literacy, such training in elocution was considered essential to citizenship in a modern republic.[31]

Leggett clearly understood patriotism as a performance. His father had witnessed the emergence of popular politics in the street theater of the Revolutionary Era, at a time when professional theater was banished as a symbol of monarchical culture. By the time Leggett was born, American theater was enjoying a revival as a forum for the kind of cultural politics earlier played out in liberty pole celebrations, tea parties, and tarring-and-featherings. The reborn playhouse became an arena of patriotic unity and raucous social strife among the servants, apprentices, and prostitutes in the gallery, the artisans and professionals in the pit, and the elites in the box seats, not to mention the English actors on stage.[32]

This was the republican theater to which Leggett turned repeatedly for inspiration, beginning with the panic of 1819. He had his acting debut that summer in a popular contemporary comedy called *The Jew*, about a money-lender whose secret gift of a dowry to a poor woman enables her to marry a wealthy merchant, overcoming the opposition of both families.[33] The hope that generosity and love could prove more powerful than greed and class antagonism stuck with Leggett long after he came to write about how money might be made a means of sympathy rather than selfishness. True love likewise triumphs over social strife in two self-styled "melo-dramas" in which he appeared that season, *The Watch-Word* and *The Blind Boy*, with revolutionary unrest in Spanish America and eastern Europe providing the backdrop for similar stories of political intrigue resolved in the end by happy marriages.[34] Leggett also delivered playhouse performances of celebrated speeches and verses, including the English theater manager William Dimond's popular reverie "The Sailor Boy's Dream," in which a seaman dreams of returning to his childhood home and reuniting with his loved ones, only to awaken to a fearsome tempest that buries him beneath the waves.[35] A newspaper notice of a public recitation by Leggett two years later included Thomas Campbell's "The Battle of Hohenlinden" and "The Soldier's Dream," William Collins's "Ode on Music," classical Roman orations on conspiracy and mortality, and climactic scenes from *Hamlet* and *Macbeth*.[36] These sentimental readings combined pastoral nostalgia and republican politics in ways that resonated powerfully in Leggett's own poetry and prose.[37]

Lackluster reviews put an early end to his acting career, but not to his identification with the theater.[38] The 1820s marked the rise in New York, Boston, and Philadelphia of the "star system" dominated by traveling actors with national and international reputations and by the urban impresarios who managed their contracts. After returning home from the navy, Leggett began a lifelong friendship with Edwin Forrest, then on the eve of becoming the first American star of the stage. He soon became Forrest's most enthusiastic admirer. (Forrest later returned the favor by subsidizing Leggett's journalistic career.) Forrest's thunderous speeches and sensational performances in historical roles written especially for him—as the charismatic leader of a slave rebellion, a peasant revolt, and an American Indian uprising—made him the embodiment of Leggett's vision of the male virtuoso as a model of freedom-fighting valor. For Leggett as for many of his contemporaries, the new role of the star actor exemplified the Jacksonian ideal of heroic individualism. Like Andrew Jackson, the statesman of the stage was to represent the popular will, much as Leggett sought to do as a journalist. He also became an enthusiast of the growth of a mass working-class audience for Forrest and similar stars in new playhouses like the Bowery Theatre in New York, where Leggett himself gave his last performance in 1826. After the Bowery was destroyed by fire two years later, he wrote the prize-winning poem for its reopening, lauding the "moral stage" as a great school of righteous action.[39]

The expressive force of Leggett's later writing derived from the theatrical conventions of melodrama that he learned as a young man. On both sides of the Atlantic, the early nineteenth century saw the emergence of melodrama as the dominant form of commercial theater and the main attraction of popular venues like the Bowery.[40] As a new genre in its own right as opposed to a long-standing element in other kinds of literature, melodrama arose from the minor theaters in eighteenth-century Paris that specialized in pantomime, spectacle, and the stirring musical accompaniment for which it was named. Its hallmarks were everywhere recognizable: courageous heroes, chaste heroines, and dastardly villains; seduction and betrayal, wrongful accusations and family secrets; thrilling action and effusive oratory.[41] But there was more to it than that. As the literary scholar Peter Brooks argues in *The Melodramatic Imagination* (1976), the mission of melodrama was to reveal the workings of elemental moral forces within the everyday lives of ordinary people. It was predicated on an ideal of total and transparent representation, in which every character, setting, and scene disclosed an unambiguous message: the eternal conflict between freedom and oppression, virtue and corruption. Reflecting its revolutionary origins, melodrama contributed to republican polemic such as the Declaration of Independence, and it inspired a wide variety of public ceremonies, celebrations, and other political performances in Europe and America.[42]

Melodrama gave form, more particularly, to the revolutionary genre of political economy, which exalted transparency in market transactions as the basis of economic equity and prosperity while regarding secrecy and deceit as the main means of monopoly, usury, and exploitation. Like melodrama, political economy brought to light the great public purposes operating through common private pursuits. It likewise uncovered the fixed principles at work beneath the flux of ordinary business, stripping away the "veil" of monetary transactions to reveal the underlying factors of production and laws of motion that governed the market economy. A fundamental materialism formed the bedrock of classical economics: market prices gravitated toward the "natural prices" of commodities determined by their real cost of production in labor and land; individual incomes were ultimately determined by the work and material wealth for which credit and currency stood.[43] Viewing market actors as representatives of intrinsic class interests driven inexorably into competition and conflict, political economy proved an ideal subject for the melodramatic imagination. And like the Shakespearean theater with which it was allied, economic theory made up a vital part of nineteenth-century popular culture before becoming the exclusive province of an educated elite.[44]

Therein lies a challenge and an opportunity for scholars of the period. The stereotyped characters, stilted speeches, and hackneyed plots of melodrama have long made it the stuff of parody, disparaged by twentieth-century writers for its heavy-handed didacticism and apparent lack of irony or ambiguity.[45] For similar reasons, it is hard to read the vernacular economics of the nineteenth century without smiling at its histrionic language, its righteous certitude, its penchant for iron laws and rigid dichotomies: right versus wrong, truth versus fiction, supply versus demand, labor versus capital, population versus subsistence. In recent years, however, film studies and feminist scholars have rehabilitated melodrama as a more complex, protean, and inventively modern form than was previously appreciated, highlighting the ways in which the far-reaching moral conflicts it portrayed inevitably exceeded the narrow boundaries of its formulaic endings. Such work suggests that its inconclusive struggles between liberty and power, honor and treachery, made the genre uniquely revealing in periods of revolutionary upheaval. At such times, its stock stories dramatized the widely felt sense of an epochal social conflict under way and delineated what was at stake, even as they failed in the end to resolve the contradictions between new social forces and inherited ideals.[46] The popular political economy that rose and fell with nineteenth-century melodrama merits similar reconsideration for what it revealed and concealed in the moments of crisis when it held greatest sway.

"A Fearful Brink": New Forms of Fiction and Risk

Leggett's work in the theater helped him to make sense of the panic of 1819, but it could not save his large family from the ruin of his father's trade. Joining an exodus of refugees from the gathering crisis in the Northeast, they headed for the new settlement of Edwardsville in southern Illinois. But the collapsing economy caught up with them there as with many migrants, and his father's blacksmith shop soon went out of business. By 1822, most of the family returned to New York, and Leggett joined the navy.[47]

Out west and at sea, Leggett became a writer, finding the material for his early poetry and short fiction. His first published works appeared in the local newspaper, the *Edwardsville Spectator*, which gave him an elementary education in political economy as well. Though Edwardsville was barely a year old with just sixty or seventy households when the Leggetts arrived, its federal land office drew a rush of settlers and speculators buying up plots of uncultivated prairie on credit with little money down. Small farmers and hunters from the backwoods of Kentucky and Tennessee joined well-heeled doctors, lawyers, and slave-owning planters from the tidewater South, along with merchants, mariners, and shopkeepers from New England and the Middle Atlantic like the Leggetts. Three main tributaries of Jacksonian democracy—western farmers, southern planters, and eastern artisans—thus came together at the outset of Leggett's career, united by hard times in a lasting suspicion of the financial system. The columns of the *Spectator* filled with anxious debates over the simultaneous spread of banking and slavery in the new state, giving the weekly paper and its antislavery editor, Hooper Warren, an outsized influence in the democratic politics of the Trans-Allegheny West.[48]

Leggett's contributions were limited to occasional poems on timeless themes such as hope and loss, death and immortality, and beauty and faith, eschewing explicit references to contemporary issues. Collected in a small, self-published volume in 1822, the pieces were less original efforts to represent social experience than formulaic exercises in self-expression, earnestly emulating popular sentimental and Romantic poets such as Byron, Campbell, Thomas Moore, and Felicia Hemans. Yet Leggett presented his poetry as a form of patriotism, akin to his recitations of famous speeches. Anticipating Walt Whitman in a "New Year's Address, Written for the Carrier of the Edwardsville Spectator," he celebrated the newsboy as a plebeian bard, singing the "crowning glories" of the young republic.[49] In an expanded compilation published after his tour in the navy, *Leisure Hours at Sea* (1825), he similarly introduced his poems as quotidian dispatches "by a youth engaged in the service of his country," from "the bustle and confusion of the steerage of a man-of-war."[50]

If Leggett intended his writing, like the ship, to enlist his life in a larger cause, it remained as yet a largely empty vessel. As he confessed in the volume's epigraph from Byron,

> 'Tis pleasant, sure, to see one's name in print;
> A book's a book, although there's nothing in't.

Byron seems to have provided the main example for Leggett's pose of wistful wandering, exuding a sense of being figuratively as well as literally at sea. The only places and people in these verses are those long lost or left behind. There are no destinations, only a "trackless course" across a fathomless ocean, no society save in the narrator's mournful memory, and no home to which the outcast might return. Smiles deceive, stars fade, lovers betray, living things decay and die. Blending neoclassical language and piety with a Romantic emphasis on personal emotion and experience, these plaintive poems chronicle an endless search for secure footing, a prominent theme in Leggett's later writing on the falsity of appearances, ephemerality of fortunes, and fragility of households and communities. At this formative stage, he sought a contemporary cause worthy of the sentiments he expressed, or a sense of how his own experience could live up to his inherited ideals.[51]

After leaving the navy, Leggett returned to New York City. There he joined in a collective effort by authors and publishers to produce a body of distinctively American literature as part of an artistic vanguard allied with the rise of Jacksonian democracy. Forming a bridge between his poetic and his political vision, the dozens of short stories that he produced in the late 1820s gained him a popular following and a rising reputation within the New York "Knickerbocker school" headed by Washington Irving, James Fenimore Cooper, and William Cullen Bryant. A long story of Leggett's called "The Rifle" was reprinted in newspapers across the country and adapted into a play. A shorter one entitled "The Main-Truck; or, A Leap for Life" was widely published in British and American newspapers as well as in German, Spanish, and French translations, and was later turned into a popular poem and ballad.[52] More stories appeared in the next few years, and most were republished in two well-received collections, *Tales and Sketches: By a Country Schoolmaster* (1829) and *Naval Stories* (1834).[53]

As these titles suggest, Leggett's fiction fell into the contemporary categories of western stories and sea stories, closely based as it was on his time in Illinois and the Mediterranean. Yet the isolated communities in which his stories take place serve as microcosms of the market society in which they were written. The western and the nautical tale first emerged as recognized subgenres in the literature of the 1820s and 1830s. While Cooper's "Leatherstocking Tales" and maritime adventures made him the preeminent novelist of the land and sea frontiers, Leggett led the way in the development of the short western and sea story. In part, the matching narrative forms reflected the nation's aggressive expansion in the "golden age of American shipping" and of Manifest Destiny, when the sailor and the settler became twin figures of American freedom. Yet for metropolitan writers like Leggett, the high seas and the backcountry represented as much a chronological as a geographical frontier, a borderland between an older agrarian economy and new forms of commodified labor and finance capital. The self-enclosed societies of Leggett's ships and towns appeared partly as pastoral throwbacks to earlier communal life, partly as windows onto a rootless and restless new world. So also, the emerging genres of the sea story and the western story brought the familiar formulas of adventure, coming-of-age, and melodrama onto uncharted terrain, where the market revolution could be climactically enacted.[54]

Central to Leggett's short fiction is the problem of frontier justice, whether in the face of autarchy and despotism aboard ship or of anarchy and lawlessness in the West. His stories feature orphans and widows, fugitives, migrants, and sailors adrift in a disorienting terrain of unclear title, mistaken identity, and ceaseless motion. Their fire-prone cabins and storm-tossed sloops reflect the precariousness of such humble characters' existence. Again and again in these stories, the man who rises in the morning prosperous and respected goes to bed destitute and in jail. Such rapid reversals are a source of perpetual hope as well as fear, expressing a profound ambivalence about the societal transformation under way. "The Rifle" refers in passing to a once-wealthy merchant from New York City "whom misfortune in business had suddenly befallen, and stripped of all his possessions," much like Leggett's father. Migrating with his family to Illinois, he finally finds "a degree of happiness that he had never known before . . . for he was rich—not in money, but in a better, a more enduring kind of wealth."[55]

The commotion of a navy ship likewise occasionally offers a fragile sanctuary for a better, more enduring kind of work, reflecting the novel forms of working-class community made possible by the new industrial order. The cast of "The Main-Truck" finds such fleeting communion in Leggett's depiction of the ordinary chores of preparing to leave port:

> The boatswain and his crew were engaged in fitting a new gang of rigging; the gunner in repairing his breeches and gun-tackles; the fo'castle men in calking; the top-men in sending down the yards and upper spars; the holders and waisters in whitewashing and holy-stoning; and even the poor marines were kept busy, like beasts of burden, in carrying breakers of water on their backs. On the quay, near the ship, the smoke of the armourer's forge . . . ascended in a thin column through the clear blue sky; from one of the neighbouring white stone warehouses the sound of saw and hammer told that the carpenters were at work; near by, a livelier rattling drew attention to the cooper, who in the open air was tightening the water-casks; and not far removed . . . sat the sailmaker and his assistants, repairing sails, which had been rent or injured by the many storms we had encountered.

Within a few days, the fresh-painted ship looks "as fine as a midshipman on liberty," a floating craft of craftsmen.[56] Yet this artisanal idyll soon yields to another kind of community, united in panic rather than labor. When the captain's young son carelessly climbs to the peak of the ship's tallest mast, he finds himself trapped atop the little wooden wheel called the "main-truck," with "nothing above him or around him but the empty air." As the horrified crew looks on, the boy heeds his father's command—"Jump! 'tis your only chance for life"—and so is saved from the sea, in a parable of risk, faith, and salvation recalling the "Sailor Boy's Dream."[57] Such a redemptive "leap for life," as the story is subtitled, forms the climax of several of Leggett's naval adventures, presenting a nightmarish vision of survival in a watery world with no safe place to stand. As in other contemporary seamen's narratives, the specter of being suspended midair above stormy seas is juxtaposed to an ideal image of collective industry, encapsulating the contrast between the solidity and solidarity of labor and the panic and peril of total liquidity.[58]

Leggett's western characters are often pitched onto a similarly terrifying threshold: "I stand upon a fearful brink, and it requires but a breath to send me toppling into the yawning gulf below"; "He knew that he stood upon the crumbling edge of an awful precipice."[59] The boundless prairie frequently appears in his fiction as "the bosom of some inland sea," alternating abruptly between a deceptive serenity and a fiery gale.[60] But the common climax of his western stories comes in a different sort of trial, reflecting the difficulty of establishing justice in the no-man's-land of the market frontier. Here the general pattern involves an innocent man convicted of a robbery or murder, followed by an ultimate exoneration along with discovery of the true culprit. Unlike other crime and proto-detective stories by Cooper and Sir Walter Scott, Leggett's tales hinge on the role of physical evidence in both incriminating and exculpating the hero.[61] Each case boils down to a question concerning the growing gap between persons and property—what belongs to whom?—that poses a problem for two revealing reasons. First, the property in question is readily exchangeable and repeatedly exchanged. Second, certain kinds of property—such as clothing, newspapers, and especially money—prove consistently misleading. The kinds of evidence that do not deceive, by contrast, are those that supposedly can be neither changed nor exchanged: the gray hair of the robber's horse, the soft white hands of the defendant, the rifle ball of the murder weapon.

Leggett makes much of the difference between such immutable physical features and the instability of monetary value. An old hunter aptly named Silversight immediately recognizes the practical worth of a fine rifle that bears but little market value, yet he blithely passes along, "without witness or receipt, an uncounted or unlimited amount of money."[62] Conversely, a rich man's son sells the family estate to a speculator "for less than half its worth," intending "to invest the proceeds in some moneyed institution, where, without any care of his own, it might yield him a regular income."[63] What is particularly troubling about money in these stories is the way it transforms personal negotiations between two parties into impersonal transactions among a widening circle of intermediaries.[64] Spiraling struggles involving multiple parties in Leggett's fiction generally culminate in either a marriage or a comparably conclusive man-to-man struggle between hero and villain, or both. Resolution is found in a return to bilateral, personal relations through a decisive two-person exchange of vows or of blows.[65]

Leggett's style accentuates the core concern of all his stories with honesty and deceit. His narrators relate events as if from the perspective of the audience for a play in which motives and meanings are reliably signified through formulaic characters, body language, and symbolic scenery. Relentless importance is placed on deciphering visual cues and clues: "His countenance indicated manliness and intelligence," "His conversation and manners were said . . . to belong to a rank in society much superior to that which he now occupied," "The character and manners of the inhabitants might, by a medi-

FIGURE 3.1. Portrait of William Leggett, engraved by A. Sealey from a painting by T. S. Cummings. Frontispiece of *A Collection of the Political Writings of William Leggett*, ed. Theodore Sedgwick Jr. (New York: Taylor and Dodd, 1840). Courtesy of the Library of Congress, E381 .L4.

tative mind, be nearly guessed at from the appearance of their abodes." The narratives feature frequent stage directions spelling out the signs and gestures through which characters convey their feelings, and even the most duplicitous rogues betray their deepest sentiments in dialogue or soliloquy.[66] A contemporary portrait of Leggett fittingly shows a serious young man with a sincere expression, posed stiffly in a dark coat and waistcoat against a plain backdrop, with an open and unadorned collar in defiance of fashionable frills (figure 3.1). "The true poet, like the true gentleman, seeks not to array himself in a fantastic garb," Leggett wrote a few years later, "but the language of the one, like the dress of the other, is rather distinguished by its propriety—by its evident adaptation to the thought which it clothes, than by singularity or profusion of ornament."[67]

The moralism of Leggett's writing made it easy for him to move from fictional depiction to critical prescription. While he was writing short stories, he was also reviewing books and plays for the *New York Mirror* and the *Merchants' Telegraph*. In the fall of 1828, he launched his own literary newspaper, the *Critic*. It lasted just eight months, enough to gain him considerable influence in literary circles.[68] Leggett shared with the other members of the Knickerbocker school a doggedly moralistic approach to literature.[69] "A novel," he wrote, "should be a sort of practical commentary on the writings of the moral philosopher."[70] Seen in this way, the new forms of fiction that drew his attention presented an unparalleled opportunity for popular education. But like the mass market on which they depended, these emerging subgenres also posed a new kind of threat to the republican values they were meant to promote. So the *Critic* pursued a dual purpose, trumpeting the invaluable potential of popular theater and literature when properly directed while railing against the degradation of such work by market mores. Leggett rejected the kind of blanket condemnation of playacting that had been a staple of conservative reaction to modernity and the market since the seventeenth century.[71] "When genius creates, and wisdom revises, and eloquence pronounces, and painting adorns, and music accompanies" the theater, he wrote, "the heart of the spectator must be callous indeed, if it thrill not in responsive acknowledgement of the potency of the combination," so that "the mind is vanquished by the united power of precept and example."[72] That mind-bending influence, however, rendered the theater a powerful instrument of deceit as well as enlightenment.

The danger lay in the tendency of drama, like money, to become an end in itself instead of a means to higher ends. Art or entertainment for its own sake appeared to Leggett an archetype of gluttony or greed. Just as "the desire for wealth is a feverish thirst, which rages with the more violence the more it is sought to gratify it," he wrote, so the desire for mere amusement was liable to fuel a vicious cycle of self-indulgence rather than self-improvement.[73] The source of such vice, however, lay not in any innate appeal to popular tastes, but in the artificial demand created by theater managers, whose control over the means of entertainment resembled that of bankers over the means of exchange in Leggett's later work. "It is too often the case that managers foist entertainments upon the public, for which the natural appetite never would have asked," he wrote. He urged agents and impresarios to "abjure French dancers and flying Indians, elephants and horses, phantom ships and real ships, and all the rest of the nonsensical trash, with which they have surfeited the public."[74]

These sensuous spectacles had their counterparts in the publishing industry, and Leggett's approach to poetry and fiction was similarly steeped in the logic of melodrama. His highest compliment was to write, as he did of a little-known poet, "what she speaks she feels. . . . Her words are used as *vehicles* of thought."[75] He applauded the increasing availability of cheap books and periodicals, and particularly the proliferation of anthologies, miscellanies, and gift books that made literature more accessible for people of limited education and means. Yet at the same time, he lamented publishers' enthusiasm for "fashionable novels" that titillated more than they taught. "Without plot, without incident, without connexion of parts," he wrote, such works "present a jumble—an anomaly in letters."[76] The result was "an increase of books without an increase of knowledge; the perusal of which, like inebriating draughts, does not quench, but inflames, the thirst of mind, and, at the same time, diminishes the delicacy of its perception."[77] Little wonder that Leggett called intemperance "the besetting sin of the country."[78] For him as for many writers, addiction symbolized the self-sustaining spiral of desire associated with commercial culture. It connoted the corruption of representation that he found in speculation and paper money no less than in ballet and fashionable novels, the means become ends.[79]

The affinity between literary and monetary representation struck Leggett even before he began writing political editorials. "'Words are things'; they are the representatives of ideas, as money is the representative of value," he wrote, quoting Byron again, in an essay on the relationship between the language of literature and its intended audience.

> The merchant who has large sums to appropriate pays them out by the signs of hundreds and thousands, while he who carries on a petty traffic deals in shillings and pence. It is the same with language: words are the coin made use of by the mind; and he who deals with the poor in understanding must use only such as the value of which cannot fail to be appreciated from their general currency; while he whose intellectual transactions are extensive must employ expressions that shall quicken its operations.[80]

Much as the common man dealt in small change, so he naturally dealt in plain language, representing ideas as simply as coins did value. The value of money itself, however, was anything but clear when Leggett wrote these words. The conventional analogy between words and coins bore the seeds of his critique of the new banking system, through which methods of payment long reserved for merchants had become the common currency of workers, shopkeepers, and family farmers.

"Plaindealing": New Forms of Nonfiction and the Language of the Market

When Bryant hired him as assistant editor of the *Evening Post* in 1829, Leggett accepted the job on the condition "that he should not be required to write upon political topics, 'on which he had no settled opinions, and for which he had no taste'; but within a few months he found himself almost wholly devoted to them," as Allan Nevins has written in his history of the New York newspaper. Bryant himself had recently made a similar move from being the nation's most celebrated poet to editing the city's leading Democratic daily.[81] He and Leggett forged an extraordinary literary and political partnership, exemplifying the deep affinity in their day between imaginative writing such as poetry, drama, and fiction and equally inventive forms of nonfiction such as journalism and political commentary.[82]

In the fray of political debate, Leggett broke through the stylistic shell of his earlier efforts, allowing the language of melodrama that he had developed over the past decade to show its full range and force. His finest editorials for the *Evening Post* and for two other papers that he founded, the *Plaindealer* and the *Examiner*, were compelling, colorful, and often devastating, with a mixture of irreverence and indignation worthy of Thomas Paine and William Cobbett. "He was truly the very Jove of editors," wrote a compatriot, recalling the burning bolts of invective that made Leggett for a time the most admired and reviled writer in New York.[83] As a preeminent practitioner of the "middling rhetoric" that reached its apotheosis in the penny press of the 1830s, Leggett pioneered the polemical style that inspired a generation of antebellum writers including Mike Walsh, George Lippard, and Walt Whitman.[84]

If he found his voice in the theater, he found his vehicle in journalism, his creed in Jacksonian democracy, and his cause in the workingmen's movement. "No one has labored more perseveringly, or in the end, more successfully, to bring the practice of American democracy into conformity with its professions," the poet John Greenleaf Whittier wrote of Leggett in 1850.[85] Leggett called his profession "plaindealing," dedicated to truthful representation in life as in literature, or in business and politics as in print. As Gary Wills has noted, the "plain speech" perfected by politicians like Jackson and Lincoln along with writers like Leggett was hardly free of figurative language. Its freedom of expression came rather from its command of the resonant figures of speech and patterns of syntax that rendered simple, straightforward, and accessible what otherwise appeared esoteric and out of reach for the common people it addressed.[86]

While "plaindealing" had long meant honesty in language, it had more recently come to denote truth and openness in trade, as "dealing" had come to mean selling as well as speaking. The key to Leggett's social philosophy lay in the implicit belief that literary expression and economic exchange operated according to the same basic principles, whether derived from the melodrama that he knew by heart or from the political economy that he learned under Bryant's tutelage. An epigraph from John Milton's seventeenth-century defense of freedom of the press, *Areopagitica*, headed the front page of each issue of Leggett's *Examiner*—"Give me the liberty to know, to utter, and to argue freely according to conscience, above all liberties"—harking back to his earlier defense of his "constitutional privelege of speech" in the navy.[87] But just as the exercise of free speech required popular mastery of the sophisticated style and rhetoric that formed the means of expression in the early republic, so his emerging understanding of "free trade" depended on democratic control of the means of market exchange. Contrary to historical depictions of Leggett as a defender of precapitalist practices, his model of plaindealing did not mean reducing exchange relations to unmediated two-person transactions akin to barter, as in the man-to-man or bride-and-groom resolutions of his short stories, but rather ensuring free and equal access to money and markets.[88]

In completing his migration from poetry to prose to politics, Leggett increasingly conceived of communication as well as commerce in collective and institutional rather than individual terms. He shifted his attention from the theatrical and literary elements of self-expression to the crucial role of the press and the post office in conveying not simply personal sentiments, but the greater good of "public opinion." Similarly, he emphasized the responsibility of business corporations and banks to represent not just individual interests, but the transcendent authority of "the market" as a whole. The specter of tyranny now appeared to arise less from evil individuals like the villains of his earlier work than from corrupt institutions that monopolized the means of expression and exchange.

In a democratic manifesto of sorts with which Leggett introduced the *Plaindealer*, he declared his utmost commitment to "the political maxim, that the majority have the right to govern" as well as "the moral maxim, that it is the duty of the majority so to govern as to preserve inviolate the equal rights of all. In this large sense, democracy includes all the main principles of political economy: that noble science which is silently and surely revolutionizing the world."[89] The main adversary of this modern, market-oriented democracy was what Jacksonians like Leggett called "special privilege," by which they meant the bestowal of corporate rights and powers on specially chartered businesses. Instead of channeling private wealth to serve public needs, the system of special charters made public servants into the agents of the private entities they created. By delegating exclusive authority to favored groups of investors, Leggett wrote, the legislatures were "bartering away the sovereignty of the People to little bodies politic, fattening on the great body."[90] His conception of such corruption was profoundly shaped by concerns about freedom of expression. His model of monopoly was rooted in the eighteenth-century opposition to the governmental establishment of religious institutions, reflected in his parallel calls for "perfect free-trade in religion" and for the "separation of Bank and State."[91]

Leggett broadened the Anglo-American intellectual tradition of resistance to state-sponsored economic enterprise, running from Adam Smith through Thomas Jefferson and John Taylor, into a sweeping indictment of virtually every form of public regulation, relief, or provision, from municipal licensing of particular trades to public postal service, ferries, insane asylums, and veterans' pensions. By subscribing to banks, railroads, canals, and other ventures, he argued, governments saddled middling taxpayers with an increasingly heavy load, while rich bondholders reaped the rewards. The states' reliance on tolls, tariffs, and taxes on transactions ensured that the bulk of the burden would be borne by the final consumers who paid in higher prices, according to Leggett, hitting urban workers especially hard in a period when the prices of basic necessities rose much faster than wages.[92] His ideal notion of the freedom of the market arose in the shadow of his trenchant critique of the "monopoly system," as he sought to unhitch the market economy from what he deemed "unnatural" enterprise. The "natural economy" he imagined was like "an equal and uniform current, never stagnating, and never overflowing its boundaries," or like the limpid streams that gurgled through the pastoral landscapes of his western tales.[93] Natural—as in "natural price," "natural right," "natural level," "natural equilibrium"—meant lawful, balanced, proportional, predictable, self-regulating. Freedom meant fixity, regularity, and stability, as opposed to addiction, inebriety, fanaticism, and frenzy.

"Convince me that a principle is right in the abstract, and I will reduce it to practice if I can," Leggett wrote.[94] For his contemporaries as for later historians, Leggett's legacy rested on his radicalism in pursuing the ideals of equal rights and antimonopoly to their furthest extent, as an advocate of the nineteenth-century ideology of "free labor" and laissez-faire. "He boldly and invariably brought public measures to a rigid comparison with fixed principles," Bryant wrote shortly after Leggett's death in 1839, and subsequent scholars have seconded that assessment.[95] Yet a reconsideration of his writings on the freedom of the press and the freedom of labor suggests that the ideal of "plaindealing" appeared much plainer in principle than in practice. His devotion to the "free market," far from being a "fixed principle," emerged from Leggett's uncertain efforts to counter new forms of market power that threatened the independence of the press and the autonomy of labor alike in ways that he struggled to comprehend.

As Jeffrey Pasley has shown, the editor as partisan leader was a peculiarly nineteenth-century creature, reaching maturity with the emergence of modern parties mobilizing a mass electorate in the late 1820s and 1830s. Leggett was typical of many young journalists who identified with the journeymen, small retailers, and petty professionals among whom they worked. Like stage acting, newspaper editing provided not only a means of political expression for men of little other means, but also a medium of representation for their avid audience in the streets and taverns.[96] "His vocation is emphatically that of a publick leader," Leggett wrote of his new calling. ". . . To discharge fully the duties of a publick journalist would be to elevate the vocation to the loftiest summit of human dignity and usefulness." In a sense, Leggett suggested, the journalist occupied a higher office than elected officials, for he represented not merely the fully formed, explicit demands of his constituents, but the embryonic, implicit will of "the people" or "the public" as a collectivity. "The duty of a legislator, and that of a journalist, are distinguished by this important difference; the one should be limited in his action by the wishes of the public; the other only by the wider boundaries of abstract truth," he wrote. "The one should follow publick opinion; the other should seek to lead it; the one should do what his constituents require, the other should endeavour so to inform their minds, that their requirements might be in exact accordance with the principles of theoretick wisdom."[97]

While he embraced the growing power of the popular press, Leggett warned over and over of the danger that "the men acting as the representatives of the people" could form "a private and sinister interest" unto themselves, in Jeremy Bentham's words. In the partisan press, such corruption as Leggett saw it took the form of a narrow-minded devotion to the immediate interests of a political party instead of the higher principles it should serve. "What more wretched slavery can there be, than to be doomed to follow forever in the track of party, to speak not the honest impulses of one's mind and heart, but what the 'party leaders'—who are oftentimes men without minds or hearts—may think or feel . . . ?" he wrote.[98]

Yet even as the political press reached the zenith of its influence, the first signs of its eclipse appeared in the expanding media market itself, centered in

New York. The development of stereotype printing, papermaking machinery, and the steam-powered cylinder press created the conditions for an exponential increase in newspaper production and circulation in the 1830s. Artisanal papers like Leggett's competed with the sudden ascendance of penny dailies, much larger in staff and readership, sustained by cash sales and advertising, and emphasizing crime, scandal, and "human-interest" stories rather than political commentary.[99] By the twentieth century, the dominance of this modern model cast the partisan press into the "dark ages of journalism," much like melodramatic literature and popular political economy.[100] By its very nature, Leggett's vocation looked backward to the Jeffersonian republic even as it looked forward to the spread of Jacksonian democracy. The market that sustained the partisan press also imperiled it, much as the market for inexpensive entertainment both supported and threatened the critical role of drama and fiction in the new republic.

In principle, Leggett viewed newspapers as the perfect medium for plain-dealing. "There is no species of literary composition so extensively read, or so eagerly sought after," as newspapers, he noted in the *Critic* in 1829. The emerging mass market for journalism dictated a distinctive literary style—or rather, a distinctive lack thereof. "Business language is fully adequate to the announcement of business transactions," he wrote, including in the realm of "business transactions" all manner of political and economic affairs. "He who relates the events of a battle, the effects of a whirlwind, or the political or commercial condition of his own, or of another country, is not looked to so much for an elegant flow of thought, or gracefulness of diction, as for accuracy of investigation and correctness of statement, and, provided he utters only the truth, the particular mode is a matter of but little importance." Such strict fidelity stemmed not only from newspapers' concern with business affairs, but also from their financial dependence on subscriptions and sales. Intensifying competition, according to Leggett, ensured that no paper could long afford to keep the truth from its readers. "Indeed, *in no branch of literature is implicit veracity more indispensably requisite* than in newspaper writing; for . . . no sooner is an error committed by one, than all the others are loud in censure or abuse," he wrote.[101]

Two months after he expressed such high hopes for the union of free speech and the free market, however, the *Critic* folded for lack of funds, like hundreds of other publications in these years. Each of his other three papers likewise capsized quickly under his command. After the *Critic* came the *Evening Post*, where Bryant soon made him his business partner and co-owner as well as coeditor. In June 1834, Bryant placed the thriving paper in

Leggett's sole hands and departed for a sojourn in Europe. Under Leggett's direction, the *Evening Post* steadily lost the support of political patrons, commercial advertisers, and other newspapers infuriated by his editorials. Bryant returned eighteen months later to find the paper close to insolvency, its revenues roughly a quarter of what they had been when he left. Leggett was forced to sell his share in order to pay off the debts he had incurred, and he left the paper shortly thereafter "without a shilling," as he confided in a letter to a friend.[102] He fared no better with the two papers that he launched after leaving the *Evening Post*, the daily *Examiner* and the weekly *Plaindealer*. Each survived for less than a year before falling victim to the panic of 1837, leaving Leggett even more heavily in debt. "I am overwhelmed with debts: in another week I shall have no roof over my head; and I see no prospect for better days," he told Edwin Forrest, who paid off his obligations, lent him enough to live on, and gave him a house in New Rochelle. As Leggett wrote to another friend in November 1838, "I have been for a twelvemonth and more without business and without resources, except such as have been supplied by the generosity of private friendship."[103]

His relentless money troubles rattled Leggett's confidence that the market rewarded plaindealing. "He who strives to be a reformer, and to discharge his high trust with strict and single reference to the responsibilities of his vocation, will be sadly admonished by his dwindled receipts that he has not chosen the path of profit," he lamented to readers in February 1837. The remedy he proposed appears surprising at first glance, given his opposition to corporate privilege. Noting that editor-owners were peculiarly vulnerable to the vicissitudes of the market, he argued that newspapers should be operated instead by joint-stock companies, as they were in Britain, diffusing the risks of ownership among a large group of investors and insulating editors from the immediate pressures of running a business. Corporate control, he hoped, would afford newspapers the security they needed to survive without pursuing the short-term profits to be made in gossip and sensationalism. "Among us," Leggett wrote, "the newspapers are the property of single individuals," who find that "consulting the passion and caprice of the hour . . . is a more profitable, as well as an easier task, than steering undeviatingly by fixed principles."[104] Plaindealing required protection against cutthroat competition, even as it depended on healthy competition to keep editors honest. As we will see, his embrace of the form of the business corporation, though not the system of special charters, extended well beyond his own industry.

A related challenge to Leggett's vision of the marketplace of ideas concerned the question of property rights in printed material. Antebellum journalists served as the gatekeepers for what Meredith McGill calls the "culture of reprinting," in which editors freely reprinted whatever they pleased from other periodicals along with poetry, fiction, and essays taken without permission from books published overseas. The law of copyright remained much more limited in the United States than in England, and it protected only works by U.S. citizens and residents. In the landmark case of *Wheaton v. Peters* (1834), the Supreme Court sanctioned the popular view of published work as presumptively common property, to which authors and publishers held only provisional claims. Congress repeatedly refused to extend copyright protection to foreign works. The looseness of the literary market mirrored in this way the free-for-all of competing currencies and wildcat banks that Leggett regarded with similar anxiety. Not until the turn of the century did the Supreme Court designate literary work as essentially private property belonging exclusively to individuals, at the same time that it privatized other kinds of "intellectual property" such as the price quotations of commodity exchanges. Like melodrama and popular political economy, the "culture of reprinting" had its heyday in the nineteenth century.[105]

Leggett's wavering response to the copyright controversy reflected his broader ambivalence about the emergence of a new kind of property in the written word, whether in a newspaper or on a banknote. When he first addressed the issue in September 1836, he was reflexively sympathetic to the concept of copyright, which seemed to him to protect individuals' "natural right" to the products of their labor. Unlike special charters for corporations, he contended, copyright "confers no new privilege or immunity," but rather secures what belongs to an author already.[106] Yet his democratic sympathies pulled him in the opposite direction. A few months later he criticized other journals for discouraging readers' common practice of borrowing or sharing the newspapers they read. Leggett welcomed his readers to share the *Plaindealer* as much as they liked, even as he continued to complain of the difficulty of selling enough papers to survive.[107]

By the following January, Leggett deemed authors' property "an equivocal right, at best." While writers were entitled to exclusive ownership of their original manuscripts, they could not monopolize the intangible products of their mental labor, their words and ideas. "The regions of thought, like those of the air, are the common property of all the earth's creatures," Leggett reasoned. "The limits of corporeal property are exact, definite, and always ascertainable. Those of incorporeal property are vague and indefinite, and subject to continual dispute," he wrote. To grant individuals private property in language was to squelch the freedom of expression that seemed to him the essence of the free market, impoverishing the great majority of readers dependent on the cheap price of uncopyrighted work. Within weeks, however, he reconsidered once again, conceding that writers might legitimately claim private property in their distinctive "language and style" after all.[108]

Leggett's difficulty in distinguishing natural right from special privilege in publishing reflected his broader problem in applying the deceptively simple standard of plaindealing to new forms of property and production. He faced that challenge most fully in his leadership of the fledgling labor movement, particularly in his shifting positions on the related issues of antislavery and antimonopoly. Spurred into political action by the panic of 1819, New York City workers had successfully campaigned for the elimination of property restrictions on voting in the 1820s. They responded to the runaway inflation of the 1830s with an unprecedented surge of trade-union organizing. Employers enlisted the aid of the courts to declare the new unions in violation of a tailor-made conspiracy law against combinations "injurious to trade," prompting the formation of the local Equal Rights Party in the fall and winter of 1835–36, devoted to working men's equal representation in economic as in political affairs.[109] The other impetus for the new electoral organization came largely from Leggett, who, in August 1834, advised voters to support only those candidates pledged to oppose any further bank charters. That fall, the Democratic candidates took Leggett's pledge and won election with workers' support, but then promptly began chartering more banks. To Leggett's constituency of laborers, artisans, and shopkeepers, nicknamed the "Loco Focos," the betrayal of labor votes appeared of a piece with the suppression of labor unions, together amounting to a denial of rightful representation. In 1836, they nominated him for mayor, but he declined to run.[110]

Leggett's leadership of the workingmen brought to a head the tensions inherent in his antimonopoly ideology. For him and his followers, any corporation established by special legislative charter constituted an illegitimate monopoly. Any business without such exclusive state support did not. Indeed, his devotion to laissez-faire was rarely more adamant than in his defense of business combinations in the winter of 1836–37, when the already inflated prices of food, fuel, and rental housing suddenly spiked. At a mass protest organized by the Loco Focos in February 1837, party leaders blamed the inflationary surge on the depreciation of the currency due to the proliferation of banks and banknotes. Outraged by reports that local merchants were hoarding flour in order to raise the price in a time of need, a large crowd left the rally to storm several flour warehouses, destroying property and hurling barrels of flour into the street.[111] But Leggett denounced the riot as a "causeless and disgraceful outrage." "It was causeless," he wrote, "as the dealers in any commodity whatever have a perfect right to fix their own price; and it was disgraceful, as it sought to effect an unworthy object by unworthy means."[112]

His condemnation of the flour riot was colored by his earlier response to the antiabolitionist riots of 1834 and 1835, which had made him the leading advocate of abolition within the Democratic Party. Much as Leggett exalted melodramatic theater while decrying mere entertainment for its own sake, much as he embraced the free market but bemoaned the self-destructive cycle of limitless competition, so he defined his own vision of popular politics against the urban riots that formed the underside of the city democracy. Like the popularity of licentious literature and hard spirits, vigilante violence signified for him a failure of rightful representation. Indeed, the riots targeted the very forms of legitimate representation that the rioters lacked, in his view: merchants' associations, for example, and the newly organized abolitionist movement in New York City led by merchants Lewis and Arthur Tappan.[113]

The printing revolution in New York City made possible the national pamphlet campaign of 1835, in which the Tappan organization deluged the mails with abolitionist literature. In response, antiabolition committees and rallies arose everywhere that summer, turning the rhetoric of equal rights into a furious reaction against what was widely described as a monstrous conspiracy led by moneyed elites in New York and London.[114] Leggett initially shared the deep hostility toward abolitionism within the Democratic Party, viewing it as a "fanatical" and "aristocratic" movement to degrade northern labor. He called the pamphlet campaign "reprehensible to a degree for which language has no terms of adequate censure."[115] Yet each time he took up the issue, he was provoked by violent efforts to suppress antislavery speech and association. When antiabolition crowds occupied the city in July 1834, he became the abolitionists' strongest defender in the press while still disavowing any agreement with their cause. The following year, his *Evening Post* became one of only three major papers in the country to condemn the U.S. postmaster general for allowing the confiscation of abolitionist literature by southern postmasters—an action that Leggett deemed tantamount to "*censorship of the press*." His growing sympathy for antislavery stemmed less from the ideology of "free labor" than from that of free speech.[116]

Yet if Leggett's support was initially much narrower than that of leading abolitionists, it grew into something broader in important ways: a vision of the emancipation of labor that extended far beyond ending chattel slavery. "The day will come," he wrote, "when the claims of the American black race to all the privileges and immunities of equal political freedom will be fully acknowledged, and when the prejudices of society will give way before the steady influence of truth, enlightened reason, and comprehensive philanthropy."[117] When local and national Democratic organizations censured the *Evening Post* for its apostasy, Leggett broke with his party and began promoting the cause of abolition with his customary vigor. When he founded the *Plaindealer* in December 1836, he proclaimed in its first editorial his intention to discuss the evils of slavery openly and constantly. Southerners who hoped to stifle antislavery agitation, he wrote, "never can induce the northern states to give up freedom for the sake of union; to give up the end for the sake of the means; to give up the substance for the sake of the shadow."[118]

Leggett continued to maintain that the Constitution did not permit the federal government to abolish slavery in the southern states, though he supported congressional abolition in the District of Columbia. But as Sean Wilentz has argued, he advanced a distinctively Jacksonian brand of antislavery, which identified southern planters with the "moneyed classes," southern slaves with northern workers, and democracy with equality under the law regardless of race.[119] New York City's African American newspaper, the *Colored American*, remembered him after his death as "a political sage," "a fearless advocate and sympathizing coadjutor" for "the oppressed of every hue and grade; from the naked and starved African of the South, up to the hoodwinked aristocratic-ridden operative of the North."[120]

While Leggett's response to the flour riot flowed partly from its association with previous riots, his position also reflected broader convictions about economic representation in the form of labor unions and business corporations. Earlier in the decade, he had strenuously supported workers' right to organize amid the anticonspiracy trials of union leaders. "The rich perceive, acknowledge, and act upon a common interest, and why not the poor?" he wrote in December 1834.[121] But when laboring New Yorkers charged coal and flour dealers with collusion in the winter of 1836–37, Leggett applied the same principle to merchants' associations as to trade unions. Business combination was nothing to fear, he argued, for as soon as merchants colluded to raise the price of flour or any other necessity, they invited competition that would "very soon let them down from their fancied elevation," restoring prices to their "natural value." "The safety of the community against extortionate and intolerant combinations is sufficiently insured by the effect of competition and the influence of publick opinion," he wrote in January 1837.[122]

Yet much as Leggett's trust in the market and public opinion faltered in the face of the "passion and caprice" of newspaper readers, so the extreme hardship in the wake of the financial panic a few months later prompted him to endorse emergency measures to prevent merchants from stifling the supply of basic necessities. "The flour of a single monopolist, which he was

[with]holding from a starving people," he now allowed, might justly "be seized by due process of law," though he emphasized that even dire deprivation did not justify lawless action such as the flour riot. "It would be '*private property taken for publick use*'; and a '*just compensation*,' estimated by an equitable comparison of the amount of supply with the amount of demand, would be awarded to the owner."[123] Still, Leggett much preferred private association to public regulation as an antidote to monopoly. The real remedy for price-gouging, he contended, was to be found not by opposing business combination, but by demanding that it be made equally accessible to working people through a general incorporation law, which would turn incorporation into a basic right of all qualified applicants. "The humblest citizens might associate together, and wield . . . a vast aggregate capital, composed of the little separate sums which they could afford to invest in such an enterprise, in competition with the purse-proud men who now almost monopolize certain branches of business," Leggett wrote.[124] "Combination," he contended in March 1837, was "an efficient weapon against the oppressor; but, like the sword bestowed by the good genius in the fairy tale, it shivers into fragments when drawn against the oppressed."[125]

Yet even the combined power of the rising working class in New York City, where two-thirds of the paid labor force was organized under the auspices of the newborn trade-union movement, was buried beneath the avalanche of insolvency and unemployment following the suspension of specie payments by the banks a few months later. For Leggett, the panic proved the prescience of his long-standing view that the ultimate cause of both inflation and depression lay in an incorrigibly corrupt banking system that monopolized the means of exchange.

"Real Bills": New Forms of Finance and the Critique of the "Money Power"

When the crash came, Leggett was ready. He had been rehearsing his response in one literary form or another for nearly twenty years, since the beginning of his career in 1819. "The time must come, nor can it be remote, when some financial or commercial revulsion will throw back the stream of paper circulation to its source, and many a goodly vessel, which had ventured too boldly on the current, will be left by the reflux stranded on its shores. . . . Wo unto them in that day who do not now take timely caution," he warned in September 1836.[126] "A vast and terrifick crash" was coming, he wrote in December, "when the treacherous and unsubstantial basis crumbles beneath the stupendous fabrick of credit, and the structure falls to the ground, burying in its ruins thousands who exulted in the fancied security of their elevation."[127]

Leggett's jeremiads derived from a tradition of antibanking discourse dating back to the advent of the widespread use of government-authorized paper currency more than a hundred years earlier. In both England and its American colonies, much if not most of the currency in circulation by the mid-eighteenth century comprised paper of one kind or another. The founding of the United States then yielded a mixed monetary legacy. On the one hand, the financial innovation of the colonial era opened the gate for the deluge of paper currency that drove the rapid economic development of the new nation, from bills of exchange and warehouse receipts to postage stamps, store vouchers, and company scrip, and particularly for the proliferation of banknotes, which became the preferred medium for retail transactions among strangers. By the panic of 1819, as the British banker Alexander Baring noted at the time, "The system of a paper currency ha[d] been carried to a greater extent in America than in any other part of the world."[128]

On the other hand, the Constitution prohibited the states from issuing their own paper money and left the federal government's authority to do so subject to judicial debate for nearly a century. The thousands of state-chartered banks that filled the breach placed the nation's currency largely under their control. Stipulations in the banks' charters determined the varying balance between public and private governance. These provisions included various degrees of public ownership and direction and a range of regulations on how ownership and liability were distributed among investors, how much discretion bank directors were granted, how much and what kind of capital banks held, and what kinds of loans they made.[129] But whatever the terms of the public-private partnership, the financial revolution in late eighteenth-century America, as in England a century earlier, meant that management of the money supply fell to commercial banks. Banks were authorized to lend out a much larger amount of currency in the form of notes and deposits than the value of their specie reserves and their real assets that could readily be sold for gold or silver to meet note-holders' and depositors' demands for payment. "The profits of [an incorporated bank] do not commence until, having loaned all its capital, it begins to loan its credit as money," as Leggett explained. "No set of men would desire a bank charter merely to authorize them to lend their money capital at the common rate of interest; for they would have no difficulty in doing that, without a charter, and without incurring the heavy expense incident to banking business. *The object of a bank charter is to enable those holding it to lend their credit at interest*, and to lend their credit too, to twice, and sometimes three times, the amount of their actual capital."[130]

Political resistance to the banking system converged from several quarters in the 1820s and 1830s—from Jeffersonian planters in the Old South, hill country yeomen in Kentucky and other western states, and artisans and journeymen in Philadelphia and New York. The rising opposition enlisted ambitious entrepreneurs, land speculators, and frontier bankers mainly resentful of the special privileges enjoyed by the Bank of the United States and its jealous control of loanable capital. But the rank and file of the bank war came from those spurred less by a desire for riches than by a fear of falling into poverty, who hated the multitude of state-chartered banks as much as they did the national bank. While many western farmers demanded relief from their debts and easier access to currency and credit, workingmen in the seaport cities sought refuge from soaring prices in tighter restrictions on bank lending and note-issue. Leggett spoke most immediately for the hard-money politics of this besieged urban stratum, but the literary logic that he brought to the currency question found a wider and more enduring appeal.[131]

The money question as Jacksonian writers conceived it appeared intrinsically melodramatic: dedicated to the truth of the free-market ideal as opposed to the fraudulence of current practice; convinced that the corruption they deplored stemmed from improper representation of the mutual interests of creditors and debtors, producers and consumers, by self-serving agents; confident that plaindealing truth would set the market free, restoring the balance of simple commodity exchange. By detaching the money supply from the "real economy" of goods and services, Leggett argued, banks sponsored overtrading, overbuilding, and reckless risk-taking at the expense of prudent investment in response to actually existing demand. They excited "a feverish and baneful thirst of gain—gain not by the regular and legitimate operations of trade, but by sudden and hazardous means."[132]

Paper money "is a curse to the poor, continually defrauding them of a portion of their hard earnings, without their knowing how or when they go," he wrote at the height of the panic. "It is a curse to the rich, introducing among them an insane desire of boundless wealth, and leading them into the most demoralizing schemes of speculation. It is a curse to the whole country, unsettling the established modes of industry, creating false notions of the relative respectability of various callings, alluring men from the steady pursuits of agriculture and the mechanick arts, and setting them in full chase after those glittering stock-bubbles, which cheat the eye with the appearance of valuable substance, but turn to nothing in the grasp."[133] Banknotes, in other words, were as volatile, seductive, and deceptive as the speculative machinery they fueled. They epitomized the tendency of money to become an overpowering end in itself instead of a mere means of exchange.

Leggett's foremost contribution to the money question concerned what he regarded as an insidious form of fraud. On its face, a banknote bore the appearance of a reciprocal agreement, which formed the basis of the reciprocal nature of market transactions in general, the exchange of equivalent values. But the face value of a note was not its actual market value: banknotes circulated at a discount, or rather at an endless series of discounts reflecting, first, the deduction that a local bank would make in cashing other banks' notes for gold or silver, and second, the varying reputations of their original banks of issue. Leggett contended that the difference between the face value and the market value of banknotes amounted to a swindle, a surplus silently expropriated in every transaction.

He began with workers' common complaint that employers paid them in "uncurrent notes" issued by backwoods banks of little repute, bought from Wall Street brokers for this express purpose. In a variant of the well-known "Gresham's law" that bad money drives out good, he argued that the most depreciated currency gravitated to those on the bottom rung, who had no choice but to accept it at face value, while their employers pocketed the difference between what they brought to Wall Street and what they paid their workers. But even if workers were paid in hard money, he contended, they were still robbed of their rightful wages by the circulation of depreciated banknotes. For the shopkeepers who sold them food and fuel had to pay off their loans in specie, not paper; and the wholesale merchants who sold to the shopkeepers paid for imported goods with gold and silver as well. The premium that shopkeepers and merchants paid to cash their banknotes, Leggett reasoned, they turned around and charged their customers in higher prices, each adding a margin of profit on top. The indirect tax on paper levied by banks and brokers trickled down "till it reache[d] the broad backs and hard hands of the mechanics and laborers," forced to bear the full burden in the end.[134]

So long as banks continued issuing small notes, Leggett encouraged workers to redeem their paper wages for gold and silver instead of passing along the bank money. Making the most of wage earners' undesirable position in the paper chain, he recommended a yet more direct remedy. "A cheap . . . method of disseminating the principles of those opposed to incorporated rag-money manufactories," he suggested, "would be for them to write upon the back of every bank-note which should come into their possession, some short sentence, expressive of their sentiments. For example—'No monopolies!' 'No Union of Banks and State!' 'Jackson and Hard Money!' 'Gold before Rags!' and the like." When called upon to endorse a bad bill, "it would be well to inscribe upon it in a clear and distinct hand, 'Wages of Iniquity!'"[135] By correcting the monetary misrepresentation in this way, wage earners could help to make the market the arena of plaindealing it was meant to be.

Behind Leggett's influential critique of the relationship between banknotes and wages lay an instinctive suspicion of "magnificent promises." A promise to pay, he held, was only fulfilled by being paid off in hard cash, not by becoming a means of payment itself. A contract between a creditor and debtor remained sacred no matter how far the debt traveled or how many hands it passed through. "The bill-holder should always be secure, whatever might become of the stock-holder," he wrote. "That which is received as money, and which is designed to pass from hand to hand as such, should not be liable to change into worthless paper in the transition."[136] Leggett would not require that banks actually hold in their vaults the gold or silver represented on their notes. The point was that note-holders should be secure in their property, knowing that a bank was no less obliged to keep its promises than an individual. His object could be achieved, he wrote, by requiring bankers to maintain sufficient capital in "real, substantial, imperishable property, such as lots, farms, houses, ships, and the like" to redeem all their notes in hard money on demand, certified by a government comptroller or other authority, and periodically reappraised to ensure that the banks' real assets remained equal in value to their paper liabilities. Then, "each holder of a note would, in point of fact, hold a title-deed of property to the full value of its amount," never subject to change.[137]

The quest for a fixed standard that would make plaindealing possible, that would allow for truthful transactions by providing a reliable measure of value, manifested a deep concern about standards of moral value as well. The differentiation of currency from commerce, closely related to the contemporaneous separation of labor from capital, epitomized for Leggett the peculiarly floating and self-referential character of market value, and therefore of all other values in a market society. Yet in what was the standard of value to be fixed? Farms, houses, and ships, like gold and silver, were themselves increasingly liable to wide fluctuations. Even if bank paper were as good as gold, Leggett noted, prices might rise steadily if the supply of gold grew faster than the demand. Paradoxically, then, a fixed standard of value—one that would keep prices relatively stable, relieving those on fixed incomes of the persistent press of inflation and the recurrent crises that came in its wake—had to rest on the watery bed of the market itself. Like postbellum *opponents* of the gold standard, who faced the converse problem of prolonged deflation, he and like-minded Jacksonians sought to peg the money supply to the demand for its services, or to the volume of buying and selling for which currency was called into use—the "real needs of trade," in the parlance of monetary theorists.

This was the burden of Leggett's articulation of the so-called real bills doctrine restricting banks to the business of discounting commercial paper, or obligations directly tied to actual purchases and sales of goods. First elaborated by Adam Smith, this conservative stricture called for banks to limit their note-issue to self-liquidating, short-term loans to merchants arising from wholesale transactions, as the early mercantile banks in American seaboard cities did after the Revolution. In a typical scenario, a merchant would buy goods from a farmer or manufacturer, paying for them with a bill of exchange drawn on another merchant to whom the goods would be shipped. The bill was payable in cash—that is, gold or silver specie—when the goods arrived at the other end. Meanwhile, the farmer or manufacturer would sell the bill to a local bank at a discount, meaning that the bank would give in exchange for it a banknote for a lesser value, which could be used to make any other payments. The bank, or another bank with which it did business, would cash the original bill for gold or silver after the goods were delivered to the second merchant, collecting the difference between the value of its own note and that of the bill in payment for its provision of credit in the form of a surrogate currency. In this way, banknotes would be based strictly on bills that were based in turn on exchanges of real goods, to be paid for in cash after a short period. In theory, the real bills doctrine would prevent banks from altering the supply of currency relative to the demands of commerce and ensure that banknotes circulated at roughly their face value in silver or gold.[138] "When bank issues are limited within this circle, the notes of the bank in circulation are founded on the security of the notes of the merchants in possession of the bank, and the notes of the merchants rest on the basis of goods actually purchased, which are finally to be paid for with the products of the soil or other articles of export," Leggett explained. "The maintaining of the currency at this point . . . would be supplying the channels of business to the degree requisite to facilitate the operations of commerce, without causing those operations to be unduly extended at one time, and unduly contracted at another."[139]

Beginning in the 1790s, however, American banking had spread from the city into the countryside and branched out into the riskier business of "accommodation loans." These were simply personal loans unconnected to any commercial transactions, typically to enable a borrower to invest in land or equipment, a new shop or a new venture. Instead of discounting bills of exchange to be paid in cash when goods were delivered, the banks would issue their notes or credit customers' accounts in exchange for written promises to repay the loans with interest, secured by borrowers' or cosigners' property. By the 1830s, the value of accommodation lending greatly exceeded that of strictly commercial lending, as banks took a leading role in sponsoring economic development.[140] The basic problem, according to Leggett, was that specially chartered banks channeled such accommodation lending away from the petty proprietors and aspiring entrepreneurs who deserved credit, into the hands of politically connected speculators and stock-jobbers instead. The free competition for funds made possible by "free banking," he believed, would naturally redirect loan capital where it was truly needed, making credit easier to obtain for "plaindealing merchants and shopkeepers" even as it cut off the flow to speculators, stock-jobbers, and rentiers.

Implicit in the Jacksonian critique of banking was a vision of commerce as a sound and fair foundation for cash and credit, a level playing field from which the financial system had dangerously departed and to which it might safely return. This ideal market was best described in the most important economic treatise of the Jacksonian era, *A Short History of Paper Money and Banking in the United States* (1833), by the Philadelphia financial journalist William M. Gouge.[141] Leggett was so impressed by Gouge's work that he reprinted it at the *Evening Post*'s considerable expense while Bryant was in Europe—ironically going into debt in order to cover the costs.[142]

Without the corrupting influence of legislative favoritism, Gouge contended, the credit system would simply function as a neutral broker, uniting those who held idle funds with those who could put such funds to productive use. In the "natural order of things," credit would be based on moral character just as currency would be based on real wealth. Those with money to lend and those in need of it would negotiate with each other directly, without the interference of government or banks. Freed from the tumult of a speculative economy, creditors would be able to judge the trustworthiness of debtors themselves, and aspiring farmers and mechanics could obtain the assistance they needed without becoming caught up in high-risk gambles. The trouble lay in the toll taken by parasitical middlemen standing between lenders and borrowers, preventing the harmonizing flow of market forces. "What would be the condition of the merchant who should trust every thing to his clerks, or of the farmer who should trust every thing to his laborers," Gouge wrote, deploring bankers' irresponsibility with their depositors' savings. "Corporations are obliged to trust every thing to stipendiaries, who are oftentimes less trustworthy than the clerks of the merchant or the laborers of the farmer."[143]

Leggett did not share Gouge's implicit distrust of both wage labor and corporate capital. But he followed Gouge's faith that proper representation could reconcile older republican principles with new market practices, agrarian democracy with industrial capitalism. "If we could only get rid of a few laws and institutions which give advantages to some men over others, we might arrive at a state of improvement which would surpass that of any country of which mention is made in history," Gouge wrote, and Leggett agreed.[144]

"The evil is legislative," as a contemporary currency reformer put it, "and the remedy must be legislative."[145] As it turned out, the panic of 1837 paved the way for the passage of the New York Free Banking Act the following year, essentially enacting the main plank of Leggett's legislative platform. Fifteen other states followed suit over the next twenty years, and the state laws contributed significantly to the framing of the National Banking Act of 1863.[146] Along with the banning of small notes, the disestablishment of the Bank of the United States, and the creation of the Independent Treasury, free banking amounted to a major achievement for Leggett's cause.

Yet these victories augured neither the demise of the "money power" nor the decline of speculation and the return to a simple market economy. The irony may be attributed, in part, to crucial aspects of the financial order that were not evident to Leggett or most of his contemporaries. Chief among these blind spots was the way in which banks augmented the money supply by making loans in the form of credits to deposit accounts, which accountholders drew on by writing checks. By the 1830s, checks and drafts on "demand deposits" already made up a large share of the means of payment with which commerce was conducted. As the former secretary of the treasury Albert Gallatin explained in 1831, "The credits in amount current or 'deposits' of our banks are also, in their origin and effect, perfectly assimilated to bank-notes. . . . The bank-notes and the deposits rest precisely on the same basis: for immediate payment on the amount of specie in the vaults; for ultimate security on the solidity of the debtors of the bank. . . . We cannot, therefore, but consider the aggregate amount of credits payable on demand, standing on the books of the several banks, as being part of the currency of the United States."[147] Leggett's single-minded focus on banknotes typified the prevailing tendency to think of the money question as a question of control over the physical means of exchange while neglecting the broader power of finance capital residing in the "credit system" that he only partially understood.[148] Similarly, in adopting the orthodox monetary faith in "real bills"—the belief that the supply of bank money could be safely constrained by tethering the issuance of banknotes to the "real needs of trade"—Leggett and the workingmen did not account for the role of banks' interest rates in determining the profitability of investment in industry and commerce to begin with. In other words, they overlooked banks' ability to manipulate the demand for credit and currency as well as the supply.[149] Selling and speculating were more tightly entwined than the stark polarities of the melodrama of the market allowed them to see.

Most importantly, Leggett could not conceive of the ways in which banks would continue to govern the main means of payment while being legally and politically treated as private enterprises rather than public servants. Like cutting the umbilical cord between government and business corporations more generally, the "separation of Bank and State" ultimately gave banks greater autonomy in exercising what had once been sovereign prerogatives. It made their power over the market economy increasingly taken for granted and off-limits to political debate. The popular political economy that emerged from the 1830s enabled contemporaries to consider the rising power of capital as an urgent constitutional question about how they were ruled, about the economic as well as political meaning of their fledgling democracy. At the same time, it inspired a widespread will to believe that financial panic and economic depression represented the corruption, not the completion, of the sovereignty of the market.

4

Nicholas Biddle and the Beauty of Banking

When Charles Dickens visited Philadelphia in 1842, he found the city still in the throes of the longest and deepest depression in the nation's history, triggered by the panic of 1837. "Looking out of my chamber-window, before going to bed," he wrote of his first night, "I saw, on the opposite side of the way, a handsome building of white marble, which had a mournful ghost-like aspect, dreary to behold." The next morning, he learned why. "It was the Tomb of many fortunes; the Great Catacomb of investment; the memorable United States Bank. The stoppage of this bank, with all its ruinous consequences, had cast (as I was told on every side) a gloom on Philadelphia, under the depressing effect of which it yet laboured." On the outskirts of the city, Dickens observed another monument to its past prosperity, "a most splendid unfinished marble structure for the Girard College . . . which, if completed according to the original design will be perhaps the richest edifice of modern times," but on which construction had halted.[1]

The stone frames of the defunct national bank and the partially built boarding school stood as the most celebrated examples of the Greek Revival in American architecture, symbolizing the tarnished prestige of the antebellum financial elite headquartered in Philadelphia. Had Dickens traveled a dozen miles farther up the Delaware River, he would have come upon a third memorial to the moneyed men of the new Athens, a brick mansion encased in a massive marble colonnade modeled on the Temple of Theseus. There lived the deposed president of both the bank and the school, the leader of the neoclassical revival, and the nation's first true central banker, Nicholas Biddle (1786–1844).[2]

At the peak of his power a few years earlier, Biddle had wielded unrivaled control over the largest business enterprise in early America and the leading regulatory agency of the federal government, directing the supply of currency and credit from New York to New Orleans through the twenty-five branches of the Bank of the United States. His widely followed speeches, reports, and letters to editors and legislators had made him the preeminent spokesperson for the rising authority of American finance. As Andrew Jackson's nemesis in the famed "bank war" of the 1830s, he had enjoyed "a degree of influence and popularity among the monied and educated classes equalled only by that of Genl. Jackson with the populace," according to the Philadelphia essayist Sidney George Fisher. ". . . How he was followed, praised, worshipped can scarcely be conceived by those who did not witness the scenes in which he was an actor."[3] In an age of Barings and Rothschilds, the Pennsylvania legislator Charles J. Ingersoll recalled, "Biddle was praised and respected in Europe as the most sagacious and successful banker in the world."[4]

His energetic sponsorship of the Greek Revival forged a lasting bond between classical beauty and modern banking, setting the sovereignty of finance in stone. Yet when Biddle died two years after Dickens's visit in 1844, his demise along with that of the national bank signified to his opponents the failure of the "money power" that he personified. "After bringing thousands to utter poverty, by the frauds and extravagances of his bank, he passed the close of his life in an elegant leisure at his country seat on the Delaware," wrote William Cullen Bryant in New York. "If he had met with his deserts, he would have passed it in the penitentiary."[5]

This chapter explores the roots of Biddle's ideological innovations as a banker in his previous career as a lawyer, legislator, and editor. Born with the new nation in 1786, he was the son of a Philadelphia merchant and prominent Federalist, rich from the West Indies trade. He entered the College of New Jersey (now Princeton University) at age ten and graduated five years later, then studied law with his older brother in Philadelphia.[6] In 1804, he accepted an appointment as secretary to the American minister in Paris, John Armstrong, followed by a brief stint in the same post with the minister in London, James Monroe. He completed his apprenticeship abroad with a grand tour of southern Europe in the manner of young English gentlemen, honing his impressions and self-reflections in a carefully crafted journal. The highlight of his travels came amid the ruins of golden-age Greece, and he established himself as an amateur authority by bringing back copious notes on the Athenian architecture that he was among the first Americans to see.

Returning home, Biddle entered a successful law practice specializing in commercial litigation. He married the daughter of a wealthy widow from whom he acquired a large country estate called "Andalusia." At the same time, he became a regular contributor to the nation's premier literary journal, the *Port Folio*, and he took over as editor in 1812. He also essentially rewrote for publication the journals of Lewis and Clark; his massive two-volume history served as the definitive account of the expedition for nearly a century, until the journals themselves were published in 1904–5.

While working on the journals, Biddle won election to the lower house of the Pennsylvania legislature, and four years later he entered the state senate, where he served a single term before retiring from elective office. His main distinction as a legislator came in a widely admired address on his twenty-fifth birthday, arguing forcefully but unsuccessfully for the recharter of the First Bank of the United States, which operated from 1791 to 1811. In 1818, Biddle accepted a commission from President Monroe to edit a comprehensive digest of the commercial laws of the nation's main trading partners. The following year, Monroe appointed him to the board of the Second Bank, chartered by Congress in 1816, and in 1823 the board elected him president, a title he held for sixteen years.

Relating Biddle's little-studied legal, legislative, and literary experience to his better-known banking career, this chapter considers in turn two fundamental problems of early American finance that Biddle confronted. One was a problem of regulation. The advent of central banking formed the second major phase of a financial revolution that began in the United States in the 1780s, when Biddle was born. The first phase saw the rise of modern commercial banking, when state governments delegated control over the main means of payment to banks, and money became a commodity produced for private profit. But while they were entrusted with quasi-sovereign authority over the monetary system in the new nation, commercial banks could not effectively control the circulation and value of the currencies they produced. They could not restrain their own tendency to overbanking and overlending, nor the resulting crises of the banking system. Central banking, as Biddle conceived it, came partly in answer to bankers' need to regulate the money supply as sovereigns once had.

The second problem was one of representation. Just when men of little or no property were gaining political power in the United States, and just when ordinary people were coming to rely on monetary transactions in qualitatively new ways, control over the supply of cash and credit was ceded to unelected bankers and faceless corporations. The logic of popular sovereignty appeared increasingly in tension with the sovereign privileges bestowed on state-chartered banks. To its Jacksonian critics, as we have seen, the banking system epitomized the corruption of rightful representation, with self-serving middlemen usurping power from those they were supposed to serve. Biddle's vision of central banking arose in large part in response to the challenge of justifying the growing authority of moneyed men in Jacksonian America.

"Let Those Who Own It Govern It": The Problem of Regulation

Like the First Bank of the United States, the Second Bank was the national government's bank, entrusted with the revenues from federal taxes, duties, and fees and with management of the government's debts to bondholders. It too was a mixed public-private corporation, in which the federal government owned a one-fifth share; in the case of the Second Bank, the U.S. president appointed one-fifth of its directors as well. But unlike the First Bank, founded by Alexander Hamilton at a time when the nation had only four other banks, Biddle's bank towered over hundreds of state-chartered banks from the Atlantic seaboard to the western frontier and the cotton kingdom. In the five years between the demise of the First Bank and the establishment of its successor, the number of banks in the United States had nearly doubled, from 117 to 232.[7]

In January 1819, much of the American banking system was collapsing under the mounting weight of its debts for the second time in ten years, bringing its far-flung network of depositors and note-holders down with it. The panic of 1819 launched Biddle's banking career, much as it gave William Leggett his start in journalism. The three-year-old Second Bank, having thrown its own credit headlong into the speculative boom that preceded the panic, was now leading the way into a full-blown depression instead of cushioning the crash. Asked by New York Congressman John C. Spencer for his views on the crisis, Biddle had two things to say in reply. First, he wrote, "the [national] govt which is so jealous of the exclusive privilege of stamping its eagles on a few dollars, should be much more tenacious of its rights over the more universal currency, and never again abandon its finances to the mercy of four or five hundred banks[,] independent[,] irresponsible[,] and precarious." Second, while continuing to serve as the fiscal agent of the federal government, the national bank must assume a new regulatory authority over the nation's banking system and the money supply it controlled. In order to do so, the Second Bank must never allow itself to be swept up in the tide of reckless lending that had jeopardized not only its own capital and credit, but that of the whole class of creditors that owned and should rightly manage the means of producing money in the early republic. Biddle blamed the crisis on a cabal of government-appointed officers and directors at the national bank's Baltimore branch who had loaned themselves more and more money with which to buy more and more stock in the bank, while pursuing policies intended to pay themselves large dividends and inflate the value of their heavily leveraged holdings—essentially creating a giant bubble in the bank itself. "This transferred the management of [the bank] from the hands of those who really [invested their own money in] it to those who had no interest but in its mismanagement—it created that solecism—a monied institution governed by those who had no money," he wrote. ". . . What should be the remedy? Simply to enable those most interested to have their due share in managing the Bank. . . . I believe it to be as true of a bank as of a country that the best security for its welfare is to let those who own it govern it."[8] For Biddle as for Leggett, the financial crisis manifested a failure of rightful representation, as we will see. More immediately, it demonstrated the inadequacy of the sprawling banking system's existing mechanism for regulating its own operations, and the need for a stronger central authority at its helm.

In principle, the self-regulation of the banking system and the money supply depended on its bimetallic basis, which pegged the legal value of the national unit of account in which prices and debts were reckoned—the dollar—to the international market value of gold and silver. In 1792, Congress designated the dollar as the basic monetary unit and defined its value as that of a specified amount of fine gold or silver.[9] The market value of the precious metals was supposed to secure the value of all dollar-denominated debts, a critical function for the entire financial system founded on the circulation of private promises to pay.

There was a hitch. In the United States as in England, the early nineteenth century witnessed a profound crisis of commercial banking and the specie standard on which it was based. The Bank of England was forced to suspend specie payments for its notes from 1797 to 1821, spurred by the spiraling costs of the Napoleonic Wars. American banks outside New England likewise suspended payments during the War of 1812, after the British occupation of Washington, DC, triggered a run on the banks by panicked depositors, and the banks did not resume redemption of their notes for several years after the war. The evident limits of the metallic standard as an automatic regulator of the supply of bank credit and currency sparked a protracted transatlantic debate, focusing on the newly important role of the national bank in safeguarding the system—a subject on which the classical political economy of Adam Smith offered little guidance. As Albert Gallatin, secretary of the treasury under Thomas Jefferson and James Madison, later wrote, "The provisions of the Constitution were universally considered as affording a complete security against the danger of paper money. . . . It was not apprehended that bank-notes, convertible at will into specie, and which no person could be legally compelled to take in payment, would generate into pure paper money, no longer paid at sight in specie. At a later date, although occasional bankruptcies had taken place, and might again be anticipated, there was no apprehension of a general failure of the banks in three-quarters of the states."[10] Simply put, commercial banks proved unable to regulate effectively their lending and the volume and circulation of paper currency they created in the form of notes and deposits redeemable on demand in specie. From the resulting conflicts surrounding the Bank of England and the Bank of the United States arose the foundations of modern monetary theory, monetary policy, and central banking.[11]

In the early United States, the thousands of different kinds of banknotes issued by hundreds of independent banks formed the main tributary of a torrent of paper payment instruments. The monetary free-for-all allowed virtually anyone with a state charter and a printing press to begin lending out notes that passed into general circulation, blurring the line between banking and fraud and spawning a booming black market in counterfeit currency.[12] Amid such a hodgepodge of currencies, the value of banknotes in practice varied widely from place to place, from bank to bank, and from month to month—not to mention from the value of silver and gold to which the dollar was legally pegged. Prices of goods fluctuated sharply and varied steeply across the country as well, reflecting the shifting value of the mishmash of money for which they exchanged. Banks and merchants in one city might decline to accept banknotes issued in another city entirely, or they might accept them only at a great discount. Even local banknotes frequently exchanged for far less than their face value in specie.[13] Individual banks had a powerful incentive to maximize their lending and to encourage customers to borrow more than they could reasonably expect to repay, banking on their ability to refinance the loans when they came due. With a couple of notable exceptions in New England and New York State, where state banks formed federations to regulate or insure their collective lending and note-issue, chaotic competition was the rule.

The result was a self-destructive cycle of pell-mell investment, hyperspeculation, and repeated panics when assets were liquidated and debts cleared in draconian fashion. Perhaps most importantly, the toll taken on small property owners and workers, in the very years when they were gaining political power for the first time, generated growing political opposition to bankers' control over the money supply, as we have seen. This was the central challenge that Biddle's pathbreaking policies as a central banker were intended to address. "If twenty-four States require a National Government to keep them steady," Biddle wrote to William Lewis, a key ally within the Jackson administration, "how much more do several hundred irresponsible independent Banks require the control of a National Bank."[14]

"The Nerves of the Whole Nation": Commercial Regulation and International Law

When Biddle became president of the Second Bank in 1823, at age thirty-seven, he had never run a business other than his wife's family estate. His sole experience in either banking or national office consisted of the four years he had spent as a government appointee to the national bank's board of directors. "Never having felt the wish to be connected with that or any other Bank," he wrote to John Spencer upon being appointed to the board, "my first intention was to decline."[15] But Biddle brought unusual expertise in a related field, international law, through which he had become well acquainted with the challenge of financial regulation that faced the ascendant creditor class.

At eighteen, Biddle became secretary to the new American minister to France, former U.S. senator John Armstrong of New York, an old friend of his father. An accomplished polemicist, Armstrong had gained renown as the Revolutionary War officer who wrote the "Newburgh Addresses," tying wealthy public creditors' demand for full payment from the new U.S. government to soldiers' threat to mutiny if they were not paid as well, an infamous part of the Hamiltonian case for creating a funded national debt along with a national bank to manage it.[16] His and Biddle's main assignment was to expedite payment of claims made by American merchants and their agents whose ships and cargo had been seized during the undeclared Quasi-War with France in the 1790s. Merchants like Biddle's father had profited from the Napoleonic Wars between Britain and France by trading heavily with both sides, particularly with the British and French West Indies. But they had lost millions of dollars to French (and British) "spoliations" of their property, and hundreds of competing claimants now clamored for reparation. The United States assumed responsibility for compensating its own citizens as part of the peace with France and the price of the Louisiana Purchase, setting up an American Board of Commissioners in Paris to adjudicate claims.[17] Armstrong's predecessor and brother-in-law, Robert Livingston, waged a long war of letters with the board on behalf of "creditors both here and in America looking with certainty to a speedy payment," and Biddle and Armstrong vigorously took up the cause.[18] Leading contestants in the French spoliation claims remained Biddle's clients for years after he returned to Philadelphia to practice law.

Biddle thus received a practical education in international finance, highlighting the difficulties of collecting debts and remitting funds in the absence of any shared financial structure or international commercial law. Debt instruments could not circulate across borders without paying a high price in exchange, with little guarantee that promises to pay would be enforced. "To send specie is almost impracticable, and if it were possible the insurance is so enormous that it would sink a great proportion of the capital," Biddle wrote to one of his clients in Paris, the American consul David Bailie Warden, in 1812. "I have therefore looked out for bills[,] but those which are now in the market by no means satisfy me"—a common complaint.[19] Another client, the Virginia tobacco merchant Fulwar Skipwith, proposed establishing an American bank in Paris to handle all payments between the two countries, much as the Second Bank came to control American interregional and international exchange when Biddle was president.[20]

The larger lesson Biddle seems to have drawn from his experience abroad concerned the failure of the eighteenth-century ideal of the "law of nations," which formed the international analog of the self-regulating market in classical political economy. As Peter Onuf and Nicholas Onuf have shown, the French Revolution and the rise of the French Imperium during Biddle's sojourn in Europe shattered liberal hopes that the natural laws of trade would promote a harmonious "balance of power," in which each nation's pursuit of its separate interest would form the basis of peaceful commerce among all. The general suspension of the specie standard, which the architects of the financial revolution had relied on to regulate currency and credit both within and among nations—what Albert Gallatin called "the catastrophe of the year 1814 which first disclosed the insecurity of the American banking system"—signaled a broader loss of confidence in the benevolent power of the "invisible hand" guiding domestic and foreign affairs. By the end of the Napoleonic Wars in 1815, lawyers and ministers on both sides of the Atlantic agreed on the need to create a positive framework of what Jeremy Bentham dubbed "international law" to secure property and markets, contain the revolutionary forces spread by Napoleon's army, and prevent the recurrence of ruinous conflicts among the commercial classes of rival nations. In similar fashion, "National Republicans" like Madison, Monroe, and Biddle united behind a commitment to large-scale, coordinated investment in the development of national and transatlantic markets, directed by financiers in league with a strong central government.[21]

Elected to the Pennsylvania legislature in 1810, Biddle pursued this expansive agenda in a state increasingly dominated by "Old School" Republicans or "unreconstructed Jeffersonians" opposed to higher taxes or public debt and suspicious of moneyed interests. He promoted state sponsorship of a network of roads, canals, and river improvements designed to make Philadelphia the metropolitan capital of an agricultural empire stretching from the Great Lakes to the Gulf of Mexico, without much success. Most notably, he delivered an impassioned three-hour speech calling on Congress to renew the charter of the First Bank of the United States in 1811, winning national attention but scant support from his colleagues in the statehouse.

Boldly extending Hamilton's original arguments for creating a national bank, Biddle stressed the need for a powerful central authority to anchor the centrifugal sprawl of state banks and interstate commerce that had arisen in the past twenty years. Drawing deeply on the writings of Adam Smith, David Hume, James Steuart, Jean-Baptiste Say, and other economic theorists, he rejected the laissez-faire principles of Ricardian and Malthusian economics in favor of a forthright defense of energetic governmental management of money and markets and active promotion of capitalist development. He argued that the growth of the national economy depended on the concomitant expansion of the federal government's constitutional power to regulate long-distance commerce, which entailed the right to define "the nature, the extent, and the means of that intercourse" as well as the "duty of guarding against the inconveniences and difficulties to which that intercourse is subject, and of providing the usual natural facilities, by which the trade of the interior may be assisted"—including a national system of currency and credit. As the nation appeared on the brink of war, Biddle warned Americans to stave off the turmoil that enveloped a divided Europe by rallying around the financial guardian of their shared prosperity. "God grant that what I am saying might alarm into prudence these spoiled children of fortune, who know not how to appreciate the blessings which are heaped upon us by the bounty of heaven. Was ever indeed prosperity so unexampled—yet was ever the happiness of a people so heedlessly guarded?" he asked. ". . . When the nerves of the whole nation should be braced and strung, are we to prepare for combat by cutting the main artery of all its resources?"[22]

A similar spirit runs through the thousand-page history of the Lewis and Clark expedition that Biddle compiled while in the state legislature. Published amid the last of the great Indian wars that formed the western front of the European imperial conflict, the work comprised in important part a catalog of the laws, natural resources, industries, trading posts, and imports and exports of native peoples, reflecting the expedition's primary purpose as part of the Act for Establishing Trading Houses with the Indian Tribes. Five years later, Biddle assembled for the president and senate an analogous digest of the commercial regulations of the nation's trading partners in Europe, primarily Britain, France, and Spain. Laying out a framework for international law at the close of the Napoleonic Wars, the book offered an encyclopedic guide to treaties and laws, coins and other currencies, weights and measures, tariffs and duties, ships and mariners, and an awesome array of commodities from all parts of the colonized globe—from Russian linens, Turkish carpets, Egyptian almonds, and Etruscan vases to scientific instruments, religious artifacts, artistic curios, and animal bones, hides, teeth, furs, feathers, and fins—all painstakingly enumerated and reduced to standard shipping rates and exchange values. Like his chronicle of Lewis and Clark, Biddle's compendium constituted a kind of panoptic regulatory authority in itself.[23]

"The Great Object Is to Control the State Institutions": Central Banking

The First Bank of the United States was chartered with the dual mission of creating credit and acting as the fiscal agent for the U.S. Treasury—helping the federal government to collect taxes, obtain loans, and sell public lands, providing a source of government revenue from the profit on the bank's lending, and managing the national debt. The Second Bank, by contrast, was also expressly empowered to regulate the money supply—that is, to act as a central bank. Whereas Hamilton's rationale for the First Bank rested on the federal government's constitutional authority to levy taxes and make public payments, the congressional debate over a Second Bank in 1816 centered on Congress's power to regulate the value of the coinage, now broadly interpreted to mean the value of bank money as well. The Second Bank, as the political scientist Susan Hoffman has written, was thus "the first organization established by Congress as an economic regulator."[24]

The bank's first two presidents, however, failed to make effective use of the novel authority that Congress had conferred. William Jones ran the Second Bank essentially like any other profit-minded commercial bank, inflating the speculative bubble in cotton and western lands, surrendering whatever leverage the bank might have had to rein in overextended lending and note-issue. Jones's successor, Langdon Cheves, swung the bank abruptly in the opposite direction. He curtailed the bank's lending by more than 50 percent and minimized its issuance of its own notes, while tripling its specie reserves and demanding rapid redemption of state banknotes, together sparking a deep deflationary spiral and helping to bring on the devastating panic of 1819. Jones and Cheves both arrived and departed in the space of just seven years, inciting popular distrust of the national bank without appreciably expanding its purview or power.[25]

Biddle was different. In several major ways, he transformed the Second Bank into the central institution governing the tumultuous growth of the market economy.[26] First and most basically, he gained effective control over the state banks and their creation of currency and credit. "The great object of the Bank is to control the state institutions," he wrote to the bank's oratorical champion, Daniel Webster.[27] In its capacity as the depository of federal revenues, the Second Bank continually accumulated the notes of the state banks, making it their biggest creditor. Immediately following the Second Bank's charter in 1816, Congress legislated that all "duties, taxes, debts or sums of money" owed to the federal government must be paid "in the legal currency of the United States [i.e., gold and silver coin], or Treasury Notes, notes of the Bank of the United States, *or in notes of Banks which are payable and paid on demand in the said legal currency of the United States*."[28] By regularly redeeming state banknotes for specie, as few other note-holders did, the Second Bank could regulate the level of reserves held by the state banks, allowing them to lend more freely or less at its discretion.

"The whole evil therefore lies in an overbanking which occasions an overtrading, and the whole remedy lies in preventing this overbanking," Biddle wrote to John White, cashier of the Second Bank's Baltimore branch, in 1828.[29] He exhorted the bank's branches to remain vigilant in this respect, maintaining their leverage over the state banks by requiring regular settlement of accounts. "It is my anxious desire to see your Office at the head of the business of N. York, and for that purpose not to suffer itself to be encumbered with State Bank balances," he instructed Campbell White, one of the directors of the New York branch, shortly after taking over as Second Bank president in 1823. "The practice here is this. Every morning the clerks from this Bank and the State Banks meet and interchange the notes received respectively on the preceding day. The Balances are struck accordingly—but no bank ever calculates on its Balance remaining for any length of time, and whenever it grows a little too large, no Bank ever hesitates to send for ten or fifteen or twenty thousand dollars from its debtor."[30] Writing to an officer of the national bank in Savannah, he likewise advised,

> In the relations between the Bank of the U.S. and the State Banks, the fundamental principle is, that when their mutual exchanges are made, the balance should be at once paid. It may not be paid in gold or silver but it should be paid in their equivalents—in drafts or stocks or some other property which the creditor is willing to receive & the debtor able to give. There should be an actual discharge & settlement of the debt in some form or other. If a Bank cannot do this—if when its notes are presented it has neither the coin which the notes promise nor the equivalents for it—if it can only pay its old notes with a new note—such an institution whatever veil may disguise its real situation is in fact insolvent. It may possess ample means—but if they are remote & unavailable, they might as well for banking purposes not exist at all since it is the condition of the existence of a Bank to be always ready to pay what it promised to pay.[31]

Biddle treaded carefully when commenting publicly, eager to point out the ways in which the Second Bank provided essential support to the state banks, yet always from a position of superiority over them. "There are very few banks which might not have been destroyed by an exertion of the [Second] bank," he told a congressional committee in 1832.[32]

Second, Biddle greatly expanded the volume of lending and note-issue by the national bank itself.[33] Meanwhile, he focused the bank's business on financing long-distance trade between the staple-growing regions of the South and West and the commercial cities of the Middle Atlantic seaboard. More particularly, he tied the growth of both the bank and the national economy as never before to the rising fortunes of southern slavery and cotton production. Under Biddle's direction, New Orleans became the busiest branch of the national bank, conducting more lending than any office other than the headquarters in Philadelphia, and supplying along with the branches in Mobile and Nashville the great river of paper that made the Mississippi the delta of capital as well as of cotton.[34] "We regard the Office at New Orleans," he wrote in 1826, ". . . as the first in the whole establishment, decidedly superior to any other Office."[35] He played a leading role in the "financialization of American slavery" that turned human chattel into the essential security for the development of financial assets and markets throughout the United States and across the Atlantic. Banking houses like Baring Brothers bundled slave mortgages into bonds sold to far-off investors, and the skyrocketing prices of cotton and slaves fueled the biggest speculative boom in the nation's history.[36]

Biddle's main vehicle in this regard was the bank's control over the business of domestic and foreign exchange—that is, the payment of debts in one place with credits in another. By actively buying commercial paper in the developing regions of the South and West and selling it in the financial centers of the Northeast, the central bank could limit arbitrage by bill brokers, so that merchants' paper IOUs could circulate throughout the country without much loss of value. Merchants in New Orleans, for example, could trade their bills of exchange drawn on people they did business with in New York for Bank of the United States notes. The New Orleans branch of the bank would remit the bills of exchange drawn on New York to the New York branch, which would credit them to the New Orleans branch's account. The New Orleans branch would then have funds to its credit with the New York branch. When the banknotes issued by the New Orleans branch found their way, after circulating through the country, to New York, they would be cashed at the New York branch and deducted from the account of the New Orleans branch there. "So that the Bank is in the South a great buyer [of bills] and in the North a great seller," Biddle wrote, "in the first case preventing too great a fall [in price], in the second too great a rise."[37]

Because the Bank of the United States notes themselves traded at close to their par value in specie throughout the country, instead of trading at various discounts in different locations as state banknotes did, the bank was effectively creating a "sound and uniform" national currency under the bank's control, as Biddle never tired of explaining. "I consider the exchange operations of the Bank as the most useful to the community—the most safe for the Bank and the country and in truth the only resource by which the Institution can maintain a circulation universally receivable," he wrote to Pennsylvania congressman Joseph Hemphill in January 1830.[38] "These operations too are fortunately of the highest benefit to the community," Biddle wrote in his 1831 report to the Second Bank stockholders. "They give the most direct encouragement to industry, by facilitating the purchase and interchange of all its products, they bring the producers and consumers into more immediate contact by diminishing the obstacles which separate them, and they specially adapt the Bank to the wants and interests of each section of the Union, by making it alternately a large purchaser among the sellers of bills, and a large seller among the purchasers."[39] Through its correspondents abroad—Baring Brothers and Company in London, Hope and Company in Amsterdam, Hottinguer and Company in Paris—the Second Bank also became the leading dealer in foreign exchange. This, in fact, became one of Biddle's main instruments for managing the money supply as a whole.[40]

By maintaining its own notes roughly at par, the national bank could limit the excesses of the state banks and keep the currency closely tethered to the specie standard, or what Biddle called "the only safe basis of a circulating medium, the precious metals and the private credits attached to them."[41] "In truth the existence of a National Bank is a question of an irredeemable paper currency or a sound circulation equivalent to specie," he wrote to his close ally William Lewis in 1829. Without the restraint of the Second Bank, he warned, "there will be no general specie payments throughout the Union—and private fortunes as well as the public revenue would relapse into a state of fluctuation and instability."

In these ways, the Second Bank under Biddle's leadership offered a powerful corrective to the problems of self-destructive competition and overbanking. The bank, as he saw it, could stave off dangerous crises in which the banking system and the specie standard broke down and popular distrust of the "money power" mounted. It could offset the economic consequences of a bad balance of trade, a late crop, a large disbursement of federal funds, a war, or a sudden drain of specie, smoothing out the trajectory of economic development and allowing for long-term planning. It could provide a uniform national currency for long-distance trade of American staples, and it could shore up the metallic standard.

In demonstrating that the system of bank credit money could be effectively regulated, however, Biddle also heightened the significance of the second main challenge that he confronted: the challenge of defending bankers' control over the money supply in the face of escalating democratic opposition. More than any immediate issue of monetary policy, it was this fundamental problem of political economy that Biddle aimed to address as banker-in-chief.

"Serving Men": The Problem of Representation

"How are we served by serving men!" Biddle wrote in an 1829 poem called "Ode to Bogle." Robert Bogle, the subject of Biddle's playful tribute, was Philadelphia's first "public waiter," who transformed the position of freelance butler and chef into a kind of public office for the city's small black elite. As the ultimate arbiter of social conduct at every major life event from baptisms to weddings to funerals, Bogle in Biddle's depiction assumed a godlike authority over those he supposedly served. "Thou social Fabius!" Biddle wrote, recalling the Roman general and dictator famous for waiting out the enemy,

> None else has found the happy chance,
> By always waiting, to advance.

By acting as the selfless agent of others, he became for Biddle a comic exemplar of disinterested public service:

> When parties rage, on thee they call
> Who seek'st no office in the State,
> Content, while others push—to wait.

Indeed, the waiter's model of duty and decorum held the selfish striving of those around him in check, ironically requiring them to wait on him:

> Let widows anxious to fulfil
> (For the first time) the dear man's will,
> Lovers and lawyers ill at ease,
> For bliss deferred, or loss of fees,
> Or heirs impatient of delay,
> Chafe inly at his formal stay;
> The Bogle heeds not—nobly true,
> Resolved to give the dead his due.[42]

Partly a tongue-in-cheek comment on the rising power of "serving men" in the age of Jackson, "Ode to Bogle" was also a reflection on Biddle's own authority as the nation's chief "public banker"—an office that he largely defined. Like the butler, the banker was supposed to be a faithful servant, advancing others' interests rather than his own. But Biddle had likewise converted this subordinate role into a position of preeminence over all who depended on his services as the ostensibly dispassionate mediator of monetary affairs. Therein lay a critical problem of representation concerning the peculiar power not only of bankers, but of the currency and credit they controlled.

What or whom bankers and bank money ultimately represented became the most hotly contested question in American politics during Biddle's career. On one level, of course, they represented the rise of the market as a power unto itself, beyond a place, process, or principle, as Jean-Christophe Agnew has written.[43] Its visible hand appeared in the multiplying congregation of so-called middlemen since the seventeenth century: in the agents, bankers, brokers, factors, lawyers, managers, and merchants who stood between buyers and sellers, creditors and debtors, and employers and employees, and in the bills, bonds, checks, deposits, drafts, and notes that increasingly mediated market relations. Contemporary observers generally presumed that the rise of the "middleman economy" reflected the growth of the "real economy" of land, labor, and goods on which it was based.[44] But the widening gap between the network of financial instruments and intermediaries, on the one hand, and the market in material goods and services, on the other, provoked growing debate over the role of the means of payment in regulating as well as reflecting economic activity.

At the same time, the state banking system represented the emergence of a constitutional order founded on the union of private property and popular sovereignty. Representative government arose in tandem with the middleman economy, based on a parallel principle of delegated authority. Representation in this sense originated as a distinctively modern means of legitimating sovereign prerogative, derived from the legal authority of agents such as procurators, attorneys, and ambassadors to make binding financial agreements in other people's names.[45] In political and economic theory, proper representation transmuted competing interests into the common good, whether by marshalling an assembly of locally elected delegates into a strong central government or by synthesizing a multitude of individual transactions into a common market valuation. The converse danger lay in the potential for representatives to pursue their personal interests in place of those of their constituents, in a political economy predicated on reliable representation. Aristotle and the Greek historian Polybius described this fateful liability as the corruption of the body politic. Their republican followers in England and America applied the metaphor of corruption to the modern merger of finance and government. They drew on Aristotle's related warning against the tendency of money, the quintessential representative of the bond between economic value and political sovereignty, to become an end rather than a means, or a self-serving "money power" rather than a subservient medium of exchange.[46]

Conceived as the betrayal of rightful representation, corruption became the main rhetorical rubric under which eighteenth- and nineteenth-century Americans articulated criticisms of political and economic power in general, of corporations in particular, and of banks most of all. Nowhere was the rhetoric of corruption more heated and the banking question more fiercely fought than in Biddle's Pennsylvania, the stronghold of both finance and democratic radicalism in the early republic.[47]

On the one hand, as the new nation's financial and political capital, Philadelphia included America's "first Wall Street," home to the Bank of Pennsylvania and the Bank of North America—the first two American banks—as well as the First and Second Banks of the United States.[48] Its unique combination of capital and political power made possible Pennsylvania's explosive proliferation of business corporations, from just one prior to the American Revolution to more than two thousand businesses individually chartered by the state legislature between 1790 and 1860.[49] There as elsewhere in the early republic, the general practice of requiring a special statute from the legislature for a corporate charter, establishing each company's constitution and bylaws, signified a closer identification between government and corporate enterprise than in England, where joint-stock companies formed by private agreement predominated. In Pennsylvania, such special charters commonly required corporations for banking and transportation to provide loans or bonuses to the state government, and many were "mixed corporations" owned jointly by the state and by private investors, like the Second Bank of the United States after it lost its federal charter and was reorganized under a state charter in 1835.[50] At the same time, however, business corporations in Pennsylvania, as throughout the nation, gained increasing autonomy during Biddle's lifetime. State and federal courts moved to grant corporations private property rights that the legislatures that chartered them could not abrogate. Thus by the 1830s, Biddle's bank operated in legal respects much like a wholly privately owned corporation responsible first and foremost to its investors.[51]

On the other hand, Pennsylvania's uniquely democratic state constitution of 1790 enfranchised all taxpayers, made all important public offices elective and without property qualifications, and provided the platform for a political alliance of Philadelphia artisans and western farmers that gained control of the state government during the presidency of Thomas Jefferson.[52] The legal profession, which supplied a large share of the new nation's political elite and was especially well established in Philadelphia, formed a natural target for radical Democrats. While popular campaigns against the bench and bar appeared in many places after the Revolution, only in Georgia and Pennsylvania did such opposition mobilize a sustained political movement for fundamental reform. Tainted by their association with the English Inns of Court and by their unpopular role in collecting debts and enforcing contracts, lawyers were charged by Pennsylvania Democrats with the cardinal sin of corruption. "In the demagogic idiom," writes Gary Nash, "[lawyers] were parasitical and superfluous agents who had arrogated an important democratic function—the administration of justice." When Biddle was beginning his legal career, the emerging farmer-labor bloc began agitating to make the judiciary responsible to the electorate, expand the jurisdiction of lay justices of the peace, replace lawyers with lay arbitrators in civil actions, codify the criminal law and simplify court procedures, and reduce as much as possible the requirements for admission to the bar or even eliminate the bar outright. The goal, shared by similar movements in revolutionary England and France, was to minimize the role of legal institutions and intermediaries, allowing litigants to settle disputes themselves.[53]

A similar suspicion of delegated authority propelled the growing opposition to corporate charters, which became a major cause of radical Democrats in Pennsylvania. Part public utility, part private property, specially chartered business corporations appeared to the rising ranks of their opponents to occupy an illegitimate middle ground between individual liberty and collective authority. They appropriated sovereign prerogatives such as eminent domain and taxation properly reserved to "the people" as a whole, even as they encroached on the equal rights of those without a charter.[54]

Like other corporations, state banks as well as the national bank were thus widely accused of serving the private interest of their investors at the expense of the public interest they were meant to uphold. But as we have seen in the previous chapter, banks posed a special problem of representation for radical Democrats because they stood not only between the state and its citizens, but between creditors and debtors, producers and consumers, inevitably tending to subvert the interests of both sides of the market exchanges they mediated. The close connection between the political economy and the art and literature of the early republic gave moral force and popular appeal to democratic criticisms of finance and banking, as exemplified by Leggett. No one responded more creatively to that ideological challenge than Biddle, turning the rhetoric of corruption back on its Jacksonian exponents.

"A Bank on Parnassus": Melancholy and Neoclassicism

Biddle's carefully crafted personal appearance reflected the genteel image of finance he cultivated. Contemporaries typically described him as "beautiful in person as Apollo; highly educated, polished in his manners, and gifted with all the grace that ever adorned the most refined court of Europe." "Wherever he appeared," one recalled, "there was a sensation and a crowd immediately formed around him. His manner was gracious, smiling, easy, gentlemanlike, a little condescending and exhibited supreme self-satisfaction and elation." He posed for at least eighteen portraits, recording his development from the rakish youth in a French drawing of 1805 into the elder statesman with the Grecian portico of the national bank in the background in 1837. Probably his best-known likeness, painted by Thomas Sully in 1826, depicts the bank president in Romantic repose, warmly lit in an open-necked shirt and fur-collared coat, his long brown locks swept forward in the Byronic style as he sits moodily at a window overlooking a cloudy seascape—the picture of a poet with more on his mind than cotton bills and discount rates (figure 4.1).[55]

Biddle drew the face of American banking with comparable aesthetic care. Along with his legal and legislative experience, he brought to the Second Bank a reputation as a man of letters dating back to his renowned travels in the Mediterranean twenty years earlier. As he mused in a whimsical poem upon becoming president,

> Alas! had the ancients, who so much surpass us,
> In their pure golden age, fixed a *bank* on Parnassus,
> What a model of wisdom and pleasure to follow!
> Only think now—to sign one's bank-notes like Apollo!

"Enclosed in my vast marble tomb," as he called the bank's new headquarters modeled on the Parthenon, he pictured himself

> 'Mid vaults of damp stone and huge chests of cold
> iron,
> That would quell all the fancy of Shakespeare or
> Byron.

In his new office, he confessed with a wink,

> I prefer my last letter from Barings or Hope
> To the finest epistles of Pliny or Pope;
> My "much-esteem'd favors" from Paris, to those
> Which brought on poor Helen an Iliad of woes;

FIGURE 4.1. Thomas Sully, *Nicholas Biddle*, 1826. Courtesy of the Andalusia Foundation.

> One lot of good bills from Prime, Bell, or the
> Biddles,
> To whole volumes of epics or satires or Idyls;
> Nay, two lines of plain prose with a good name
> upon it,
> To the tenderest fourteen ever squeezed in a sonnet.[56]

Biddle's wry obituary for his love of literature proved premature. His cultural credentials were crucial to his efforts to rebrand the bank. If he could not quite sign his banknotes like Apollo, knowing from personal experience the distance between the glory of the ancients and the disreputable role of the

FIGURE 4.2. Drawing by Charles Burton, *United States Bank, Philadelphia*, engraved by Fenner, Sears, and Co. (London: Hinton, Simpkin, and Marshall, 1831). Courtesy of the American Antiquarian Society.

middleman in modern society, he aimed to bridge that divide in his classical temple for money changers on Chestnut Street (figure 4.2).

Art and money had been Biddle's passions ever since he had returned from college to study law with his brother in Philadelphia, the literary and financial capital of the early republic. There he joined a close circle of doctors, lawyers, scientists, ministers, and teachers called the Tuesday Club, dedicated to the twin pursuits of literary appreciation and professional advancement. He formed a lasting association with the society's unofficial leader, Joseph Dennie, the acid-penned editor of the *Port Folio*. The nation's foremost literary journal wedded an archconservative contempt for democratic politics and "vulgar" hucksterism to the establishment of belles lettres as a prestigious vocation in the young republic, akin to law and finance. While Dennie scorned popularity and profit, he made the weekly magazine more widely subscribed and successful than any previous American publication, launching the careers of a prominent stable of authors including Biddle.[57]

Biddle contributed a couple of revealing essays in "mock criticism," as the editor called it—one poking fun at the pseudo-military "manœuvres" and "reconnoitring" of "valourous knights" and "damsels" at a tea party, another satirically describing "Jack and Gill" as a tale of heroism and tragedy illustrating the "fall of men" and "instability of all things." Like his later comic verses, these pieces ridiculed the humdrum routines of post-Revolutionary society by contrast to classical ideals, parodying melodramatic efforts to find the workings of great moral forces within the everyday affairs of ordinary people—the favored literary mode of democratic discourse, as we have seen in Leggett's writings.[58] Yet as he showed in a tribute to his uncle and namesake, Captain Nicholas Biddle, who had served with distinction as a naval officer in the Revolution, the young Biddle shared with Leggett the quest for a cause worthy of the ideals of the Revolutionary Era.[59]

The ironic detachment that Biddle affected in these early writings bespoke a budding patrician sensibility, as did the copious classical allusions. At Princeton he had excelled in Latin and Greek and taken a leading role in a debating society as "Grammaticus," deeming the ancient languages, as he wrote in a college essay, essential for "those who intend to move in a higher sphere and those whose business require it," though "highly unnecessary" for "those who expect to be brought up as tradesmen."[60] His studied balance of alienation and ambition found full expression in the travel journal he kept of his grand tour of southern Europe several years later, which he patterned after the Roman poet Horace. "I look from my window so coolly on the noise of Trieste that I seem like one of Plato's wise men who sees the vanity of the shadows which deceive the people in the hole," he wrote. As one of the first of many Americans to visit Greece in the early nineteenth century, he felt himself heir to the valor of the Roman legal sage Cicero, whom he read as he roamed the ruins. But he deplored the squalor and servitude of the modern Greeks under Turkish rule. He prayed for their deliverance, perhaps with foreign assistance, at the hands of what he called the "higher classes" who still remembered their long-lost glory—meaning the Hellenic diaspora of grain merchants and liberal administrators who aimed to ally with local bandits and clans in liberating their ancient homeland. "Society has at the close of the last century received a great and glorious movement," he wrote, "which promises to become general."[61]

Biddle's response to the stirrings of the Greek Revolution set the pattern for the Napoleonic nationalism that became his signature as he developed close political and social ties to the community of wealthy French expatriates in Philadelphia, including the banker Stephen Girard and Napoleon's older brother and would-be heir, Joseph Bonaparte.[62] He embraced the republican spirit of the age of revolution while finding its exemplars not in the common people themselves, but in the enlightened emancipators who led in their name. In Athens, he dedicated himself to the career of a classical orator and statesman. "I believe the turn of my mind, or what may properly be called my genius, has at length decided itself," Biddle wrote to his brother. "To govern men, and particularly by means of eloquence[,] seems to me the object most worthy of ambition in a free govt. It is the avenue which leads to glory," he wrote, ". . . Yet much, very much is to be done in order to acquire glory. The routine of [an] attorney, pleading, is beneath imitation."[63]

The routine of an attorney proved lucrative enough on his return to Philadelphia in 1807, but Biddle longed to find a higher calling in his career. In a letter to his friend and fellow lawyer Benjamin Rush, he rejoiced at the widening purview of the American legal profession, reaching far beyond litigation, mediation, and law enforcement. "There has in fact been reproduced here a state of things which has scarcely any example since the best days of Rome, when the citizen accomplished in every branch of science passed from the forum to the highest duties of war[,] of religion[,] or of civil magistracy," Biddle wrote, "and if our bar would only cultivate more deeply the severer studies they might realize what their great model asserts of the Roman orators: 'non solum ut de jure civili ad eos verum etiam de omni aut officio aut negotio referratur.'" That is, lawyers who trained broadly in rhetoric, literature, history, and politics might attain the singular stature of those whom Cicero, in the passage that Biddle loosely quoted, said citizens would "consult [not only] on points of law but also about marrying off a daughter, buying a farm, tilling their estates, and in short every sort of liability or business." In answering the pressing need of their countrymen for wise counsel in the broadest sense, Biddle wrote, lawyers could represent not merely the narrow interests of their clients, but the common standards and sympathies of the nation as a whole. They could "twine together the scattered cords which should bind us to the country" and "build up a system of national opinions."[64] Though he later transferred its locus from the practice of law to that of central banking, his Ciceronian ideal stayed the same.

Over the next ten years, however, Biddle pursued the role of oracle of public opinion in a literary direction. He became a regular contributor of essays, sketches, poems, and reviews for the *Port Folio* and took over as editor when Joseph Dennie died in 1812. He remade the journal into a platform for the kind of impassioned patriotism that he associated with classical oratory, cleansed of Dennie's penchant for partisan attacks—"a *national* work," as Biddle called it, devoted to "the literary splendour of the country at large." Not "cold and prudent calculation" but "kindred feelings" must bind Americans in common cause, he told his readers on the eve of the War of 1812, calling for poetry and song to "make us not merely know, but feel that we have a country."[65]

Biddle's dominant mode of expression recalled the blend of disdain and determination in his youthful essays, bewailing the loneliness of the modern "philosophical statesman" amid the ashes of his ancient forebears while heralding the dawn of a new Athens or Rome.[66] Since the time when he gazed at the Athenian ruins and reflected "with a melancholy satisfaction that we [Americans] may one day be as great and as miserable" as the Greeks, "melancholy" became one of Biddle's favorite words, ritually invoked on public occasions.[67] In his poems identifying the role of the public banker with that of a funeral director or marble-tombed spirit, as in his frequent eulogies for family members, friends, and national leaders like Washington and Jefferson, he adopted a sentimental idiom that transcended the petty pursuits of political ambition and economic interest, much like patriotic art, architecture, and literature. Like other self-styled aristocrats in revolutionary Europe and America, he embraced the Aristotelian notion of melancholy as a mark of genius, identifying the natural nobility in a time of social upheaval. He cultivated the character of the gentleman of feeling who takes upon himself the suffering of a strife-torn world, manifested in effusive despair and foreboding.[68] So in an 1811 Fourth of July oration he surveyed the desolated kingdoms of wartime Europe and anticipated a similar fate for the American republic, now in its "golden age."[69] And so in an 1835 commencement address he recalled seeing Napoleon crowned emperor in Paris, only to end up exiled and alone—"the great moral lesson of our age," as he said, perhaps more prophetically than he realized.[70] Seen from this plaintive perspective, the evanescence of paper wealth and fragility of fortune in the new financial order seemed sublimely in tune with the eternal cycle of creation and destruction depicted in Thomas Cole's celebrated series of landscape paintings, *The Course of Empire* (1834–36), in which the Second Bank building prominently appears (figure 4.3).[71]

Elegy and epic came together in Biddle's nationalist history of the Lewis and Clark expedition, tracing the destiny of the new republic from Athens to Oregon. Commissioned in 1810 to edit the journals that the two commanders had kept of their journey, he completely reworked the chronicle, adding extensive material based on his own interviews, correspondence, and study of related reports. Among the most influential works of literary nationalism in this period, his *History of the Expedition of Captains Lewis and Clark* (1814) appeared in twenty-two editions over the next ninety years. It set the standard for later western adventure stories, hitching a heroic odyssey of Euro-American exploration to the expansion of the national economy and the national government. Submerging the confusion, disarray, and disease of the original Corps of Discovery, he fashioned a seamless narrative whose genteel prose generally bore faint resemblance to the raw material. Though William Clark hired him as editor, Biddle's style more closely matched that of Meriwether Lewis, whose world-weary, soul-searching journal resembled Biddle's

FIGURE 4.3A. Thomas Cole, *The Course of Empire: Consummation*, ca. 1835–36, oil on canvas, 51 ¼ × 76 inches, Object No. 1858.3, New-York Historical Society. Photo courtesy of the New-York Historical Society. The Second Bank building appears on the left.

FIGURE 4.3B. Thomas Cole, *The Course of Empire: Desolation*, 1836, oil on canvas, 39 ¼ × 63 ¼ inches, Object No. 1858.5, New-York Historical Society. Photo courtesy of the New-York Historical Society.

own travel notes from the same years. Like Leggett's melodramatic naval stories and western tales, Biddle's melancholic accounts of the Mediterranean and the Far West frontiers framed his writings on the metropolitan Middle Atlantic.[72]

The most striking way in which Biddle joined commemoration of past causes to consecration of new ones appeared in his long campaign to create modern antiquities, lasting monuments of his own era comparable to those of classical Greece and Rome. "Amidst the numerous advantages to be derived from travelling, the greatest, and most essential are those moral reflections which naturally present themselves to the mind at the sights of what is great, grand, or magnificent," Biddle wrote in an undergraduate essay on the pyramids of ancient Egypt.[73] Calling for the construction of a memorial to George Washington in 1811, he noted that the relics of such structures "will exist long after the republic is in ashes."[74] They will endure "unmoved by all the revolutions of the changing world," he said in 1833, dedicating the cornerstone of Girard College in Philadelphia as president of its board of trustees.[75] Presiding over the nation's financial order from his "marble tomb," Biddle looked forward to the ruins of his own realm. Freed from the political tumult in which it was born, the bleached remains of the bank might finally attain the supreme authority for which it stood.

Greco-Roman classicism formed a keynote of Biddle's career, joining poetry, politics, and his inspirational vision of the banker as statesman and sage. "The two great truths in the world are the Bible and Greek architecture," he wrote.[76] The vogue of neoclassical art and rhetoric in the new United States reflected the Janus face of merchant-gentry families like his and their planter-class counterparts, perched precariously atop the tide of revolution. Courtly in style and self-image, aggressively entrepreneurial in business, bankers and planters looked to antiquity as a surrogate pedigree and a testament to their republican allegiance. Perhaps the "premier Grecophile of his era," as art historians have suggested, Biddle brought this compound of aristocratic and bourgeois elements to the system of early American banking.[77]

Designed by his friend William Strickland with Biddle's approval and built between 1818 and 1824, the Second Bank building in Philadelphia became the most acclaimed example of the Greek Revival that swept American architecture under the bank's twenty-year tutelage. It was rivaled only by his country house at Andalusia and by Girard College, whose Doric design he also supervised.[78] European architects had been copying Greek temple remains since the mid-eighteenth century, but the Greek Revival made little headway in the United States before the 1820s. Earlier Americans' enthusiasm for the ancients ran strongly toward republican Rome, and the architecture of the new nation clung to the stately red-brick boxes of British and Dutch colonialism—with the notable exception of Jefferson's classical Roman plans for the University of Virginia and Monticello. But as chair of the Second Bank's building committee and then as its president, Biddle saw to it that branches of the national bank across the country—and scores of state banks as well—came to be modeled on Greek temples. From the new north portico of the White House to "thousands of gabled white frame buildings" across the country, as a leading scholar of the revival has written, what Biddle called the "refined simplicity" of the Grecian style epitomized the union of nostalgia and enterprise, draping the new riches of financiers and planters in a classically republican mantle.[79]

"The Bank is undoubtedly the most faultless monument of its size in the United States," wrote the architect James Gallier in 1836. "We cannot avoid noticing the peculiar aptness of the Grecian architecture for banking-houses," he added, explaining that its exceptional strength and grandeur "form a befitting temple for the worship of the blind goddess. And this style of building . . . prevails throughout the country, wherever an edifice is erected expressly for a banking-house."[80] Biddle sponsored the spread of the Greek Revival from its hub in Philadelphia throughout the Second Bank's principal dominion, extending along the Atlantic seaboard from Washington and Baltimore to New York, westward across the "inland empire" of canal towns to the riverbank cities and frontier communities of the Northwest Territory, and southward through the old tobacco country of Virginia and North Carolina. Cotton planters brought neoclassical architecture to the Deep South, following the lead of Biddle's nemesis, Andrew Jackson, who had his Tennessee manor rebuilt to fit his image as a latter-day Cincinnatus. But the white-columned mansions of the cotton kingdom only loosely resembled the "blockier, simpler, more massive" Greek models that Biddle promoted in the North, which were regarded by the 1830s as "the 'official' style of financial Whiggery," in the words of the architectural critic Roger G. Kennedy.[81]

Biddle was hardly the first to connect the form of the classical temple with the functions of finance. Even in ancient Greece, temples had received valuables and coins offered as tokens of devotion, then lent these funds at interest to the state and possibly to individuals as well.[82] In Renaissance Italy, Venetian merchants-turned-planters had adapted the classical designs of Greek civic and religious structures to their country estates, providing a veneer of rural repose for their financial fortunes. Bankers had also been the leading patrons of the Greek Revival in Augustan Britain.[83] In the solid geometry of pillars and planes, Biddle found an analog for his notion of banking as the poetry of capital, distilling the Platonic ideals concealed within the commotion of market relations. From what he regarded as the savage "arts of traffic," banking abstracted the simple yet profound principles of exchange and value, much as Greek architecture epitomized the eternal truths of beauty and utility implicit in even the most primitive dwelling.[84]

Indeed, the Panhellenic revival arose along with political economy in eighteenth-century Edinburgh, twin progeny of the Scottish moral philosophy of Adam Smith and David Hume, among others. Biddle began promoting an amalgam of finance and fine art as editor of the *Port Folio*. He published articles by disciples of the Scottish school such as the Virginian lawyer and author George Tucker, who contributed a series of essays in 1814 and 1815 entitled "Thoughts of a Hermit"—a familiar figure in early American political discourse, signaling a lofty detachment from contemporary society akin to that of "Plato's wise men" in Biddle's travel journal. Tucker's pieces found a timeless beauty in works of art, music, poetry, and architecture that appealed to the deep aesthetic sense inherent in human nature across all ages and cultures, exemplified in the perfect "simplicity" of classical Greece. In a similar way, Tucker suggested that modern banking best answered the age-old need of a circulating medium of exchange, especially when administered by disinterested boards of directors regulating the money supply more wisely than self-interested individuals could.[85]

In an 1811 manifesto that Biddle published as a special addendum, the architect Benjamin Henry Latrobe wrote that American artistic development was stunted by provincial prejudice against the fine arts and the concentration of funds needed to support them, which were similarly stigmatized as unproductive and unrepublican. To the contrary, Latrobe contended, "A propensity to the fine arts is an instinctive property of human nature," liberty and art flourished together, and they had attained their highest stage of mutual improvement in Periclean Athens. Noting that the groundwork for the Greek Revival had been laid with the marble facade of the First Bank of the United States and his own Grecian design for the Bank of Pennsylvania, Latrobe called for Philadelphia to capitalize on its financial wealth and become "the Athens of the Western world."[86]

Biddle shared Latrobe's enthusiasm for public architecture. He hoped the beauty of the Second Bank and its branches—representing, as an architectural historian has noted, "the first widespread introduction into the states . . . of public buildings associated with the central government"—could awaken in Americans a visceral sense of unity, rooted in a common system of currency and credit.[87] Like the Whig party, which split from the Democrats after Jackson vetoed the recharter of the national bank, the Greek Revival both participated in and departed from the revolutionary movements that swept across the Atlantic around 1830. The democratic ferment from Poland to Paris to the English Parliament reached furthest in the United States, inspired in part by the recent triumph of the Greek Revolution in the ancient birthplace of Western democracy.[88] In eighteenth-century England and Continental Europe, the Greek Revival had been an exclusively elite and conservative movement, mainly restricted to the private country residences of wealthy industrialists and financiers. In antebellum America, by contrast, the "refined simplicity" of the Grecian style acquired a far more popular and public character, associating the growth of commercial banking with the ascendance of democratic politics.[89] Yet at the same time, as Caroline Winterer has shown, classics scholars came to identify Greek architecture, sculpture, and rhetoric with a sophisticated appreciation for beauty, truth, and genius as opposed to the moneygrubbing mediocrity of Jacksonian America.[90]

Such superiority naturally appealed to profit-driven southern planters, who owned most of the stock in Biddle's bank held by U.S. citizens.[91] In much the same way, the antimodern character of the Greek Revival lent itself to Biddle's image of banking as a critical check on the irresponsibility of businessmen and their representatives in government. "Landed proprietors," Biddle told the Philadelphia Society for Promoting Agriculture in 1822, "well educated, brave, and independent—the friends of the government, without soliciting its favors—the advocates of the people, without descending to flatter their passions; these men, rooted like their own forests, may yet interpose between the factions of the country, to heal, to defend, and to save."[92] The next year, Biddle became president of the Second Bank, where he devised a similar role for central banking as the balance wheel of market society.

"Places of Refuge": The Pastoralization of Finance

Even as he waxed rhapsodic about the natural nobility of "men of the soil," Biddle called for intensive agricultural development of the Pennsylvania backcountry. He disparaged the prevalence of extensive but poorly capitalized and underutilized estates maintained by absentee landlords more interested in owning land than in effectively farming it. "The natural feelings belong to all times, but science is necessarily progressive," he told the Philadelphia agricultural society, endorsing increased investment in techniques of systematic irrigation, "efficient cultivation," and employment of hired labor, for "an ill-stocked farm can be no more profitable than an empty factory." "Now an English farmer, with a certain capital, rents a farm, as a manufacturer rents a house, and devotes his capital to extract from it the greatest possible produce," Biddle said approvingly. He urged the Middle Atlantic gentry to emulate its British cousin whose "combinations of wealth and skill" formed the modern foundation of "good husbandry," as capital improvements designed to maximize productivity took on the pastoral virtues associated with leisured landownership in an earlier age.[93] At the same time that he mobilized the resources of the national bank to promote the capital-intensive cotton kingdom in the Deep South, he supported North Carolina and Virginia planters turning from traditional tobacco cultivation to invest in the growth of retail operations across the Upper South, as well as the development of the domestic slave trade linking the Atlantic seaboard to the Mississippi Delta in an expanding empire of finance and human capital.[94]

A centralized system of national banking, as Biddle conceived it, enabled such diversification and maximization of returns on agricultural investment. It turned planters into financiers and made bankers into veritable modern-day planters, paternal lords of the market economy itself. "Pastoralization" is what Jeanne Boydston has called a form of ideology first described by the literary theorist Raymond Williams, whereby the capitalist transformation of agricultural land and labor ironically came to be identified with nostalgic ideals of rural life and the virtues of stability, community, and caretaking. In much the same way, as Boydston argues, the Victorian domestic sphere or "home" came to be conceived as a haven from or antidote to the market forces that it actually advanced. Something similar might be said of Biddle's "bank on Parnassus" and the ongoing financial revolution it came to lead.[95]

Public credit and paper money had long been associated with the strength of social ties and communal feelings, and particularly with the cultivation of a sentimental form of national identity or "public opinion" in the early United States.[96] Biddle invoked this familiar bond between finance and patriotism in identifying the national bank with a moral reaction against the shallow materialism and individualism of his age—the "worship of cunning" and single-minded pursuit of creature comforts, as he typically put it, which "have tended to unspiritualize the understanding."[97] Like critics of banking such as Leggett, Biddle welcomed what he deemed the salutary discipline imposed by the panic of 1837, bringing an abrupt end to the speculative spree of the preceding years. But unlike his opponents, he associated the authority of the national bank itself with a new spirit of collective responsibility embodied in the full and prompt repayment of debts. In an open letter to John Quincy Adams in 1838, Biddle boasted of the bank's "active agency in collecting the debts" that Americans owed to foreign creditors. "If the universal distress which pervaded the community could not be witnessed without a painful sympathy,—its melancholy was redeemed by the high and manly spirit which it roused throughout the country," he wrote. "For never, on its most glorious fields of battle, was there displayed a more lofty sentiment of honor and courage than was then exhibited. The honest payment of debt,—the homely duty of private life—was elevated by its universality into a sentiment of honor,—as the whole country in mass pressed forward to its performance, as to some sacred and patriotic obligation." In the crucible of hard times, the strict enforcement of private contracts between wealthy creditors and impoverished debtors was thus made a test of national unity and resolve. International debt collection, the task with which he had been charged in his first public office many years earlier, appeared to Biddle as the moral equivalent of military service. "A civil glory this," he wrote, "worth a thousand victories."[98]

Biddle had learned his lesson from his disappointing foray into Pennsylvania politics, where he had seen his empire-building plans stymied in the state legislature and his two bids for Congress defeated. "The district is in truth a perfect chaos of factions," he wrote to President James Monroe in 1820, "and as I have shunned all participation in their intrigues I do not anticipate the slightest chance of being elected."[99] In the coming years, he found frequent occasion to decry the decline of the "scholar and statesman" whose classical learning made him a leader rather than a follower of his constituents.[100] "Undoubtedly the public councils should reflect the public sentiment," he said in a eulogy for Jefferson in 1827, "but that mirror may be dimmed by being too closely breathed on."[101] A free people depended on the "personal independence" of leaders able to represent its real interests rather than its "crude opinions," Biddle argued in a public rebuke to Jackson several years later. The danger to democracy came from demagogues who followed too faithfully the caprice of popular excitement, who "flatter us until they can betray us—as men praise what they mean to sell."[102]

Politicians and salesmen alike, said Biddle, obeyed the destructive dictates of parochial self-interest. As he saw it, the dollar democracy of the market followed the same logic as popular politics, under a misguided faith that the free play of competing interests automatically assured the general welfare of all. Indeed, his Jacksonian opponents typically did apply the same basic conception of faithful representation to market exchange and electoral politics—and to art and literature as well. They implicitly recognized no legitimate role for public officials or financial intermediaries beyond obediently carrying out the wishes of their constituents and customers. For Biddle, however, true representation meant rising above the "chaos of factions" and the base "arts of traffic," or "that selfishness . . . which *intense devotion to the world of business* is too prone to inspire." Of those "finer intellects" whose "literary pursuits" and "love of study" prepared them for public service, he wrote, "From that outer scene of contention with the passions and interests of others, their retreat is to the fountain within, calming by its repose and freshening with its coolness the overstrained energy of the mind."[103] This was the Ciceronian sovereignty that had eluded Biddle as a lawyer and legislator, and that he finally claimed as the nation's first central banker.

The presidency of the Second Bank afforded a unique form of unappealable power in a constitutional republic, comparable only to the Supreme Court as it came to define its role in these same years. As Biddle confided to a political supporter near the end of his tenure at the national bank in 1837, "I have been for years in the daily exercise of more personal authority than any [U.S.] President habitually enjoys."[104] Unlike even Supreme Court justices, the president of the bank was not appointed by any elected official. He was chosen by the bank's board of directors, which mainly comprised bankers appointed by other bankers, who were responsible solely to private investors. The president was the only member of its board of directors who served an unlimited term; he generally controlled sufficient votes among the stockholders to decide the election of the other directors; and in practice, he selected the directors and officers of all the branches as well.[105]

Far from disguising this virtually unlimited authority in his public statements and private correspondence, Biddle made the autonomy of the national bank and its chief executive their most precious asset. The president of the bank, he wrote shortly before taking the job, should be someone with a "*talent* for business rather than what is commonly called a man of business," for businessmen lacked "liberal habits of thinking." He should likewise "stand well with the Govt" without being "an active partizan," for "I am far from thinking that the govt should have any direct or indirect influence over the Bank."[106] In nearly everything he said about the Second Bank, he walked this ideological tightrope, emphasizing the bank's vital service to the national government and promotion of economic development while staunchly defending its political and economic independence.

To those, like Jackson, who questioned the constitutionality of the Second Bank's charter, he responded that it was simply a vehicle for the performance of several of the federal government's constitutional powers, including the authority to tax, borrow, and regulate interstate commerce and currency.[107] Yet its public responsibilities emphatically did not mean that the central bank should be answerable to the citizens or elected officials it served. Biddle's constant refrain was the bank's "complete estrangement from politics"—a theme he stressed increasingly as the bank came under attack for allegedly favoring anti-Jackson candidates in state and national elections.[108] "We believe that the prosperity of the Bank and its usefulness to the country depend on its being entirely free from the control of the Officers of the Govt—a control fatal to every Bank, which it ever influenced," he wrote to Senator Samuel Smith of Maryland, chair of the Senate Finance Committee, in December 1828. ". . . The truth is that with us, it is considered that we have no concern in politics. Dean [Jonathan] Swift said you know, that money is neither Whig nor Tory, and we say with equal truth, that the Bank is neither a Jackson man nor an Adams man. It is only a Bank."[109]

With a similar logic, Biddle affirmed the Second Bank's strict allegiance to the so-called real bills doctrine, to which Leggett subscribed as well. The doctrine meant limiting the bank's lending to short-term, self-liquidating loans secured by actual purchases and sales of goods, as opposed to longer-term, riskier loans to farmers and entrepreneurs. "The great advantage and the great security of a Bank paper is that it rises and falls with the business wants of the community," Biddle wrote to Albert Gallatin in 1830.[110] When responding to congressional investigators, he pointed with pride to the discipline with which he maintained the bank's "true business character as a Counting House," promoting "a thorough identification of the Bank with the real business and exchanges of the country."[111]

Yet just as the bank's fealty to the federal government did not warrant government oversight, according to Biddle, so its responsiveness to the needs of trade did not mean that it should simply do its customers' bidding. The fatal mistake of his predecessors was to have too readily accommodated growing demands for credit as the national economy expanded. "The fact is that the misfortunes of the Bank . . . were occasioned by the men of business and their errors were precisely the faults into which the men of business were most likely to fall. They trusted the Western people with money as they trusted them with goods," he wrote before taking office. "It is no doubt very unpleasant and even painful to decline good business paper," he instructed the president of the New York branch of the Second Bank, Isaac Laurence, in April 1825, "but . . . beyond a certain limit the convenience of the customers of the Bank[,] however desirable it may be to promote it, is only a secondary consideration."[112] Indeed, the very purpose of the central bank, in Biddle's view, was to regulate the market rather than be regulated by it, as the state banks largely were. He regarded his leverage over the money supply as an essential instrument of economic planning, not simply service to business and government. And he justified that authority as a fulfillment of the national bank's duty to look out for the long-term health of the economy as a whole rather than the immediate interests of various stakeholders.

As much as he deplored the irresponsibility of the state banks, Biddle's arguments on behalf of the national bank extended in many ways to the system of commercial banking in general. "Banks are essentially popular and republican institutions. They are the places of refuge from the overweening dominion of very rich men," he wrote in March 1831. Properly organized and operated, banks served as impartial umpires of the contest of political and economic self-interest, providing a crucial buffer between creditors and debtors, rich and poor, while safeguarding the interests of all contending parties. "A bank," he said, "is an unambitious and passionless rich man lending for money not for power."[113] It was, in fact, "the most natural way of protecting the poorer classes," preventing the activity of predatory moneylenders by providing loans at moderate interest. "As to a monied aristocracy, is it not obvious that the funds of a bank are of all other kinds of property the least calculated to promote the influence which is feared?" Biddle argued. "An extensive proprietor of land may oppress his tenantry; the holder of mortgages may influence and control a whole neighborhood; but a large stockholder in a bank sees interposed between him and his debtors an association of individuals whose private or political feelings are merged in the ruling passion of such companies, pecuniary gain."[114] In other words, properly regulated banking provided an essential antidote to personal exploitation in creditor-debtor relations. And the Second Bank fulfilled the promise of banking on a national and international scale, according to Biddle. It united in a single transcendent public interest what market and contractual relations otherwise set apart as opposing interests—not just creditor and debtor, but labor and capital, agriculture and industry, northeast and southwest—much as his Lewis and Clark narrative united the patchwork of polities across the continent, and the promise of international law bound together the warring nations of Europe and America. In this way, Biddle advanced an influential argument for the increasing autonomy of bankers in general and the central bank in particular. What critics viewed as a betrayal of representation, the rise of the "money power" as an authority in its own right rather than a dutiful servant of business and government, he championed as a measure of disinterested loyalty to the common good.

"An Undertaker Overtaken": The Banker's Fall

Biddle's was a delicate stance to sustain even in prosperous times, when the fortunes of finance rose along with those of planters, merchants, and industrialists, as they did for much of his tenure at the Second Bank. The pose of the Platonic guardian was always in tension with the bank's role as an active and interested participant in the speculation and enterprise it governed. Biddle recognized the difficulty from the start. As he wrote of his alter ego in "Ode to Bogle,"

Unstumbling foot was rarely given
To man or beast when quickly driven;
And they do say—but this I doubt,
For seldom he lets things leak out—
They do say—ere the dances close,
His, too, are "light fantastic toes."
Oh, if this be so, Bogle! then,
How are we served by serving men!
A waiter by his weight forsaken!
An undertaker overtaken![115]

The expiration of the bank's federal charter in 1836, following Jackson's famous veto, freed the bank of many of the restrictions on its private actions attached to its public responsibilities. Under a new charter from the State of Pennsylvania, the bank lost its power to restrain the state banks and the boom-and-bust economy they fueled, but it retained its matchless resources of private capital and credit, enabling it to join in the speculative boom of the Jacksonian era with new abandon. Vastly extending its lending, Biddle turned his reborn "United States Bank" into an exuberant investor in economic enterprise on its own account, while buying shares in a wide variety of businesses including toll roads, bridges, canals, railroads, and more than twenty other banks across the country. When the bottom fell out of the cotton market on which domestic and foreign commerce depended in the prelude to the panic of 1837, Biddle rushed into the void. Seizing control over an extensive chain of transactions normally conducted by countless merchants and creditors from New Orleans to Liverpool, he made the United States Bank itself effectively the single major buyer of cotton in the South, shipper of cotton across the Atlantic, and seller of cotton abroad. He sought to restrict the international supply of cotton in order to force up its price, and he financed the audacious venture by selling large volumes of bank stock in London. "Departing from the legitimate province of banking," the London *Times* editorialized, the United States Bank "constituted itself a great trading and speculating corporation" in its own right.[116]

The gamble failed as spectacularly as it had begun. As the transatlantic depression deepened and cotton prices plummeted, Biddle retired in March 1839. Six months later, unable to pay its debts, the bank was forced to suspend specie payments. In 1841, it closed permanently amid accusations of gross financial fraud, shortly before Charles Dickens spent the night across the street from "the Tomb of many fortunes." Banks were legally prohibited from buying and selling commodities, so Biddle had borrowed heavily from the United States Bank himself and had made many of the high-stakes transactions of its final years in his own name and those of other senior officers. Sued by the stockholders and indicted on charges of conspiracy and embezzlement, he paid part of what he owed by selling off what remained of his personal fortune, even melting into bullion a silver service of plate that the stockholders had earlier given him as a gift. He was spared a trial when the court dismissed the criminal charges, and he lived the remainder of his life secluded on his wife's family property at Andalusia, supported largely by the trustees of her estate.[117] "There have been few instances of a more complete reverse of fortune," wrote the Philadelphia author Sidney George Fisher upon Biddle's death in February 1844. ". . . The vast operations and extensive connections of the Bank, which in the day of its success had been the cause of Mr. Biddle's power and popularity, now that its downfall carried ruin as extensive as its influence, became the source of the storm of indignation and abuse which was raised against him."[118]

From the ruins of Biddle's bank arose a large legacy. His politically divisive policies as president of the Second Bank helped to pave the way for the large-scale organization and management of corporate enterprise during the long depression of the late nineteenth century. He established an important precedent for what came to be called "countercyclical policy," regulating the money supply to mitigate the violent vicissitudes of the business cycle, amid the greater depression of the twentieth century. He prefigured the rise of bankers as rulers rather than servants of industry and commerce, as well as their tendency to become overwhelmed by the speculative forces they aim to harness. Today, Biddle's Olympian vision of finance lives on. Its classical facade has yielded to strip-mall and office-park designs, signifying the banality rather than the beauty of banking even as its power has never been more starkly displayed.[119]

PART THREE

Big Business and the Problem of Association in the Gilded Age and Progressive Era

5

Charles Macune and the Currency of Cooperation

One morning in November 1883, the small ranchers and farmers of Coleman, Texas, found an anonymous notice posted on the street:

> Down with monopolies, they can't exist in Texas, and especially in Coleman county; away with your foreign capitalists; the range and soil of Texas belong to the heroes of the South; no monopolies, and don't tax us to school the nigger; give us homes as God intended, and not gates to churches and towns and schools and above all give us water for our stock.

Though the broadside took aim at several targets, the main objects of protest were real estate companies backed by eastern and English investors that had recently bought up tens of thousands of acres of the vanishing open range. Absentee owners speculating in land and longhorns had enclosed their sprawling claims with trainloads of newly invented barbed wire, cutting off access to pastures and streams amid a drought that struck that summer. Fences stranded churches, schools, and towns like Coleman, a stop on the Western Trail for cattle drovers headed to northern markets. All along the central Texas borderland between the fertile prairies and the arid Great Plains, stockmen and yeomen were taking up wire clippers in a fence-cutting war. They were arming themselves as well with a rhetoric of resistance drawn from the antimonopoly tradition and white-supremacist southern sectionalism, along with a sense of solidarity born on the frontier of a new kind of farm country.[1]

In the foothills east of Coleman known as the Cross Timbers, the previous decade had seen the emergence of a secret society called the Land League, soon renamed the Farmers' Alliance. Organized in the mid-1870s in opposition to so-called land sharks—company agents pursuing contested titles to smallholders' plots through the courts—the group had spread by 1883 across a dozen counties filling with migrants from the Old South and Midwest. With subsistence farming and stock-raising rapidly giving way to cultivation of cash crops, the formerly isolated upcountry was being drawn into ascendant industrial agriculture.[2]

As the Farmers' Alliance expanded eastward from the edge of cattle country into the widening cotton and wheat belt, its purpose shifted from defending the means of small-scale production to taking control of the means of large-scale exchange. The movement that grew into the last great agrarian uprising in American history sought to overcome the financial rather than physical fences enclosing the market for the crops farmers sold and the supplies they purchased. Yet while striving to construct cooperative arrangements to control markets, farmers contended with deep racial and regional divides within their own ranks, inscribed on the sign in Coleman. In the end, they vested their hope of surmounting both internal and external divisions in a vision of common access to a different kind of liquidity than water for livestock: a free-flowing currency that could wash away sectional, sectoral, and class boundaries and create a truly free market in the mass produce of modern agriculture, a monetary equivalent of the open range.[3]

The battleground of the agrarian conflict lay not in the exponential increase of cultivated farmland on the fading frontier, but in the proliferation of backcountry towns along the network of railroad lines, which supplanted the port cities as the locus of commerce and credit in the postbellum South. As the contested meeting place between rural labor and urban capital, the small town in the interior formed the cradle of a rising generation of Main Street professionals who made up much of the alliance leadership. Foremost among these friends of farming was the preeminent economic theorist of the agrarian movement, Charles Macune (1851–1940), who joined the alliance as a charter member of the local chapter in the central Texas town of Cameron in early 1886. Never a farmer himself, Macune pursued a wide variety of vocations including medicine, law, and journalism, but his longest calling was to the Methodist ministry and the broader evangelical tradition from which he drew inspiration.[4]

Macune united the fractious membership of the Texas alliance behind an ambitious agenda of agricultural cooperation, aiming to unite all farmers across the South (and soon the West as well) in taking collective command of the commodity markets on which they depended. He championed the monetary reform that became the alliance's central cause, "by far the most radical idea placed on the political agenda by a major social organization" in the late nineteenth and early twentieth centuries, as a leading scholar of the movement has written.[5] It called for the creation of a federal system of "subtreasuries" to take the place of merchants, mortgage companies, and banks in providing farmers with low-interest credit and a flexible currency backed by land and crops instead of silver and gold. As founder and editor of the alliance's official organ, the *National Economist*, Macune directed an extensive effort in popular education aimed at fostering a radical understanding of history, economics, and politics throughout agricultural America. "The organization man par excellence," as another historian has described him, he identified his calling wholeheartedly with the Farmers' Alliance and designed its pathbreaking model of agrarian association. This chapter follows his intellectual migration through a series of pivotal shifts in his views in the face of repeated frustrations, culminating in his embrace of currency reform as the key to the farmers' cause.[6]

In the commercial cooperation and political mobilization of cotton and grain growers, and in the subsequent movement of bankers and industrialists on behalf of the gold standard and central banking (the subject of the next chapter), the money question became bound up with efforts to comprehend mass production and mass distribution on an unprecedented scale. As farmers and financiers alike struggled to create centralized institutions such as corporations, cooperatives, and government bureaucracies capable of controlling national and international markets, the organization of currency and credit came to stand for opposing conceptions of association, reflecting the pervasive socialization of modern life. In the conflict between a vision of agricultural collectivism inspired by the ideal of Christian fellowship, on the one hand, and a model of corporate administration developed from the tradition of fiduciary trusteeship, on the other, the monetary system formed the central subject of social struggle for perhaps the last time.

"A White Man's State": Democracy and Development in the Hill Country

"Don't tax us to school the nigger": the agrarian resistance bore within it the political alliance of laissez-faire and white supremacy that had arisen from the ruins of the Confederacy. The ideology of the "New South," which served to justify the racial and class structure that supplanted slavery, also set the terms for the strongest challenge to the ascendant capitalist order of the Gilded Age. Southern Populism emerged from and reflected the southern democracy it came to rival, sharing a dual devotion to Adam Smith and Jim Crow.

Ten years before it appeared on the sign in Coleman, the identification of high taxes on struggling smallholders with public benefits for former slaves delivered the Texas statehouse into the hands of a popular Democratic coalition in which the Grange, the organizational forerunner of the Farmers' Alliance, played a leading part. Fifty miles from the capital of Austin, in the granite hills of Burnet County, the "rule of the taxpayer" found a fiery new advocate in a recent arrival from the western cattle range. Taking over the editorship of the local Democratic newspaper, the *Burnet Bulletin*, in September 1874, the twenty-three-year-old Charles Macune launched his public career with a country town defense of the party's winning platform, which was basically no taxation with black representation. "If Texas would have towns and cities ever flourishing, and ever free from burdens of taxation, added to the cost of goods, and finally paid by farmers, the Constitution of Texas should be so amended, and at once, that the Legislature may restrict suffrage, in all town, city and county elections, to freeholders," he wrote, so that propertyless black voters could not lay claim to the value of white men's land by means of taxing and spending. An onerous "five per cent. is the average rate of taxation upon property wherever taxes are imposed by blacks, or by people elected by blacks," he wrote. ". . . The best population of the whole South and of the Middle and Northwestern States seek homes in Texas" due to "the simple fact that Texas is a white man's State," and the state constitution should preserve that fact.[7]

Unlike in the southeastern states of the Black Belt, white settlers predominated in Texas, especially in frontier hill districts such as Burnet County, which had no plantations and few slaves at the time of the Civil War. In the war-ravaged region from which many of Macune's neighbors had migrated, the abolition of slavery had eliminated the major source of tax revenue. Republican programs for Reconstruction had been funded with drastically increased land taxes that fell hardest on cash-poor white farmers, whose property had been largely exempted from taxation until the late 1850s. In the years since the war, many small farmers in the Lower South had faced forfeiture of their property for nonpayment of taxes, which lent a desperation born of dispossession to the resistance to Republican rule in the Texas hill country.[8]

There the southern refugees joined a smaller stream of debt-driven migrants from the Midwest like Macune. His parents had moved to Illinois from upstate New York amid the depression of the early 1840s, much like William Leggett's family twenty years earlier, drawn by cheap land and the prospect of a new start. After struggling to patch together a living as a farmer, blacksmith, and itinerant preacher, his father had lost his latest job as a traveling salesman for a farm equipment manufacturer when Charles was born in Kenosha, Wisconsin, in 1851. Heading west once more in search of work, his father had died of cholera less than a year later en route to the California gold fields, leaving behind a total estate valued at $41.24, including fifty cents in his pocket when he died.[9]

With the aid of other family members, Macune's mother had somehow managed to support him and his sister through the 1850s in the rural community of Freeport, Illinois. He grew up at the heart of the mounting sectional conflict over "free soil," land ostensibly reserved for white homesteaders of modest means rather than rich planters and their slaves. He attended public school in Freeport, worked on a neighboring farm when he was ten, and was apprenticed to a pharmacist when he was fifteen. In 1869, at the age of eighteen, he left home for California, where he labored as a ranch hand, then took a job with a circus in Kansas. By 1871, he was working as a cattle drover on the plains of northwest Texas where the rural rebellion would ignite a few years later. In 1874, Macune settled in Burnet, a county seat of several hundred people on the eastern edge of the hill country, where he took on a new identity as editor of the local paper. He became a leader in the local Masonic Lodge and the Democratic Party, married the daughter of a successful builder, and leased a hotel in a nearby community, anticipating a rush of new development with the arrival of the railroad.[10]

Like many of the country editors who became popular apostles of the New South, Macune devoted his seven-month tenure at the weekly *Burnet Bulletin* to promoting aggressive development of the surrounding counties, extolling the virtues of their fertile soil, healthy climate, and eagerness to attract money and migrants. Touting the area's deep quarries of limestone and pink marble, its rich veins of silver, gold, iron, and lead, its powerful rivers destined to fuel "great and diversi[fi]ed industries" and provide "a highway for our internal commerce," he foresaw a bright future "as soon as capitalists turn their attention this way." "The impression is fast gaining ground that the mountain or hill country of Western Texas is more desirable . . . for its varied elements of wealth, than the planting regions," he wrote, and it "may, in time, become the most populous, refined and healthy portion of Texas." Even the dry western climate could be improved by careful cultivation of the soil, Macune imagined, so that "fifty years from now a drouth will never be thought of in the State of Texas."[11]

The ensuing decade of depression and drought narrowed the economic prospects for the hill country, where the path to prosperity came fenced with barbed wire. The kernel of the Populist critique of merchants, monopolists, and moneyed men could already be seen in Macune's editorials in response to hard times. The tax revolt that spurred backcountry opposition to Reconstruction had its roots in the decade before the Civil War, when the Lower South planter class had begun shifting the incidence of taxation from slaveholders to smallholders by enacting "uniformity clauses" that required real property to be taxed at a flat percentage of its value, regardless of whether it was a family farm or a large plantation. Macune's first published commentaries in 1875 drew on the well of antebellum resistance to efforts to compel those least able to pay to support rising public expenditures. But he reframed the agrarian position in postbellum terms by railing against real estate speculators instead of planters, advocating not subsistence agriculture but industrial development. Uniform property taxes on land were "detrimental to the vital interest of a new country immigration," stifling entrepreneurship and improvement, he contended. "The injustice of an equal taxation upon value of real estate is shown by the difference between the benefits derived from A, who pays taxes on $40,000 worth of wild land which he is holding for the purpose of speculation, and B, who pays taxes upon the same but has his divided among buildings and improvements. The one a draw back to his country, the other exactly the opposite," he wrote, following a similar logic to that of Henry George's contemporaneous critique of taxes on improvements as opposed to ground rent. "Now the rational and most expedient way to obviate this wrong as well as to guarantee great stimulus and enterprise in improvements upon real estate, is for the State to exempt property from a certain amount of tax for every hundred dollars['] worth of improvements put upon it."[12]

Macune was acutely attentive to the question of who would bear the cost of the commercial, industrial, and agricultural improvements that he endorsed. He called for Austin's taxpayers to pay for building better roads to transport the produce of the hill country to market. Likewise, while welcoming plans for extending the Austin and Pacific Short Line Railroad, Macune opposed the prevailing practice of taxing local residents to pay for it. "The cry of the honest producer! the bone and sinew of the whole country on which everybody else depends, is God deliver us from being bled to death by a railroad tax," he wrote. Instead of taxpayer subsidies for private railroads charging monopoly prices to settlers in remote regions, he favored government ownership of "all public means of transportation," charging consumers only the actual cost of construction and operation.[13]

Mining, manufacturing, and transportation loomed much larger than farming in Macune's program for upcountry economic development. "We want men of capital" was the restless booster's refrain. "Mechanical power is wealth," he wrote, contrary to pastoral paeans to the natural bounty of agriculture as the basis of all wealth and industry. "We have it, and we have the material upon which to work. Our stone, and marble, and lime and minerals will find their way to the coast country by a cheap transit. While every five miles, for over two hundred miles on the Colorado [River] furnishes water power for manufacturing cities of 10,000 to 30,000 population each." When he did turn his attention to agriculture, Macune's ranching experience showed in his enthusiasm for the recent boom in sheep-raising, tied to the new technology of New England woolen mills. He also argued against shifting from the mixed farming of corn, wheat, cattle, and hogs primarily for local consumption to specialized production of a cash crop such as cotton, which accounted for a small fraction of the county's farmland in the 1870s.[14]

Macune excerpted with approval a recent speech by the Democratic politician and former Confederate leader Benjamin H. Hill at an agricultural fair in Georgia, cautioning small farmers against becoming dependent on merchants as they produced more for the market. "Make cotton your surplus crop! In these five words lie the Samson locks of your future power," Hill told his listeners.

> Make your own fertilizers by resting, cropping, grassing and manuring your land. Thus you become independent of the guano merchants. Raise your own provisions. Then you become independent of the provision merchants. Your cheapest and safest line of transportation runs from [your] own fields and hog-pens to your own barns and meat house. With no debts for your supplies, you will need no accommodation credit at two per cent. per month. Thus you become independent of brokers, cotton factors, and lien merchants. You can then sell your cotton at your own time, to your own chosen buyers, and will get your own money.[15]

Macune sympathized with Hill's hope for a New South in which the interior would take the place of the coast and the tidewater, emancipating the upcountry yeomanry from its previous subservience to the plantation economy—or what Hill called, without apparent irony, the Old South's "bondage to the negro."[16] At the same time, Macune shared Hill's fear that as poor white farmers were drawn into production for national and international markets, they would become slaves of a new master class of southern merchants and their Yankee backers. "Without a great change," Hill warned, "the Southern States are destined to become so many plantations practically owned by the Northern people, and Southern people so many hireling slaves to work them."[17]

Over the next ten years, the fate of white freeholders would be joined to that of black freedpeople in ways that Macune dimly discerned in the mid-1870s. Once sharply divided as subsistence farmers and slaves, white and black farmers were converging on a shared status as market-oriented family farmers bound by a new system of debt servitude. If the new tax structure appeared to place the interests of landowning white yeomen in opposition to those of propertyless black croppers, the emerging credit system drew both into dependence on merchants or landlords. By the mid-1880s, the development of the hill country became bound up with that of cotton in ways that Macune had hardly anticipated when he arrived. As Sven Beckert has shown, the decades after the Civil War witnessed a tremendous growth in the worldwide demand for the leading southern staple along with an even more impressive increase in its supply, depressing prices and profits for producers while enriching merchants and manufacturers. Most of the increased output came from a vast enlargement in the amount of land and labor devoted to raising cotton. The greatest territorial expansion came in the southwestern states of Arkansas, Louisiana, and especially Texas, the fertile triangle of the Farmers' Alliance. Cotton spread from the lowlands into the upcountry, carried by the extension of the railroad and the telegraph.[18]

Along with the changed terrain came a different structure of labor in place of the plantation. The family farm, an old mode of production, became harnessed to the voracious world market for cotton. The reconstruction of cotton cultivation in the postwar South, like the explosive growth in grain production from the Midwest, depended largely on farm families working land that they owned, rented, or managed themselves, rather than on the waged workforce mobilized by modern industry. The conjunction of small-scale, household-based production with the mass market for agricultural staples shaped Macune's combination of social conservatism and economic radicalism first expressed in Burnet. More important for Macune than the production and exchange of commodity crops, however, were the novel forms of credit at the center of the new economy. For the tethers that bound the labor of isolated farm families to the capital of landlords and merchants were not wages but debts. Debt, moreover, gathered together grain growers and cotton cultivators, whether yeomen, tenants, or sharecroppers, into what he called the "whole class" of agricultural producers.[19]

The plantation economy of the antebellum era had given rise to the highly developed financial system of the Second Bank of the United States and its extensive facilities for long-distance investment in cotton and slaves. Just as chattel slaves had constituted the primary form of taxable property in the Lower South, they also had served as the main form of security for the credit that planters obtained from the merchants who acted as their commercial agents in the riverside and seaboard cities. These commission merchants, known as factors, had sold the slave mortgages in turn to banking houses that had packaged them into bonds to be purchased by investors around the country and across the Atlantic.[20] The upcountry economy of subsistence farming, meanwhile, had operated largely on the basis of reciprocal exchanges among neighbors, personal loans from planters, and purchases from country stores paid for in labor or in corn, wheat, eggs, hides, and other surplus of farmers' households, with relatively little need of cash or formal credit.[21]

Emancipation overturned not only the mode of producing cotton, but also the financial structure it had supported. The elimination of slaveholders' property in four million persons, the most valuable asset in the cotton kingdom, caused the collapse of the whole supply chain of credit based on human collateral. Many southern banks went out of business, and the high capital requirements of the new National Banking System, which was established to fund the northern war effort, made banking even scarcer in the postwar South. Those banks that survived restricted their business mainly to short-term lending to merchants, including the small retailers serving the growing economy of the interior, who demanded "cash or cotton" rather than labor services or "country produce" for their goods.[22]

To acquire the means of paying for essential provisions, backwoods farming families had to devote more and more of their labor to cultivating the cash crop. More time for cotton meant less time for producing their own food and other necessities, which they had to purchase by producing still more cotton. To carry them through each year until the cotton could be harvested and sold, farmers bought their food, fertilizer, tobacco, wagons, harvesters, and other supplies on credit, giving the local storekeeper a lien on their future crop. The country merchants, in addition to becoming their customers' main creditors, took charge of weighing, grading, selling, and shipping the cotton directly from interior towns via the railroads, replacing the urban factors who had handled the trade before the war.[23]

Unlike antebellum planters, postbellum growers could not use slaves as collateral, nor were their small farms valuable enough to mortgage, unlike midwestern homesteads. The only sufficient security that they could offer the furnishing merchant was their cotton. With exclusive control over the cotton from their communities, local merchants monopolized the supply of virtually everything farmers required, charging a markup of 40–70 percent for purchases on credit rather than in cash throughout the year, then adding 10 percent or more in interest when the bills came due. In order to meet their own obligations to local banks, the storekeepers called for the entire crop to be delivered as soon as it was harvested, flooding the market each fall so that the price of cotton fell to a fraction of what it might have sold for otherwise. "The result of these conditions and others may be generalized and condensed into a few words," as Macune recalled in a brief memoir of the Farmers' Alliance, written in 1920. "Men had been encouraged and enabled to become cotton farmers by the extension of credit. When they became established in that occupation the crop sold so low, and the supplies necessary to make the crop cost so much, that they could not pay out but found themselves very often deeper in debt at the end of the year, with nothing to show for labor expended during the whole year. This was a new kind of slavery which they did not understand."[24] As he said in a speech to the Farmers' Alliance in 1887, the cotton crops "would not pay hireling's wages to the one who produced them, and were really grown at a loss."[25]

After editing the Burnet newspaper, Macune trained as a physician and began practicing medicine in ranching communities along the edge of the southern plains. In 1881, he settled in Cameron, another county seat perched on a new branch of the Santa Fe Railroad amid the blackland prairie and cotton fields east of Burnet. His medical practice apparently did well enough to allow him to buy several town lots along with a nearby farm, though he lost part of what he had purchased a few years later in a court-ordered foreclosure.[26]

Meanwhile, his observations of the rise of the crop-lien system made Macune reconsider his earlier commitments to white solidarity and business boosterism. His growing awareness of white and black farmers' similar subjection suggested to him that the racial divide served to bolster an emerging financial and commercial order that bound smallholders, tenants, and sharecroppers alike. "It is impossible to skim the cream from agriculture, to select a part and secure prosperity for them, leaving the balance to suffer. . . . All must go together, or none can go at all," he wrote in the *National Economist*, the newspaper he founded and edited, in 1890. ". . . From a business standpoint the colored farmer in the South must be recognized and extended the hand of co-operation, because the sacrifice of his crop at a ruinously low price injures his neighbor as much as it does him."[27] Macune was no convert to the cause of racial equality, and he staunchly resisted calls to integrate black and white farmers in a single organization. But he insisted that the whites-only alliance must seek to work with and uplift black farmers as well. Macune elaborated this crucial lesson in another editorial:

> The Alliance movement in the South has demonstrated more clearly than was before realized, that the farmer, in order to prosper, must take with him all engaged in that occupation. He cannot organize the thrifty and well-to-do and make a success of any effort to increase the price of his products or decrease the price of the commodities he buys. He must take the poor man who is in debt and the renters, both white and colored, along and enable them to secure like prices, or he cannot get them. . . . The necessities of the poor are taken

> advantage of to maintain high prices in the sale of commodities and low prices in the purchase of farm products. Therefore a move calculated to benefit the farmer, to be a true success, must reach the poorest, both black and white.[28]

The demand to restrict the vote to white landowners, which Macune and the Grange had endorsed as a critical component of yeoman resistance to ruinous taxes under Reconstruction, appeared at odds with the need for cross-racial resistance to debt servitude by the time of the Mississippi Plan for disfranchising black voters, which Macune and the alliance opposed. "A citizen must own property to the value of $150, or be able to read or understand the constitution" in order to vote under the provisions of the new state constitution of Mississippi, Macune observed in making the case against property qualifications that he had earlier supported, but which now threatened to disfranchise a growing number of poor white farmers along with their black counterparts. "Who will pass upon the important question, does a poor man understand the constitution? A rich man doesn't have to know anything under the theory of the Mississippi sub-committee."[29]

The failure of the New South to uplift small farmers likewise led Macune to disavow his earlier faith in the economic development of the hill country. Noting that "the doctrine of diversified industries . . . has been the theme of political economists from the time of Adam Smith," he called it "the fullness of cold-blooded selfishness." For it pinned the prosperity of the upcountry on its ability to produce more cheaply than the lowlands, and it pitted the South against the West and the country against the city. Such regional rivalry eventually depressed prices across the country, condemning farmers to compete for a rapidly diminishing share of the fruits of their labor. "It is a mistake to urge the people of the cotton belt to raise less cotton and more corn," Macune argued, rejecting the call for farmers to make cotton their "surplus crop" that he had advocated at the *Burnet Bulletin*. "The real object in diversifying industries is to make the products of labor cheaper. That is exactly what the farmer, laborer, and planter should try to avoid," he wrote. "It is not cheap products that will benefit, it is dear products that will bring a reward. While the people are laboring to diversify their industries in order to reduce the price of their products, they are forging the chains which in the end will bind them to a relentless system of wage slavery."[30] What southern farmers really needed was to "devise means whereby a fair price can be obtained for what they now produce," Macune argued, increasingly turning his attention to the problem of markets, prices, and ultimately, the means of exchange.

If one took the production of cash crops to be essential to the maintenance of an independent livelihood, the question became how farmers could gain control of the marketing process dominated by furnishing merchants, warehouses, commodity exchanges, and bankers. Though he remained committed to racial segregation and low taxation, Macune's "business standpoint" moved him to embrace a broader class of producers called into being by the commercialization of agriculture throughout the American interior. For market-oriented small farmers—white and black, South and West—the unrealized promise of emancipation required a new kind of cooperation, which Macune made the main business of the Farmers' Alliance.

"A Business Organization for Business Purposes": Cooperation in the Cotton Belt

Macune entered the alliance at a pivotal moment, and not just for hill country farmers. From stockmen battling cattle barons in the Panhandle to striking coal miners in West Texas, construction workers in Austin, dockworkers in Galveston, and thousands of railroad workers across the state who joined the Great Southwest Strike of 1886 led by the Knights of Labor, Texas became a battleground of labor conflict in the mid-1880s as never before. The Lone Star class war ushered in a critical phase in the careers of Macune and the farmers' movement.[31]

In the aftermath of the fence-cutting uprising of 1883, Farmers' Alliance chapters formed in dozens of counties. Thousands of suballiances sprouted across Texas over the next three years, including Friendship Alliance Number 1963 of Milam County, which Macune joined as a founding member in early 1886. As one of three delegates from his suballiance to a stormy state convention in Cleburne that August, Macune saw the alliance bitterly divide over whether to mobilize behind a broad political platform demanding state and national legislation to "secure to our people freedom from the onerous and shameful abuses that the industrial classes are now suffering at the hands of arrogant capitalists and powerful corporations." The convention's "Cleburne Demands" included reserving western lands for actual settlers, regulating interstate railroads, and ensuring that the nation's money supply expanded in step with the growth of population and business. But the first and foremost plank of the platform called for "the recognition by incorporation of trade-unions, co-operative stores, and such other associations as may be organized by the industrial classes to improve their financial condition, or to promote their general welfare."[32]

Organization on a new basis was the fundamental imperative. The shared outrage that had joined a few hundred frontier farmers in fighting the enclosure of land and water a few years earlier could not hold the allegiance of the legions of small growers in the cotton belt. The alliance broke in two after Cleburne, and its top officials resigned. Macune stepped into the breach as acting president, calling both sides to a meeting at Waco in January 1887. He found the source of dissension in the comparatively disorganized state of farming itself. "All the different classes and occupations of society are engaging in organization for mutual advancement and protection to a greater extent than ever before in the history of the world," he told the delegates. "In fact, we may say that every calling is organized. This thorough organization has created a new order of things."[33] If the alliance's original methods were unequal to the needs of commercial cultivators, it was because family farmers' traditional methods of operation gave them little leverage in commodity markets. The common farmer "still lives isolated and alone and follows in this particular the traditions and customs of his ancestors in that he strives to be a segregated, independent factor in production, while in consumption he practices the most modern patronage of improvements caused by the division of labor," Macune explained in a subsequent essay. "Organization is now the order of the day," he wrote in another piece. "It is the motive power that rules and guides the world. . . . If the farmers of America would organize as intelligently and solidly as the Standard Oil Company has, and then use the power of such organization as unscrupulously, they would in a few years become the dictators of the world. Nothing could withstand their power."[34]

Macune dedicated the reunited alliance to a two-track agenda of expansion and cooperation, aiming to assemble a powerful national association for commercial farmers and, at the same time, create a new mode of marketing their produce. As he wrote in his own history of the organization, "the Alliance movement embraced two different lines of activities; first, the extension of the alliance by the organizers and lecturers, and the local, State and National papers devoted to the movement," and "Second, the organization and conduct of the business co-operation within the order."[35] Both enterprises were hobbled by deep divisions among farmers along lines of race, region, party, and property, as well as by the limits of their ability to control capital and credit. But the principle of cooperation that animated the alliance under Macune reached beyond these dual organizing campaigns, inspiring a major effort in popular education and a final crusade for financial reform focused on the money question.

Macune met the threat of disunion that brought him to power with a call for expansion. The problem as he saw it was not that the alliance had grown too big to hold together, but that it was not big enough to survive in a new environment. In order to meet the needs of its members, the organization itself had to expand to include those with whom they increasingly competed.

"All must go together, or none can go at all": the logic of his case for cross-racial cooperation extended to the need to mobilize all cotton growers, and ultimately all farmers. Macune's and the membership's enduring commitment to racial segregation led to the establishment of a separate Colored Farmers' National Alliance, closely tied to the whites-only organization. Still, he wrote in 1889, "the present condition in our own country, the dominance of capital and the subjugation of the masses by it, is proof now and here of the necessity for the rallying of the people under one banner. The time has come when division means ruin to all. . . . Force must be met by force, organization by organization."[36]

Under Macune's direction, teams of organizers and lecturers fanned out from Texas in a mirror image of the migration to the southwestern frontier, drawing in hundreds of thousands of new members. In his inaugural action as president in 1887, Macune arranged the first of a series of mergers with associations in other states, moving east to combine with the Louisiana Farmers' Union in forming the auspiciously named National Farmers' Alliance and Co-operative Union. In 1888, the alliance moved up the Mississippi River valley to join with a more class-conscious organization called the Agricultural Wheel, based in Arkansas and its northern neighbors, Tennessee, Kentucky, and Missouri. Renaming itself the National Farmers' Alliance and Industrial Union in 1889, the group forged an agreement to work together with the Knights of Labor, though farmers and workers remained in separate organizations. Having expanded across the cotton belt, the alliance set its sights on the grain-growing states of the Midwest, recruiting heavily among the homesteaders of Kansas, Nebraska, and the Dakotas, while declining to unite with a smaller western federation also called the National Farmers' Alliance, based in Chicago—in part because of the latter group's inclusion of black and white members alike. By 1891, the "Southern Alliance," as it had become commonly known, actually extended across thirty-two states from New York to California. Three-quarters of its roughly 1.5 million members were southerners, concentrated in recently developed or economically depressed areas.[37]

"Let the Alliance be a business organization for business purposes," Macune declared at the first meeting of the National Farmers' Alliance and Co-operative Union, which he called "the first organization of the real cotton-raisers ever inaugurated on a plan calculated to assist the poor man." The "business" of the alliance, as he conceived it, meant more than a means of making cotton cultivation financially sustainable for poor farmers. It represented a way of binding farmers together in a common purpose, overcoming the political, religious, and regional divides that separated them, and transcending self-destructive conflict and competition. "The dissensions spoken of in the early history of the order, in regard to politics and other subjects, have entirely died out, and given place to an enlightened effort to achieve something grand—a business organization," Macune told his audience in Shreveport, Louisiana, in October 1887. The exalted significance of "business purposes" for Macune helps to account for the ardor with which the alliance promoted modern marketing and accounting methods for its members. Macune's National Economist Publishing Company, for example, distributed a "Standard Outfit" of business supplies for suballiances, including the alliance's seal (a five-pointed star with the word "unity" in the center) along with a record book, two account books, a book of blank forms of various kinds, a book of "rituals," the alliance constitution, and complementary issues of the *National Economist*, among other items.[38] Even in strictly economic terms, business for Macune meant large-scale purchasing of supplies and selling of crops on a fundamentally different basis than contemporary capitalist enterprise.

What contemporaries came to call the "Macune business system" or "Macuneism" represented a singular form of social solidarity, constituted by cooperation in commercial practices. The "one great battle-cry of co-operation," Macune proclaimed, would serve "as the universal principle upon which all could unite; co-operation in its broadest sense, that is, that we will assist one another, that we will stand shoulder to shoulder in bearing the crosses and burdens of life, that we will intelligently pull together in everything; *in buying and selling, in producing and consuming*. There is a necessity for enlightened co-operation in everything."[39] Macune's ideal of the business cooperative derived from the traditions of European Christian socialism, antebellum communes such as New Harmony and Brook Farm, and the famed social experiment of the textile weavers of Rochdale, England, who established a cooperative store in 1844 and published their principles for worker-owned cooperatives in 1860.[40] At the heart of the cooperative idea was the hope for an "equitable capitalism" in which labor and capital could be harmoniously united, abolishing the inequities and exploitation within industrial capitalism while preserving private property rights and market relations.[41]

The cooperative vision appealed strongly to postbellum farmers' traditions of self-help. The National Grange, founded after the Civil War, had created cooperative purchasing agencies and stores dealing in farm equipment, expanded into marketing livestock, grains, tobacco, wool, and cotton, and eventually established joint-stock companies owned and run by farmers. Operated entirely on a cash basis, these enterprises were of no use to the growing majority of farmers who could not afford to patronize them, and most failed by the late 1870s.[42] The Grange stores were "conducted at about the same profit demanded by other stores, and the profits arising from the business were the dividends paid to the stockholders. This was very satisfactory in many cases; especially to the stockholders," as Macune drily noted. "But in 1885 the general mutterings of discontent were so strong that these methods only seemed to whet the appetites of the farmers for something that promised a more general relief."[43]

The alliance's own cooperative efforts began modestly in the mid-1880s. County trade committees negotiated agreements with local merchants, promising that their members would exclusively patronize selected stores in exchange for low prices for supplies. Such arrangements still only benefited farmers who could pay cash. The informal agreements tended to break down when wholesalers pressured storekeepers not to deal with the alliance or when selected storekeepers drove their competitors out of business so that alliance members had no choice but to deal with them. Cooperatively owned, cash-based country stores, which the suballiances tried next, similarly could not cater to the mass of farmers who bought their supplies on credit. Even among farmers who could pay cash, there was a significant divergence of interests between poorer patrons, who needed the lowest possible prices, and more prosperous shareholders, who demanded higher dividends from their investments, though this entailed charging members more for supplies. When such joint-stock retail outlets succeeded in both turning a profit and offering lower prices than local merchants, the merchants often reduced their own cash prices in order to compete and then made up for it by charging higher "time prices" to customers who had to buy on credit. Thus the consumer cooperatives in many cases actually worsened conditions for farmers who most needed help.[44] County alliances also sought to cooperate in storing, ginning, and selling crops. Like the trade agreements and the cooperative stores, however, such schemes could not work for debt-driven farmers who had no choice but to sell their entire crop to the merchants who extended them credit. In addition, small groups of farmers rarely could bulk enough cotton to compel buyers to compete for their business.[45]

These early experiments thus proved unable to challenge effectively the power of furnishing merchants over most farmers. Aware of the limits of previous efforts at the local and county levels, Macune launched a statewide cotton exchange cooperative in 1887. He hoped to mobilize its larger scale of operations to succeed where smaller efforts had failed, supplanting the existing cotton exchanges. County business agents were to inspect, weigh, and grade members' cotton in their local suballiances, and then send samples and reports to the state headquarters of the exchange in Dallas. There Macune, as state business agent, would negotiate sales of the cotton crop directly with eastern and European buyers, charging farmers a commission of only twenty-five cents per bale, far less than country merchants typically charged. At the same time, the exchange would replace the merchants in providing the farmers with fertilizer, cloth, plows, wagons, and other supplies. The local agents would collect and forward their members' orders for supplies to Dallas, where the exchange would arrange purchases directly from manufacturers, charging members only a little more than wholesale prices. To underwrite these purchasing contracts, Macune planned for an initial capitalization of $500,000, to be financed by requiring each member to pay a two-dollar assessment fee.

Aside from its unprecedented scale, the major innovation of the exchange was Macune's plan for collectively extending credit to farmers who could not pay in cash. Along with their purchase orders, the county agents were to issue IOUs for the total amount of credit required by the members of each sub-alliance. These notes were to be signed jointly by farmers in need of credit and "responsible farmers," who would serve as cosigners in exchange for mortgages on their poorer neighbors' crops. The "joint notes" pledged cotton worth at least three times the value of the required credit, and the farmers were to be charged a mere 1 percent interest every six months, as compared with as much as 60 percent per year under the crop-lien system.[46]

Alliance lecturers trumpeted the democratic virtue and financial promise of the Texas exchange as they spread out across the South. Similar efforts soon arose in other states, forming magnets for new members. "This plan is pure and simple co-operation, with no joint stock features whatever and differs from similar plans before introduced in several important particulars," Macune explained in his annual address in 1888. "It is calculated to benefit the whole class and not simply those who have surplus money to invest in capital stock," and to enable "the poor man to make a crop without mortgaging to the merchant."[47]

In practice, however, the exchange soon fell short of capital and credit. The original plan called for the Dallas office to purchase in cash the supplies that farmers had ordered on credit with the joint notes, using the capital it raised from the two-dollar assessment fee. But by April 1888, the exchange had received just over $20,000 in assessment fees, while the directors had authorized joint notes for purchases worth more than ten times that amount. With farmers in immediate need of supplies, the exchange began making large-volume purchases, totaling more than $100,000. Macune tried desperately to borrow the money to pay for them using the joint notes as collateral. But city bankers in Dallas, Houston, Fort Worth, Galveston, and New Orleans balked at backing the obligations of backcountry farmers whom they neither knew nor could supervise. Meanwhile, the state alliance called for mass meetings to raise additional capital from the membership, but the $30,000 that came in was not nearly enough to save the exchange from insolvency. In January 1889, Macune was forced to resign as business manager, and by December the Texas exchange was out of business.

As the sociologist Donna Barnes has explained, the basic problem was that many alliance members could not afford the two-dollar assessment fee, while their better-off brethren had little financial incentive to invest any more than was required since the exchange paid no dividends. Despite its democratic design, the exchange could not overcome the wide divide between poor and prosperous farmers.[48] Similar agricultural cooperatives failed across the country in the following few years, leading to renewed conflict over what should take their place at the core of the alliance program. "The subsequent history of the movement shows that no other system for either selling produce or buying supplies was encouraged," Macune noted, "and this accounts for the fact that the Exchange movement declined from that date on to its final collapse."[49]

The failures of the cooperative effort led to enduring doubts about the combination of social solidarity and collective marketing that Macune had made the main endeavor of the alliance. For critics at the time as well as subsequent historians, the key question was whether the farmers' drive to manage marketing had fatally undermined their dedication to transforming the social order. In rebutting the charge that the exchange represented simply an effort to beat capitalists at their own game, Macune was at pains to point out that the exchange was "not that kind of a trust." "Trusts are wholly combinations of capitalists made for the purpose of using the power of money to oppress labor in order to extort all that labor produces over a mere subsistence," he wrote. ". . . God forbid that the Union [the Farmers' Alliance] should ever be a similar organization, or use like methods, or desire such purposes. . . . Selfishness is in no sense the object of its effort but pecuniary gain up to a standard of exact justice to labor is demanded as a right. Instead of pooling the wealth of its members, it pools their heads and hearts, their strong right arms, and leaves the property of each undisturbed."[50] Indeed, the exchange had no absentee investors, no board of directors, no bottom line of profit maximization and capital accumulation. The tension between brotherhood and business was precisely what the cooperative movement aimed to overcome by modeling a different kind of large-scale commercial enterprise at a time when the basic structure of corporate consolidation appeared up for grabs.

Nevertheless, the practical shortcomings of cooperation led Macune to push for a more radical plan of attack. Much as he had earlier shifted his allegiance from New South industrialization to agrarian cooperation, he began to pursue a broader ideological critique and a more direct political crusade to reform the capitalist system itself. By December 1889, Macune had concluded that producers' cooperatives could not adequately address the systemic factors that inevitably inflated the prices of farmers' supplies, deflated the prices of their crops, and left them chronically short of cash. For the root causes lay not in the market for either supplies or crops themselves, but in the structure and supply of the money with which they were bought and sold. Cooperation required a different currency. To achieve it, farmers needed a new outlook on the emerging commercial and financial order as a whole. They needed to reorganize the nation's banking and monetary system, not just cotton and wheat farming. With these parallel goals in mind, Macune moved in 1889 from Dallas to Washington, DC. There he charged the alliance with a new mission of education and legislation, aimed at the federal level, shifting the focus of his critique from merchants and shippers to bankers.[51]

"A Citadel of Pure Economics": The Education of the "Producing Classes"

The goal of the great organizing drive that Macune led was more than the expansion of the alliance. It was the personal transformation of its gathering flock. Joining the order meant converting to a cause. Like the southern Baptist and Methodist churches whose methods it adopted—including circuit-riding preachers, Sunday schools, camp meetings, testimonials, rites and rituals, hymns and songs, picnics and rallies—the alliance's organizing efforts were intended to create a cohesive new community of belief, fostering a changed sense of self in its followers. They built on the traditions of fraternal lodges, vigilante groups, agrarian societies, and country churches like the ones Macune's father had visited as a preacher, which had long joined farmers in fellowship. Of the nine aims of the alliance stated in its constitution, six concerned the moral and spiritual ideals it sought to instill, including the development of "a better state mentally, morally, socially, and financially," the promotion of "harmony and good will to all mankind, and brotherly love among ourselves," and the suppression of "personal, local, sectional, and national prejudices, all unheathful rivalry, and all selfish ambition." The Declaration of Purposes concluded:

> The brightest jewels which it garners are the tears of widows and orphans, and its imperative commands are to visit the homes where lacerated hearts are bleeding; to assuage the sufferings of a brother or sister; bury the dead; care

> for the widows and educate the orphans; to exercise charity towards offenders; to construe words and deeds in their most favorable light, granting honesty of purpose and good intentions to others; and to protect the National Farmers' Alliance and Co-operative Union until death. Its laws are reason and equity; its cardinal doctrines inspire purity of thought and life; its intention is, "Peace on earth and good will to man."[52]

A deep religiosity was vital to the order. "Let us remember that the last sentence in the declaration of purposes is a reiteration of the song of the heavenly hosts that praised God in the presence of the shepherds for the birth of Jesus Christ," Macune wrote in an essay titled "The Purposes of the Farmers' Alliance."[53]

Macune described the alliance as "a living, active, practical, and present embodiment of the cause of Jesus Christ." Indeed, in Texas as throughout the cotton belt, the Methodist Episcopal Church, South, enjoyed a period of spectacular growth in the mid-1880s along with the alliance, fueled by a great wave of "gracious revivals." Macune's methods as leader of the alliance were closely bound up with those of the southern Methodists. They combined a highly centralized, tightly controlled leadership with a zealous dedication to spreading the word in far-flung rural communities through itinerant preachers, local societies and lay exhorters, an elaborate structure of popular education and periodicals, an intense sense of personal witness, and an increasingly broad commitment to the "social gospel." Macune called Christianity "the only organization that has stood the test of time." Though he did not become a Methodist minister until 1901, his previous work in the farmers' movement was profoundly evangelical, and his conception of cooperation owed more to the tradition of Christian fellowship than it did to big business and corporate capital.[54]

Macune and his allies found the new life of the gospel in the educational awakening of the late nineteenth century associated with the growth of public schools, agricultural colleges, research universities, and religious seminaries. As Charles Postel has written of the Populists, "Few political or social movements brought so many men and women into lecture halls, classrooms, camp meetings, and seminars or produced such an array of inexpensive literature."[55] The intellectual coordinates of the alliance's educational mission came from the postbellum emergence of the modern social sciences. From contemporary sociology and psychology, Macune drew an understanding of societal evolution according to which "the social organism" was becoming increasingly complex and interdependent due to modern technologies of communication and transportation and the great extension of market relations they made possible. Yet while individuals had become bound up in an intricate web of economic exchange, their mental and social relations had lagged behind, beholden to outdated notions of individual independence and self-interest. "The development of those characteristics of our nature which tend most certainly to fit us to enjoy this complex social condition is the end to which social and moral training should tend," Macune wrote. ". . . This high moral development secured, the mere physical accompaniments will naturally follow." Drawing on the work of the English sociologists Herbert Spencer and William Kingdon Clifford, Macune argued that "the building up of the most perfect social system" depended on "the elimination of the quality of *selfishness*," or on the cultivation of a more encompassing "social self" that identified its own happiness and welfare with the progress and prosperity of the burgeoning market society of which it was part.[56]

For Macune as for many contemporary social reformers, the widest horizon of social selfhood was the nation, transcending local and regional interests along with the racial and class conflicts of the Gilded Age. To embody such a more perfect union was Macune's highest aspiration for the National Farmers' Alliance as he moved its headquarters to the nation's capital and founded the *National Economist* as its organ in 1889. Convinced that the success of the movement rested on its unity in belief as well as in action, Macune led a systematic effort to make "education in its broadest sense . . . the bulwark as well as the hope of the Alliance."[57] Hundreds of traveling lecturers brought the message to new recruits. Tens of thousands of suballiances served as the schools in which members learned the leading ideas of the alliance, fostering face-to-face discussions of complex issues in small rural communities. The *National Economist* boasted a circulation of one hundred thousand subscribers at its peak and probably reached several hundred thousand other readers, serving as the flagship of a "Farmers' Newspaper Alliance" of roughly one thousand state and local alliance journals. Each paper took its news and editorials from the state newspapers, which got them in turn from the national organ, compiled by Macune. "A united effort on the part of all Alliance newspapers and lecturers in advocating fearlessly and intelligently the whole platform of Alliance demands, will so instruct and unify the people upon the great principles which they contain, that every sub-Alliance would be a citadel of pure economics, and every member its true defender," the *National Economist* exhorted its readers.[58]

"The crying necessity of the hour is for the people to think for themselves," Macune wrote in the newspaper's first editorial. To this end, he announced, "It will be a part of the mission of the paper to simplify and express in plain and easily understood language the present and proposed methods and policies of this government and compare them to historical precedents when possible and show the teachings of political economy on the same subject."[59] Macune's intention was not simply that "the people" should learn to think for themselves individually; it was that they should come to think of themselves collectively. The *National Economist* directed American farmers to see themselves as the core of a unified social, economic, and political entity, "the producing classes," comprising the three subclasses of agricultural, manufacturing, and commercial "producers."[60] Key to the paper's purpose was teaching its readers to transcend divisions between North and South, Democrat and Republican, country and city, and embrace their shared class identity. While the ideology of "producers" as opposed to "nonproducers" continued a tradition born of the defense of self-employment by urban artisans and yeoman farmers in the early republic, it took on new significance for commercial farmers and wage workers in the industrial age. What Rosanne Currarino has called "industrial producerism" developed in dialogue with and opposition to the dictates of big business and finance capital in the late nineteenth century.[61] The Farmers' Alliance system of education and publication formed the main ideological arsenal of the producing classes in modern American agriculture.

From the fields of history and political economy, Macune provided the collectivity he helped to create with both an ancient ancestry and a contemporary basis in the structure of the new industrial order. The past and present of the producing classes formed the subjects of two book-length series of essays that ran in the *National Economist* over several years. The themes of these courses were recapitulated in twenty installments of "Economist Educational Exercises," designed by Macune to introduce members to basic concepts in ways that related concretely to their lives and livelihoods. They covered literacy, numeracy, political theory, class analysis, the social gospel, the distribution of wealth in the United States and abroad, the condition of the common people in various countries, railroad systems, radical movements, and related topics. In his series "History and Government," Macune contributed to a wave of contemporary scholarship on the collective biography of "the people" or "the masses," intended to illuminate the social and political unrest of the Gilded Age.[62]

Observing that history as it had been previously written focused exclusively on the actions of rulers and military leaders while neglecting "the social, political, and financial status of the masses of the people," Macune offered a sweeping alternative narrative. He chronicled the successive modes of religious, military, and commercial oppression through which the "speculative element" concentrated the wealth of the many in the hands of the few. Like his social scientific contemporaries, Lewis Henry Morgan and Thorstein

Veblen, he gave the producing classes a quasi-racial character rooted in the "Aryan, or Indo-European, stock, from which have sprung all the historic races of Europe," making its first appearance in the city-states of classical Greece. But the rise of individual ownership of land, which formed the cornerstone of ancient Greeks' liberty, ironically provided the means of their eventual enslavement. As Americans' agrarian ancestors prospered through trade, a "commercial aristocracy" came to monopolize the supply of gold and silver coin. Exclusive control of the "royal metals," which had facilitated the power of monarchs and their courtiers, now transferred to merchants, who used it to gain control of land and labor. The "two monopolies" of land and money thus proved "the curse of Greece, as they were of all the nations which succeeded them."[63]

Postbellum America marked a familiar stage in the rise and fall of republics, according to Macune. The age-old divide between producers and nonproducers had come to dominate the new order of agriculture, industry, and commerce, forming the central axis of exploitation. In his series of essays, "Political Economy," Macune aimed to show that the various subsets of the producing classes, particularly wage-earning workers and smallholding farmers, had practically merged into a single social body; so had, on the other hand, the formerly distinct elements of the nonproducing classes, landlords and lenders. He began with the classical political economy of Adam Smith and its eighteenth-century version of the divide between what Smith had similarly termed "productive and nonproductive employments." As Macune explained, for Smith and his nineteenth-century successors, the fundamental form of exploitation of productive labor was land rent. While merchants and moneylenders earned their income principally from *trade*, the key classes engaged in *production* were the respective owners of land, capital, and labor, dividing among them the surplus derived from industry and agriculture as rents, profits, and wages. Of these three class claimants, Macune continued, Smith and company had considered both hired labor and commercial farming and manufacturing as "productive employments," whose wages and profits were directly proportional to productivity. Landlords appeared as the prototypical nonproducers whose rents were essentially tolls for access to the land on which workers and employers depended. This earlier conception had informed the classical economists' critique of rent, which tended to consume more and more of the surplus as productive land became increasingly scarce relative to the demand for it, leaving diminishing returns for the active industry of farmers, manufacturers, and workers. Allowing just enough for their tenants to support themselves and their hired hands, landlords demanded the rest in rent.[64]

Macune argued that a transformation in class relations separated the late nineteenth-century United States from eighteenth-century Britain, calling for a critical revision of Smithian political economy. Real estate had become an essentially financial asset that could be traded like "any other commodity that could be purchased and placed in the coat pocket." As land had become a form of security for credit, effective control had shifted from farmers or planters to the mortgage companies and furnishing merchants who held the lien on their land or crops. As the new ruling class in the countryside, moneylending merchants extracted the surplus mainly through charging interest on loans, not rent on land. "This is true because the compounding of interest on the aggregated capital goes faster than the industry of a nation can create values, and in a certain time it will absorb all created values and go on increasing in geometrical progression until the time will come when the surplus values will not only be absorbed, but all the annual creations of values," Macune explained, implicitly drawing on the work of earlier nineteenth-century critics including Edward Kellogg and Alexander Campbell.[65]

Rent had been effectively subsumed by interest, as merchant-creditors had become lords of the land as well as lords of the market. "Is it not misleading and useless to longer keep up a finespun distinction between rent and interest since the complete capitalization of lands?" Macune wrote. Smith's three classes had thus been reduced to two: "capital," by which Macune meant the merchant class that had come to control both land and money, and "labor," by which he meant the "producing classes" including family farmers, tenant farmers, sharecroppers, and paid laborers. "Land having become merged in capital, the two great factors of production are labor and capital," he wrote. So conceived, "labor" was seen to receive in "wages"—by which Macune meant commercial farmers' and manufacturers' profits as well as employees' paychecks—a declining fraction of the proceeds from the sale of what it produced, while "capital" claimed the remainder of the surplus as interest. The common economic interest of the producing classes lay in maximizing the prices of the commodities they sold and minimizing the cost of the credit they required. "All producers are alike interested in high prices for everything," he wrote.[66]

Macune's conception of farmers' class interest clearly spoke to their need to raise the prices of farm goods and lower the interest they paid to their merchant-creditors. How it reflected the interests of paid laborers, who were generally supposed to benefit from relatively *low* prices as consumers, required strenuous explanation. Macune argued that since wage earners, like family farmers, produced more than they consumed, they likewise stood to gain from rising prices overall; even if they paid more for their purchases, they would more than make up for it in increased income. "The consumers of butter would be better off if butter was [raised to] one dollar per pound if everything else was enhanced in proportion, provided such consumers were producers, because their revenues would be increased accordingly," Macune wrote.[67] Of course, this reasoning overlooked the fact that wage earners were not paid more in proportion to rising revenues resulting from higher prices on their products. This critical blind spot was largely responsible for the weak support of wage earners for agrarian financial reforms designed to raise prices and lower interest rates, despite Macune's and his allies' efforts to convince them that farmers and workers shared the same class interests.

Macune had been trying to comprehend and respond to the growing power of corporate capital ever since he had been a cattle drover. Early on, he had sought to draw "men of capital" to the ranching and farming frontier. When absentee investment had impoverished rather than enriched many backcountry settlers, he had aimed to make cooperative businessmen of small farmers themselves. The frustration of these efforts led him in the late 1880s to take a broader view of modern business practices as marking not merely a new form of private enterprise, but a new stage of market relations in which the old rules of private property and competition no longer applied. Along with the combination of land and capital under the control of the merchant-creditor class in the countryside, he believed, the rise of corporations with the power to govern the market instead of being governed by it called for a fundamental rethinking of the premises of classical political economy. As Macune's *National Economist Almanac* for 1890 instructed readers, "The law of supply and demand becomes an absurdity when it is comprehended that capitalism controls both."[68]

His name for the new structure of market exchange was "monopoly," an old word that acquired new meaning in the industrial age, like "producerism." While Macune identified with what historians have called the "antimonopoly tradition," he did not intend to abolish monopoly itself, restoring the competitive conditions that the classical economists had described and Jacksonian critics had defended. Neither did he seek to wrest the mantle of corporate capital from big merchants and bankers in order to bestow it more broadly on small producers, conceiving of antimonopoly as basically just a decentralized brand of business, as some local and regional business owners did.[69] Indeed, Macune's critique of monopoly reflected his loss of faith in producers' cooperatives as an adequate solution to the scarcity of capital and credit that held small farmers in thrall. By 1890, he refused either to reject monopoly per se or to accept the terms of the ascendant corporate order. He insisted instead on viewing monopoly as a natural stage of economic evolution, but one whose progressive potential had been hijacked by predatory capitalists.[70]

The crux of the issue for Macune lay in public versus private control over the infrastructure of market relations. "Monopoly," he explained, "is, in a general way, the manufacture, production, or control of some article, thing, or service of prime necessity, under conditions that prevent a healthy competition." Such essential goods and services entailed large, long-term investment and planning as well as public responsibility. In the household economy of the early United States, he continued, the common commodities that had been supplied under monopolistic conditions included the minting of coins and the postal service, which the Founders had wisely reserved for the exclusive control of the national government. Since then, however, the development of the railroad and the telegraph and the extension of market relations had vastly extended the domain of "prime necessities" on which the whole society depended. "Telephones, gas-works, water-works, street-car lines, express companies, and electric-light plants are all examples of lines of business that are by their very nature monopolies," Macune wrote, adding elsewhere insurance and banking. Yet governance of this commercial infrastructure had devolved upon privately owned corporations. "These great inventions are the property of the world, and yet they have been monopolized by a few, and through them the industry of the world is controlled."[71]

The problem with monopolistic corporations was not that there was too little competition between them, according to Macune. It was that there was too much, or rather too much "destructive warfare," for "there can be no such thing as competition pure and simple between combinations." The cutthroat struggle of corporate titans represented to Macune a perilous transition to true monopoly, which was "the function of government and government alone." Combinations of farmers and laborers such as trade unions and cooperatives might "temporarily perform the duties of true government, but the better plan would be for the government to do its whole duty and assume control of such lines of business as are essential to all and are or can be monopolized." Seizing the reins of the new corporate order therefore meant not just reorganizing the business of farming, but reforming the state. "Let the government be the embodiment of all the combined action society finds necessary," Macune wrote, "by saying that all kinds of business or effort susceptible of being monopolized shall be conducted by the whole society and not by a favored few."[72]

The ultimate monopoly for Macune was the supply of money, the fundamental means of market exchange and thus the supreme prerogative of the state. "I believe it is admitted that the reason why the Government should coin or issue money is that it is one of the most perfect illustrations of a monopoly pure and simple," he testified before the Committee on Ways and Means of the U.S. House of Representatives in 1890, "and a monopoly is a species of business in which there can be no competition, and any business which can not be regulated by the effects of competition is peculiarly in the province of the Government, because if allowed to be exercised by individuals it carries with it power to levy tribute at will, and this could never be tolerated in a free government."[73]

Money also posed a special challenge beyond that of simple monopoly, which Macune called "monopoly price." A commodity need not be monopolized in order to command an artificially high price, he explained. Any time that a fluctuating demand for a commodity ran up against an inflexible supply, its price would be liable to soar far above its natural market value. If the commodity in question was a basic necessity, those who owned it would be in a position to extort those in need of it even if the sellers did not exclusively control the supply. When the commodity was the standard of value for all other commodities, its monopoly price could depress the prices of everything for which it exchanged. Unlike actual monopolies of goods or services, monopoly prices typically resulted from local and transient conditions, making them far more difficult for government to regulate. Therein lay what he called the "great secret" of modern finance, the key to the corporate economy in which finance reigned supreme: "*Money commands a monopoly price.*"[74]

"Eureka!": The Subtreasury Plan and the Financialization of Cash Crops

In late December 1889, former President Grover Cleveland spoke at a banquet held by the Boston Merchants' Association. "When I see about me this gathering of business men and merchants," Cleveland told his hosts, "I find it impossible to rid myself of the impressive thought, that here is represented that factor in civilized life which measures the progress of a people, which constitutes the chief care of every enlightened government, and which gives to a country the privilege of recognized membership in the community of nations." The following week, Macune responded in the pages of the *National Economist*. Cleveland's speech nakedly revealed the "policy of this government for the last quarter century, including his own administration. The policy, 'the chief care,' of our national government has been to foster the trading, the banking and the speculating interests. And it has developed them to an abnormal extent at the expense and to the abnormal depletion of other interests," Macune wrote. ". . . The results of that policy are seen in the present depressed condition of producers throughout the Union. They are seen in the deserted farms of New England, whose former owners and tillers have fled to the cities or to the West. They are seen in many counties of the West with rural population stationary or decreasing. They are seen in the deserted agricultural colleges where youths can not either be coaxed or paid to learn practical farming. It does not pay."[75]

Why did the prodigious production of cash crops not generate sufficient profits for those who grew them? The answer that Macune arrived at was that farmers did not create the money for which their crops exchanged. "No question is of greater interest or importance to the American citizen than the money question," the *National Economist* editorialized in 1889. Yet while "the question of finance" was the "subject which most directly affects the masses of the people," it was also "the one on which they are least of all informed." The operations of currency and credit appeared "so subtle and so sure as to produce the most startling results, and at the same time defy the tracing of the effect to its primitive cause," the newspaper observed.[76] In focusing on financial reform, Macune threw the alliance into the paramount political contest in the period between the end of Reconstruction and the turn of the century, an issue that divided both major political parties, spawned several third parties, and mobilized the activism of workers and business leaders as well as farmers for more than twenty years.[77]

The Populist currency crusade found its chief intellectual inspiration before Macune in two antebellum exponents of "fiat currency," paper money irredeemable in gold or silver and secured solely by government fiat. From the New York merchant Edward Kellogg's 1849 tract, *Labor and Other Capital*, postbellum reformers learned that money was purely a creature of law, that its value derived from the legislation that authorized it rather than from the precious metals on which it was based, and that it became the main means of exploitation when its legally determined interest rate was allowed to rise more rapidly than the prices of the products of labor.[78] As Macune put it, Kellogg's later followers understood that "any substance can be used [as money] and to any extent of value the people may determine," and that "it is dangerous to the best interests of the people to allow it to be made a commodity for speculation."[79] They also took the encouraging message that if "the power of money to oppress" came from legislation, then labor could be liberated by reforming the laws regulating the means of exchange.

Along with Kellogg's work, which gained a wide readership in the 1860s, the political economist Henry Carey's *Principles of Social Science* (1858–59) lay the foundation for postbellum monetary reform. An acerbic critic of the power of merchants and moneylenders, Carey drew from utopian socialism and the sociology of Auguste Comte a countervailing ideal: a harmonious market society in which the growth of market relations, freed from the grip of parasitic middlemen, would knit people together spiritually and materially in increasing mutuality, solidarity, and "association." When Macune envisioned an economy in which commerce would be mediated only by a publicly governed supply of currency and credit with no need for the intervention of bankers and brokers, enabling "a direct exchange without the friction of a middleman," he was echoing Carey.[80] The ultimate embodiment of the power of society itself as an organic whole for Carey was a democratically controlled fiat currency, the "great instrument of association," transcending class differences and rendering speculation and exploitation obsolete. It was Carey who made "association" the grand ideal of postbellum currency reform.[81]

Kellogg and Carey's hopes were partly and temporarily realized during the Civil War with the creation of the first national paper currency in the United States. Skyrocketing demands for cash quickly compelled northern banks to suspend specie payments for their banknotes at the outset of the war, and gold and silver virtually disappeared from circulation as in previous crises. As an emergency means of paying soldiers and suppliers, the U.S. government issued $400 million in Treasury notes, much as the American colonies had created the first "bills of credit" initially as a wartime expedient. Known as "greenbacks" because they were backed solely by the green ink declaring them legal tender, the non-interest-bearing notes could also be used to buy interest-bearing government bonds, more than $2 billion of which were sold to fund the Union effort. Partly to provide a market for the war bonds, Congress established a whole new network of federally chartered banks, the National Banking System, whose members were required to hold part of their capital in U.S. Treasury bonds. Concentrated heavily in the Northeast, the national banks were authorized to lend out their own banknotes, creating a second national paper currency alongside the greenbacks, while a steep federal tax on state banknotes drove out of circulation the multitude of locally issued paper currencies that had made up the main circulating medium before the war. After the war, Congress and the Treasury pursued a series of measures that effectively contracted the currency by withdrawing greenbacks, resumed specie payments and returned the nation to a specie standard by 1879, and paid back both the principal and the interest on the war bonds in gold at taxpayers' expense. Together, these policies enriched wealthy bondholders and concentrated control over the currency in the banking centers of the Northeast, while depressing the prices and deepening the debts of farmers in the South and West. The stage was thus set for the third and final act of the long conflict over the means of producing the means of payment in early America.[82]

As Macune and the Farmers' Alliance saw it, the wartime introduction of a fiat currency for the first time since the Founding Era had "created a decided sensation among the bankers of this country," who "were not slow in discovering that by reason of this issue of non-interest-bearing treasury notes the government had invaded their special privilege, that of furnishing a currency to the people." He quoted Treasury Secretary Hugh McCulloch, who had worried that "a permanent government currency" would keep "the question of the currency constantly before the people as a political question, than which few things would be more injurious to business." In Macune's view, the creditor class had lobbied for the establishment of the National Banking System as an alternative to popular control over currency and credit, then had campaigned successfully for contraction of the "people's money," the greenbacks. But Macune concluded, "A government violates its most sacred obligation—a guarantee of life, liberty, and the pursuit of happiness—when it delegates to a certain class of its citizens the right to issue money, and then by contracting and withdrawing from circulation its own money it offers such a class so great a premium to hoard its dollars to the end that the inadequate volume may possess the power to oppress all other classes."[83]

In opposition to the National Banking System and the return to a specie standard, a rising Greenback movement united northern workers, manufacturers, and mining companies in the 1860s and 1870s. Its leading theorist was an Illinois state legislator with interests in iron and coal named Alexander Campbell. His short book *The True American System of Finance* (1864) provided the platform for a resurgent labor movement in the aftermath of emancipation. Drawing extensively on Kellogg, Campbell proposed a panacea for the crushing burden on small producers and debtors created by the contraction of the currency: declaring the nation's paper money redeemable not in specie but in government bonds paying a modest interest rate of 3 percent, which he estimated to be the average rate of economic growth. He argued that his "interconvertible bond scheme" would establish a currency designed to expand and contract automatically with the volume of business for which it was called into use. For when the production of commodities grew faster than 3 percent per year, leading to a relative scarcity of currency and falling prices, bondholders would trade in their bonds for money; and when economic growth fell below 3 percent, so that too many dollars were chasing too few goods, money-holders would buy bonds, withdrawing currency from circulation. Campbellite Greenbackism spread south and west in the 1870s, gaining a following among farmers struggling against falling prices and rising debts. By the 1880s, however, the movement had stalled.[84]

"EUREKA!" the *National Economist* cried in December 1889, reprinting a blockbuster report by a special Committee on the Monetary System, appointed by the Farmers' Alliance and led by Macune. In the report and in dozens of speeches and articles over the next three years, Macune offered an original explanation of the causes of agricultural depression, not just in the United States but in all "thickly populated agricultural countries." Previous currency critics, while recognizing the hardship imposed on producers as the supply of money grew more sluggishly than the demand for it, had assumed that the demand for money rose steadily from year to year in step with the growth of the market economy. What was needed, by this logic, was a mechanism for similarly increasing the money supply at the rate of economic growth, along the lines of Campbell's interconvertible bond scheme. By continually balancing the supply of money with the demand for it, the argument went, prices could be kept constant, or rather allowed to rise and fall in relation to the supply and demand for particular commodities without being distorted by inflation or depression in the economy as a whole.[85]

What others had missed, according to Macune, was that the demand for money did not increase uniformly with the total volume of monetary transactions. Monetary demand *varied* qualitatively from one economic sector to another, and it *fluctuated* steeply over the course of each year, particularly for farmers, whose market activities ebbed and flowed with the natural cycle of planting, growing, and harvesting. Macune held that the sectoral variations and seasonal fluctuations were as critical as economic growth in determining the demand for money, especially in farm country. Yet the supply of money remained basically constant across the economy and throughout the year, with dire consequences for prices and prosperity. He argued that previous writers' neglect of the variability of monetary demand comported reasonably well with the conditions of manufacturing, which produced a relatively unvarying output of goods in all seasons. The demand for money in the agricultural sector, however, was far more volatile. Commercial growers of durable staples such as wheat and cotton marketed the great majority of their annual produce in the few months following the harvest. As Macune explained, this seasonal rush had become more marked than ever in the late nineteenth century, partly due to the development of the railroad and the telegraph, and partly due to the pressures of the crop-lien system, under which farmers were compelled to put their entire crop up for sale as soon as it was harvested. "Never before in the history of the world has the product of the farm, the day it was prepared for the market, been offered for sale in the great markets of the world," Macune told the House Ways and Means Committee. ". . . It is therefore no surprise that the entire crop of agriculture in this country is within a few weeks' time, placed upon the market demanding money."[86]

The surge in agricultural demand for the means of exchange in the late summer and fall created a severe scarcity of money just when farmers were selling, dramatically depressing the prices of cash crops. The subsequent fall in monetary demand led to a great glut of money in the winter and spring, sharply inflating the prices of farmers' supplies. The maintenance of a relatively inelastic currency thus discriminated against farmers. Macune estimated that the combined toll of artificially low prices for farm goods and high prices for provisions amounted to as much as 40 percent of the value of farmers' purchases and sales each year. Not only farmers suffered the consequences, however. The flood of farm goods each fall placed such an outsized burden on the nation's money supply that the prices of all other goods were violently disturbed as well, chaining the whole economy to the vicissitudes of the farm sector.[87] While all the producing classes paid the costs of the disjuncture between the mode of farming and the mode of payment, Macune wrote, the sole benefits accrued to the merchants and bankers who lent money at interest and "who desire by means of this scarcity to depress prices and purchase the products of agriculture for speculative purposes."[88]

Though Macune and the alliance supported Populist calls for the free coinage of silver along with gold in order to increase the total volume of money in circulation, a bimetallic money standard appeared to them less important than a bifurcated money supply. For any increase in the overall ratio of monetary supply to monetary demand could not eliminate the discrimination against farmers stemming from the seasonal fluctuation in demand.[89] Anticipating twentieth-century theorists of "concurrent currencies" and "multiple monies," Macune therefore urged the dual creation of a stable money supply sufficient to meet the demands of the manufacturing sector supplemented by an elastic supply tied to the seasonal cycle of the agricultural sector.[90] Only by operating in tandem to supply the different demands of agriculture and industry, he argued, could the two segments of the money supply "guarantee actual uniformity of volume as compared to its only measure—demand—throughout the year."[91]

While advocating the establishment of a two-track public money supply, Macune argued that the privately controlled creation of currency by banks should be abolished. "The greatest evil . . . is that which delegates to a certain class the power to fix the price of all kinds of produce and of all commodities," Macune wrote. "This power is not delegated directly, but it is delegated indirectly by allowing such class to issue a large per cent of the money used as the circulating medium of the country, and having the balance of such circulating medium, which is issued by the Government, a fixed quantity that is not augmented to correspond with the necessities of the times." What was needed was "a Government issue, the volume of which, shall be increased to correspond with the actual addition to the wealth of the Nation presented by agriculture at harvest time, and diminished as such agricultural products are consumed."[92]

Such an elastic currency was the main economic goal of the subtreasury plan devised by Macune's Committee on the Monetary System. The plan called for replacing the National Banking System with a federal system of subtreasuries, establishing one office in each county in every state that marketed at least $500,000 worth of leading cash crops per year. The subtreasuries were to operate public warehouses in which farmers could store their crops. In return for the crops they deposited, farmers would be able to borrow a new kind of paper currency equal to a maximum of 80 percent of the value of the goods stored in the subtreasuries. They would be charged a nominal 1 percent annual interest. The subtreasury notes would circulate freely as cash, and the farmers could use them to pay for their supplies. The farmers would also receive warehouse certificates listing the quantity, quality, and value of the crops they had stored in the subtreasuries as well as the amount of subtreasury notes that they had been lent. They could then sell the crops whenever they chose to do so simply by transferring and endorsing the warehouse receipts. The purchasers would pay the agreed-upon price minus however much the sellers had already received as a loan as well as the government's costs of insuring, processing, and storing their crops.[93]

The subtreasury plan became for several years the centerpiece of the agrarian cause. "The shibboleth of the true reform movement," in Macune's words, it divided its fervent supporters from those willing to compromise in the face of furious opposition from merchants, bankers, and moneyed interests. The most basic features of the plan, as Macune conceived it, concerned its provisions for the marketing of farmers' staples. It provided for the government to construct and maintain storage facilities in a thousand counties across the South and West, allowing farmers to store their goods locally instead of in the cities, without paying the owners of warehouses or elevators. Most importantly, it would allow farmers to trade their crops for cash without having to sell them as soon as they were harvested; they could store the crops and sell them throughout the year, alleviating the seasonal depression of prices. The subtreasury notes, loaned at low interest, would allow farmers to buy supplies in cash instead of on credit from furnishing merchants. Speculators would no longer be able to corner the market by buying up agricultural staples in large quantities at low prices at harvest time and selling them at much higher prices throughout the year. The subtreasury plan would also eliminate the incentive for merchants and financiers to hoard money, encouraging them to invest it productively instead. "Money, stripped of its 'power to oppress,' would no longer be hoarded away from legitimate productive effort that it might secure the greater gains that flow from such doubtful methods," Macune said. ". . . As the freebooter when he finds robbing no longer practicable goes to work and becomes a useful citizen, so money, when production became its most practicable channel, would join labor as its true adjunct."[94]

Further, the subtreasury plan was designed to enable farmers rather than speculators to use the credit system to hedge against changing prices. With crucial support from the federal government, farmers would be able to manage the risks associated with the volatility in the markets for their goods, doing for themselves what the rise of corporate commodity exchanges had allowed brokers and investors to do by trading in futures contracts. Just as the Chicago Board of Trade, established in 1848, had made it possible for traders to bet on rising and falling grain prices; and just as the New York and New Orleans Cotton Exchanges, established in 1869 and 1871, respectively, had created a booming market in cotton futures; so the subtreasury plan would enable farmers to become dealers in their own financial derivatives, treating their crops as fungible financial assets that could be bought, sold, and borrowed against without actually exchanging their goods.[95]

As Macune testified before the House Committee on Agriculture during its hearings on "fictitious dealings in agricultural products," large companies and traders made a practice of selling huge volumes of cotton futures just before the harvest, greatly exacerbating the downward pressure on the "spot prices" of farmers' goods at harvest time. "Now, this system does not result from the little buyer who buys a few hundred bales and sells against it while his cotton is going to market," Macune said. "It is not from legitimate business men at all, but it is done by these combinations that manipulate, that squeeze the crops out of the hands of the producer and hold it through the season and deal it out in dribbles as they need it at a high price." For that reason, he said, the alliance opposed the current system of commodity options and futures trading and sought to prohibit speculators from dealing in large quantities of commodities that they never actually held. But the subtreasury plan would effectively allow small growers to buy and sell futures of their own crops. "If there were any way to encourage the producer to go on the market," Macune said he would favor it, ". . . but as long as this middle influence has got the power to squeeze it out of the producer and horn off the consumer until he is compelled to have it, they are masters of the situation."[96]

In mobilizing new financial instruments on farmers' behalf, Macune aimed to foster a relationship of essentially "direct exchange" between producers and consumers under modern conditions of mass production and distribution. Macune called his commercial ideal "equivalence of service," meaning that commodities should exchange for other commodities of equal value, determined by the labor required for their production. Commodities exchanging directly for commodities, producers trading directly with consumers—this was a vision in which the mechanisms of finance and exchange theoretically disappeared, as they ceased to distort the natural operations of simple and direct market transactions.

The spirit of his ideal came closest to what Macune called the "scientific anarchy" of the French radical Pierre-Joseph Proudhon, whose ideas he admired.[97] Kellogg had sent Proudhon his *Labor and Other Capital*, and its influence was most evident in Proudhon's writings on credit and banking, which emerged from his participation in the Revolution of 1848 in France—including a brief experiment in banking that Macune claimed as a key precedent for the subtreasury plan. In his *Solution of the Social Problem* (1849), Proudhon articulated his "principle of reciprocity," which he said was essentially the Golden Rule applied to market relations: "*Products exchange for products*." "What must we do to make possible direct exchange, not only among three, four, six, ten or one hundred traders, but among one hundred thousand, between all producers and all consumers?" Proudhon asked. He answered: "Let all merchandise become current money, and abolish the royalty of gold." Gold was the ultimate despot in modern market society, according to Proudhon. His goal was to overthrow its absolute power by effectively monetizing all commodities. "If all the products of labor had the same exchange value as money, all the workers would enjoy the same advantages as the holders of money: everyone would have, in his ability to produce, an inexhaustible source of wealth." The Midas-like power to make all merchandise as good as gold would be tantamount to dethroning money as a power unto itself.[98]

Macune shared Proudhon's animus toward what he similarly referred to as the tyranny of gold, which he regarded as a vestige of the original basis of commercial oppression in ancient merchants' exclusive control over the precious metals. "Now, had no such arbitrary measure of value been established," he wrote of classical Greece, "but a currency been issued based on the products of labor and equally accessible to all citizens who could produce such evidences of value, it would have been impossible for one class to have absorbed all values, because labor would have continued to create the means of supplying its own requirements."[99] As it did for many agrarian radicals, the gold standard for Macune stood for the age-old practice of conferring special privilege upon the scarce assets of moneyed men, over against the values created by the producing classes. Yet unlike the partisans of "free and unlimited coinage of silver," he did not simply seek to make the monetary standard broader. He sought to make it more truly universal by conferring the status of money on the leading commodities of the country, making cotton as good as the "white gold" with which it was frequently equated.

The subtreasury plan, as Macune often noted, based the new circulating medium it created on the leading exports, particularly wheat and cotton, whose international prices were denominated in gold. Thus, he reasoned, the subtreasury notes would circulate at par with gold, for when cotton was worth more in gold on international markets than it was worth in subtreasury notes at home, the holders of those notes would exchange them for cotton in the warehouses and export it abroad. Whereas, when the purchasing power of the subtreasury notes that farmers could obtain for a bale of cotton was greater than the purchasing power of the gold that they could sell it for abroad, they would logically tend to keep the cotton in the government storehouses. "Therefore the deposits would be regulated by the parity of the circulating medium with gold," Macune wrote. ". . . Instead of issuing certificates based on gold and silver bullion deposited in the treasury, where it sometimes will become greatly depreciated, the sub-treasury plan proposes to issue certificates upon wheat and cotton that represents foreign gold." In substituting a cotton and wheat standard for the gold standard, the subtreasury plan promised to make cotton truly a cash crop for farmers themselves.[100]

The subtreasury plan was never enacted. Adamant bipartisan opposition to the plan played a key part in spurring the formation of the People's Party in 1892—a course that Macune strongly opposed, convinced that partisan politics would compromise the independence and organizational goals of the Farmers' Alliance. He was pushed out of the order he had built up the following year. By the presidential election of 1896, Macune's fears had been borne out by the collapse of the alliance and by the Populists' tactical decision to abandon the subtreasury plan and unite behind the Democratic demand for a return to the bimetallic standard. But while less radical in its immediate proposals, the mass mobilization against the gold standard led by William Jennings Bryan upheld the long-range vision of a plentiful and popularly controlled currency for which Macune had fought. The campaign for "free silver" advanced as well the agrarian indictment of the geographical inequity and instability of the National Banking System and the rising "power of money to oppress" not only farmers on the nation's periphery, but the nation's workers and producers more generally.

Bryan's epochal defeat in the "battle of the standards" marked the beginning of the end of the money question as a popular cause. The organization of currency and credit became much less open to broad-based political challenge thereafter. Nevertheless, the education and radicalization of the farmers' movement that Macune had led deeply influenced the agenda of agrarian Democrats in the Progressive Era. They found considerable success in their campaign for a qualitatively greater role for the regulatory state in controlling public utilities and the infrastructure of market relations, as Elizabeth Sanders has shown. The agrarian call for an elastic currency responsive to geographical and seasonal variability in monetary demand shaped the structure of the Federal Reserve System established in 1913. But the new system left the nation's money and credit squarely in the hands of bankers and bondholders, and the Federal Reserve became increasingly immune to political pressure from below. The call for public provisions for low-interest loans to farmers was answered partly in the Federal Reserve Act and more extensively in the Federal Farm Loan Act of 1916 as well as later New Deal reforms. But such legislation assisted mortgage companies, merchants, and agribusiness trusts in extending their control over land and crops at the expense of family farmers. The crusade against what Bryan famously called the "cross of gold" paved the way for a series of steps away from the gold standard and toward a fiat currency over the course of the twentieth century, allowing wider latitude for social provision and countercyclical policy in response to unemployment and depression. But the power of finance capital depended less on the precious metals than agrarian reformers imagined, as we will see.[101]

As in previous eras, the questions about capitalist development that arose from the conflict over currency in the late nineteenth century were more profound than the available answers and alternatives. Macune often said that the specific details of the subtreasury plan were far less important than the general principles it embodied. "The central idea underlying the industrial movement is the establishment of economic systems that will insure equivalence of service in the exchanges and business transactions between man and man," he wrote. He explained that "the expenditure of labor in production means the expenditure of a part of the life forces in the product. A portion of the toiler's life is blended, woven, and embodied in every article of wealth he produces. Those stately mansions that line our streets, those piles of goods that fill those warehouses, all this wealth really means so many human lives crystallized by labor." Macune and his followers envisioned a market economy in which commercial exchange would be the vehicle for the fulfillment of the ultimately religious ideals of mutuality and reciprocity. "Under an equitable exchange system every worker would receive for his product or services an equitable amount of the labor or services—that is, the life of others. Under an unjust system of exchange he is robbed of a part of his life," Macune wrote. "The average pay of the workingman of the country is about $350 per annum. The man who by the aid of unjust economic systems or class laws obtains an income of $500,000 per annum and spends it, actually—not literally but actually—devours 10,000 workingmen during his life."[102] Denouncing what he called "economic cannibalism," he concluded, "Monopolists manufacture the muscle, blood, and brain of the workers into wealth without rendering an adequate return."[103]

While Macune's plans for democratizing the means of market relations were largely disappointed, the broader ideal he championed continued to inspire social reform. When he left the alliance at the age of forty-two, he had spent less than seven years in the agrarian cause, and he never reentered the fray of national political debate. After returning to Texas and practicing law and medicine for a few years in the mid-1890s, Macune entered the Methodist ministry, becoming licensed to preach in 1901. He spent the next two decades mainly working as an itinerant supply preacher for a circuit of small communities in central Texas. Moving through hardscrabble towns like Copperas Cove, Thurber, Florence, Hillsboro, and Rising Star, he ministered to the same struggling family farmers who had been at the heart of his mission in the alliance. He joined his son, Dennis Macune, who also became a prominent minister, in missionary work in northern Mexico, and he ended his career as pastor for a Methodist church in Miami, Arizona. Amid the defeat or cooptation of its broadest political aims, the agrarian movement channeled much of its imaginative energy and spirit into the evangelical church. But its cause was not utopian in any pie-in-the-sky sense. From a sustained and sophisticated engagement with the changing political economy of southern farming, Macune and his allies drew a vision of cooperation and fellowship that reached far beyond the hill country.

6

Charles Conant and the Fund of Trust

The power of money comes from its conjunction of credit and law. People accept money in payment because of their confidence that they can use it to pay other prices and debts and because the government compels them to do so through taxation and legal-tender laws. In 1864, Congress manifested the combination of faith and fiat by introducing the motto "In God We Trust" on U.S. coins above the striped shield of the federal government.[1] Nearly two hundred years earlier, Massachusetts had created the first public "bills of credit," vesting the sacred trust on which they were based in a special "fund for the repayment of all such sums" from tax revenues. The 1694 law marked one of the earliest uses of the word "fund," meaning the base or bottom of something, for a stock or sum of money.[2] In the half century after the Civil War, the nation's currency came to be based on a different kind of fund, the fund of capital available for investment, governed by a new form of corporate trust.

Among the chief architects of that new structure of money and capital was the financial journalist, currency reformer, and exponent of empire Charles A. Conant (1861–1915). Born with the greenback and the National Banking System at the start of the Civil War, he lived just long enough to see the establishment of the Federal Reserve System on the eve of the First World War. His earliest American ancestor had been the governor of the first permanent English settlement in what became Massachusetts, who had migrated to the Puritan colony at Plymouth in 1623. Conant's family had remained in New England and active in the church, contributing a long line of elders to the First Congregational Church in Mont Vernon, New Hampshire, until his parents moved to the Boston suburb of Winchester, Massachusetts, the year before he was born. Census records indicate that his father had initially followed Conant's grandfather into the carpentry trade, but had become a "trader" by 1860, when Conant's mother was working as a seamstress. Ten years later, his father was working with Conant's uncles who owned a Boston shop engaged in manufacturing and wholesaling "Looking-Glasses, Fancy Boxes, Portable Writing Desks, &c." After graduating from Winchester High School, Conant went to work as a reporter for the *Boston Daily Advertiser* at the age of eighteen, beginning a twenty-year journalistic career with a series of Boston, Springfield, and New York newspapers that brought him to prominence in political and financial circles.[3]

"There are probably few living Americans who have made so careful a study of the science of money and finance and have done so much constructive work," the *Bankers' Magazine* commented in a 1908 profile of Conant. "Apart from two or three University Presidents," the editors wrote, "it would be perhaps not too much to say that Mr. Conant has a wider reputation, abroad as well as at home, than any other living economist."[4] As a preeminent theorist of capitalist crisis in a period of protracted depression, Conant became an influential advocate for monetary and banking reform. He was also a major proponent of colonialism and "dollar democracy" as outlets for the overaccumulation of savings seeking profitable investment, a problem that drew bankers and industrialists to the money question at the turn of the twentieth century much as the surplus of goods depressing the price of staple crops spurred the monetary activism of American farmers. As the creator of a new currency for the Philippines under American rule and instigator of related monetary reforms in other countries, he pioneered the profession of foreign financial adviser, which became central to U.S. foreign policy.

Most importantly, as a prolific author and trust company treasurer, Conant played a leading part in making financial trusteeship a dominant model of corporate ownership and enterprise, of overseas investment and colonial governance, and of class relations and capitalist rule. He led the way toward a radical reconception of what Adam Smith called "the wealth of nations" as a social fund to be administered by bankers as trustees for a society of beneficiaries, directing its combined savings so as to maximize the returns on each additional dollar invested. Through Conant's career, this chapter explores the transformation of trust into a fiduciary ideal of financial management of a monopolistic market economy, arising in response to economic crisis and in counterpoint to the democratic vision of the cooperative commonwealth.

"Congested Capital": Crises of Surplus

In the summer of 1892, Jane Addams gave a talk to the Ethical Culture Society in Plymouth, Massachusetts, describing a common personal crisis inciting the new social settlement movement. "We have in America a fast-growing number of cultivated young people who have no recognized outlet for their active faculties," said the thirty-two-year-old Addams, just a year older than Conant. "They hear constantly of the great social maladjustment, but no way is provided for them to change it, and their uselessness hangs about them heavily." She and her peers bore "traces of the starvation struggle which for so long made up the life of the race," and they felt instinctively the brutality and privation of life for so many in their midst. Yet a growing gulf separated them from "the stream of laboring people [that] goes past you as you gaze through the plate-glass window of your hotel," creating a hunger born of privilege rather than poverty. Shut off from "half the race" and "half the humanity to which we have been born heir," affluent, educated young people found no "outlet for that sentiment of universal brotherhood, which the best spirit of our times is forcing from an emotion into a motive." As their social aspirations turned inward in high society and higher education, despair only deepened under the burden of unfulfilled ideals. "Many are buried beneath this mental accumulation with lowered vitality and discontent. . . . This young life, so sincere in its emotion and good phrases and yet so undirected, seems to me as pitiful as the other great mass of destitute lives. One is supplementary to the other, and some method of communication can surely be devised," Addams wrote. The social settlement afforded a means of productively employing their faculties by transplanting young people like herself into poor communities, where their overabundance of education and cultivation could find fertile soil. "It is an attempt to relieve, at the same time, the overaccumulation at one end of society and the destitution at the other," she wrote, "but it assumes that this overaccumulation and destitution is most sorely felt in the things that pertain to social and educational advantages."[5]

Many contemporary Americans were spurred into social action by similar crises of abundance, even as they decried the growth of poverty in the shadow of unprecedented wealth. Amid mounting class strife, Progressive reformers saw the signs of a societal coming-of-age in which the nation's surging productivity and population had outgrown the social structures of its youth.[6] Two years after Addams's talk on the need for social settlements, Frederick Jackson Turner described the closing of the frontier of western expansion that had long provided the main outlet for surplus labor and enterprise as American society had grown. "He would be a rash prophet who should assert that the expansive character of American life has now entirely ceased," Turner told his fellow historians, predicting that "the American energy will continually demand a wider field for its exercise."[7] Five years later, in 1899, Thorstein Veblen published his scathing study of idle wealth, *The Theory of the Leisure Class*, and Theodore Roosevelt urged "over-civilized" Americans to find a new frontier for "the strenuous life" in overseas colonies instead of degenerating into the "slothful ease" of a people that no longer needed to struggle for its collective subsistence.[8]

Such concerns reflected an increasingly pervasive discourse of "crisis" in the industrialized world, as new technological forces and economic conditions were seen to strain the limits of the social order that had given rise to them. Traditionally associated with fateful struggles of the body and the soul, the concept of crisis had been extended in the late eighteenth century to revolutions in the body politic. Admirers and detractors alike interpreted the American and French Revolutions as the results of a structural conflict between the ossified institutions of monarchy and mercantilism and the growth of colonies and estates that the old regimes could no longer contain. A century later, influential observers in Germany, France, England, and the United States viewed the financial panics and commercial convulsions of their era as manifestations of a comparable crisis of the international economic regime.[9]

The distinguishing feature of capitalist crisis was the paradox of plenty. Unlike premodern eras of hunger and hardship due to diseases, wars, and poor harvests, the depressions of the modern market economy were rooted in surplus rather than scarcity. They were crises of distribution rather than production, in which the rising capacity of factories and farms brought falling prices and profits, fueling a vicious cycle of business failure, unemployment, and declining demand that contemporaries dubbed "overproduction." The major industrial nations had each "overstocked itself with machinery and manufacturing plant far in excess of the wants of production," wrote the U.S. commissioner of labor Carroll D. Wright in 1886, concluding that "this full supply of economic tools to meet the wants of nearly all branches of commerce and industry is the most important factor in the present industrial depression." The "great enigma of our times," wrote the land reformer Henry George in 1879, was this: "Where the conditions to which material progress everywhere tends are most fully realized—that is to say, where population is densest, wealth greatest, and machinery of production and exchange most highly developed—we find the deepest poverty, the sharpest struggle for existence, and the most of enforced idleness." Idle wealth accumulated alongside idle workers, spurring a restless search for a remedy among business leaders and their political allies no less than among agrarian and labor organizers by the 1890s. A quarter century of intensifying crisis and class struggle caused a general loss of faith in the self-regulating capacity of the competitive market even among those who reaped the lion's share of the rewards.[10]

If the existing mechanisms of market exchange could not bring the supply of labor, capital, and commodities into balance with the demand for them, neither could classical economics account for the crisis. According to the conventional "law of markets" formulated by the French economist Jean-Baptiste Say in 1803, the production and sale of commodities automatically created a corresponding demand for other commodities of equal value, as profits and wages were spent on purchases. While the supply of particular goods and services would temporarily exceed or fall short of the effective demand for them, triggering the movement of prices and reallocating production accordingly, the aggregate supply of all commodities would naturally tend toward equilibrium with overall demand, preventing a "general glut." Chronic overproduction, which preoccupied economic theorists during the "long depression" from the mid-1870s to the mid-1890s, thus represented a crisis of economics as well as an economic crisis. The "invisible hand" that had reigned in economic theory since Adam Smith's day appeared unable to regulate supply and demand under modern industrial conditions. Perhaps the most fully developed theory of capitalist crisis to emerge on either side of the Atlantic came from Conant's work between 1896 and 1905, a century after Say.[11]

What Say's law neglected was savings, Conant wrote, well before John Maynard Keynes made much the same point. If part of the profits and wages from production were saved in the bank rather than spent in the market, then the supply of goods and services would not create equivalent consumer demand. If the bank invested the savings in building new factories, railroads, and other productive enterprises or expanding existing ones, it would create a supply of capital instead. But the supply of capital, like that of commodities, did not create its own demand. "If saving in any community no more than kept pace with new demands for capital which proved legitimate and profitable, the happy situation of a constantly progressive industrial condition would be realized," Conant wrote. "Saving is applied in too many cases, however, to the reproduction of machinery which is already sufficient and the creation of enterprises which do not prove productive." Invested in "needless duplication of what already exists," such "surplus capital" fueled surplus production of commodities in excess of demand. Overproduction, he argued, resulted from "oversavings" and excess investment in redundant means of production and exchange, creating the conditions of crisis. "The salient feature of nearly every crisis has been the sinking of capital in unproductive enterprises," he wrote. "These enterprises have usually been in new fields, whose limitations have not been accurately measured by investors or even by capitalists of presumed judgment and experience. The opening of such a field has been followed by a rush in that direction, which has quickly exhausted all its possibilities and resulted in overproduction and the loss of the capital invested."[12]

The tendency for risky investments in anticipation of demand to promote reckless expansion followed by panic and depression had long been a target of critics of finance such as William Leggett. But Conant contended that such waves of speculation and retrenchment were unavoidable phases of a predictable cycle. Laying the foundation for modern studies of the business cycle, he argued that periodic crises were not aberrations from the normal tendency of the market economy toward an equilibrium of production and demand, but rather inherent dynamics of capitalist development. "The seeking of special causes may be of value to enable the business community to guard against the repetition of old mistakes," he wrote, "but the belief that conditions can be produced which will put an end to the regular cycle of credit contraction and expansion has not been justified by any theory of banking, of trade, or of public finance which has yet been tested." Public policy should aim not to prevent crises, but rather to moderate and regulate them so that they served their vital role in curtailing unproductive investments without spiraling out of control and destroying healthy enterprises and industries. We will examine Conant's influential agenda for empowering banks to pursue such "countercyclical policy" later in this chapter.[13]

Beneath the business cycle, however, Conant discerned a more troubling secular trend toward the accumulation of savings with fewer and fewer outlets for its profitable investment. Each upswing of the business cycle required a fresh field of economic expansion in which the surplus savings accumulated in the previous round could be gainfully employed. Capital, like cotton, was a restless crop, needing new regions, markets, and technologies to develop as it inexorably exhausted the demands of existing enterprises and industries and yielded diminishing returns on additional investment. But in the Old World and increasingly in the New World as well, Conant saw that the frontier of new opportunities for productive investment was closing by the late nineteenth century, even as the supply of savings was growing larger and faster than ever. While short-term spikes in speculation led to painful but passing crises, the long-term buildup of what he called "congested capital" was creating a profound structural crisis for the system itself, threatening its ability to recover from ever-deeper depressions. Deprived of its vital mobility, capital was sinking under its own growing weight.

The congestion of capital had not been unknown in earlier economic eras, according to Conant. In fifteenth-century Florence, sixteenth-century Holland, and seventeenth- and eighteenth-century England, growing stores of surplus wealth had gone idle in the absence of sufficient demand for loanable funds, imperiling the earning capacity of restive fortunes. "In each of these cases the world was far from rich, and savings could not be said to exist in excess in the sense that there was more than enough for all," Conant acknowledged. "But the question of congested capital is a practical one and not a sentimental one. The few who then saved, the many who save now, will not hand over their whole savings to the needy, except under compulsion of taxation, or under the cruel stress of an economic crisis which wipes out dividends and shrivels the value of investments." Never before the nineteenth century, however, had a whole society—indeed, the entire industrialized world—come to depend for its prosperity on the profitable investment of savings. The advent of modern modes of production and transportation had led to an unprecedented level of savings as incomes had risen more rapidly than the cost of living for large numbers of small savers. The development of commercial banking had made possible the pooling and investment of savings on a mass scale for the first time. At the same time, the extraordinary expense of equipping industrializing nations with railroads and mass-production machinery had provided profitable employment for the phenomenal growth of savings, Conant wrote.[14]

By the late nineteenth century, the infrastructure of modern industry and the transcontinental railroads had largely been constructed across Europe, the United States, and the British Empire, but the investment fund continued to multiply. While productivity soared, the need for capital to support basic economic development began to soften relative to its supply. "This process of equipment was substantially completed in 1873, with which year the long period of depression set in which some have ascribed, by a natural error, to changes in the monetary standard," Conant wrote, referring to the congressional demonetization of silver that year. As the accumulation of savings accelerated while the growth of demand for new factories and railroads slowed, the interest earned from investments declined sharply, obeying the "law of diminishing returns" for capital established by the contemporary Austrian economist Eugen von Böhm-Bawerk. "In other words, capital becomes less productive in earning power where it is abundant, because less productive use can be found for the excess above a certain limit. And it is this excess which fixes the rate for all," Conant explained. From the French economist Paul Leroy-Beaulieu, he cited turn-of-the-century statistics showing that European interest rates had trended downward since at least the 1870s, as capitalists anxious to invest their mushrooming savings competed with each other to purchase industrial, railway, and government securities at higher prices with lower yields. Americans, he noted, were facing similarly shrinking prospects for investing their savings at home by the 1890s. "A given capital which earned six per cent. a decade or two ago now earns but three or four per cent. and double the accumulation is required to render the same return," he wrote in 1896, much as a recent reporter on Populist politics had observed that the wheat farmer was "struggling hopelessly with the question how to get as much for two spears of grass as he used to get for one."[15]

Nor were the consequences of congested capital confined to a small class of moneyed men as in ages past. "The congestion has on previous occasions reduced interest rates as low as the past few years," Conant wrote, "but never before has the accumulation of capital been so enormous, nor have so many millions of individuals—those of modest means as well as the typical 'capitalist' of socialistic dreams—been confronted by the condition that their savings must be greatly multiplied in order to afford the old return, and that even such savings as they had could with difficulty find safe lodgment in productive enterprises." During a depression, Conant argued, "accumulated capital suffers more than productive industry," as wage-earners benefited from lower prices or from "public charity, contributed by taxation upon the accumulated earnings of capital." Enterprises that were forced to operate at a loss in order to stay in business effectively transferred their profits to "the consumers of the community," whose "wealth is enhanced at the expense of the owners of inherited or accumulated capital." By consuming the surplus that had kindled the crisis, such short-term destruction of savings cleared the way for recovery. But Conant rejected calls for a longer-term redistribution from capital to labor or from savings to current consumption as "a reversal of the lessons taught by five centuries of civilization," which had shown that the accumulation and reinvestment of capital formed the engine of economic progress and prosperity. In the "long period of stagnation" after 1873, "broken only by brief periods of activity after surplus goods had been consumed," Conant saw the future if the profitability of savings could not be sustained. The fortunes of market society as a whole had come to rest on ensuring adequate returns to the "fund of capital seeking investment."[16]

Classical economics had been predicated on the general principle that the total wealth of market society would naturally be maximized if each household or firm was enabled to pursue its self-interest in free competition with all other enterprises. The revisionist lesson that Conant drew from his theory of crisis was that with the growth of savings, the efforts of individual businesses in pursuit of their own short-term profits actually undermined the long-term profits of capital overall, ultimately endangering the system itself. Unregulated competition maximized the production of wealth all too well, manifested in the prodigious productivity of industrial farms and factories, but in so doing it increasingly impaired the profitability of the growing mass of loanable capital on which the modern economy depended. What was needed was an autonomous institutional agent for the fund of loanable savings that would systematically maximize its returns across the economy, emancipating capital from the control of individual enterprises while regulating investment and production in lieu of the "invisible hand." If the recurrent crises of the late nineteenth century were rooted in a structural crisis of savings, the remedy for Conant lay in the establishment of a new structure for the fund of capital itself: the modern investment trust.[17]

"The Price Takes the Place of the Object": The Transformation of Trust

In February 1889, the *North American Review* featured an essay by Andrew Carnegie on a new social movement among big businessmen, comparable in some ways to the social settlement movement described by Jane Addams. "We must all have our toys," the steel magnate began, and the latest hobby among his peers was the creation of "trusts," corporate combinations of competing firms to control the prices of their products. Oil and coal, sugar and salt, copper and lead, lumber and brick, railroads and telegraph lines—all the main materials of the new industrial order were suddenly subject to strenuous joint efforts to control the market. But the cutthroat competition giving rise to the trusts was more than a high-stakes game in which the best businesses triumphed, as Carnegie explained. It was a collective crisis for manufacturers drowning in a flood of their own goods, driving down prices below the costs of production for even the fittest competitors. Unlike the glut of crops afflicting small farmers, the problem for major manufacturers and railroads lay in the vast size of their operations, requiring large, long-term investments to build and maintain their facilities, and compelling them to continue running at full capacity despite falling prices, indeed even at a loss, in order to pay their fixed costs. "While continuing to produce may be costly, the manufacturer knows too well that stoppage would be ruin," he wrote, articulating what became known as "Carnegie's law of surplus." Seeking a way out of the cycle of production beyond effective demand, industrialists were uniting to maintain the prices of their goods at remunerative levels. But Carnegie predicted that such monopolistic methods would prove futile as new firms offering cheaper products were inevitably drawn into the market. "The fashion of Trusts has but a short season to run," he assured readers.[18]

Four months later, Carnegie returned to the pages of the *North American Review* to consider the related problem of what he called "surplus wealth" as opposed to surplus goods. Calling for a longer view of corporate trusteeship than that of price-fixing schemes, he advocated redirecting surplus wealth from industry into philanthropy, protecting private profits from both self-destructive competition and popular outrage. Like Conant a few years later, he argued that the increasing concentration of wealth was as vital to social progress as the consolidation of manufacturing, so long as large fortunes no less than large factories were wisely managed. "It is well, nay, essential for the progress of the race, that the houses of some should be homes for all that is highest and best in literature and the arts, and for all the refinements of civilization," Carnegie wrote. Yet he shared, for different reasons, Addams's concern that the houses of a few had become so far removed from the homes of the many that "all intercourse between them is at an end," and "often there is friction between the employer and the employed, between capital and labor, and between rich and poor." The antidote to rising class strife for Carnegie lay not in a more equitable distribution of wealth, but in its more munificent management. Or as he put it, "The problem of our age is the proper administration of wealth, so that the ties of brotherhood may still bind together the rich and poor in harmonious relationship." Carnegie aimed to persuade those troubled by widening inequality to "intrust" men like himself with "a great part of the increased wealth of the community," while convincing his fellow capitalists to treat their private savings as a public resource. The "duty of the man of Wealth," he wrote, beyond providing "moderately" for his family, was "to consider all surplus revenues which come to him simply as trust funds, which he is called upon to administer, and strictly bound as a matter of duty to administer in the manner which, in his judgment, is best calculated to produce the most beneficial results for the community—the man of wealth thus becoming the mere agent and trustee for his poorer brethren, bringing to their service his superior wisdom, experience, and ability to administer, doing for them better than they would or could do for themselves."[19]

Carnegie envisioned a union of big business and philanthropy entailing a far-reaching reconstruction of the Anglo-American institution of the trust, which had long provided a vehicle for large estates to be privately administered for public purposes. Born of the bequests of wealthy families, the older charitable trusts that had governed hospitals, universities, libraries, museums, and other cultural institutions since William Douglass's day had been strictly limited by the directives of their donors, like early corporations restricted by their charters. The new philanthropic foundations endowed by Carnegie and like-minded corporate leaders, by contrast, exercised far greater autonomy in funding an ever-changing array of causes, from science and medicine to art and education. At the same time, their ongoing ability to support public projects derived from their latitude in investing their endowments in an equally diverse and flexible portfolio of assets calculated to produce the best earnings on behalf of the masses of recipients of their largesse. Viewing the market economy as a whole as the source of the funds that they administered, boards of trustees regarded the pursuit of the highest returns as their fiduciary responsibility to the society they served. If "the fashion of Trusts" proved more enduring than Carnegie at first foresaw, it was because it found a broader foundation than any enterprise or industry in the financial fund itself, and in the ethic of investment that he called "the true Gospel concerning Wealth."[20]

"Observe that metaphor of 'investment,'" wrote the English legal historian Frederic Maitland in 1904, recalling that the word originally referred to the act of putting on clothes. "We conceive that the 'trust fund' can change its dress, but maintain its identity. Today it appears as a piece of land; tomorrow it may be some gold coins in a purse; then it will be a sum of Consols; then it will be shares in a Railway Company, and then Peruvian Bonds. When all is going well, changes of investment may often be made; the trustees have been given power to make them. All along the 'trust fund' retains its identity. 'The price takes the place of the object,' we might say, 'and the object takes the place of the price.'" While Maitland proudly claimed the trust fund as the offspring of an idea conceived centuries earlier in English law, he acknowledged that the trust had gained unprecedented power in modern America through its marriage to corporate capital. "Of late years under American teaching, we have learned to couple together the two terms 'corporations' and 'trusts,'" he wrote, even as he contended that the aristocratic ancestor of the modern trust had contained at its core a contract not unlike that of its corporate descendant. But like the corporation, the trust had been fundamentally transformed by its capitalist reincarnation. It had evolved from an arrangement under which family estates controlled land into an agreement through which corporations combined to control prices, and finally into a fund with which financiers controlled savings. The price indeed took the place of the object, but only as the result of a long revolution in the basis of trust.[21]

What gave the trust unparalleled command over capital at the turn of the twentieth century was what had made it a "most powerful instrument of social experimentation" since its emergence in medieval England, according to Maitland: its extraordinary "elasticity." "It is an 'institute' of great elasticity and generality; as elastic, as general as contract," he wrote in his landmark lectures on the legal tradition of equity, in which the trust appeared as the most important English innovation.[22] Descended from the principles of "equity" and "conscience" with which the Roman Empire and the medieval church had administered their dominions over a diverse panoply of peoples, equitable jurisprudence manifested both the supremacy of the sovereign and his compassion and solicitude for the varying circumstances of his subjects. Equity conferred open-ended discretion on the king's chancellors to execute "extraordinary remedies" outside of the general rules, procedures, and protections of civil, canon, and common law, with special regard for the needs of those deemed incapable of exercising rights on their own behalf such as children, married women, paupers, foreigners, and the mentally ill.[23]

In inventing the trust, the English Court of Chancery brought the paternal authority at the heart of equity to bear on the institution of property. The trust created a structure under which one party legally owned property on another's behalf. It separated the legal right to *control* property, which reposed in the trustee, from the equitable right to *benefit* from it, which belonged to the beneficiary. It established between the two parties a fiduciary relationship—a bond based in principle on caretaking and confidence, like that between parents and children, guardians and wards, or lords and vassals. The idea of property as a trust, an office in which ownership formed the means of fulfilling social obligations, reflected its origins in a feudal system in which all English land officially belonged to the king, who entrusted it to his subjects in return for their service and allowed them to subdivide their holdings among tenants under a similar manorial responsibility. By the fourteenth century, legal restrictions and heavy taxes on the inheritance of land, originally enacted to enforce the Crown's claim on the lands of the kingdom, conflicted with its interest in encouraging the growing power and prosperity of the landowning class. Thus the trust was born, deploying the earlier notion of property as a social estate while enabling owners to devise land indirectly to their families by transferring title to trustees, bypassing legal limits on testamentary power. In granting increasing independence to landholders, the innovation of the trust further supported aristocratic families by providing a way for wealthy women to retain rights as beneficiaries to property that they brought into marriage, circumventing the common law of coverture under which married women could not own property in their own name.[24]

Charles Dickens's satire in *Bleak House* of an interminable trust case in Chancery captures the conservatism of the family trust in general: "Innumerable children have been born into the cause; innumerable young people have married into it; innumerable old people have died out of it."[25] Indeed, the flexible framework of the trust provided a cocoon for the conservation and transformation of wealth not just across generations, but across historical epochs and class regimes. Just as the locus of trust transferred from the king to landowning families in early modern England, so it shifted again in the early American republic, when both land ownership and families ran up against the limits of their capacities for accumulation under the changing rules of an emerging market society. Inheritance laws that had preserved landed estates in England—prohibiting heirs from selling off property held in "fee tail," preventing creditors from seizing land in settlement of debts, barring the division of estates among several sons when fathers died without a will—were abolished in the new nation, much as monarchical limits on devising land had fallen into abeyance with the development of the testamentary trust centuries before. As large landholdings became subject to partition, sale, and debt collection, the separation of legal rights to real property from beneficial rights to its economic value made the trust the model for American probate courts exercising equity powers in presiding over a sweeping reform of family estates. Treating land as a financial asset valued mainly for its market price, judges developed what Elizabeth Blackmar terms a "discipline of investment," requiring court-appointed trustees and executors to assume an active role in reorganizing estates as profit-making portfolios.[26]

Trust administrators heeded the rising mandate to make savings pay, providing a constant stream of revenues for beneficiaries, enhancing the value of trust assets, and maximizing estates' earnings from interest, dividends, and the buying and selling of properties. Aided by the liberality of trust law in Massachusetts, the mercantile families of Boston proved especially versatile in mobilizing their savings, giving rise to a new vocation of professional trustees to manage their investments. "Bostonians from the first showed their ability to adapt themselves to changing conditions. Wealth garnered from ventures associated with one type of enterprise was used to spur on and create new wealth in succeeding business undertakings," as Donald Holbrook wrote in his study of the "Boston trustee." A landmark Massachusetts Supreme Court ruling in 1829 released trustees from any continuing commitment to specific investments, instructing them instead to redistribute the savings under their charge as widely as they thought "prudent" to keep up with changing financial conditions. As Holbrook wrote of his profession, "No trust manager should be tied to a prescribed or set form of investment whose character or even substance itself might be altered or entirely disappear with the course of time."[27]

In detaching trusts from the financial constraints of the land and other assets they traditionally had held, the courts freed them from the families they had long served as well. Consolidating the fortunes of many families under centralized management, trustees gained authority to act in the collective interests of the estate itself, defying the demands of beneficiaries when they conflicted with the growth of the endowment. In a broader sense, trust managers were empowered to act on behalf of the whole class they helped to call into being as opposed to the narrow interests of individuals and families. As the Boston physician and writer Oliver Wendell Holmes Sr. wrote of the Brahmin elite in 1859, "The millionocracy, considered in a large way, is not at all an affair of persons and families, but a perpetual fact of money with a variable human element." The modern investment trust was distinguished from earlier family trusts by the breadth of the capital that it collected and directed, by the flexibility and diversity of its investments, and by its paramount devotion to the perpetuation of principal rather than payouts to beneficiaries. It embodied the impersonality and mutability of socialized savings like no other nineteenth-century institution, save for the modern business corporation with which it became enduringly linked.[28]

The limited-liability corporation, which gradually supplanted the family firm and the joint-stock company as the dominant form of business enterprise, arose from the same search for a new basis of trust with which to pool the savings and plan the investments of large numbers of unrelated individuals. Its defining characteristic, like that of the trust, was the separation of the income rights of shareholders (or beneficiaries) from the administrative rights of directors (or trustees). Trusts and corporations thus converged on a shared endeavor in the second half of the nineteenth century. Trusts played a central part in channeling the savings of northeastern capitalists into the new corporate securities of western railroads, mines, stockyards, and farm mortgages, while Boston trustees fanned out onto boards of directors throughout the country, much as "financial missionaries" like Conant soon spread the Yankee gospel of wealth to Latin America and Asia.[29]

Just as the trust had formed the model for the financial reform of land ownership in the early republic, so it provided the template for a reorganization of factory and railroad ownership in the Gilded Age. Arising in answer to the pervasive problem of overproduction, the "trustee device" found its first major use as a means of corporate consolidation in the oil industry, in which the need to limit output in order to maintain prices at profitable levels was both chronic and acute. In an 1879 agreement orchestrated by John D. Rockefeller, the stockholders of roughly forty companies controlling more than 90 percent of the nation's oil refining transferred their shares to a single board of trustees that would preside over the entire industry on their behalf, setting prices and production limits, opening and closing plants, distributing interest and dividends, and using surplus funds to buy out remaining competitors. Within a decade, the success of Standard Oil spawned similar agreements in other refining industries including cottonseed oil, linseed oil, sugar, and whiskey along with tobacco, cordage, lead, steel, and machine-making. By the time that Carnegie wrote "The Bugaboo of Trusts" in 1889, the word had taken on a new meaning. A "trust" meant an industrial monopoly, defined by the possession of sufficient control over production to control prices as well.[30]

Carnegie wrote in response to a rising antimonopoly movement that saw in the new combinations an arrogation of the powers of equity and a corruption of the office of trusteeship into a vehicle for private profit instead of social service. "The courts have no other function so high as the enforcement of equity, and when private enterprise puts on the cloak of chancery, calling itself a 'trust,' it is guilty of a species of imposition, one which at least justifies the presumption of fraud," the *Chicago Daily Tribune* commented in 1887. "The execution of a trust is not only the highest office of the judiciary, but one of its more sacred prerogatives. It is contrary to public policy, as the phrase is, for private corporations, or corporations organized for private gain, to assume the place reserved for the bench." In the late 1880s and early 1890s, a spate of state laws prohibiting agreements "in restraint of trade" along with a series of related state court cases marked the advent of the "trust question" in public discourse and the rise of what was popularly called "antitrust law," including most importantly the Sherman Antitrust Act passed by Congress in 1890.[31]

As stockholder agreements using the trustee device were struck down for violating the original corporate charters or for restraint of trade, business leaders created instead "holding companies" that owned outright either the financial securities or the physical assets of a host of smaller firms. Though they were often not trusts strictly speaking, the industrial behemoths that came to dominate mass production and distribution by the early twentieth century were predicated on the separation of ownership and management that originated in the law of trusts. The Supreme Court in the 1880s and 1890s bolstered the autonomy of boards of directors by granting their corporations full legal personhood as "natural entities," endowed with the same constitutional rights and due process protections as individuals. At the same time, the court extended property rights to encompass intangible assets, sanctioning stockholders' ownership of shares in the earnings of the enterprises in which they invested, or their beneficial claims to a "reasonable return on investment." The delineation of the respective rights of directors and investors provided the legal basis for the emergence of a mass market in industrial securities around 1900, representing what contemporaries dubbed the "trustification" of the corporation.[32]

Conversely, the same years witnessed the ultimate corporatization of the trust, with the rise of the trust company at the center of the new structure of investment on which the corporate reorganization of industry depended.[33] A distinctively American institution, the "corporate fiduciary" was born with the business of fire and life insurance in the 1820s and 1830s, when corporations entrusted with individuals' long-term savings were authorized to execute trusts and administer estates as well. As trust companies gained the power to receive deposits after the Civil War, they became essentially savings banks for the rich, paying 2–5 percent interest to depositors while investing their money in land mortgages and government bonds at higher rates. Commercial banks' "demand liabilities"—banknotes and deposits payable in coin on demand—generally barred them from engaging in long-term lending and from paying interest to account-holders, making trust companies more attractive to those with large savings to invest. Meanwhile, as bank loans more and more commonly took the form of credits to deposit accounts rather than banknotes in the postbellum era, national banks' exclusive power of note-issue declined in importance. Trust companies therefore increasingly competed with banks in short-term as well as long-term lending, creating "active accounts" paying lower interest rates from which borrowers could draw on demand along with "certificates of deposit" paying higher interest rates in exchange for depositors' forgoing the right to withdraw funds for a fixed term. As banking became their main business, trust companies accumulated enormous funds from corporate and individual depositors amid the spectacular growth of savings in the late nineteenth century. But the real ascendance of the trust company as the "department store of finance" came in the decade following the crisis of the mid-1890s, with the opening of a vast new field for investing surplus savings. The rapid development of the market for industrial stocks and bonds that fueled the great merger movement of the turn of the century thrust trust companies into a preeminent position in the new financial order, far outpacing state and national banks in their growth in numbers and deposits in the decade after 1895.[34]

Conant's career on the national and international stage rose with them. When he became treasurer of the Morton Trust Company of New York in 1902, he took charge of one of the country's largest investment funds. That same year, he heralded the reign of the trust company in an enthusiastic exposition of its vital new role for the *American Review of Reviews*, a leading journal of Progressive social thought. "The work of reorganizing old corporations and organizing new ones, taking up old securities and issuing new, which has been made necessary by the new enterprises, the consolidations, and the 'mergers' of the last few years, has fallen in a large measure to the trust companies of New York and one or two other large cities," Conant wrote. When a joint-stock company reorganized as a limited-liability corporation or when a new corporation formed, he explained, it naturally turned to a trust company as intermediary and "guardian for interests of the public on the one hand and the corporation on the other." National banks, whose notes, drafts, and checks served as the currency of everyday commerce, were prohibited by law from lending more than 10 percent of their capital to any single individual, firm, or corporation, and they were required to restrict their lending so as to be able to pay their depositors and note-holders in cash at any time. Trust companies' larger long-term deposits, concentrated in New York, gave them greater ability to advance investors the funds for the new securities, making them leading lenders on Wall Street.[35]

Almost overnight, it seemed, the trust companies had become the trustees of a great and growing share of the nation's surplus savings, planning and directing investment in factories, farms, railroads, and mines across the country, regulating the nascent corporate economy as a whole. "The savings, which the people of the entire country are realizing from increased production and improved trade, are poured into the New York money market almost as promptly and directly as a current of oil through one of the Standard Oil Company's pipe-lines," Conant wrote in 1907. ". . . The control of these vast sums, in the form of deposits and money for investment, has placed power in the hands of the men at the head of New York finance such as has seldom been possessed by the financiers of any country."[36]

The trust company stood as the institutional embodiment of an emerging social ideal, one that harked back to the paternal principles of equity while making the investment fund rather than the king, the court, the family estate, or even the business corporation the ultimate repository of trust. "The purely trust functions of the old-fashioned trust company are undoubtedly the highest development of the principle of credit and of confidence. They are the highest application of that principle to the relation of man to man in business," the U.S. comptroller of the currency, William Ridgely, told the recently formed Trust Company Section of the American Bankers Association in 1904, anchoring the new system of savings and investment in the venerable ideal of trust.[37] "Coincident with this tendency to great consolidations," wrote one of the leading authorities on the trust companies, Clay Herrick, in 1909, ". . . is the growing recognition among all classes of people of the value of associated effort. Here again the trust company finds itself in harmony with the times. . . . The trust company is emphatically an institution of the people. . . . It enables us to reap most of the advantages claimed for community of ownership, without the dangers that would come with the systems proposed by dogmatists."[38] In Conant's words, the individualism of classical political economy was giving way to "the principle of association and coöperation" embodied in the corporate fiduciary.[39]

More than a form of inheritance, business, or finance, the transformed trust represented a universal principle of social authority. It embodied a model of fiduciary relations not just between investors and directors, but between labor and capital, as Carnegie suggested, and between rich and poor countries, as Conant contended. Espoused in different ways by Carnegie and Conant, the ethic of investment formed a financial successor to what Ellen Meiksins Wood calls the early modern "ethic of improvement." Arising as an ideology of the landowning gentry in seventeenth-century England, improvement meant making land profitable by consolidating private property and employing the productive labor of tenants and their hired hands. It was both a general ethical ideal, eschewing waste and valuing work, and a specific rationale for landowners' property in the products of the labor and land they "improved."[40] The ethic of investment, by contrast, meant making savings profitable by consolidating and mobilizing surplus capital in the form of financial securities rather than landed estates. It likewise conceived a new "ethical subject," "the trustee as Economic Man," as Ritu Birla has written of late-imperial India at the turn of the century, while validating financiers' control of the funds they collected and invested.[41]

"How mighty is the influence of these few minds,—the inventors, the captains of industry, the resourceful authors of new combinations,—upon national economic progress is realized by few," Conant wrote in an essay titled "The Trusts and the Public" in 1904, comparing the earlier work ethic to a new wealth ethic.

> Plodding industry, which must ever be the virtue of the mass of men, accomplishes much; it is the foundation upon which all else is built. But plodding industry alone does not utilize new forces; it does not harness Niagara; it does not keep a nation at the forefront in the race with industrial rivals. The Chinese and several of the Latin peoples are perhaps to-day the equals, if not the superiors, of the Americans in their willingness to work and save; but these qualities are not sufficiently supplemented by those great powers of invention, initiative, and combination which give dominance in the modern world.[42]

In other words, the new basis of the wealth of nations was not simply productive industry but profitable investment. The wealth ethic joined the growing mass of savers to the rising class of money managers, and it linked the peoples of Asia and Latin America to the "great powers" of the United States and its European counterparts, in fiduciary relations defined by the transformation of trusteeship. "When enterprises became national and international in their scope, it was inevitable that they should look to the fund of free capital of the entire country for their support," Conant wrote three years later in "The Concentration of Capital in New York, and Those Who Manage It." ". . . It was natural also that such demands should develop a special type of men trained to deal with them—the masters of finance, upon whose decision depends the creation of new enterprises which promise benefits to the community, the abandonment or reorganization of old enterprises, whose benefits have ceased or have been surpassed by more modern and efficient machinery."[43]

The triumph of the trust fund required a parallel transformation of the currency and credit that it controlled. Calling for the establishment of "sound money" and an "elastic currency," Conant became a leading exponent of a federal reserve system in the United States and a "gold-exchange standard" abroad. Aiming to model the national and international monetary order on the creation of a community of capital in place of a producers' republic, he traced the century-long development of a society of investors.

"Pioneers of Credit": The Banking Frontier

For Conant, the roots of modern investment lay in small-town banking. Metropolitan "masters of finance" marshalling the nation's concentrated capital were fulfilling the same basic role as backcountry bankers administering the savings of their local communities. "In distributing between depositors, borrowers and his vaults the money intrusted to him," "the modern banker has become arbiter of the direction of investment, the organization of industry, and even of the fate of nations," Conant wrote, highlighting bankers' systematic selection of those borrowers who would generate the greatest return on depositors' savings. He continued, "In every growing community much of the real burden of deciding upon the course of its future development lies with the banker. It is for him to determine the relative marginal utility of one enterprise as compared with another and to grant his support to the enterprise which promises the highest utility and therefore the most certain profits. There rests upon the banker in a sense the vital function of trustee for the community in its dealings with itself. This trusteeship is especially sacred if he deals with the money of others, and not purely with money of his own." But the bank's responsibility extended beyond its circle of depositors to encompass all those who accepted its banknotes in payment, indirectly lending the value of their goods and services to the bank's borrowers. By using bank currency, every household, farm, and shop became an implicit investor in all the businesses to which bankers chose to lend. The local banker, Conant wrote, "is the trustee of the mechanism of credit for the entire community, whether its members are individually depositors with him or not."[44]

From the vantage of Wall Street, Main Street bankers appeared as the "pioneers of credit in their respective localities" whose banknotes "paved the way for other systems of credit which appealed to the direct initiative of the small capitalist," such as the stocks, bonds, and other negotiable securities in which trust companies specialized.[45] Small banks formed the tributaries of a long stream of savings flowing from depositors and note-holders like a "stream of water from a vast storage basin through mammoth supply pipes," fostering local enterprise, while larger banks channeled the surplus into investment in big business.[46] From Conant's perspective in the 1890s, the history of banking appeared as the story of the development of ever more efficient mechanisms for mobilizing savings and "transferring it from place to place and from industry to industry" in search of the most profitable investment for each additional dollar saved, beginning with banknotes and culminating with stock and commodity exchanges "by which the change of a fraction of one per cent in the rate indicating the demand for credit in one market would put at its command the surplus resources of other markets."[47]

By the mid-1890s, however, the multiplying means of capital mobility that formed the main theme of Conant's *History of Modern Banks of Issue* (1896) were proving unable to accommodate the staggering growth of surplus savings. As the main conduit for the accumulation of capital, the banking sector formed the crucible of crisis—though not its underlying cause, as Conant emphasized.[48] Hundreds of national, state, and private banks closed or collapsed in the panic of 1893. The ensuing depression galvanized a political movement among business leaders and bankers seeking fundamental reform of the system of banking and currency.[49] The controversy over the role of banking in the crisis sparked intellectual innovation as well, marking a pivotal period in monetary economics comparable to the seminal debate over bullion and banknotes in England at the beginning of the nineteenth century.[50] By his own account, Conant's two-volume treatise, *The Principles of Money and Banking* (1905), was one of the first comprehensive studies of the subject, based on his role as a leading theorist of banking reform.[51]

In 1894, Conant had run for Congress from the wealthy Eighth District of Massachusetts, including Boston's Back Bay and Cambridge, having established his reputation as an authority on financial issues through his work as Washington correspondent for the *New York Journal of Commerce*. He joined the gold-standard wing of the Democratic Party aligned with President Grover Cleveland, who had pushed Congress to repeal the Sherman Silver Purchase Act of 1890, eliminating one of the last vestiges of bimetallism. Though defeated in 1894 as part of a historic Republican landslide, Conant was elected as a delegate to the convention of dissident "Gold Democrats" in 1896, organized in opposition to the free-silver candidacy of William Jennings Bryan for president.[52] "The decision which has been made by the majority of voters in favor of the gold standard is, in some sense, only a negative decision, and merely clears the ground for the radical reforms which are needed, in order to place our currency system upon a scientific basis and make it responsive to the legitimate needs of business," Conant wrote in the aftermath of Bryan's loss to William McKinley, explaining the immediate motive for his study of the history of banking. "The financial ills from which the United States have suffered in recent years cannot be permanently cured by a political victory over the forces of discontent. A defective currency system has undoubtedly been one among several causes which have contributed to recent agitation, and the political party which has the judgment and the courage to reform the system will do much to commend itself to the intelligent support of the American people."[53] Indeed, the business leaders' and bankers' campaign for currency reform, which propelled Conant from journalism into a powerful policy-making role, arose in direct response to the Populist movement. Co-opting agrarian calls for an elastic currency and low-interest loans for farmers, the corporate movement countered more radical demands for public, democratic, legislative control of currency and credit by advancing a far more conservative model of financial trusteeship by bankers in league with the executive branch of the federal government.

Seeking to frame the agenda for financial reform on their own terms, representatives of boards of trade, chambers of commerce, and other business groups from twenty-six states and the District of Columbia gathered in January 1897 for a monetary convention headed by the Indianapolis manufacturer Hugh H. Hanna. The convention led later that year to the appointment of a private commission to devise a platform, with Conant playing a critical part as Hanna's assistant. But Conant's major contribution to the new movement came in his two treatises and numerous articles on banking, in which he systematically related the glut of savings depressing investment and industry in the metropolitan Northeast to the scarcity of currency and credit sparking Populist protest in the rural South and West. He found a solution in staking out a new financial frontier on the border between country banking and corporate investment, much as Jane Addams viewed social settlements as an ideal answer to "the overaccumulation at one end of society and the destitution at the other."[54]

Conant's equivalent of the settlement house was a commercial bank setting up shop in a "new country" such as the southern upcountry or the midwestern plains. With little capital and few if any depositors, the bank would simply lend out its own banknotes in exchange for the short-term IOUs of small farmers and traders, collecting the principal and interest in specie when borrowers sold their goods and their notes came due. As long as its officers ensured that money flowed into the bank's coffers as steadily as its notes flowed out, it would stand ready to redeem its notes in cash whenever note-holders demanded it, and the bank could safely increase or decrease its lending as needed to meet the demands of local trade. Such a system was ideally suited to meet "the needs of rural districts and especially of the producing and laboring classes," who had the least savings and familiarity with banking but the most need for short-term credit and cheap currency. In principle, Conant noted, their extraordinary elasticity could make banknotes an especially important instrument for farmers, alleviating the seasonal stringency that depressed the prices of cotton and other crops at harvest time, which the subtreasury plan of the Farmers' Alliance had been designed to address. So too, an elastic supply of banknotes could free cash-poor farmers from "serfdom to the storekeeper" and the crop-lien system afflicting the southern states in particular. By "introducing the use of credit and stimulating the production of commodities and the transfer of capital" in the agricultural hinterland, the note-issuing country bank "paves the way for deposit banking" and other more sophisticated means of mobilizing savings for investment, Conant wrote. "The bank-note," he quoted the contemporary French economist Léon Say (grandson of the author of "Say's law"), "is the deposit account of humble citizens and small merchants."[55]

In practice, however, banknotes were in increasingly short supply relative to the demand for them in the South and West, even as surplus savings piled up in the East. Conant agreed with the Populists that the dearth of currency and credit severely suppressed consumer demand for the excess output of farm staples and manufactured goods. "This poverty of the means of carrying on transactions is a striking feature of the condition of many parts of the Southern and Western sections of the United States," Conant wrote, "and the remedy lies in an expansive currency which shall make exchange easier and afford the buyer of credit an instrument which he can readily use."[56] What constricted the currency was a set of restrictions on the issuance of banknotes under the National Banking System established during the Civil War: a 10 percent tax on notes issued by state banks, which effectively limited the power of note-issue to national banks; a requirement that national banks hold a share of their capital in U.S. Treasury bonds, which, along with other capital requirements, made national banks scarce in capital-poor regions of the country; and a requirement that the banks limit their note-issue to 90 percent of the face value of the bonds they held. As the price of government securities rose steadily in the late nineteenth century—the government sought to borrow less, while the glut of savings made bondholders willing to pay more—the supply of bond-based banknotes contracted relative to the volume of transactions for which they were required. "The public, under these circumstances," Conant wrote, "have looked to other sources than the banks for a circulating medium, and found it, until the repeal of the purchasing clause of the Sherman law, in purchases of silver bullion, by the Treasury, and the issue of government paper money in payment for the bullion."[57]

Contrary to agrarian currency reformers, however, Conant argued that the real remedy for the inadequate supply lay in reforming the legal basis of the banknotes, not in returning to the old alternatives of government-issued greenbacks or silver coins. The "chief object" of his history of banking was to "convince thinking Americans of the axiomatic truth that—*The currency of a commercial country should be regulated by commercial conditions and not by the whims of politicians*." Only a paper currency issued by banks in the course of commercial lending was actually created by the transactions for which it was called into use. Only a "banking currency, when not disturbed by the public authority, except to enforce uniformity, safety, and convertibility with coin, is automatically responsive to the demands of business." Only banks, through the interest rates that they charged for commercial loans, controlled the market price of currency itself (as opposed to the price of precious metals or government bonds), which was the most powerful instrument for regulating as well as responding to commercial demand for the means of exchange. Finally, only well-managed banks, through their control of "quick assets" such as short-term commercial paper that could be quickly converted into cash, always stood ready to pay cash for their own notes. Banks were therefore uniquely capable of maintaining the currency that they issued at parity with coin, which was essential to upholding the role of money as a standard of value.[58]

"The touchstone of a sound banking currency is redemption in standard coin on demand," Conant wrote. It was the necessity of redeeming their notes in cash on demand that compelled banks to limit their loans to the value of their capital and cashable assets, or in other words, to tether the supply of bank currency to the needs of trade, which were represented by the commercial bills against which banknotes were issued. Conant stressed that redemption in coin did not call for tying the supply of currency tightly to the supply of coin, as Populist advocates of silver coinage and more conservative defenders of gold-based currency did. It rather entailed requiring banks to maintain in specie reserves just a fraction of the value of their deposit accounts and circulating notes, while allowing the currency they created to fluctuate freely with the volume of commercial IOUs presented for discount in exchange. In keeping with the so-called banking principle espoused by most contemporary bankers and economists, Conant explained that banknotes were essentially no different than the commercial bills for which they were exchanged, except that they were more widely accepted. They were promises to pay coin on demand, just as commercial bills were promises to deliver wheat, cotton, or other commodities. "It is not necessary in either case that the signer of the engagement should possess the full amount of the commodity which he promises; it is only necessary that his reputation and other forms of property should inspire confidence in his ability to fulfill the promise." Like that of any other business, the solvency of a bank depended on the sufficiency of all of its assets or credits, not just what it kept in its vaults, to cover its debts. Commercial banks were properly restricted in the *kinds* of assets they could acquire or loans they could make, according to Conant; they could not make long-term loans backed by land or real property in industrial enterprises because such securities could not be turned into cash whenever it was demanded. But banks should not be limited any more than any other business in the *amount* of their assets (including loans) and liabilities (including deposits and notes), so long as the former could cover the latter. In other words, banks should not be restricted in the quantity of currency they pumped into circulation, so long as they did so in the course of responsible short-term commercial lending. Freed from undue restrictions regarding their cash or capital in government bonds, banks could supply the "expansive currency" that an expanding economy and its seasons and cycles demanded.[59]

The merits of such an "expansive theory" of banking had become increasingly apparent, Conant argued, as banks had developed more sophisticated forms of credit and currency to mobilize the growing fund of savings. Since the Civil War, the use of demand deposits and checking accounts had risen much faster than that of banknotes, constituting "much the most important part of the medium of exchange" by the 1890s. Unburdened by the outdated laws that constricted the supply of banknotes in the South and West, the proliferating paper currency arising from the growth of deposits in the Northeast was much more responsive to the vicissitudes of business activity. Forming "the great element of elasticity in the tool of exchange," the burgeoning bank currency born of surplus savings for investment provided a model for the reform of banknotes as well. "Such currency under sound business conditions is convertible into metallic money, just as are the more formal kinds of currency in the form of printed notes," Conant wrote, but the circulation of checks, drafts, and other transferable credit instruments based on deposits was displacing coins in all but the smallest retail transactions. Modern banking methods "have reduced the demand for gold to a very small percentage of the total demand for currency and a still smaller percentage of the total demand for means of payment. Gold has come to be required chiefly for cash payments of small amount in retail trade and for bank reserves." Further "economies in the use of gold" were made possible by modern means of communication including the cable, the telegraph, and the telephone, allowing credits to cross the country and the ocean almost immediately so that more and more long-distance transactions could be conducted on the basis of "a given sum of gold."[60]

Dedicated to the dual promise of "sound money" and an "elastic currency," the movement for banking reform achieved its first major success in the Gold Standard Act of 1900, informed partly by Conant's work. Intended to extend the soundness and elasticity of deposit banking to banknotes, the act required the Treasury to maintain parity between gold and all forms of legal money while reducing the federal tax on banknotes, permitting national banks to issue notes up to 100 percent of the face value of the government bonds that they held (instead of up to 90 percent), and refunding many bonds at lower rates so as to provide a broader base for banknotes.[61] The Gold Standard Act marked the beginning of a larger corporate reform designed to entrust the currency of the "producing and laboring classes" wholly to note-issuing commercial banks, liberated from the lingering constraints of government-issued greenbacks, bonds, and coins, while trust companies took charge of the deposit savings of capitalists and corporations. Conant and his allies envisioned a parallel form of trusteeship in which bigger banks would increasingly control the gold reserves of smaller ones, so that the solvency of each bank and its community of creditors would come to rest on that of the banking system as a whole. "It may prove advisable to concentrate the actual coin holdings in the hands of a few strong banks, whose notes are substituted for coin in redemptions by the smaller banks," Conant wrote in 1896. ". . . The essential point is that there shall be an ultimate coin reserve somewhere, upon which the circulation of all the banks actually rests."[62]

After the development of banknotes and the subsequent shift toward checks and deposits, the third stage in Conant's history of modern banking consisted of the concentration of capital in a small number of big banks as well as insurance and trust companies located in the "chief reserve cities," including Chicago, St. Louis, and especially New York. The centralization of bank funds reflected and facilitated the corporate consolidation of other industries, which demanded financial institutions capable of accumulating the resources and distributing the risks of mass production for a world market.[63] But while the management of savings had become increasingly concentrated, the issuance of currency had remained fragmented since the demise of the Second Bank of the United States in the 1830s, even under the aegis of the National Banking System, which governed a declining share of the means of exchange due to the growth of deposit banking in the late nineteenth century. England and France, Conant noted, had each granted exclusive control over banknotes and currency issues more generally to central banks since the

1840s. With its vast fund of surplus savings, he argued, the sprawling banking system of the United States required a comparable central authority to manage currency and credit and respond to crises. Its main instruments would be its control of the nation's gold reserves and its influence over interest rates as a lender to smaller banks, representing the fourth and final stage in the progress of banking.[64]

In December 1905, the New York Chamber of Commerce, which included among its members the nation's largest financial institutions, appointed Conant and four other financiers to a commission on the currency. The commission issued its report the following year, recommending the establishment of a central bank with branches in leading cities. A special commission of the American Bankers' Association (ABA) advocated a similar plan, likewise calling for self-regulation of the banking sector by leading banks. The panic of 1907 spurred the creation of a National Monetary Commission (NMC) under the direction of Senator Nelson Aldrich of Rhode Island, hiring Conant as a key staff member.[65] The combined efforts of the chamber of commerce, the ABA, and the NMC were channeled into what became the "Aldrich bill," calling for a highly centralized structure dominated by bankers and business leaders, which would issue currency, set national discount rates, and supervise branch banks.

In 1909, Conant wrote an influential fourteen-part series for the *Wall Street Journal*, making the case for a central bank. One of its primary purposes, he wrote, would be "giving elasticity to the currency" by issuing its own notes, which the central bank would put into circulation by exchanging them for the notes of smaller banks ("rediscounting"), which would exchange them in turn for commercial bills. "Moderate and reasonable provisions for the gradual substitution of the notes of the central bank for those of the local banks would soon bring order and a sense of security into our currency system," he wrote. At the same time, the "centralization of reserves" by the bank "would greatly increase the financial power of the country by permitting the use of those reserves at all times where they were the most effective." The bank would "afford a reservoir of unimpeachable credit and adequate currency resources in time of stress." It would "regulate the ebb and flow of capital" through "changes in the discount rate," the interest rate it charged to other banks. "In these matters a central bank would exercise the function of leadership—of giving definite form and substance without delay to policies obviously sound, but which nobody under the present system has power to inaugurate effectively," Conant wrote. Crucially, as he saw it, the effectiveness of such a central bank depended on its independence from government in its ownership and largely in its management as well. While representatives of the federal government might serve on the bank's managing board, their "essential function," he insisted, "should be negative rather positive—not to devise constructive policies, but to check unwise policies."[66]

Created by Congress in 1913, the Federal Reserve System (FRS) represented a compromise between the New York–centered corporate banking reform movement and agrarian interests from the South and West that had been pushing since the Populist campaigns of the 1890s for public accountability, monetary flexibility, provisions for moving funds to the agricultural periphery at harvest time, and access to affordable loans for family farmers. The law created a more decentralized structure than the Aldrich bill, with greater public oversight and significant concessions on agricultural credit. The new currency of Federal Reserve notes was made an obligation of the U.S. government rather than the issuing banks, and the Federal Reserve Board comprised five members appointed by the U.S. president along with the comptroller of the currency and the secretary of the treasury serving ex-officio. These public officials were granted broad supervisory authority over the twelve regional reserve banks, and only a third of the board of directors of each regional bank could be stockholders, directors, or employees of banks themselves. Yet the establishment of the FRS decisively removed monetary policy from the legislative arena, creating a powerful administrative agency that insulated the banking system from popular challenges. As James Livingston has argued, the Federal Reserve was designed "to depoliticize issues of money and banking, to place such issues beyond the reach of political debate," while empowering the reserve banks to act on behalf of the banking system as a whole and the total fund of savings it directed.[67]

Nevertheless, Conant sounded a cautionary note regarding the limits of what the banking system alone could achieve. Reflecting on the passage of the Federal Reserve Act, he noted in 1914 that the reserve banks were like other commercial banks in being limited by law to short-term commercial lending. "Even if completely successful in its proper field, of giving flexibility and sufficiency to short-term credit for commercial purposes, the law will affect only in a way very indirect the market for investment credit for long terms."[68] Indeed, his own work in monetary theory pushed strongly against the idea that commercial interest rates could effectively regulate the supply and demand for savings and goods along with the supply and demand for money. The "organization of capital" through the banking sector could ameliorate seasonal fluctuations, geographical disparities, and periodic crises. But Conant believed such reforms could not address the long-term crisis posed by the accumulation of surplus savings without also opening new avenues for profitable investment abroad, which required comparable restructuring of currency and banking in the developing countries of Latin America and Asia to which American capital now turned.[69]

"The Rule of Gold": The Empire of Investment

The ascendance of gold as the standard of value went hand in hand with its increasing obsolescence as a medium of exchange. Surveying the reign of the international gold standard in 1930, John Maynard Keynes observed that the more the gold basis of currency came to be universally respected, the more gold itself tended to disappear from use in favor of paper notes and token coins, aside from occasional transfers of gold reserves among central banks. "It is not a far step from this to the beginning of arrangements between Central Banks by which, without ever formally renouncing the rule of gold, the quantity of metal actually buried in their vaults may come to stand, by a modern alchemy, for what they please, and its value for what they choose," Keynes wrote. "Thus gold, originally stationed in heaven with his consort silver, as Sun and Moon, having first doffed his sacred attributes and come to earth as an autocrat, may next descend to the sober status of a constitutional king with a cabinet of Banks; and it may never be necessary to proclaim a Republic."[70]

No less powerful for being increasingly invisible, the gold standard indeed represented a new form of global governance by the cabinet of bankers who ruled in its name. Two months after the Gold Standard Act was signed into law in 1900, Conant associated the dawning era of economic integration with another golden rule: "the rule taught by the Saviour of men—'All things whatsoever ye would that men should do unto you, do ye even so to them'; or, in its simpler form, 'Thou shalt love thy neighbor as thyself.'" In a Memorial Day address in his native Winchester, Conant implicitly identified the spread of the gold standard with "that high standard which makes every man one's neighbor," embodied in "those economic laws under which are being worked out the vital problems of our time." He celebrated the abolition of slavery and the passage of protective labor laws ensuring that "the door stands open" for the American worker to "attain the highest position for which he is fitted." But he declared that these recent achievements would remain incomplete until the United States extended like opportunities to its "neighbors" across the Caribbean and the Pacific. Much as Jane Addams urged affluent Americans to make new homes in poor immigrant neighborhoods, Conant called for an "open door" not simply for free trade and immigration but for direct investment in the economic development of the nation's new colonies and dependencies. Unlike older forms of commercial empire, the new empire of investment would provide much-needed employment for American capital as well as labor while "carrying order, civilization, and justice to the distant islands of the sea."[71]

A precursor of the more critical theories of John A. Hobson and Vladimir Lenin, Conant's enthusiastic vision of imperial investment depended on the spread of the gold standard from the Atlantic core to the Pacific periphery of capitalist development at the turn of the twentieth century. Integrating the silver-based economies of Mexico, China, and their respective regions into the gold-based economy of international finance appeared essential in order to make long-term investment in the colonies attractive for metropolitan capital, and, he suggested, in order to liberate colonial producers from a predatory pattern of staple production without industrial development.[72] But the golden rule of empire for Conant was equity, not equality. In the nation's island possessions as on the American mainland, the ethic of investment was bound up with the ideal of trusteeship. "American liberty, like English liberty, has been a plant of slow growth," which cannot be "torn up by the roots and transplanted in its entirety to foreign soil," he wrote.[73] "When a Statute declared that the Herrschaft [rule] which the East India Company had acquired in India was held 'in trust' for the Crown of Great Britain, that was no idle proposition but the settlement of a great dispute," as Frederic Maitland observed in 1904. "It is only the other day that American judges were saying that the United States acquired the sovereignty of Cuba upon trust for the Cubans."[74]

Colonial trusteeship was central to a broader revival of the tradition of equity at the turn of the century. As Nancy Buenger has shown, the American adoption of equitable procedures and paternalistic principles in the colonies of Puerto Rico and the Philippines was closely linked to parental notions of municipal governance in Chicago and other cities. Under the banner of "home rule," Progressive reformers campaigned for special treatment of women, children, and immigrants before the law, broadly modeled on familial government of household dependents, as in Chicago's new juvenile and municipal courts. At the same time, the Supreme Court and the Bureau of Insular Affairs employed the same rationale regarding the colonial government's role as *parens patriae* in administering the former Spanish territories.[75] While specifically applied to the "unincorporated territories" conquered in the Spanish-American and Philippines War, notions of trusteeship provided the justification for U.S. control over the protectorate of Cuba, the canal zone of Panama, and the custom houses in the Dominican Republic as well for colonial governance of Puerto Rico and the Philippines. "Only by the firm hand of the responsible governing races . . . can the assurance of uninterrupted progress be conveyed to the tropical and undeveloped countries," Conant wrote. "This duty, imposed upon the superior races by the evolution of events, if not by the moral order, affords the opportunity for the absorption of the surplus of savings not applied to current consumption which is going on under the existing social system."[76] While white racism divided the ranks of agrarian and Populist reform, posing perhaps the greatest internal obstacle to a united movement for democratic finance, notions of Anglo-Saxon supremacy were integral to the ideology of investment imperialism that Conant articulated. As the author of a new currency system in the Philippines that became a model for other countries in Latin America and Asia, and as the preeminent exponent of "dollar diplomacy," he predicated his vision of Progressive foreign policy on the principles of financial trusteeship.

"The necessity of sending capital abroad to obtain profitable returns is the salient economic lesson of the closing days of the nineteenth century," he wrote in one of a series of articles on what he called "the economic basis of imperialism" during the Spanish-American and Philippines War. There were logically three possible ways of resolving the "congestion of capital in excess of legitimate demand," the fundamental cause of economic crisis in the advanced industrial countries, according to Conant. One was "the socialistic solution of the abandonment of saving, the application of the whole earnings of the laborer to current consumption," which he dismissed as unlikely and unwise. A second was "the creation of new demands at home for the absorption of capital," but "the proportion of capital to be absorbed was so great in proportion to possible new demands" that he deemed this an inadequate solution as well. "Aside from the waste of capital in war, which is only a form of consumption, there remains, therefore, as the final resource, the equipment of new countries with the means of production and exchange," he wrote.[77]

In line with the theory of marginal utility at the heart of neoclassical economics, Conant explained that capital would wield the greatest "earning power" in countries with little accumulated savings of their own, and increased returns abroad would raise the "rental" value of capital at home as well. The growth of international finance had made it possible for capitalists to invest in "new countries" not simply by lending money, but by selling the materials required for the means of production, transportation, and communication on credit. Developing countries "have not only to obtain buildings and machinery,—the necessary elements in producing machine-made goods,—but they have to build their roads, drain their marshes, dam their rivers, build the aqueducts for their water supplies and sewers for their towns and cities," Conant wrote. He foresaw a great wave of railroad construction across Asia and Africa comparable to the rise of the transcontinental railroads in advanced countries in the mid-nineteenth century, along with a building boom in mines and factories. "These openings for capital promise to absorb many millions within the next ten or twenty years." As Great Britain, Germany, France, Belgium, and Russia raced to invest in colonial economic development, it became urgent for the United States to stake its own claim so as "not to be crowded to the wall by the efforts of the other great civilized powers." "The people which has invested considerable amounts of its surplus capital in foreign countries has cast off its swaddling clothes and is ready to take rank among the financial powers of the world," Conant wrote, warning in 1907 that "the United States will not become a first-class financial power until its investments abroad are much more extended than at present."[78]

Such a long-term commitment of American savings in undeveloped countries would require a close partnership of finance capital and colonial government, Conant noted. Earlier international loans had often been jeopardized by "revolutionary governments, where unwise financiering, official corruption, and the adoption of an irredeemable paper currency have wrecked business and frightened away foreign capital," he wrote on the heels of the revolutions in Cuba and the Philippines. "A new era is opening for such investments, under the protection of responsible powers, whether a direct guarantee of the interest is given by the powers themselves, or reliance is placed upon the governing capacity of the men of the Anglo-Saxon or other European races, who exercise indirectly the control over the finances of the protected country."[79] Along with provisions to ensure that taxes were collected and public debts were paid, the paramount requirement was the establishment of colonial currency systems that would guarantee "that investments there can be realized upon at any time in the standard money of the world," that is, gold, as Conant wrote in a 1901 report on the currency of the Philippines. "In this respect the proper regulation of the currency is more important than the regulations governing almost any other single branch of the public administration or those affecting any one or several industries."[80] The danger of depreciation of local currencies based on silver threatened the principal and dividends of any international loans made in gold-based dollars. Reconstructing colonial currencies on the basis of the gold standard was therefore more fundamental than safeguarding systems of taxing and spending in attracting foreign investment, as Conant explained in an article ten years later on monetary reform in Latin America. "Fiscal reform means the restoration of a favorable balance to the budget and the prompt payment of interest on public obligations. Monetary reform reaches deeper into the heart of commercial affairs, because it alone makes possible the free interchange of products and the investment of foreign capital upon a basis which ensures its permanency in gold value."[81]

In the wake of the Gold Standard Act of 1900 and the U.S. conquests in the Caribbean and across the Pacific, Conant's work on the importance of extending the gold standard to silver-based colonies became central to American foreign policy. Secretary of War Elihu Root commissioned him to study the currency system in the Philippines, where he worked closely with the U.S. territorial governor, William Howard Taft (a major promoter of the legal tradition of equity in colonial governance), in devising a plan for monetary reform. Enacted by the U.S. Congress in 1903, Conant's plan for the Philippines formed the template for parallel currency reforms in Mexico, Nicaragua, Panama, and the Dominican Republic over the next few years, and for extensive efforts to bring China onto the gold standard. As Emily Rosenberg has written, Conant became the principal founder of the profession of foreign financial advising in the United States.[82]

The financial face of American empire was the "gold-exchange standard," a formula for a gold standard of value with a silver means of exchange that Conant developed in the Philippines and espoused with an evangelical zeal comparable to Charles Macune's promotion of the subtreasury plan.[83] First introduced in British India in 1893, the gold-exchange standard came to represent for Conant "a new monetary system" that "blazed a new path in the principles of money," promising to revolutionize monetary theory and practice not only in peripheral countries, but in advanced industrial nations as well. It was, he wrote, essentially "an extension of the banknote system to token coins," carrying to its conclusion the logic of the campaign for "sound money" and "elastic currency" in the United States.[84] Indeed, the idea of creating a managed currency of token silver coins convertible into gold-standard money at a fixed rate was actually a systematization of a practice that had arisen in a piecemeal fashion in the United States and other bimetallic countries as they converted to the gold standard in the late nineteenth century. "Events are stronger than theories in shaping economic tendencies," as Conant wrote.[85] Yet the theory that emerged from the practice of a token currency with a fixed standard anticipated the advent of an entirely token or "fiat" currency controlled by central bankers in the twentieth century, revealing that the "rule of gold" hardly required gold itself. For the real basis of the currency that Conant helped to create was not the market value of gold, but the fiat of organized capital.[86]

"Belief in the gold standard was the faith of the age," Karl Polanyi wrote of "nineteenth-century civilization."[87] Yet until the 1870s, Britain was virtually alone in making gold its sole monetary standard, and silver coins circulated as legal tender in most of Europe and the United States until the 1890s. Bimetallism had enjoyed broad support in the French and American republics since the Revolutionary Era, allowing for unlimited coinage of both gold and silver while defining the unit of account—the dollar or franc—as a legally fixed quantity of either metal. Since a fall in the market value of gold strongly tended to be balanced by a rise in the value of silver and vice versa, a bimetallic standard was designed to prevent the value of money from fluctuating with that of either precious metal, so long as their legal ratio was occasionally adjusted to reflect changes in the ratio of their respective market values, which hovered around 15.5 ounces of silver to 1 ounce of gold for more than seventy-five years. By the mid-nineteenth century, however, the rising dominance of London and the British pound sterling in international trade and finance had spurred European and American import-export merchants and financiers to favor an international gold standard. In the 1870s, they got their wish, as large silver discoveries in the United States triggered a steep decline in the gold price of silver that continued for the remainder of the century. Germany converted to gold in 1871, and France and its allies in the so-called Latin Monetary Union (Belgium, Switzerland, Italy, and Greece) followed suit in order to avoid losing all their gold and becoming de facto silver-standard countries at a growing commercial disadvantage. The United States ceased free coinage of silver dollars in 1873 and made greenbacks and banknotes redeemable in gold in 1879. By 1880, every major trading nation had adopted the gold standard in swift succession, beginning a period of unprecedented integration of international markets that lasted until the First World War.[88]

While silver ceased to serve as a standard of value, it still circulated as currency in gold-standard countries. Responding to mining interests and to the demands of interior manufacturers and farmers for cheap currency to counter falling commodity prices, the United States and the nations of the Latin Monetary Union continued to mint silver coins. Like copper coins and the small-change silver coins that had been issued earlier, the silver dollars minted in the 1880s and early 1890s were "token" coins: though they were still legal tender, their output was controlled by the Treasury ("on government account"), and their metallic content was reduced well below their face value, which derived from the government's promise to redeem them in gold-standard money at a fixed rate. "Silver limps along behind gold, without enjoying the privilege of free coinage accorded to the standard metal, but nevertheless finding a large use as money, and kept at par with the standard," as Conant explained in a 1903 article on "the limping standard." The French economist Léon Walras in 1886 gave systematic sanction to the ad hoc policy of maintaining a sound fractional (as opposed to "full-bodied") coinage legally redeemable in gold, akin to banknotes based on fractional reserves. In 1899, the Indianapolis Monetary Commission, for which Conant served as a key adviser, codified the "laws of token money": controlled coinage of limited quantities of a subsidiary metal on government account, redeemable in the standard money with which it was kept at par. This "standard formula" for an elastic token coinage for domestic commerce coupled to a gold standard for international trade provided the basic structure for Conant's vision of colonial currency.[89]

By the turn of the century, the gold standard reigned over the north Atlantic homelands of industrial capitalism. But the silver standard prevailed across the Pacific from Central America to Southeast Asia, a legacy of the circuit of Spanish silver from American mines to Chinese merchants that had fueled world trade since the sixteenth century.[90] When Conant took up his three-month commission in the Philippines in the summer of 1901, he arrived in a vast commercial region where the Mexican silver dollar served as the international standard of value and the main means of market exchange, stretching from the Dutch colonies of Sumatra and Borneo to British Hong Kong and Singapore, French Indochina, and coastal China. The spread of the gold standard in all the major imperial powers and the rapid depreciation of silver in terms of gold had created a widening monetary gulf between East and West.[91]

"The rupture of the par of exchange between gold and silver countries has undoubtedly done much to divide the world into two halves, those using gold and those using silver," Conant wrote. "It has tended to congest unused capital in the rich countries, with a depressing effect upon rates of interest . . . and has left the silver countries to struggle along with insufficient means for developing the treasures of nature which are locked in their soil."[92] Trade between gold and silver countries was seriously hampered by fluctuations in the exchange rate, so that transpacific merchants were forced either to run large risks or to price their goods so high as to cover any potential losses. But the more damaging consequence of the growing gap between the silver and gold worlds, according to Conant, was its deterrence of direct international investment in new enterprises and the expansion of existing ones. Western investors who borrowed money to buy negotiable securities at 3–5 percent interest could not afford to see their profits swallowed up by the comparable cost of exchange between revenues earned in silver and debts owed in gold. Filipino or Mexican farmers, industrialists, and bankers who borrowed in U.S. dollars or British pounds likewise found the costs of transferring capital prohibitive. "For this reason the accumulated capital of the great civilized countries has in recent years refused to seek investment in silver countries," Conant wrote, while "the borrower in a silver country can under present conditions look for no aid abroad" and is therefore "prevented from taking any steps to develop the natural resources of the country." He concluded: "Since it is in the gold-standard countries that the great surplus of capital has been accumulated, which is now being offered in the world's money markets for the development of the tropical countries, it is absolutely essential that monetary legislation . . . should be such as to attract the investors of these countries. Experience has demonstrated that capital seeking investment can be attracted in no other way than by the adoption and maintenance of the gold standard."[93]

Conant recognized, however, that simply converting from a plentiful silver currency to a scarce gold currency was no more practical in Asia or Latin America than it had been in the American South and West. Whereas monetary reform in the United States had arisen in response to economic depression and agrarian resistance, in the Philippines it was imposed in the face of a five-year revolutionary struggle against colonial rule, which had just ended when Conant arrived. The new colonial government complained of exorbitant losses from paying soldiers, laborers, and suppliers in U.S. dollars while receiving revenues in Spanish or Mexican coins. At the same time, British, German, and American merchants in Manila, sugar, hemp, and tobacco planters in the provinces, and the Chinese traders who managed most of the trade between them sought to protect the competitive advantage they enjoyed by paying workers and suppliers in silver while selling their exports for gold-based dollars and pounds.[94] "The American Government found in the Philippine Islands upon their cession by Spain a condition as chaotic in monetary affairs as in civil administration," Conant reported in 1902, highlighting the need for a new currency to serve as a means of rule as well as a means of exchange.[95]

Conant sympathized with Filipino planters and entrepreneurs who warned that a shift from silver to gold currency would incite workers to demand higher wages, as had recently occurred in a wave of strikes in Puerto Rico. Gold could not be subdivided into small enough coins to provide a practical means of paying wages as low as forty cents a day in silver for skilled labor, he wrote. Filipino workers, many of whom had served in the defeated fight for independence, would likely resist being paid fifty cents in gold instead of a dollar in silver even though that was the rate of exchange in foreign trade, rightly expecting that local storekeepers would not lower the prices of food and other basic necessities accordingly. "Silver is the natural money of undeveloped countries, where the scale of wages is low, and such countries can only be given the benefits of the gold standard, without detriment to their interests, by some system which combines the large use of silver with measures for linking it closely to gold values," Conant wrote.[96]

In principle, an expansive banknote currency backed by gold in reserve banks, such as Conant advocated in the United States, could best meet the requirements of new colonies as well, offering "a much greater economy" by obviating the need for either silver or gold in most market transactions. "The practical problem, however, with which statesmen have to deal, is the prejudice of the peoples of the East, and many of those of the West, for a currency of ringing metal rather than one of paper," he wrote. "The recognition of money as a commodity is instinctive among primitive peoples, and leads them to prefer a form of money which possesses tangible value in itself, and permits a more satisfying form of ostentation than the display of a roll of bank bills." With its need for a "firm hand" to regulate the supply of currency more stringently than the banknote system allowed, the colonial context called for the creation of what Conant called a "metallic bank-note," a token coinage closely based on the silver coins that had played a supplementary role in the currency of the United States and other countries under the "limping standard." "The adoption of a token coinage . . . promises to be the most important step which can be taken in our time in educating the undeveloped peoples to the true function of money and credit, and the final evolution of a bank note currency resting upon an adequate gold reserve," he wrote.[97]

In collaboration with the U.S. secretary of justice and finance (and later governor-general) in the Philippines, Henry Clay Ide, Conant worked out a plan for a token silver coinage. The official standard of value would be a gold peso worth fifty cents in U.S. money, but the principal currency would be a silver peso convertible into gold at a fixed rate. The Philippine finance minister would control the quantity of silver coins, and their metallic content would be kept lower than that of Mexican silver dollars to prevent their being exported, so that they would serve exclusively as a domestic currency. Since gold would only be required for international payments, and since the United States intended all such payments to flow through New York, the gold reserves on which the silver coinage was to be based, derived from the seigniorage charged by the Philippines mint, would be kept in New York. When merchants in the Philippines made payments abroad, they would deposit silver pesos in the Philippines treasury in exchange for drafts on the New York reserves. In this way, the gold-exchange standard would represent "the extension of the banking principle to the foreign exchanges," allowing fund managers in New York to fulfill the role of reserve and central banks in the United States and other advanced industrial countries.[98] "If the use of silver money can be continued while it is given a fixed and unquestioned relation to gold,

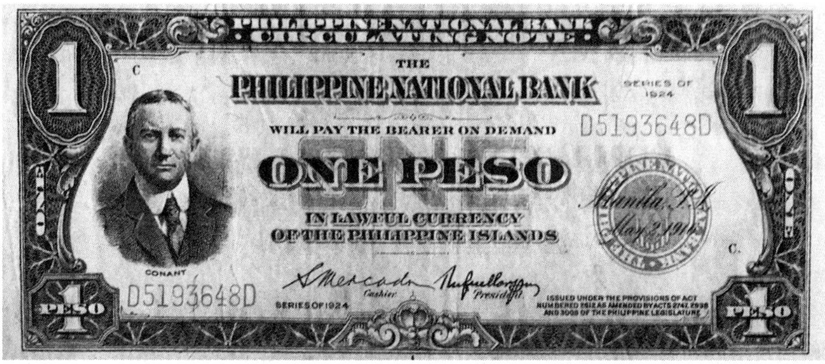

FIGURE 6.1. One-peso Philippine National Bank note, 1924. Photo courtesy of Cesar Alano.

the double result will be accomplished of leaving undisturbed the present customs of the people"—especially the existing structure of low wages—"and of extending a tempting invitation to American and foreign capital to enter and develop the islands," Conant wrote. Thus the gold-exchange standard "may be made the effective means of restoring the par of exchange between the countries of the East and West, so long broken by the fall in the gold price of silver, and thereby of forging anew the link of commercial relationship which is so vital to the prosperity of both hemispheres."[99]

Approved by the War Department, Conant's plan for the coinage was enacted by Congress in 1903. The new silver coins and Philippine National Bank notes were colloquially called "conants," and his portrait appeared on some of the bills (figure 6.1). The Morton Trust Company, for which Secretary of War Elihu Root served as legal counsel and Conant worked as treasurer, became the reserve bank for the Philippines, as well as subsequently for Panama and the Dominican Republic.[100] Appointed by President Theodore Roosevelt as one of three members of a Commission on International Exchange in 1903, Conant consulted with European leaders on an agenda for extending the gold-exchange standard to Mexico, China, and other countries in their respective orbits, a plan that succeeded in transforming the monetary systems of Mexico, Nicaragua, and Panama. When Conant died of stomach cancer in 1915, he was in Havana, advocating for a similar reform of the Cuban currency.[101]

As a token of exchange value, currency always rests on confidence. Its value derives from the debts and taxes it can pay, the goods and services it can purchase, or the gold and silver for which it can be redeemed, and on the system of exchange that makes these promises possible. The promissory character of currency has led to a common conception of the growth of monetary relations as founded on trust in the impersonal market itself. "A growing reliance on mutual promises," a leading historian wrote in 1979, "comes very close to the heart of what we mean by 'the rise of capitalism.'" "Confidence was the engine of economic growth, the mysterious sentiment that permitted a country poor in specie but rich in promises to create something from nothing," writes a recent scholar of money in early America. "At its core, capitalism was little more than a confidence game."[102]

But money is a creature of government fiat as well as public faith. Its power, like that of the market it mediates, depends on compulsion as much as confidence. For early Americans, money signified sovereignty. The rising power of the modern investment trust actually reflected the *loss* of trust in "the market" in the abstract, and the increasing authority of bankers, fund managers, and their close colleagues in the executive branch of the federal government, managing the market economy through their administration of currency, credit, and savings. In contrast to agrarians and Populists who viewed monetary reform as the means of the emancipation of productive labor and democratization of finance, Conant and his allies fought for the emancipation of capital from popular politics and "plodding industry," in the name of a paternalistic ideal of trusteeship that provided the major rationale for colonialism and corporate capitalism. Their campaign for a national and international monetary order governed by the imperative to maximize profits on each additional increment of investment reflected the particular problems of surplus capital and heavy industry that rose to the fore in the late nineteenth century. Early nineteenth-century exponents of central banking like Nicholas Biddle had grappled with the rather different demands of scarce capital, plantation agriculture, and internal improvements, whereas eighteenth-century critics of paper money like William Douglass had approached the money question with the distinctive needs of transatlantic merchants and colonial creditors in mind. But like their predecessors, turn-of-the-century "masters of finance" framed their ideas in the context of the two-hundred-year struggle over the means of payment as the means of class rule.

Much of the industrial landscape that they inhabited has long since declined or disappeared. Abandoned or converted to other uses are many of the mills and mines, the railroads and streetcars, the mammoth manufacturers, department stores, and mail-order houses, along with the colonial order in the Caribbean and Pacific islands and the international gold standard that presided over the global market economy. What remains above all is the fund of trust: the "giant pool of money" seeking investment, as National Public Radio called it in the midst of the financial crisis of 2008; the many successors of the trust company, from mutual funds to pension funds to real estate investment trusts to hedge funds and other vehicles of asset securitization; the administrative and regulatory authority of central bankers and bondholders over households, corporations, and governments; and the ethic of investment that identifies fund managers' fiduciary responsibility to investors and endowments with the pursuit of public as well as private interests.[103] The foundations endowed by Carnegie, Rockefeller, and Henry Ford now appear as powerful as the industries from which they arose. Carnegie scarcely anticipated that big businesses would prove to be the passing playthings of the trusts rather than the other way around. But Conant recognized that the long swings of investment and disinvestment, industrialization and deindustrialization, formed the violent rhythm of capitalist development no less than the cycles of speculative boom and bust. The structure of financial trust that he helped to bring into being was designed not to halt but to harness the systemic instability that produced recurrent panics and depressions as well as longer-term crises.

Conclusion

The Magician's Glass

The long conflict over currency reflected a deeper struggle to comprehend and control the hidden source of the power that money wielded in modern society. Two centuries after John Taylor's *Shilling* (1621) and Thomas Hobbes's *Leviathan* (1651), Herman Melville's *Moby-Dick* (1851) chronicled the quest of a shipboard society of "mariners, renegades and castaways" for another leviathan represented by a coin. Nailed to the main mast of the *Pequod* as the prize for whoever first sights Moby Dick, a gold doubloon serves as "the white whale's talisman." As an instrument of circulation, representation, and association, the coin propels the epic journey, symbolizes what is at stake, and binds the crew to the captain in a fateful social contract.[1]

The reverse side of the doubloon is described in detail based on an actual Ecuadorian coin from the period, and each of the novel's main characters finds his own meaning in its iconography (figure C.1). "This round gold is but the image of the rounder globe, which, like a magician's glass, to each and every man in turn but mirrors back his own mysterious self," says Captain Ahab, who sees in it a sign of man's ego. "This coin speaks wisely" to the first mate, Starbuck, who takes from it a message of divine providence. It appears to successive observers as a cheering sermon, a foreboding portent, and an occult fetish, among other symbols. "Here's the ship's navel, this doubloon here," says the cabin boy, Pip, "and they are all on fire to unscrew it." Yet the coin remains ultimately inscrutable, like the elusive sovereign beneath the sea. "Set apart and sanctified to one awe-inspiring end," it rises above its origins as a means of market exchange and measure of monetary value, much as the men leave their lives on land behind. "Though placed amongst a ruthless crew and every hour passed by ruthless hands," it is never stolen or spent. So too, though born of the market for whale oil, the hunt is dedicated to a

FIGURE C.1A. Ecuadorian eight-escudo doubloon, 1843, as described in *Moby-Dick* (front side). Photo courtesy of Heritage Auctions, ha.com.

FIGURE C.1B. Ecuadorian eight-escudo doubloon, 1843, as described in *Moby-Dick* (reverse side). Photo courtesy of Heritage Auctions, ha.com.

higher purpose. "Nantucket market! Hoot!" Ahab scoffs, disavowing the pecuniary calculus that makes the globe a "great counting-house" even as he raises the doubloon above the deck like a flag.[2]

Melville shared something of his protagonists' paradoxical ambition for their endeavor. "Dollars damn me," he wrote to Nathaniel Hawthorne on the eve of completing *Moby-Dick*, praying both for a commercial success to release him from the onerous debts he had incurred in writing it and for the kind of literary achievement he believed destined to fail in financial terms.[3] Like their author, his characters are "fast-fish" themselves, as the laws of the industry term a whale tied "by any medium" to an occupied boat or ship.[4] Possessed by an irresistible instinct to take to the sea, the sailors are bound by the faceless force pulling them in like an obligation they cannot escape. Their dream of redemption might be silently signified by the goddess of liberty on the front side of the real doubloon, though it goes unmentioned in the novel. The coin on the mast becomes instead their cross of gold, as the voyage approaches its apocalyptic end. "And so they'll say in the resurrection," Pip prophesies, "when they come to fish up this old mast, and find a doubloon lodged in it, with bedded oysters for the shaggy bark. Oh, the gold! The precious, precious gold!"[5]

To Melville's characters and his contemporaries, money appeared as a "magician's glass" with a power both alluring and dreadful, revealing an unfathomable enigma below the stormy surface of market society. What made currency such a compelling *question* as well as quest for early Americans? The capacity of the money question to define the stakes of social struggle for more than two hundred years did not simply reflect the conditions of capitalist development from which it stemmed. It rather gained force from what the philosopher R. G. Collingwood terms the "logical efficacy" of the "presuppositions" on which any live question is predicated—the implicit or explicit beliefs that cause a question to arise in the first place—without which the social basis of money ceased to be seriously questioned and contested for much of the century since the Federal Reserve Act of 1913.[6] What were the presuppositions that animated debates over the means of payment for so long, why did they lose their efficacy in political discourse in the twentieth century—and what are the prospects for a revival in the twenty-first?

The money question arose from the prevailing conviction that both the demand for money and the supply of money were creatures of class rule. Neither the supporters nor the opponents of colonial paper currency wanted to live in a society without a common standard of exchange value and means of market transactions; they based their opposing positions on their shared view of the barbarity of barter. Yet both sides understood that the colonists' desires and demands for money did not emerge spontaneously from their exchanges of goods and services. The need for money was rather created and controlled by government through taxes, like the property tax that the Ipswich "insurrectioners" refused to pay in the 1680s, and by merchants and creditors through their state-sanctioned demands for payment in specie or specie-backed bills, like "the tyranny of the Usurers and Misers" that the promoters of paper money resisted in the following decades.[7] In a society dominated by family farmers who conducted most of their exchanges with informal credit and required money mainly to pay taxes, settle long-distance debts, and buy land or imported goods, rising demands for currency clearly emanated from outside agrarian communities like Ipswich rather than welling up from within. Yet in antebellum New York City as well, the workingmen's movement traced workers' increasing need for money to a coordinated combination of taxes and tolls taken by state-chartered banks leading to inflated prices, rather than simply to greater demand relative to the supply of basic necessities like food and fuel. So too in postbellum Texas, hill country farmers blamed a creditor coalition of tax collectors and furnishing merchants for the crushing cost of living and the spread of debt peonage, hoping that producers' cooperatives could reverse the vicious cycle of dependence on commercial credit. The first presupposition on which the money question was predicated was that shifting demands for money were determined by changing class relations rather than merely by market exchange.

Along with their efforts to combat capitalist manipulation of the demand for money, critics contended with class control of the money supply. Early Americans generally recognized that the demand for money did not create its own supply—a fact plainly apparent in colonies with far too few coins (and too costly bills of exchange) to pay rising taxes and debts at the beginning of the eighteenth century, and all too familiar in upcountry regions drawn into industrial agriculture with a paucity of banks and banknotes at the end of the nineteenth century. The long series of strenuous efforts to create new mechanisms of payment—including bills of credit and Treasury notes, banknotes and checks, warehouse receipts and corporate securities—manifested the common understanding that currency and other widely circulating means of payment did not grow naturally with the crops and other commodities for which they exchanged. Money had to be manufactured. Hence the persistent concern of reformers on all sides of the currency question with the gap between changes in the money supply and variations in the volume of monetary transactions, or what economists called the "real needs of trade."

Whether they thought money must be redeemable on demand in gold or silver or that it could be based on nothing more than fiat and faith, early

Americans viewed money as an intrinsically political resource. Individuals could "make money" in the sense of accumulating it, but they could not produce it and cause it to circulate without concerted action and political power. Colonists could agree to accept each other's bills in payment, banks could make loans by issuing notes or crediting borrowers' accounts, and farmers could cooperate in buying and borrowing with IOUs secured by cotton or wheat instead of gold or silver. But they needed the state to turn their paper promises into legal tender and make them anonymously transferable, allowing bills and notes to circulate free and clear of the original transactions from which they arose. Born of the financial revolution that joined public authority and private profit, the money question was at heart a question about sovereignty. From John Wise's communitarian conception of civil and church government to William Douglass's defense of royal prerogative, from William Leggett's ideal of the tribune of the people to Nicolas Biddle's vision of the disinterested statesman, and from Charles Macune's model of democratic cooperation to Charles Conant's advocacy of fiduciary empire, debates about the basis of money were informed by rival views of the basis of political authority. The second presupposition underlying the money question was that the rules governing the creation and circulation of money played a critical part in determining how market society more broadly was ruled.

The third presupposition was that the contest for control of the money supply created new class divides as well as new forms of class solidarity. Wise (or a close associate) saw the scarcity of specie as "the great Source" of the emerging "divisions and sub-Divisions" in colonial New England and the extortion of small householders like his Ipswich congregants by moneyed men in Boston.[8] Public provision of paper currency controlled by townships and provincial legislatures, by contrast, could bind farmers, shopkeepers, and local traders in a plebeian community of cash and credit. Douglass expressed a similar sense of what was at stake from the other side, decrying the defrauding of creditors by assemblies of debtors who made cheap paper currency legal tender for the repayment of private debts. "When poor People can have present Money (tho' only nominal) on so easy Terms," he lamented, they became less "assiduous in Labour to increase our Produce and Manufacture."[9] Like Wise, Douglass viewed creditors' and merchants' monopoly of silver, on the one hand, and debtors' and freehold farmers' creation of paper currency, on the other, as opposing means of class rule.

A century later, Leggett found the source of the exploitation of the emerging working class not in the wage relation but in the "uncurrent bills" in which wages were paid, and in the commercial banking system that issued the currency. He urged workers to strike against the banks by refusing to use their notes, oust from office the legislators who granted their charters, and democratize the banking system itself. Responding aggressively to the rise of organized labor, Biddle sought to marshal the forces of finance by effectively regulating the supply of notes and loans issued by the sprawling system of state banks, while draping their class rule in the mantle of neoclassical architecture. Conant took up Biddle's project of class consolidation at the turn of the twentieth century, campaigning successfully for monetary reform at home and abroad as the key to the creation of a structure of savings and investment designed to emancipate capital from both popular resistance and self-destructive competition. But perhaps the most comprehensive view of the monetary basis of class relations came from Macune, who argued that the monopoly of the money supply called into being the "whole class" of agricultural labor, bridging earlier divides based on race, region, and land ownership. The banking system, he wrote, forged the financial bonds of industrial labor as well, united with its country cousin in subjection to the "speculative element." Like colonial bills of credit and antebellum "free banking," the subtreasury plan of the Farmers' Alliance was intended to seize the means of production of money on behalf of the cash-poor, debt-driven households of farmers and laborers.

The management of money was closely associated with the management of a household, together defining what "economy" meant to early Americans. The presuppositions that gave rise to the money question were bound up with paternalistic presumptions about family and domesticity as well as race and empire. Conquest and colonization formed the original terrain of conflict over paper money in eighteenth-century New England, where Wise and Douglass contrasted their equally expansive versions of British Empire and colonial finance to the primitive barter that they attributed to Native Americans. So too, Wise modeled his vision of a commonwealth bound by public confidence in a common currency on the marriage bond, urging family farmers like himself to honor their bills as they did their wives, as twin pillars of household autonomy. Douglass advanced a competing conception of paternalism in which professional medicine and philanthropy supplanted familial caregiving, while money formed the foundation for surrogate households of merchants, migrants, and unmarried men such as himself. Imperial expansion likewise framed the currency question in the early nineteenth century, when Leggett and Biddle developed their opposing views of the metropolitan Middle Atlantic through their parallel writings on the western frontier and the Mediterranean. But it was southern slavery that increasingly dominated the Jacksonian bank war: Leggett's antislavery politics inspired his broader antimonopoly ideology, while Biddle hitched the fortunes of the national bank to those of the cotton empire and its human capital. After the Civil War, emancipation created the context for Macune's upcountry ideal of a "white man's state" as well as his subsequent leadership of a climactic crusade for financial democracy in the name of both white smallholders and black sharecroppers. Conant's countervailing coalition of bankers, merchants, and manufacturers rallied around a revamped racial logic of financial trusteeship, promoting a model of class and colonial relations in which the publicly traded corporation took the place of the household as the repository of paternal trust. Conceived as a contest among heads of households for control of financial resources, the money question rose and fell with the early American household economy and the familial, racial, and imperial structures on which it depended.

In the decades after Conant's death in 1915, the conflict over the political constitution and class basis of the monetary system gradually receded from the center of American public discourse. To be sure, Wall Street and the "money trust" remained recurrent targets of political agitation, as in Louis Brandeis's influential exposé *Other People's Money: And How the Bankers Use It* (1914) and Franklin D. Roosevelt's diatribe at the 1936 Democratic Convention against "economic royalists" who had "concentrated into their own hands an almost complete control over other people's property, other people's money, other people's labor, other people's lives."[10] The monetary *policies* of the Federal Reserve continued to be widely debated, especially in crises like the Great Depression, though they attracted far less public attention than fiscal policies of taxing and spending, and they sparked far less opposition than they had in previous centuries. But the monetary *system*—particularly bankers' control of credit and currency (through deposit and checking accounts) as commodities produced for private profit—became largely off-limits to popular politics. Despite repeated reforms of *how* bankers governed the system of payment, their right to rule was no longer really open to debate.

The reasons for the decline of the money question were complex, and I can only suggest a few contributing factors. First and most importantly, fundamental alternatives to banking as the main source of the money supply had been decisively defeated. After two centuries of conflict over the union of bank and state, the Populist movement marked the last systemic and credible challenge to the sovereignty of finance capital. Agrarian radicalism faded by the mid-twentieth century, and the labor movement never again made monetary reform central to its agenda, as it had throughout the nineteenth century.[11] Theoretically, it was still possible to envision the abolition of private property in the means of producing money and the establishment of a system in which currency and credit would be controlled democratically as public resources rather than private assets, just as modern Americans might continue to imagine alternatives to private ownership of land and other productive resources. But after the Progressive Era, such ideas appeared increasingly utopian even in retrospect, beyond the horizon of what social movements could realistically aspire to achieve. Calls for structural reform of money and banking continued to find a following on the radical fringes of American politics, but they no longer mobilized the mainstream.

Second, and partly as a result, democratic demands came to focus on greater elasticity, more equitable distribution, and easier access to monetary and financial resources instead of contesting the control of bankers over the means of monetary production. The sources of the demand for money and the supply of money came to be largely taken for granted, even as liberal economists, labor leaders, and consumer advocates called for Keynesian spending to stimulate demand, monetary policies aimed at full employment, and public provision of low-interest loans for farmers, homeowners, college students, and other constituencies. In his study of the eclipse of the "labor question" in the mid-twentieth century, Steve Fraser writes that "the struggle over power and property . . . was superseded by the universal quest for more—goulash capitalism. Mass politics replaced class politics."[12] The money question met a related fate, as earlier assaults on the banking system mutated into consumerist demands for more money rather than for control of the means of producing it.

Third, the popular discourse of political economy gave way to the advent of academic, neoclassical economics. As with Shakespearean theater, Greco-Roman classicism, natural history, and folk medicine, among other aspects of early American culture with which the money question was associated over the course of its career, the rich tradition of amateur economic theory yielded to the exclusive claims of professional expertise. Macune and Conant represented the last generation of nonacademic economic theorists, the diverse social stratum that had sustained the money question since the seventeenth century. Without a strong foothold in popular culture, the subjects of money and banking lost the broad spiritual, philosophical, and cultural resonance that they had held earlier. For early Americans, the establishment or disestablishment of a bank, the suspension or resumption of specie payments in exchange for paper currency, and the demonetization or remonetization of silver had signified no less than the difference between civilization and savagery, slavery and freedom, the dark ages and the millennium. Later students of the battles over bills of credit, state banks, and the gold standard found it hard to recapture the heat and passion that had once enlivened those conflicts.

In recent years, however, the conditions may have emerged for a revival of the money question in new form. Much as paper money and the hard metallic standard arose in tandem in the late seventeenth century, the late twentieth century appears to have marked their dual demise. The United States finally went off the gold standard in 1971, signaling the end of the Bretton Woods system established during the Second World War under which the currencies of other advanced industrial economies had been convertible at a fixed exchange rate into U.S. dollars, and dollars had been convertible in turn into gold. The decades since then have seen a rising number of obituaries for the "cash era," as paper currency and coins have increasingly been supplanted by a widening variety of forms of electronic payment.[13]

For the most part, the new payment technologies have continued to rely on national or international currencies like dollars and euros, the supply of which is largely controlled by banks through their lending operations. Indeed, the three-hundred-year reign of banking over the means of payment has never appeared more powerful than in the past thirty years. Debt has become a big business in its own right, making finance arguably the leading "industry" of twenty-first century capitalism. As the overall level of debt in the United States has grown much faster than the production of commodities since the 1970s, corporate creditors and institutional investors have gained unprecedented command over property, industry, and public policy. All but the richest households have struggled to make up for stagnant or declining real incomes by racking up credit cards, car loans, student loans, and home loans. Leveraged buyouts and hostile takeovers have likewise loaded major corporations with mounting debt burdens, while declining tax revenues have driven local, state, and national governments into the arms of the bond markets as well. By far the biggest borrowers, however, have been the banks and other financial institutions that are also the leading lenders, leaving behind their comparatively tame traditional roles as brokers and agents to engage in high-stakes trading on their own behalf. As the new master rather than servant of the business world, the financial sector has claimed the lion's share of the profits made under its direction, trading places with manufacturing to become the most profitable segment of the U.S. economy.[14] An increasingly important part of those profits derives from banks' control of the burgeoning infrastructure of electronic payment and the tolls that they charge on every transaction using a credit card, computer, or cell phone.[15]

Along with new methods of payment based on conventional currencies, a growing range of alternative currencies and credit networks have arisen outside the auspices of national governments and banks, including community currencies such as local exchange trading systems and "time dollars," "peer-to-peer" lending circuits, and digital currencies like bitcoin. Much of the revived impetus for currency and credit cooperatives has come from environmentalist, feminist, and communitarian efforts to create means of exchanging goods and services without money borrowed from banks, enabling local and virtual communities to assign their own economic value to activities and enterprises instead of deferring to the profit-driven determinations of absentee investors, employers, and creditors.[16] Interest in alternatives to standard money has surged since the global financial crisis of 2008, reflecting a broader loss of confidence in the partnership of government and banking across the political spectrum. Even the most successful unconventional currencies still circulate in the shadows and interstices of mainstream markets, complementing rather than replacing the money in which taxes must be paid and debts are legally due. Yet such experiments have helped to create an opening for renewed debate on both sides of the Atlantic about the whole monetary structure that originated in England and America between 1700 and 1900.[17]

From libertarian appeals for privately issued currency to be freed from state sponsorship and supervision to social democratic demands for a fully public currency spent rather than lent into circulation without the intervention of banks, rising theoretical and political challenges have called the social basis of money into question once again. Enthusiasts of digital money herald "a profound societal upheaval" comparable to the early modern financial revolution, promising to transfer control over the money supply from "centralized financial institutions" to "a network of autonomous computers."[18] Currency collectives see themselves as micropolitical "precursors to a new twenty-first century economy founded on alternative forms of money, which will give rise to new economic opportunities to provide livelihoods focused on need rather than profit."[19] Proponents of "debt-free money" as opposed to "a money system based on bank debt" call for currency to be "reclaimed as a Commons, subject to a commons regime of democratically determined use."[20] Writers inspired by antiglobalization activism and Occupy Wall Street advocate a radical reconception of economic value and its money form, proclaiming that "in the coming years the money question is likely to assume central importance in the emerging anti-capitalist movement."[21] At the same time, social scientists discern deeper transformations of selfhood and social life embedded in new forms of finance, for better or worse. Dystopian depictions of the "financialization of daily life" and "the making of the indebted man" contrast with utopian anticipations of the "repersonalization of the economy" made possible by the advent of the Internet and the mobile phone, "so that money may be more meaningful to each of us as a means of participating in the multiple associations we choose to enter."[22] Long regarded as a narrowly technical subject of concern mainly to specialists, the study of money and banking seems to be regaining the broader social significance it held for early Americans.

How might the history of the money question illuminate current questions about the future of money? Eighteenth- and nineteenth-century campaigns reflected a basic tension in the thinking of monetary reformers in every era, including ours. Their vital insight was that money in a market society forms a fundamental means of class rule and subject of class struggle. Yet they paradoxically held out hope for a monetary standard that could fly above the fray of political contestation and economic competition, imposing its impartial authority over political leaders, financial intermediaries, buyers and sellers, and borrowers and lenders. The fiercest critiques of corruption, exploitation, and class privilege were counterposed to an implicit ideal of money as an automatic, apolitical arbiter of market relations, transcending the turmoil from which it arose. Opposing sides of the currency question envisioned money as a vehicle of natural circulation, governed in its inexorable operation by natural law or by natural history; as an agent of faithful representation, reflecting the transparent needs of trade or the dictates of growth and development; and as a bond of harmonious association, designed to transmute industrial strife into cooperative enterprise or fiduciary trust.

Even as they railed against the engrossment of the means of payment by wealthy merchants and moneylenders, the colonial pioneers of paper money believed that their invention would allow power and wealth to flow freely through the channels of trade like rains and rivers from a "Common Fountain."[23] Their imperial adversaries portrayed paper currency by contrast as the artificial creature of class legislation while upholding the self-regulating circulation of silver and gold as the natural lifeblood of a healthy economic organism. In the early nineteenth century, Jacksonians condemned the corruption of commerce by the rise of state-sponsored banks. But they contended that once freed from the grip of monopoly and "special privilege," money would serve the mutual interests of the masses of plaindealing producers instead of a parasitical class of middlemen—"if we could only get rid of a few laws and institutions which give advantages to some men over others."[24] At the same time, proponents of central banking deplored the demagoguery of politicians and the selfishness of business owners alike, while hailing the higher authority of an Olympian monetary tribunal that could oversee the "chaos of factions" and "arts of traffic."[25] Finally, late nineteenth-century agrarian radicals coupled their critique of the financial expropriation of the "producing classes" to their advocacy of a series of technical mechanisms intended to ensure that the supply of money automatically expanded and contracted with the demand for its services. From the "interconvertible bond scheme" to the subtreasury plan and "free silver," Populist proposals aimed to purify money of its "power to oppress," beating the sword of class oppression into a plowshare of cooperation.[26] In response, corporate capitalists advanced a similarly irenic vision of financial trusteeship as a means of obviating cutthroat competition and class conflict. They conceived the Federal Reserve System and "dollar diplomacy" as a peaceful, progressive alternative to both democracy and despotism.

Imagining what money could be gave early Americans a critical vantage from which to view what it actually was. They saw the class basis of money more clearly because they did not accept it as natural or foreordained. But the persistent faith that money could constitute an independent authority or autonomous sovereign of the market contradicted two hard-won lessons of the currency crusades.

The first lesson was that the political character of money as a means of rule depended on who made it, not what it was made of or based on. A fiat paper currency could be a means of popular self-rule in the hands of townships and elected assemblies, or a means of financial autocracy in the hands of bankers and bondholders. A specie standard could be a means of securing workers' wages and restraining reckless speculation, or a means of depressing producers' earnings and inflating their debts, depending on the class structure of coinage and banking. Like a magician's glass, money gets its power from those who control it, and from the illusion that power emanates from money itself.[27]

The second lesson was that the social relations that determined who made money depended in turn on a broader struggle over labor and land as well as currency and credit. The power of small farmers and traders in colonial New England came from their control of farms and shops no less than of bills of credit and public loan offices. So too, the ascendance of corporate capital two hundred years later entailed a sweeping reconstruction of property in the means of production, transportation, and communication along with the means of payment. The organization of money is hardly the lone or essential basis of economic exploitation, nor is financial reform a panacea for systemic conflict and crisis. We would do well to remember what early Americans recognized, that the money question was always about more than money.

Acknowledgments

John Kenneth Galbraith once wrote that the subject of money is really much simpler than economists make it seem. That has not been my experience. The more I have sought to understand what money once meant, the more multidimensional it has appeared, taking this study far beyond the bounds of economics. The challenge and excitement have come in following the money wherever it leads, tracking the movements of such a shape-shifting subject. I have gained much-needed guidance at every turn from friends and colleagues, and I am happy to thank them here, however inadequately.

Many people have generously read and responded to portions of this work at various stages. For their sharp questions and careful critiques, I thank Jean-Christophe Agnew, Ken Alder, Susanna Blumenthal, Charles Capper, Joanne Chaisson, Marisa Chappell, Pamela Cytrynbaum, Tracy Daugherty, Christine Desan, Carolyn Eastman, Andrew Edwards, Stephen Engelmann, Paul Farber, Walter Friedman, Joshua Greenberg, David Hall, Daniel Walker Howe, William Husband, Daniel Immerwahr, Jonathan Katz, Amy Kittelstrom, James Kloppenberg, James Livingston, Ruth MacKay, Noam Maggor, Simon Middleton, Catherine Molineux, Mary Jo Nye, Robert Nye, Jennifer Ratner-Rosenhagen, William Robbins, David Robinson, Marjorie Sandor, Lisa Sarasohn, Mark Schmeller, James Shaw, Elizabeth Shermer, Eric Slauter, Stacey Smith, Dror Wahrman, Barbara Welke, Elizabeth Wingrove, Caroline Winterer, Keith Wrightson, Alfred Young, and Michael Zakim. I am especially grateful to Elizabeth Blackmar, Leon Fink, Ben Mutschler, and Adam Rubin, whose friendship, encouragement, and interest have sustained me as a scholar.

I have been fortunate to receive funding and time for research and writing from several wonderful scholarly institutions. For their crucial support,

I am indebted to the American Antiquarian Society, the American Council of Learned Societies, the Center for the Humanities at Oregon State University, the Charles Warren Center for Studies in American History at Harvard University, the Institute for the Humanities at the University of Illinois at Chicago, the Library Company of Philadelphia, and the National Endowment for the Humanities. I am grateful to several chairpersons of the history departments at OSU and UIC—Paul Farber, Laura Hostetler, and Chris Boyer—for allowing me to take advantage of these outside opportunities, and I thank both my department and the College of Liberal Arts and Sciences at UIC for a book subvention. Last and most, I thank the Newberry Library, which has given this project a home for much of its life.

For kind invitations to present my work-in-progress and for countless helpful comments, I thank the organizers and participants in the Ancients and Moderns Seminar at the Stanford Humanities Center, the Business History Seminar at Harvard Business School, the Colloquium on Political Economy at the University of California at Santa Barbara, the "Markets, Law, and Ethics, 1300–1832" conferences at Sheffield University and the Huntington Library, the Science in Human Culture Program at Northwestern University, the "Money Matters: The Law, Economics, and Politics of Currency" conference at Tel Aviv University, the "Panic of 1837" conference at the Library Company of Philadelphia, the Science, Technology, and Society Program at the University of Michigan, the University of Minnesota Law School Program in Law and History, the Vanderbilt History Seminar, and the Yale Center for the Study of Representative Institutions.

At the University of Chicago Press, Robert Devens gave me confidence in this work long before it was done, Timothy Mennel provided wise counsel and, along with Rachel Kelly, graciously guided me through the process of publication, and Mark Reschke improved the manuscript throughout with his careful copyediting. I am grateful to Edward Gray, Stephen Mihm, and Mark Peterson for including my book in the American Beginnings series. Two anonymous reviewers gave the manuscript exceptionally incisive and constructive reviews.

Portions of chapters 3 and 4 previously appeared in two articles: "William Leggett and the Melodrama of the Market," in *Capitalism Takes Command: The Social Transformation of Nineteenth-Century America*, ed. Michael Zakim and Gary J. Kornblith (University of Chicago Press, 2012), 199–222; and "The Moneylender as Magistrate: Nicholas Biddle and the Ideological Origins of Central Banking in the United States," *Theoretical Inquiries in Law* 11, no. 11 (January 2010): 319–59. My thanks to their publishers for permission to reprint material from those publications.

As always, my greatest gifts have come from my family. My brothers, David and Mark, have been my constant confidants, my father my strongest support, and the memory of my mother my guide. My daughter, Leah, has grown up with this book, leavening its long gestation with happiness and love. In the final few years of this project, Helen Thompson has been my closest reader as well as my joy, my hope, and my soul mate. This book is for her.

Notes

Introduction

1. John Taylor, *A Shilling; or, The Trauailes of Twelue-Pence* (London: Printed by Edward Allde for Henry Gosson, 1621), n.p. On Taylor's career, see Laurie Ellinghausen, "The New Bourgeois Hero: The Self-Presentation of John Taylor 'The Water Poet,'" in her *Labor and Writing in Early Modern England, 1557–1667* (Burlington, VT: Ashgate, 2008), 93–120; Alexandra Halasz, *The Marketplace of Print: Pamphlets and the Public Sphere in Early Modern England* (Cambridge: Cambridge University Press, 1997), 191–203. On Taylor's *Shilling* and other tales of traveling coins, see Deborah Valenze, *The Social Life of Money in the English Past* (Cambridge: Cambridge University Press, 2006), 73–78. On fictional memoirs of commodities more generally, see Liz Bellamy, "It-Narrators and Circulation: Defining a Subgenre," in *The Secret Life of Things: Animals, Objects, and It-Narratives in Eighteenth-Century England*, ed. Mark Blackwell (Lewisburg, PA: Bucknell University Press, 2007), 117–46.

2. Taylor, *Shilling*, n.p.

3. R. W. K. Hinton, "The Mercantile System in the Time of Thomas Mun," *Economic History Review*, n.s., 7, no. 3 (1955): 277–90, quoted passages at 281; J. D. Gould, "The Trade Crisis of the Early 1620's and English Economic Thought," *Journal of Economic History* 15, no. 2 (June 1955): 121–33; Carlos Eduardo Suprinyak, "Trade, Money, and the Grievances of the Commonwealth: Economic Debates in the English Public Sphere during the Commercial Crisis of the Early 1620's" (Belo Horizonte: Cedeplar, 2011).

4. Adam Smith, *An Inquiry into the Nature and Causes of the Wealth of Nations*, vol. 1, ed. R. H. Campbell and A. S. Skinner (Indianapolis: Liberty Fund, 1981), 429.

5. Hinton, "Mercantile System," 282; Valenze, *Social Life of Money*, 63; Carl Wennerlind, "Money: Hartlibian Political Economy and the New Culture of Credit," in *Mercantilism Reimagined: Political Economy in Early Modern Britain and Its Empire*, ed. Philip J. Stern and Carl Wennerlind (Oxford: Oxford University Press, 2014), 74–93; Natasha Glaisyer, "'A due Circulation in the Veins of the Publick': Imagining Credit in Late Seventeenth- and Early Eighteenth-Century England," *Eighteenth Century* 46, no. 3 (Fall 2005): 277–97.

6. R. D. Richards, *The Early History of Banking in England* (London: P. S. King & Son, 1929), 23–61; James Steven Rogers, *The Early History of the Law of Bills and Notes: A Study of the Origins of Anglo-American Commercial Law* (Cambridge: Cambridge University Press, 1995), 94–170;

J. Keith Horsefield, *British Monetary Experiments, 1650–1710* (Cambridge, MA: Harvard University Press, 1960), xii–xviii; A. E. Feaveryear, *The Pound Sterling: A History of English Money* (London: Oxford University Press, 1931), 91–108. On the revolution in the social basis of money, see especially Christine Desan, *Making Money: Coin, Currency, and the Coming of Capitalism* (Oxford: Oxford University Press, 2014).

7. Feaveryear, *Pound Sterling*, 86–89; Horsefield, *British Monetary Experiments*, xi–xii.

8. Philip J. Stern and Carl Wennerlind, "Introduction," in Stern and Wennerlind, *Mercantilism Reimagined*, 5.

9. Michael Warner, *The Letters of the Republic: Publication and the Public Sphere in Eighteenth-Century America* (Cambridge, MA: Harvard University Press, 1990), 43–49, 58–63.

10. My formulation of the money question is modeled on Peter Kolchin's elegant articulation of the "labor question": "Who should work for whom, under what terms should work be performed, and how should it be compelled or rewarded?" Peter Kolchin, "The Big Picture: A Comment on David Brion Davis's 'Looking at Slavery from Broader Perspectives,'" *American Historical Review* 105, no. 2 (April 2000): 468.

11. Glyn Davies, *A History of Money: From Ancient Times to the Present Day* (Cardiff: University of Wales, 1994), 471.

12. Edwin Canaan, "Early History of the Term 'Capital,'" *Quarterly Journal of Economics* 35, no. 3 (May 1921): 469–81; Jean-Christophe Agnew, *Worlds Apart: The Market and the Theater in Anglo-American Thought, 1550–1750* (Cambridge: Cambridge University Press, 1986), 54.

13. Craig Muldrew, "'Hard Food for Midas': Cash and Its Social Value in Early Modern England," *Past and Present* 170, no. 1 (2001): 78–120.

14. E. P. Thompson, "Eighteenth-Century English Society: Class Struggle without Class?," *Social History* 3, no. 2 (1978): 133–65, quoted passage at 138.

15. See Andrew Edwards, "Grenville's Silver Hammer: Silver Stamps and a Reinterpretation of America's Founding Crisis," forthcoming in *Journal of American History*.

16. See Michael Merrill, "The Anticapitalist Origins of the United States," *Review: A Journal of the Fernand Braudel Center* 13 (Fall 1990): 465–97.

17. John Kenneth Galbraith, *Money: Whence It Came, Where It Went*, rev. ed. (Boston: Houghton Mifflin, 1995 [1975]), 44.

18. Paul Krugman, "Who Was Milton Friedman?," *New York Review of Books* 54, no. 2 (February 2007).

19. See Christopher Clark, ed., "The Transition to Capitalism in America: A Panel Discussion," *History Teacher* 27, no. 3 (1994): 263–88; Eli Cook, *The Pricing of Progress: Economic Indicators and the Capitalization of American Life* (Cambridge, MA: Harvard University Press, 2017).

20. Geoffrey Ingham, *The Nature of Money* (Cambridge: Polity Press, 2004), 13; Desan, *Making Money*, 5.

21. Giovanni Arrighi, *The Long Twentieth Century: Money, Power, and the Origins of Our Times*, new ed. (London: Verso, 2010); David Graeber, *Debt: The First 5,000 Years* (New York: Melville House, 2011).

22. Bruce H. Mann, *Republic of Debtors: Bankruptcy in the Age of American Independence* (Cambridge, MA: Harvard University Press, 2002); Louis Hyman, *Debtor Nation: The History of America in Red Ink* (Princeton, NJ: Princeton University Press, 2011); Stephen Mihm, *Nation of Counterfeiters: Capitalists, Con Men, and the Making of the United States* (Cambridge, MA: Harvard University Press, 2007); Scott Reynolds Nelson, *A Nation of Deadbeats: An Un-*

common History of America's Financial Disasters (New York: Alfred A. Knopf, 2012); Robert E. Wright, *One Nation under Debt: Hamilton, Jefferson, and the History of What We Owe* (New York: McGraw-Hill, 2008); Edward E. Baptist, "Toxic Debt, Collateralized and Securitized Human Beings, and the Panic of 1837," in *Capitalism Takes Command: The Social Transformation of Nineteenth-Century America*, ed. Michael Zakim and Gary Kornblith (Chicago: University of Chicago Press, 2012), 69–92, at 71.

23. On the relation between new work on the history of finance and older work in labor history, see Jeffrey Sklansky, "Labor, Money, and the Financial Turn in the History of Capitalism," *Labor: Studies in Working-Class History of the Americas* 11, no. 1 (Spring 2014): 23–46.

24. See especially William M. Reddy, *Money and Liberty in Modern Europe: A Critique of Historical Understanding* (Cambridge: Cambridge University Press, 1987), chap. 1, "The Crisis of the Class Concept in Historical Research," 1–33.

25. Karl Marx, *Capital: A Critique of Political Economy*, vol. 1, trans. Ben Fowkes (London: Penguin Books, 1976), 188.

26. Karl Marx, *Grundrisse*, ed. and trans. David McLellan (New York: Harper and Row, 1971), 61.

27. Marx, *Capital*, 1:247.

28. Marx, *Capital*, 1:188, 247, 266, 272.

29. Marx, *Capital*, 1:256. See also the analysis of "fictitious capital" in Karl Marx, *Capital: A Critique of Political Economy*, vol. 3, trans. David Fernbach (London: Penguin Books, 1981), 525–42, 607–25.

30. See Robert J. Steinfeld and Stanley L. Engerman, "Labor—Free or Coerced? A Historical Reassessment of Differences and Similarities," in *Free and Unfree Labour: The Debate Continues*, ed. Tom Brass and Marcel van der Linden (Bern: Peter Lang, 1997), 107–26; Seth Rockman, "The Unfree Origins of American Capitalism," in *The Economy of Early America: Historical Perspectives and New Directions*, ed. Cathy Matson (University Park: Pennsylvania State University Press, 2006), 335–61.

31. See especially Viviana A. Zelizer, *The Social Meaning of Money* (New York: Basic Books, 1994), and Craig Muldrew, *The Economy of Obligation: The Culture of Credit and Social Relations in Early Modern England* (New York: St. Martin's Press, 1998).

32. Reddy, *Money and Liberty*, xi.

33. For critiques of the barter-to-bills story, see Jean-Michel Servet, "Le troc primitive, un mythe fondateur d'une approache économiste de la monnaie," *Revue Numismatique*, 6th ser., 157 (2001): 15–32; Desan, *Making Money*, 23–69; Graeber, *Debt*, 21–42. For a helpful theoretical exposition of the basis of money in the power to determine "that which is needed to pay taxes," see L. Randall Wray, *Understanding Modern Money: The Key to Full Employment and Price Stability* (Cheltenham: Edward Elgar, 2006).

34. My argument for the historical priority of class relations builds on Robert Brenner's critique of Marxian accounts of the transition to capitalism based on the expansion of commerce and world trade. Robert Brenner, "The Origins of Capitalist Development: A Critique of Neo-Smithian Marxism," *New Left Review* 1, no. 104 (1977): 25–92; Robert Brenner, "Bourgeois Revolution and Transition to Capitalism," in *The First Modern Society: Essays in English History in Honour of Lawrence Stone*, ed. A. L. Beier, David Cannadine, and James M. Rosenheim (Cambridge: Cambridge University Press, 1989), 271–304. For Marxist efforts to move beyond the commodity theory of money, see Fred Moseley, ed., *Marx's Theory of Money: Modern Appraisals* (New York: Palgrave Macmillan, 2005).

35. Seth Rockman, *Scraping By: Wage Labor, Slavery, and Survival in Early Baltimore* (Baltimore: Johns Hopkins University Press, 2009), 11.

36. Joseph A. Schumpeter, *History of Economic Analysis* (New York: Routledge, 1954), 281, 283. Cf. E. P. Thompson, "The Moral Economy of the English Crowd in the Eighteenth Century," *Past and Present* 50 (February 1971): 76–136.

37. On the relation of intellectual history to the history of capitalism, see Jeffrey Sklansky, "The Elusive Sovereign: New Intellectual and Social Histories of Capitalism," *Modern Intellectual History* 9, no. 1 (April 2012): 233–48.

38. Thomas Hutchinson, *The History of the Province of Massachusetts-Bay, From the Charter of King William and Queen Mary, in 1691, Until the Year 1750*, vol. 2, 2nd ed. (London: J. Smith, 1768), 437.

39. Raymond Williams, *Modern Tragedy*, ed. Pamela McCallum (Toronto: Broadview Press, 2006 [1966]), 94–95.

Chapter One

1. Frederick Lewis Gay Transcripts, 1632–1786, State Papers, Vol. III, Massachusetts Historical Society, 64–65.

2. John Langdon Sibley, *Biographical Sketches of Graduates of Harvard University, in Cambridge, Massachusetts*, vol. 2 (Cambridge, MA: Harvard University Press, 1881), 429–33; Raymond P. Stearns, "John Wise of Ipswich Was No Democrat in Politics," *Essex Institute Historical Collections* 97 (1961): 2–18, esp. 8–11; Thomas Franklin Waters, *Ipswich in the Massachusetts Bay Colony*, vol. 1 (Ipswich, MA: Ipswich Historical Society, 1905), 237–64.

3. Moses Coit Tyler, *A History of American Literature*, vol. 2 (New York: G. P. Putnam's Sons, 1879), 104; Clinton L. Rossiter, "John Wise: Colonial Democrat," *New England Quarterly* 22, no. 1 (March 1949): 3–32, at 13; Vernon Louis Parrington, *Main Currents in American Thought*, vol. 1, *The Colonial Mind, 1680–1820* (Norman: University of Oklahoma Press, 1987 [1927]), 119.

4. Isaac Newton, *Philosophiæ Naturalis Principia Mathematica* (London: Joseph Streater, 1687).

5. Robert Brenner, *Merchants and Revolution: Commercial Change, Political Conflict, and London's Overseas Traders, 1550–1653* (Princeton, NJ: Princeton University Press, 1993), 276–80, 713–14.

6. Bernard Bailyn, *The New England Merchants in the Seventeenth Century* (New York: Harper & Row, 1955), 189–90, 194; Mark Valeri, *Heavenly Merchandize: How Religion Shaped Commerce in Puritan America* (Princeton, NJ: Princeton University Press, 2010), 41–42, 122–24; Owen Stanwood, *The Empire Reformed: English America in the Age of the Glorious Revolution* (Philadelphia: University of Pennsylvania Press, 2011), 85–86, 114.

7. On "the refusal of Massachusetts to become a part of the British colonial system" in the 1660s, 1670s, and 1680s, see Viola Florence Barnes, *The Dominion of New England: A Study in British Colonial Policy* (New Haven, CT: Yale University Press, 1923), 5–26.

8. "Fighting the king to defend the King": Ernst H. Kantorowicz, *The King's Two Bodies: A Study in Mediaeval Theology* (Princeton, NJ: Princeton University Press, 1957), 23.

9. Leslie V. Brock, *The Currency of the American Colonies, 1700–1764: A Study in Colonial Finance and Imperial Relations* (New York: Arno Press, 1975), 2–3, 5, 9; Edwin J. Perkins, *The Economy of Colonial America*, 2nd ed. (New York: Columbia University Press, 1988), 165, 168; Jennifer J. Baker, *Securing the Commonwealth: Debt, Speculation, and Writing in the Making of Early America* (Baltimore: Johns Hopkins University Press, 2005), 21; Margaret Ellen Newell,

From Dependency to Independence: Economic Revolution in Colonial New England (Ithaca, NY: Cornell University Press, 1998), 115, 119.

10. Tyler, *American Literature*, 115–16; Rossiter, "Colonial Democrat"; Vernon Louis Parrington, "John Wise, Village Democrat," in *Main Currents in American Thought*, vol. 1, *The Colonial Mind, 1680–1820* (Norman: University of Oklahoma Press, 1987 [1927]), 118–25; George Allan Cook, *John Wise: Early American Democrat* (New York: Octagon Books, 1966). Cf. Stearns, "John Wise."

11. See, for example, the discussion of Wise's work as epitomizing "the emergence of modern economic attitudes" as well as of secular, enlightened, liberal political ideas in Ronald P. Dufour, *Modernization in Colonial Massachusetts, 1630–1763* (New York: Garland Publishing, 1987), 206–9, 262–63, 271–72.

12. Perry Miller, *The New England Mind: From Colony to Province* (Boston: Beacon Press, 1953), 300, 317.

13. In the most comprehensive survey of the currency debate in provincial New England, Margaret Ellen Newell thus describes Wise's advocacy of paper money as exemplifying the emergence of economic liberalism that lay the ideological groundwork for American independence. Newell, *Dependency to Independence*, 157–58, 162–63, 166, 171, 180–81, 190, 195.

14. See, for example, T. H. Breen, "John Wise: A Country Writer," in Breen, *The Character of the Good Ruler: A Study of Puritan Political Ideas in New England, 1630–1730* (New Haven, CT: Yale University Press, 1970), 251–61; Stearns, "John Wise," 17; Dufour, *Modernization in Massachusetts*, 208–9.

15. See Alison Games, "Migration," in *The British Atlantic World, 1500–1800*, ed. David Armitage and Michael J. Braddick, 2nd ed. (Basingstoke: Palgrave Macmillan, 2002), 31–50.

16. Details of Wise's early life are from Cook, *John Wise*, 1–10; John Langdon Sibley, *Biographical Sketches of Graduates of Harvard University*, vol. 2 (Cambridge, MA: Harvard University Press, 1881); 428–41; D. Hamilton Hurd, ed., *History of Essex County, Massachusetts, with Biographical Sketches of Many of Its Pioneers and Prominent Men*, vol. 2 (Philadelphia: J. W. Lewis & Co., 1888), 1162–65; William Pencak, "John Wise," *American National Biography*.

17. John Winthrop, "A Modell of Christian Charity" (1630).

18. Francis S. Drake, *The Town of Roxbury: Its Memorable Persons and Places* (Roxbury, MA: Francis Drake [self-published], 1878), 363.

19. John Eliot, *The Christian Commonwealth: or, The Civil Policy of the Rising Kingdom of Jesus Christ* (London: Livewell Chapman, 1659).

20. Amicus Patriæ [John Wise], *A Word of Comfort to a Melancholy Country. Or the Bank of Credit Erected in the Massachusetts-Bay, Fairly Defended by a Discovery of the Great Benefit, accruing by it to the Whole PROVINCE; With a Remedy for Recovering a Civil State when Sinking under Desperation by Defeat on their Bank of Credit* (Boston, 1721), 11.

21. John Fea, "The Way of Improvement Leads Home: Philip Vickers Fithian's Rural Enlightenment," *Journal of American History* 90, no. 2 (September 2003): 462–90; David Jaffee, "The Village Enlightenment in New England, 1760–1820," *William and Mary Quarterly*, 3rd ser., 47, no. 3 (July 1990): 327–46; Stephen Foster, *The Long Argument: English Puritanism and the Shaping of New England Culture, 1570–1700* (Chapel Hill: University of North Carolina Press, 1991), 16–20.

22. David D. Hall, *The Faithful Shepherd: A History of the New England Ministry in the Seventeenth Century*, 2nd printing (Cambridge, MA: Harvard Theological Studies, 2006), 186–93. "Cosmopolitan rootedness" is from Fea, "Way of Improvement."

23. Cook, *John Wise*, 25–30; Wise, *Word of Comfort*, 13–14.

24. On "contention" in the late seventeenth-century New England churches, see Hall, *Faithful Shepherd*, 187.

25. Robert Crowell, *History of the Town of Essex, from 1634 to 1700* (Boston: C. C. P. Moody, 1853), 95, 107, 123–24; Hurd, *History of Essex County*, 1162; Cook, *John Wise*, 34, 41–42.

26. Joseph B. Felt, *History of Ipswich, Essex, and Hamilton* (Cambridge, MA: Charles Folsom, 1834), 33.

27. Waters, *Ipswich in Massachusetts*, 1:21–22, 75–76; Christopher M. Jedrey, *The World of John Cleaveland: Family and Community in Eighteenth-Century New England* (New York: W. W. Norton & Co., 1979), 58–68; Gary Nash, *The Urban Crucible: Social Change, Political Consciousness, and the Origins of the American Revolution* (Cambridge, MA: Harvard University Press, 1979), 54–75.

28. Brendan McConville, *The King's Three Faces: The Rise and Fall of Royal America, 1688–1776* (Chapel Hill: University of North Carolina Press, 2006), 29–35; J. R. Pole, *The Gift of Government: Political Responsibility from the English Restoration to American Independence* (Athens: University of Georgia Press, 1983), 1–2; Waters, *Ipswich in Massachusetts*, 225–33; Stanwood, *Empire Reformed*, 25–48, 123.

29. Elizabeth V. Mensch, "The Colonial Origins of Liberal Property Rights," *Buffalo Law Review* 31, no. 1 (Winter 1982): 635–735, at 644–45.

30. David Thomas Konig, *Law and Society in Puritan Massachusetts: Essex County, 1629–1692* (Chapel Hill: University of North Carolina Press, 1979), 162–64; Valeri, *Heavenly Merchandize*, 70.

31. Brenner, *Merchants and Revolution*, 666–70.

32. Cook, *John Wise*, 42–43; Waters, *Ipswich in Massachusetts*, 228, 233.

33. Barnes, *Dominion of New England*, 82–83, 91–92.

34. Edmund S. Morgan, *Inventing the People: The Rise of Popular Sovereignty in England and America* (New York: W. W. Norton & Co., 1988), 24, 43–44, 239; J. R. Pole, *Political Representation in England and the Origins of the American Republic* (Berkeley: University of California Press, 1966), 4, 33; Cook, *John Wise*, 43–44.

35. Sibley, *Graduates of Harvard University*, 431–32.

36. On slavery in seventeenth-century New England, see Wendy Warren, *New England Bound: Slavery and Colonization in Early America* (New York: Liveright, 2016).

37. Mary Sarah Bilder, *The Transatlantic Constitution: Colonial Legal Culture and the Empire* (Cambridge, MA: Harvard University Press, 2004).

38. Valeri, *Heavenly Merchandize*, 70–72.

39. Stanwood, *Empire Reformed*, 114.

40. "Black coats and redcoats": Stephen Saunders Webb, *Lord Churchill's Coup: The Anglo-American Empire and the Glorious Revolution Reconsidered* (New York: Alfred A. Knopf, 1995), x.

41. On Mather's leadership at this juncture, see Foster, *Long Argument*, 243–44, 249–50.

42. *Two Narratives of the Expedition against Quebec, A.D. 1690, under Sir William Phips: The One by Rev. John Wise, or Ipswich, Mass., and the Other by an Unknown Writer* (Cambridge, MA: John Wilson and Son, 1902), 18.

43. Newell, *Dependency to Independence*, 128–29; Perkins, *Economy of Colonial America*, 169–70; Elizabeth E. Dunn, "'Grasping at the Shadow': The Massachusetts Currency Debate, 1690–1715," *New England Quarterly* 71, no. 1 (March 1998): 54–76, esp. 55–56.

44. Paul Boyer and Stephen Nissenbaum, *Salem Possessed: The Social Origins of Witchcraft* (Cambridge, MA: Harvard University Press, 1974), 200–202.

45. Increase Mather, *Cases of Conscience Concerning Witchcrafts* (ms., Special Collections, Newberry Library, Chicago, ca. 1700; orig. signed October 1692), n.p.

46. Waters, *Ipswich in Massachusetts*, 290.

47. On the Salem witch trials as the climax of "the crisis of the interregnum" in Essex County, see Konig, *Law and Society*, 144–54, 168–85.

48. Parrington, *Main Currents*, 120.

49. Waters, *Ipswich in Massachusetts*, 89; Pole, *Political Representation*, 34; Edmund S. Morgan, *Visible Saints: The History of a Puritan Idea* (New York: New York University Press, 1963).

50. Pole, *Political Representation*, 36–37, 55–56; Valeri, *Heavenly Merchandize*, 123–24; McConville, *King's Three Faces*, 33–35.

51. Williston Walker, *A History of the Congregational Churches in the United States*, 6th ed. (New York: Charles Scribner's Sons, 1907), 170–75, 179; James F. Cooper Jr., *Tenacious of Their Liberties: The Congregationalists in Colonial Massachusetts* (New York: Oxford University Press, 1999), 151–69; J. William T. Youngs Jr., *God's Messengers: Religious Leadership in Colonial New England, 1700–1750* (Baltimore: Johns Hopkins University Press, 1976), 64–66; Hall, *Faithful Shepherd*, 199–225.

52. Youngs, *God's Messengers*, 69–73; Cooper, *Tenacious of Their Liberties*, 160–66; Walker, *History of Congregational Churches*, 198–204; Hall, *Faithful Shepherd*, 220–23.

53. Felt, *History of Ipswich*, 33.

54. John Wise, *The Churches Quarrel Espoused: or a Reply in Satyre, to certain Proposals made, in Answer to this Question, What further Steps are to be taken, that the Councils may have due Constitution and Efficacy In supporting, Preserving, and Well-Ordering the Interest of the Churches in the Country*, 2nd ed. (Boston: Nicholas Boone, 1715), 8, 9, 11.

55. Wise, *Churches Quarrel*, 24.

56. Cook, *John Wise*, 84–85.

57. Wise, *Churches Quarrel*, 30, 34.

58. Wise, *Churches Quarrel*, 10, 57–58, 31.

59. Wise, *Churches Quarrel*, 19–20.

60. On the discourse of "arbitrary government," see David D. Hall, *A Reforming People: Puritanism and the Transformation of Public Life in New England* (New York: Alfred A. Knopf, 2011), 22–52; Stanwood, *Empire Reformed*, 117.

61. Wise, *Churches Quarrel*, 93, 21, 94; John Wise, *A Vindication of the Government of New-England Churches. Drawn from Antiquity; the Light of Nature; Holy Scripture; its Noble Nature; and from the Dignity Divine Providence has put upon it* (Boston: J. Allen, 1717), 62–63.

62. Wise, *Churches Quarrel*, 40.

63. Wise, *Churches Quarrel*, 38, 28.

64. Allen D. Boyer, *Sir Edward Coke and the Elizabethan Age* (Stanford, CA: Stanford University Press, 2003), 83–107; James R. Stoner, *Common Law and Liberal Theory: Coke, Hobbes, and the Origins of American Constitutionalism* (Lawrence: University Press of Kansas, 1992), 6, 14–18; Edward S. Corwin, "The 'Higher Law' Background of American Constitutional Law," *Harvard Law Review* 42, nos. 2–3 (1928–29); John Underwood Lewis, "Sir Edward Coke (1552–1634): His Theory of 'Artificial Reason' as a Context for Modern Basic Legal Theory," in *Law, Liberty, and Parliament: Selected Essays on the Writings of Sir Edward Coke*, ed. Allen D. Boyer (Indianapolis: Liberty Fund, 2004), 107–20; J. G. A. Pocock, *The Ancient Constitution and the Feudal Law: A Study of English Historical Thought in the Seventeenth Century*, 2nd ed. (Cambridge: Cambridge University Press, 1987 [1957]), 30–69.

65. Parrington, *Main Currents*, 120–21; Benjamin Fletcher Wright Jr., *American Interpretations of Natural Law: A Study in the History of Political Thought* (Cambridge, MA: Harvard University Press, 1931), 49–57.

66. Richard Olson, *The Emergence of the Social Sciences, 1642–1792* (New York: Twayne, 1993), 139.

67. James Tully, "Editor's Introduction," in Samuel Pufendorf, *On the Duty of Man and Citizen according to Natural Law*, ed. James Tully, trans. Michael Silverthorne (Cambridge: Cambridge University Press, 1991), xiv–xxiv; Knud Haakonssen, *Natural Law and Moral Philosophy: From Grotius to the Scottish Enlightenment* (Cambridge: Cambridge University Press, 1996), 1–7, 15, 36–42, 61.

68. Terence Hutchinson, *Before Adam Smith: The Emergence of Political Economy, 1662–1776* (Oxford: Basil Blackwell, 1988), 5.

69. Leonard Krieger, *The Politics of Discretion: Pufendorf and the Acceptance of Natural Law* (Chicago: University of Chicago Press, 1965); Mark A. Peterson, "*Theopolis Americana*: The City-State of Boston, the Republic of Letters, and the Protestant International, 1689–1739," in *Soundings in Atlantic History: Latent Structures and Intellectual Currents, 1500–1830*, ed. Bernard Bailyn and Patricia L. Denault (Cambridge, MA: Harvard University Press, 2009), 329–70.

70. Haakonssen, *Natural Law*; Tully, "Introduction."

71. Wise, *Vindication of Government*, 33, 34, 36, 37.

72. Wise, *Vindication of Government*, 44, 45, 67, 86, 78.

73. Wise, *Churches Quarrel*, 90.

74. Wise, *Churches Quarrel*, 101.

75. Wise, *Churches Quarrel*, 36–37.

76. Hurd, *History of Essex County*, 1163.

77. See Robert C. Ritchie, *Captain Kidd and the War against the Pirates* (Cambridge, MA: Harvard University Press, 1986); Peter Linebaugh and Marcus Rediker, *The Many-Headed Hydra: Sailors, Slaves, Commoners, and the Hidden History of the Revolutionary Atlantic* (Boston: Beacon Press, 2000), 143–73.

78. Wise, *Vindication of Government*, 65.

79. Wise, *Churches Quarrel*, 59.

80. Baker, *Securing the Commonwealth*; Mark Peterson, *The Price of Redemption: The Spiritual Economy of Puritan New England* (Stanford, CA: Stanford University Press, 1997); Valeri, *Heavenly Merchandize*.

81. *Boston Gazette*, 13 February 1721, n.p.

82. *Boston Gazette*, 6 March 1721, n.p. Letter dated 29 September 1719.

83. *Boston Gazette*, 13 March 1721, n.p.

84. Amicus [John Wise], *A Friendly check, from a Kind Relation, To the Chief Cannoneer, Founded on a Late Information* (Boston, n.p., 1721), 1, 5–6.

85. John Wise, *The Freeholder's Address to the Honourable House of Representatives, March 15, 1720* (Boston: J. Franklin, 1721), 3, 4.

86. Nash, *Urban Crucible*, 112–13.

87. *A Letter to An Eminent Clergy-Man in the Massachusetts Bay. Containing some Just Remarks, and necessary Cautions, relating to Publick Affairs in that Province* (Boston: n.p., 1720), 5, 7, 11–12, 9, 6, 10. The historian and bibliographer Andrew McFarland Davis notes that the clergyman to whom this "letter" was addressed appears to have been Wise. A. M. Davis, *Colonial Currency Reprints, 1682–1751*, vol. 2 (Boston: John Wilson and Son, 1910), 243–44. The anonymous

author says the clergyman was very pleased with the pamphlet, which replicates both Wise's style and several extended passages from Wise's own work.

88. [John Blackwell], "A Discourse in Explanation of the Bank of Credit . . . ," unpublished ms., 1687, in Davis, *Colonial Currency Reprints*, 1:121–51, quoted passage at 125–26.

89. [John Woodbridge], *Severals relating to the Fund* (1682), 4–5.

90. Blackwell, "Bank of Credit," 144.

91. Woodbridge, *Severals relating to the Fund*, 5.

92. Blackwell, "Bank of Credit," 129, 144.

93. See Margaret Schabas, *The Natural Origins of Economics* (Chicago: University of Chicago Press, 2005).

94. Nuala Zahedieh, "Economy," in *The British Atlantic World, 1500–1800*, ed. David Armitage and Michael J. Braddick, 2nd ed. (Basingstoke: Palgrave Macmillan, 2009), 51–68.

95. Farley Grubb, "Is Paper Money Just Paper Money? Experimentation and Variation in the Paper Monies Issued by the American Colonies from 1690 to 1775," *NBER Working Papers*, no. 17997 (Washington, DC: National Bureau of Economic Research, 2012).

96. Bailyn, *New England Merchants*, 194.

97. Wise, *Word of Comfort*.

98. Wise, *Word of Comfort*, 21.

99. Wise, *Word of Comfort*, 24.

100. Wise, *Word of Comfort*, 35.

101. Wise, *Word of Comfort*, 18–19.

102. See William Pietz, "The Problem of the Fetish, I," *Res* 9 (Spring 1985): 5–17.

103. Wise, *Word of Comfort*, 4.

104. Wise, *Word of Comfort*, 38.

105. Wise, *Word of Comfort*, 2.

106. Wise, *Word of Comfort*, 33.

107. Wise, *Word of Comfort*, 4–5.

108. Wise, *Word of Comfort*, 5.

109. Wise, *Word of Comfort*, 44–45.

110. Wise, *Word of Comfort*, 33, 6.

111. Amicus Republicæ [John Wise], *Trade & Commerce Inculcated; in a Discourse Shewing the Necessity of a Well-governed* Trade, *in order to a Flourishing Common-Wealth. With some* Proposals *for the bringing* Gold & Silver *into the country for a Medium of* Trade, *as also for the better Supporting the Credit of the* Paper Currency (Boston: n.p., 1731), 20–21.

112. Wise, *Word of Comfort*, 54–55.

113. Wise, *Word of Comfort*, 52–53.

114. Wise, *Word of Comfort*, 10. See Ann Louise Kibbie, "Monstrous Generation: The Birth of Capital in Defoe's *Moll Flanders* and *Roxana*," *PMLA* 110, no. 5 (October 1995): 1023–34.

115. Wise, *Word of Comfort*, 29–30.

116. Wise, *Word of Comfort*, ii.

117. John Wise, *The Freeholder's Address to the Honourable House of Representatives* (Boston: J. Franklin, 1721); Wise, *Word of Comfort*, i.

118. Nash, *Urban Crucible*, 112.

119. Wise, *Trade and Commerce*, 12–14, 37.

120. John White, *The Gospel Treasure in Earthen Vessels: A Funeral Sermon On the Mournful Occasion of the Death of That Faithful Servant of God, the Reverend Mr. John Wise, Pastor*

of the Second Church in Ipswich, *Preached to his Flock, On the 11th Day of April, 1725* (Boston: N. Boone, 1725), 8, 36, 13.

Chapter Two

1. [William Douglass], letter to the editor, *Boston News-Letter* (17–24 July 1721), 3; William Douglass, *The Abuses and Scandals of Some Late Pamphlets in Favour of Inoculation of the Small Pox . . .* (Boston: J. Franklin, 1722), n.p. On the smallpox inoculation controversy in Boston and Douglass's role in it, see John T. Barrett, "The Inoculation Controversy in Puritan New England," *Bulletin of the History of Medicine* 12 (1942): 169–90; John D. Burton, "'The Awful Judgments of God upon the Land': Smallpox in Colonial Cambridge, Massachusetts," *New England Quarterly* 74, no. 3 (September 2001): 495–506; John B. Blake, *Public Health in the Town of Boston, 1630–1822* (Cambridge, MA: Harvard University Press, 1959), 52–59; Maxine Van de Wetering, "A Reconsideration of the Inoculation Controversy," *New England Quarterly* 58, no. 1 (March 1985): 46–67; James M. Schmotter, "William Douglass and the Beginnings of American Medical Professionalism: A Reinterpretation of the 1721 Boston Inoculation Controversy," *Historical Journal of Western Massachusetts* 6, no. 1 (Fall 1977): 23–36; Perry Miller, *The New England Mind: From Colony to Province* (Cambridge, MA: Harvard University Press, 1953), 345–66; Raymond Muse, "William Douglass: Man of the American Enlightenment, 1691–1752" (PhD diss., Stanford University, 1948), 41–72.

2. On Douglass's life and work, see Muse, "William Douglass"; Charles J. Bullock, "The Life and Writings of William Douglass," *Economic Studies* 2, no. 5 (October 1897): 265–89; Moses Coit Tyler, *A History of American Literature*, vol. 2 (New York: G. P. Putnam's Sons, 1879), 151–57.

3. R. H. Campbell, *Scotland since 1707: The Rise of an Industrial Society* (Oxford: Basil Blackwell, 1965), 2–3; Malcolm Gray, "The Impact of Agrarian Change in the Rural Lowlands," in *People and Society in Scotland*, vol. 1, *1760–1830*, ed. T. M. Devine and Rosalin Mitchison (Edinburgh: John Donald, 1988), 53–69.

4. T. M. Devine, *Scotland's Empire, 1600–1815* (London: Allen Lane, 2003), xxv–xxvii, 98, 164–65; Ned. C. Landsman, "Introduction: The Context and Functions of Scottish Involvement with the Americas," in *Nation and Province in the First British Empire*, ed. Landsman (Lewisburg, PA: Bucknell University Press, 2001), 15–35, esp. 21; Roger L. Emerson, "The Scottish Literati and America, 1680–1800," in Landsman, *Nation and Province*, 183–220, esp. 190–91.

5. Robert G. Frank Jr., "The Image of Harvey in Commonwealth and Restoration England," in *William Harvey and His Age: The Professional and Social Context of the Discovery of the Circulation*, ed. Jerome J. Bylebyl (Baltimore: Johns Hopkins University Press, 1979), 122.

6. Joyce E. Chaplin, *The First Scientific American: Benjamin Franklin and the Pursuit of Genius* (New York: Basic Books, 2006), 78.

7. Theodore M. Brown, "Medicine in the Shadow of the *Principia*," *Journal of the History of Ideas* 48, no. 4 (October–December 1987): 629–48, quoted passages at 632–33; Anita Guerrini, "Archibald Pitcairne and Newtonian Medicine," *Medical History* 31 (1987): 70–83, quoted passage at 75.

8. Muse, "William Douglass," 5.

9. Devine, *Scotland's Empire*, 98, 164–65; Richard D. Brown, "The Healing Arts in Colonial and Revolutionary Massachusetts: The Context for Scientific Medicine," in *Medicine in Colonial Massachusetts, 1620–1820*, ed. Colonial Society of Massachusetts (Boston: Colonial Society of

Massachusetts, 1980), 35–47; G. B. Warden, "The Medical Profession in Colonial Boston," in Colonial Society of Massachusetts, *Medicine in Colonial Massachusetts*, 145–57; Muse, "William Douglass," 50; [Douglass], letter to the editor, *Boston News-Letter* (17–24 July 1721), 3.

10. Miller, *New England Mind*, 347.

11. Douglass, *Abuses and Scandals*, 8.

12. Ben Mutschler, "Illness in the 'Social Credit' and 'Money' Economies of Eighteenth-Century New England," in *Medicine and the Market in England and Its Colonies, c. 1450–c. 1850*, ed. Mark S. R. Jenner and Patrick Wallis (Basingstoke: Palgrave Macmillan, 2007), 175–95.

13. Douglass, *Abuses and Scandals*, 5.

14. Schmotter, "Douglass and Medical Professionalism," 22–36; Muse, "William Douglass," 32–36.

15. Alexander Hamilton, *Gentleman's Progress* (10 August 1744), 137.

16. William Douglass, *A Practical Essay Concerning the Small Pox* (Boston: D. Henchman and T. Hancock, 1730), iii.

17. Douglass, *Dr. Douglass's Practical History of A New Epidemical Eruptive Miliary Fever, with an Angina Ulcusculosa, Which Prevailed in* Boston *New-England in the Years 1735 and 1736* (Boston: Thomas Fleet, 1736), ii.

18. Douglass, *Practical Essay Concerning the Small Pox*, 6.

19. Douglass, *A Summary, Historical and Political, Of the first Planting, progressive Improvements, and present State of the British Settlements in North America*, vol. 1 (Boston: Rogers and Fowle, 1749–51), 383.

20. Douglass to Colden, 20 February 1721, in "Letters from Dr. William Douglass to Cadwallader Colden of New York," *Collections of the Massachusetts Historical Society*, vol. 2, 4th ser., 164–65; Douglass to Colden, 1 May 1722 and 25 July 1722, in "Letters from Douglass to Colden," 170, 171.

21. Mark Harrison, *Contagion: How Commerce Has Spread Disease* (New Haven, CT: Yale University Press, 2012), xii–xiii, 8–9.

22. Blake, *Public Health*, 10, 32–36.

23. Blake, *Public Health*, 11–12, 23–25; Harrison, *Contagion*, 10, 46.

24. *Boston News-Letter*, 17–24 July 1721, 1–2. The author was likely the editor of *The Political State of Great Britain*, the French-English journalist Abel Boyer.

25. Richard Mead, from *A Short Discourse Concerning Pestilential Contagion: and the Methods to Be Used to Prevent It*, excerpted in *Boston News-Letter*, 6–10 July 1721 and 17–24 July 1721.

26. Gareth Williams, *Angel of Death: The Story of Smallpox* (Houndmills: Palgrave Macmillan, 2010), 29–32; Genevieve Miller, *The Adoption of Inoculation for Smallpox in England and France* (Philadelphia: University of Pennsylvania Press, 1957), 26.

27. Williams, *Angel of Death*, 112; Blake, *Public Health*, 54–55; Muse, *William Douglass*, 41.

28. William Douglass, *A Dissertation Concerning the Inoculation of the Small-Pox* (Boston: D. Henchman and T. Hancock, 1730), 1–2; Emanuel Timonius and John Woodward, "An Account, or History, of the Procuring the Small Pox by Incision, or Inoculation; As It Has for Some Time Been Practiced at Constantinople," *Philosophical Transactions of the Royal Society of London* 339 (1714): 72–82; Perrot Williams, "On the Method of Procuring the Small Pox, in South Wales," *Philosophical Transactions of the Royal Society of London* 375 (1723): 262; Richard Wright, "A Further Account of Buying the Small Pox," *Philosophical Transactions of the Royal Society of London* 375 (1723): 267; Williams, *Angel of Death*, 53–61; Blake, *Public Health*, 53–54; Muse, "William Douglass," 43–44.

29. Douglass to Cadwallader Colden, 28 July 1721, in "Letters from Douglass to Colden," 166.

30. Douglass, *Abuses and Scandals*, n.p., 8.

31. Douglass, *Dissertation Concerning Inoculation*, 20, n.p.

32. Douglass to Colden, 1 May 1722, in "Letters to Colden," 170; Douglass, *Dissertation Concerning Inoculation*, n.p.

33. Douglass, *Essay Concerning Small Pox*, 5–8, 11–12, 15, 16–20.

34. Brian W. Ogilvie, *The Science of Describing: Natural History in Renaissance Europe* (Chicago: University of Chicago Press, 2006), 1–8; Raymond Phineas Stearns, *Science in the British Colonies of America* (Urbana: University of Illinois Press, 1970), 6, 19, 46–47; David Elliston Allen, *The Naturalist in Britain: A Social History* (Princeton, NJ: Princeton University Press, 1976), 3.

35. Harold J. Cook, "Physicians and Natural History," in *Cultures of Natural History*, ed. N. Jardine, J. A. Secord and E. C. Spary (Cambridge: Cambridge University Press, 1996), 91–105, here 92.

36. Cook, "Natural History," 104; Susan Scott Parish, *American Curiosity: Cultures of Natural History in the Colonial British Atlantic World* (Chapel Hill: University of North Carolina Press, 2006), 7–8, 103–4; James Delbourgo, "Science," in *The British Atlantic World, 1500–1800*, ed. David Armitage and Michael J. Braddick, 2nd ed. (Basingstoke: Palgrave Macmillan, 2009), 92–112.

37. Katie Whitaker, "The Culture of Curiosity," in Jardine, Secord, and Spary, *Natural History*, 75–90; Keith Thomas, *Man and the Natural World: A History of the Modern Sensibility* (New York: Pantheon Books, 1983), 52–58.

38. Whitaker, "Culture of Curiosity," 82; Cook, "Natural History," 99–100.

39. Stearns, *Science in the Colonies*, 481.

40. Douglass to Colden, 20 February 1721, in "Letters from Douglass to Colden," 166.

41. S. Todd Lowry, "The Archaeology of the Circulation Concept in Economic Theory," *Journal of the History of Ideas* 35, no. 3 (July-September 1974): 429–44; Paul P. Christensen, "Fire, Motion, and Productivity: The Proto-Energetics of Nature and Economy in François Quesnay," in *Natural Images in Economic Thought: "Markets Read in Tooth and Claw,"* ed. Philip Mirowski (Cambridge: Cambridge University Press, 1994), 249–88, quoted passages at 271, 276–77; Margaret Schabas, *The Natural Origins of Economics* (Chicago: University of Chicago Press, 2006), 25–26, 29; James Delbourgo, *A Most Amazing Scene of Wonders: Electricity and Enlightenment in Early America* (Cambridge, MA: Harvard University Press, 2006).

42. Schabas, *Natural Origins of Economics*, 5–6, 29–30; Lowry, "Circulation Concept"; Joseph A. Schumpeter, *History of Economic Analysis*, ed. Elizabeth B. Schumpeter (New York, 1954), 242. See also the foundational work of Michel Foucault, *The Order of Things: An Archaeology of the Human Sciences* (New York: Pantheon Books, 1971), 125–65.

43. David Hume, *Dialogues Concerning Natural Religion, and Other Writings*, ed. Dorothy Coleman (Cambridge: Cambridge University Press, 2007), 59. Quoted in Schabas, *Natural Origins*, 4. Hume began writing the *Dialogues* around 1750, though the work was not published until 1779. The quoted passage is spoken by Philo, the persona in the dialogues generally considered closest to Hume's own views.

44. "Perpetual Motion in Matter, Exercise and Temperance necessary to Health, and Virtue necessary to Happiness," *American Magazine and Historical Chronicle* (June 1744), 1.

45. William Nadir [William Douglass], *Mercurius Nov-Anglicanus: or an Almanack* (Boston: Rogers and Fowle, 1743), title page.

46. [Douglass], *Mercurius Nov-Anglicanus*, 9.

47. [Douglass], *Mercurius Nov-Anglicanus*, 19.

48. William Douglass, *Plan of the British Dominions of New England in North America*, engraved by R. W. Seale (London: Executors of William Douglass, 1755); Matthew H. Edney, "New England Mapped: The Creation of a Colonial Territory," in *La Cartografia Europea tra Primmo Rinascimento e Fine Dell'Illuminismo*, ed. Diogo Ramada Curto, Angelo Cattaneo, and André Ferrand Almeieda (Florence: Leo S. Olschki Editore, 2003): 155–76.

49. Edney, "New England Mapped," 168, 170.

50. Gary Nash, "The Failure of Female Factory Labor in Colonial Boston," *Labor History* 20 (1979): 165–68, here 166–67; Alvin Rabushka, *Taxation in Colonial America* (Princeton, NJ: Princeton University Press, 2008), 575–78, 584.

51. "Letter from Dr. Wil. Douglass to the Assessors of Boston, Asking an Abatement of His Tax, 1747," *Boston Medical and Surgical Journal* 104, no. 23 (9 June 1881): 537–38.

52. C. W. Tuttle, "William Douglass, M.D.," *New England Historical and Genealogical Register* 31 (January 1877): 118; *Biographical Sketches of the Founders of the Scots' Charitable Society, 1657* (Cambridge, MA: General Microfilm Co., 1980), 51.

53. Samuel Adams Drake, *Old Boston Taverns and Tavern Clubs* (Boston: W. A. Butterfield, 1917), 10, 12–14, 46–48, 110.

54. John Winthrop, "A Modell of Christian Charity," in *The Puritans: A Sourcebook of Their Writings*, ed. Perry Miller and Thomas H. Johnson, 2 vols. bound as one (Mineola, NY: Dover, 2001), 195; Cotton Mather, *Bonifacius: An Essay Upon the Good, That is Devised and Designed, By Those Who Desire to Answer the Great End of Life, and to Do Good While They Live* (Boston: B. Green, 1710), 101; Christine Leigh Heyrman, "The Fashion among More Superior People: Charity and Social Change in Provincial New England, 1700–1740," *American Quarterly* 34, no. 2 (Summer 1982): 107–24, at 121, 117; Conrad Edick Wright, *The Transformation of Charity in Postrevolutionary New England* (Boston: Northeastern University Press, 1992), 13–47; Kathleen D. McCarthy, *American Creed: Philanthropy and the Rise of Civil Society, 1700–1865* (Chicago: University of Chicago Press, 2003), 15.

55. McCarthy, *American Creed*, 17; Robert A. Gross, "Giving in America: From Charity to Philanthropy," in *Charity, Philanthropy, and Civility in American History*, ed. Lawrence J. Friedman and Mark D. McGarvie (Cambridge: Cambridge University Press, 2002), 29–48; David Owen, *English Philanthropy, 1660–1960* (Cambridge, MA: Belknap Press of Harvard University Press, 1964), 12–14; Nash, "Factory Labor"; Daniel J. Boorstin, *The Decline of Radicalism: Reflections on America Today* (New York: Random House, 1963), 4–68.

56. Peter R. Virgadamo, "Douglass, William," in *Biographical Dictionary of Social Welfare in America*, ed. Walter I. Trattner (New York: Greenwood Press, 1986), 247–50; Peter Dobkin Hall, "The Model of Boston Charity: A Theory of Charitable Benevolence and Class Development," *Science and Society* 38 (Winter 1974): 464–77.

57. Douglass, "Letter to Assessors," 538.

58. William A. Emerson, *History of the Town of Douglas (Massachusetts), from the Earliest Period to the Close of 1878* (Boston: Frank W. Bird, 1879), 17–19.

59. Though the two volumes were dated on their covers 1749 and 1751, the second was actually published in 1752. Lawrence C. Wroth, *An American Bookshelf, 1755* (Philadelphia: University of Pennsylvania Press, 1934), 87–91, 176–77. For appreciative historical assessments of Douglass's *Summary*, see David Freeman Hawke, "William Douglass's *Summary*," in *The Colonial Legacy*, vol. 2, *Some Eighteenth-Century Commentators*, ed. Lawrence H. Leder (New York: Harper and Row, 1971), 43–74; and John M. Bumsted, "Doctor Douglass's *Summary*," *New England Quarterly* 37 (1964): 242–50.

60. Douglass, *Summary of Settlements*, 1:392.

61. Douglass, *Summary of Settlements* 1:231, 214.

62. Douglass, *Summary of Settlements* 1:310; 2:383–84. On the "miscellaneous" style in natural histories, see Whitaker, "Culture of Curiosity," 84.

63. Douglass, *Summary of Settlements*, 1:2, 208, 510n.

64. Nash, "Factory Labor," 167.

65. Douglass, *Summary of Settlements*, 1:356.

66. Douglass, "Letter to Assessors," 538.

67. Peter R. Virgadamo, "Douglass, William," *American National Biography Online*, February 2000, http://www.anb.org.proxy.cc.uic.edu/articles/12/12-00225.html.

68. Douglass, *Summary of Settlements* 1:214.

69. Thomas, *Natural World*, 60–66, 89; Schabas, *Natural Origins*, 31; Dror Wahrman, *The Making of the Modern Self: Identity and Culture in Eighteenth-Century England* (New Haven, CT: Yale University Press, 2004), 3–6, 127–53.

70. Douglass, *Summary of Settlements*, 1:153–54, 161, 156.

71. Douglass, *Summary of Settlements*, 1:206–7.

72. Douglass, *Summary of Settlements*, 1:252.

73. Douglass, *Summary of Settlements*, 1:227.

74. Douglass, *Summary of Settlements*, 1:257, 256.

75. Bumsted, "Douglass's *Summary*," 245.

76. Douglass, *Summary of Settlements*, 1;241–60, quoted passages at 243, 249–50.

77. Bray Hammond, *Banks and Politics in America: From the Revolution to the Civil War* (Princeton, NJ: Princeton University Press, 1957), 16; Rabushka, *Taxation in America*, 577.

78. Rabushka, *Taxation in America*, 577.

79. Valenze, *Social Life of Money*, 66.

80. Schabas, *Natural Origins of Economics*, 42.

81. See Jonathan Sheehan and Dror Wahrman, *Invisible Hands: Self-Organization and the Eighteenth Century* (Chicago: University of Chicago Press, 2015).

82. Douglass, *Summary of Settlements*, 1:228, 212–13.

83. Douglass, *Summary of Settlements*, 1:310–11.

84. Adam Smith, *An Inquiry into the Nature and Causes of the Wealth of Nations* (Hamburg: Management Laboratory Press), 216.

85. *Wealth of Nations*, section II.2.100.

86. Douglass to Colden, 20 February 1721, in "Letters from Douglass to Colden," 164–65.

87. John L. Brooke, *The Heart of the Commonwealth: Society and Political Culture in Worcester County, Massachusetts, 1713–1861* (Cambridge: Cambridge University Press, 1989), 42, 49–50.

88. Margaret Ellen Newell, *From Dependency to Independence: Economic Revolution in Colonial New England* (Ithaca, NY: Cornell University Press, 1998), 214–31.

89. See Joyce Oldham Appleby, "Locke, Liberalism, and the Natural Law of Money," *Past and Present* 71 (1976): 43–69.

90. [Paul Dudley], *Objections to the Bank of Credit Late Projected at Boston. Being a Letter upon that Occasion, to John Burril, Esq.; Speaker to the House of Representatives for the Province of the Massachusetts-Bay, in New-England* (Boston: T. Fleet, 1714), 14, 20, 22, 24.

91. *The Present Melancholy Circumstances of the Province Consider'd, and Methods for Redress humbly proposed, in a Letter from one in the Country to one in Boston* (Boston: B. Gray and J. Edwards, 1719), 9, 11–12.

92. [William Douglass], *An Essay, Concerning Silver and Paper Currencies. More especially with Regard to the British Colonies in* New-England (Boston: S. Kneeland and T. Green, 1738), 3.

93. Douglass, *Discourse Concerning Currencies*, 5.

94. Douglass, *Discourse Concerning Currencies*, 61.

95. Douglass, *Discourse Concerning Currencies*, 4.

96. Douglass, *Essay Concerning Silver and Paper*, 6.

97. Douglass, *Essay Concerning Silver and Paper*, 6.

98. Douglass, *Essay Concerning Silver and Paper*, 8–9.

99. Douglass, *Discourse Concerning Currencies*, 20.

100. Douglass, *Essay Concerning Silver and Paper*, 14.

101. Douglass, *Discourse Concerning Currencies*, 27.

102. Douglass, *Discourse Concerning Currencies*, 55–56.

103. Douglass, *Essay Concerning Silver and Paper*, 23–24.

104. Douglass, *Essay Concerning Silver and Paper*, 6–7.

105. Douglass, *Discourse Concerning Currencies*, 30.

106. Douglass, *Discourse Concerning Currencies*, 30.

107. Douglass, *Discourse Concerning Currencies*, 29.

108. Douglass, *Discourse Concerning Currencies*, 30, 20–21.

109. Douglass, *A Letter to —— Merchant in London, Concerning a late Combination in the Province of the Massachusetts-Bay in New-England, to Impose or Force a Private Currency called Land Bank Money* (Boston, n.p., 1741), 8–9.

110. Douglass, *Letter to Merchant*, 10.

111. William Douglass, *A Second Letter to —— Merchant in London, Concerning a late Combination in the* Massachusetts-Bay *in* New-England, *to impose or force a private Currency, called* Land Bank Money (Boston, n.p., 1741), 9–10.

112. Douglass, *Letter to Merchant*, 11.

113. Douglass, *Discourse Concerning Currencies*, 31.

114. Douglass, *Letter to Merchant*, 11.

115. Cf. E. P. Thompson, "The Moral Economy of the English Crowd in the Eighteenth Century," *Past and Present* 50 (February 1971): 76–136.

116. Douglass, *Summary of Settlements*, 1:239.

117. Douglass, *Discourse Concerning Currencies*, 50.

118. Douglass, *Discourse Concerning Currencies*, 51.

119. Newell, *Dependency to Independence*, 230–32; Rabushka, *Taxation in America*, 579.

120. Elizabeth E. Dunn, "'Grasping at the Shadow': The Massachusetts Currency Debate, 1690–1751," *New England Quarterly* 71, no. 1 (March 1998): 54–76, at 54.

Chapter Three

1. Daniel Walker Howe, *What Hath God Wrought: The Transformation of America, 1815–1848* (New York: Oxford University Press, 2007), 501–5; Scott Reynolds Nelson, *A Nation of Deadbeats: An Uncommon History of America's Financial Disasters* (New York: Alfred A. Knopf, 2012), 101–7.

2. *Plaindealer*, 13 May 1837, 369; *Plaindealer*, 29 July 1837, 546.

3. On religious and political radicalism sparked by the panic, see John Stauffer, *The Black Hearts of Men: Radical Abolitionists and the Transformation of Race* (Cambridge, MA: Harvard University Press, 2001), 114–17.

4. Jeffrey L. Pasley, *"The Tyranny of Printers": Newspaper Politics in the Early American Republic* (Charlottesville: University Press of Virginia, 2001), 1–23; Edward Pessen, *Most Uncom-*

mon Jacksonians: The Radical Leaders of the Early Labor Movement (Albany: State University of New York Press, 1967), 57; Helen L. Sumner, "Citizenship," in John R. Commons et al., *History of Labour in the United States*, vol. 1 (New York: Macmillan Co., 1918), 167–332; Edwin G. Burrows and Mike Wallace, *Gotham: A History of New York City* (New York: Oxford University Press, 1999), 513–14; Sean Wilentz, *Chants Democratic: New York City and the Rise of the American Working Class, 1788–1850* (New York: Oxford University Press, 1984), 61–105.

5. Wilentz, *Chants Democratic*, 107–42; Edward B. Mittelman, "Trade Unionism," in Commons et al., *History of Labour*, 347–49; John B. Clark, "Introduction," in *A Documentary History of American Industrial Society*, ed. John R. Commons et al. vol. 5 (Cleveland: Arthur H. Clark Co., 1910), 19–20.

6. On the lower middle-class political tradition that the workingmen's movement inaugurated, see Bruce Laurie, "'Spavined Ministers, Lying Toothpullers, and Buggering Priests': Third-Partyism and the Search for Security in the Antebellum North," in *American Artisans: Crafting Social Identity, 1750–1850*, ed. Howard B. Rock, Paul A. Gilje, and Robert Asher (Baltimore: Johns Hopkins University Press, 1995), 98–119.

7. The only extended treatment of Leggett's early writings that I know of is Page S. Procter Jr., "The Life and Works of William Leggett (1801–1839)" (PhD diss., Yale University, 1949), but it focuses on the artistic merits and weaknesses of this work by mid-twentieth-century standards.

8. "Address to the Mechanics and Working Men of the State of New York," *New York Evening Post*, 23 July 1836, quoted in Mittelman, "Trade Unionism," 462.

9. Morgan, *Inventing the People: The Rise of Popular Sovereignty in England and America* (New York: W. W. Norton and Co., 1988), 49–50. See also the discussion of the "mandate-independence controversy" in Hanna Fenichel Pitkin, *The Concept of Representation* (Berkeley: University of California Press, 1967), 145–46.

10. *Plaindealer*, 3 December 1836, 1.

11. On the spread of chartered corporations for municipal, eleemosynary, and business purposes in the early United States, see Pauline Maier, "The Revolutionary Origins of the American Corporation," *William and Mary Quarterly*, 3rd ser., 50, no. 1 (January 1993): 51–84.

12. Jerome Hall, *Theft, Law and Society*, 2nd ed. (Indianapolis: Bobbs-Merrill Co., 1935), 35–40, 65–69.

13. Leggett, "The Monopoly Banking System," *New York Evening Post*, December 1834, in *A Collection of the Political Writings of William Leggett*, ed. Theodore Sedgwick Jr., vol. 1 (New York: Taylor & Dodd, 1840), 103.

14. Edward Kellogg, *Labor and Other Capital: The Rights of Each Secured and the Wrongs of Both Eradicated; or, An Exposition of the Cause Why Few Are Wealthy and Many Poor, and the Delineation of a System, Which, without Infringing the Rights of Property, Will Give to Labor Its Just Reward* (New York: Edward Kellogg, 1849), xxxv.

15. William Leggett, "Rich and Poor," *Evening Post*, 6 December 1834, in *Political Writings*, 1:110.

16. For an overview of the "banking question" as it figured in the Jacksonian labor movement, see Walter Hugins, *Jacksonian Democracy and the Working Class: A Study of the New York Workingmen's Movement, 1829–1837* (Stanford, CA: Stanford University Press, 1960), 172–202.

17. Pitkin, *Concept of Representation*. On the dual discourse of literary and political representation in the early republic, see Carolyn Eastman, *A Nation of Speechifiers: Making an American Public after the Revolution* (Chicago: University of Chicago, 2009); Jay Fliegelman, *Declaring Independence: Jefferson, Natural Language, and the Culture of Performance* (Stanford, CA: Stanford

University Press, 1993); Christopher Looby, *Voicing America: Language, Literary Form, and the Origins of the United States* (Chicago: University of Chicago Press, 1996); Thomas Gustafson, *Representative Words: Politics, Literature, and the American Language, 1776–1865* (Cambridge: Cambridge University Press, 1992); Larzer Ziff, *Writing in the New Nation: Prose, Print, and Politics in the Early United States* (New Haven, CT: Yale University Press, 1991).

18. Pasley, *Tyranny of Printers*, 1–23; Pessen, *Uncommon Jacksonians*, 57.

19. William Cullen Bryant, "William Leggett," *United States Magazine and Democratic Review* 6, no. 19 (July 1839): 20.

20. Leggett suffered from serious but amorphous infirmities for much of his life, and the precipitating cause of his early death is unclear, variously attributed to rheumatism and "high grade bilious fever." Stanley Nelson Worton, "William Leggett, Political Journalist (1801–1839): A Study in Democratic Thought" (PhD diss., Columbia University, 1954), 18–20.

21. Records of General Courts Martial and Courts of Inquiry of the Navy Department, 1799–1867, National Archives Microfilm Publications, Microcopy No. 273, Roll 19, Vol. 17, Cases 430 ¼–434, 21 June–5 September 1825, 0098, 0100, 0121, 0134; James E. Valle, *Rocks and Shoals: Order and Discipline in the Old Navy, 1800–1861* (Annapolis, MD: Naval Institute Press, 1980), 3, 259–60.

22. Records of Courts Martial, 0076–0077, 0078, 0065.

23. Records of Courts Martial, 0148–0149, 0124–0125, 0090–0094, 0076–0077, 0078, 0171.

24. On the pervasive discourse of conspiracy and corruption in the early American republic, see Gordon Wood, "Conspiracy and the Paranoid Style: Causality and the Eighteenth Century," *William and Mary Quarterly*, 3rd ser., 39, no. 3 (July 1982): 402–41; John M. Murrin, "Escaping Perfidious Albion: Federalism, Fear of Aristocracy, and the Democratization of Corruption in Postrevolutionary America," in *Virtue, Corruption, and Self-Interest: Political Values in the Eighteenth Century*, ed. Richard K. Matthews (London: Associated University Presses, 1994), 103–47.

25. Abraham Leggett, *The Narrative of Major Abraham Leggett, of the Army of the Revolution, Now First Printed from the Original Manuscript Written by Himself*, ed. Charles I. Bushnell (New York: n.p., 1865; reprinted 1924 as Extra No. 101, *The Magazine of History*).

26. Records of Court-Martial, 0081.

27. Andrew Lawson, *Downwardly Mobile: The Changing Fortunes of American Realism* (New York: Oxford University Press, 2012).

28. Charles I. Bushnell, "Introduction," in *Narrative of Abraham Leggett*, 41–42; Procter, "Life of Leggett," 1–7; Harry Ammon, "William Leggett: Equal Rights Editor" (MA thesis, Georgetown University, 1940), 7–9.

29. See Maurice Hindle, "Introduction," in Mary Shelley, *Frankenstein; or, The Modern Prometheus*, ed. Maurice Hindle, rev. ed. (New York: Penguin Books, 2003), xliv–xlv.

30. Sean Wilentz, *The Rise of American Democracy: From Jefferson to Lincoln* (New York: W. W. Norton & Co., 2005), 206–13.

31. Eastman, *Nation of Speechifiers*; Noah Webster, *An American Selection of Lessons in Reading and Speaking: Calculated to Improve the Minds and Refine the Taste of Youth: To Which Are Prefixed, Rules in Elocution, and Directions for Expressing the Principal Passions of the Mind*, 4th ed. (Philadelphia: David Hogan, 1809), x.

32. Bruce McConachie, "American Theatre in Context, from the Beginnings to 1870," *The Cambridge History of American Theatre*, ed. Don B. Wilmeth and Christopher Bigsby, vol. 1 (Cambridge: Cambridge University Press, 1998), 127–32.

33. T. Allston Brown, *A History of the New York Stage, from the First Performance in 1732 to 1901*, vol. 1 (New York: Dodd, Mead and Co., 1903), 83.

34. *The Watch-Word; or, Quito Gate: A Melo-Drama, in Two Acts* (London: Effingham Wilson, 1816); *The Blind Boy: A Melo-Drama, in Two Acts* (London: Longman, Hurst, Rees and Orme, 1808). Authors are not listed for either play.

35. William Dimond, "The Mariner's Dream," in *The Household Book of Poetry*, ed. Charles A. Dana (New York: D. Appleton and Co., 1903), 522–23.

36. *Edwardsville (Illinois) Spectator*, 24 April 1821, n.p.

37. Cf. Katie Trumpener, *Bardic Nationalism: The Romantic Novel and the British Empire* (Princeton, NJ: Princeton University Press, 1997).

38. Ammon, "William Leggett," 25; Procter, "Works of Leggett," 117, 119–20.

39. Christopher Bigsby and Don B. Wilmeth, "Introduction," in *The Cambridge History of American Theatre*, ed. Wilmeth and Bigsby, vol. 1 (Cambridge: Cambridge University Press, 1998), 1–19; McConachie, "American Theatre"; Joseph Roach, "The Emergence of the American Actor," in Wilmeth and Bigsby, *American Theatre*, 338–72; Jill Lepore, *The Name of War: King Philip's War and the Origins of American Identity* (New York: Alfred A. Knopf, 1998), 191–226; William Leggett, "Address at the Re-opening of the Bowery Theatre in New York City, 20 Aug. 1828," New-York Historical Society Mss. Collection (Thanks to Jan Hilley for transcribing Leggett's address). On the long association of the market and theater in Anglo-American culture, see Jean-Christophe Agnew, *Worlds Apart: The Market and the Theater in Anglo-American Thought, 1550–1750* (Cambridge: Cambridge University Press, 1986).

40. Gary A. Richardson, "Plays and Playwrights: 1800–1865," in Wilmeth and Bigsby, *American Theatre*, 258; David Grimsted, *Melodrama Unveiled: American Theater and Culture, 1800–1850* (Chicago: University of Chicago Press, 1968); Bruce A. McConachie, *Melodramatic Formations: American Theatre and Society, 1820–1870* (Iowa City: University of Iowa Press, 1992).

41. Peter Brooks, *The Melodramatic Imagination: Balzac, Henry James, Melodrama, and the Mode of Excess* (New Haven, CT: Yale University Press, 1976), 85, 14; Allardyce Nicoll, *A History of Early Nineteenth-Century Drama, 1800–1850*, vol. 1 (Cambridge: Cambridge University Press, 1930), 101–2.

42. Michael T. Gilmore, *Surface and Depth: The Quest for Legibility in American Culture* (Oxford: Oxford University Press, 2003), 43–45; James R. Lehning, *The Melodramatic Thread: Spectacle and Political Culture in Modern France* (Bloomington: Indiana University Press, 2007).

43. Joseph A. Schumpeter, *History of Economic Analysis*, ed. Elizabeth Moody Schumpeter (New York: Oxford University Press, 1954), 264–65, 277, 282; D. Foley, "Money in Economic Activity," in *The New Palgrave: A Dictionary of Economics*, ed. John Eatwell, Murray Milgate, and Peter Newman (London: Macmillan, 1987), 519–25; Ronald L. Meek, *Studies in the Labor Theory of Value*, 2nd ed. (New York: Monthly Review Press, 1956).

44. On the popularity of Shakespeare in nineteenth-century America, see Lawrence Levine, *Highbrow/Lowbrow: The Emergence of Cultural Hierarchy in America* (Cambridge, MA: Harvard University Press, 1988), 11–81.

45. The playwright James Rosenberg wrote that melodrama was "just about the dirtiest word in the lexicon of the modern critic. . . . In fact, it seems to have become a sort of universally applicable term of abuse; like 'communism,' roughly speaking, it seems to mean 'bad.'" James L. Rosenberg, "Melodrama," in *Tragedy: Vision and Form*, ed. Robert W. Corrigan (San Francisco: Chandler Publishing Co., 1965), 232–44, quoted passage at 232.

46. Susan Gillman, *Blood Talk: American Race Melodrama and the Culture of the Occult* (Chicago: University of Chicago Press, 2003), 14–16, 21–23; Jacky Bratton, Jim Cook, and Christine Gledhills, eds., *Melodrama: Stage, Picture, Screen* (London: British Film Institute, 1994).

47. Procter, "Works of Leggett," 10, 11, 14.

48. Procter, "Works of Leggett," 14–32; James T. Hair, *Gazeteer of Madison County* (Alton, IL: James T. Hair, 1866), 54–56; W. L. Norton, ed., *Centennial History of Madison County, Illinois, and Its People, 1812 to 1912* (Chicago: Lewis Publishing Co., 1912), 101, 138, 141; *History of Madison County, Illinois* (Edwardsville, IL: W. R. Brink & Co., 1882), 91, 95, 200–202; Solon J. Buck, *Illinois in 1818*, 2nd ed., rev. ed. (Urbana: University of Illinois Press, 1967 [1917]), 118–58.

49. William Leggett, *Poems* (Edwardsville, IL: William Leggett).

50. William Leggett, *Leisure Hours at Sea: Being a Few Miscellaneous Poems; By a Midshipman of the United States Navy* (New York: George C. Morgan, and E. Bliss & E. White, 1825) vii, viii.

51. Leggett, *Leisure Hours*, 26, 15, 102, 48; Procter, "Works of Leggett," 89–102; Michael T. Gilmore, "The Literature of the Revolutionary and Early National Periods," in *The Cambridge History of American Literature*, vol. 1, *1590–1820*, ed. Sacvan Bercovitch and Cyrus R. K. Patell (Cambridge: Cambridge University Press, 1994), 539–694, at 591–97; Kendall B. Taft, *Minor Knickerbockers: Representative Selections, with Introduction, Bibliography, and Notes* (Freeport, NY: Books for Libraries Press, 1970 [1947]), xxxvii–xxxix, xl, xciii.

52. Procter, "Works of Leggett," 137–38, 231.

53. *Tales and Sketches* (New York: J. & J. Harper); *Naval Stories* (New York: G. & C. & H. Carrill).

54. On Leggett's leading part in the rise of western and sea stories, see Fred Lewis Pattee, *The Development of the American Short Story: An Historical Survey* (New York: Harper & Bros., 1923), 54–55; John D. Seelye, "'Spontaneous Impress of Truth': Melville's Jack Chase; A Source, an Analogue, a Conjecture," *Nineteenth-Century Fiction* 20, no. 4 (March 1966): 367–76; Thomas Philbrick, *James Fenimore Cooper and the Development of American Sea Fiction* (Cambridge, MA: Harvard University Press, 1961), 104–14; Hester Blum, *The View from the Masthead: Maritime Imagination and Antebellum American Sea Narratives* (Chapel Hill: University of North Carolina Press, 2008), 79–80. On the relation between the parallel development of the two genres and the political and economic transformations of the early nineteenth century, see Peter Antelyes, *Tales of Adventurous Enterprise: Washington Irving and the Poetics of Western Expansion* (New York: Columbia University Press, 1990); Sanford E. Marovitz, "Frontier Conflicts: Villains, Outlaws and Indians in Selected 'Western' Fiction: 1799–1860" (PhD diss., Duke University, 1967); Hugh Egan, "Cooper and His Contemporaries," in *America and the Sea: A Literary History*, ed. Haskell Springer (Athens: University of Georgia Press, 1995); Cesare Casarino, *Modernity at Sea: Melville, Marx, Conrad in Crisis* (Minneapolis: University of Minnesota Press, 2002).

55. *Tales and Sketches*, 154.

56. *Naval Stories*, 113–14.

57. *Naval Stories*, 122, 125.

58. Blum, *View from the Masthead*, 1–2. See also "A Night at Gibraltar" and "Fire and Water" in *Naval Stories*.

59. *Tales and Sketches*, 36, 65

60. *Tales and Sketches*, 15.

61. John D. Seelye, "Buckskin and Ballistics: William Leggett and the American Detective Story," *Journal of Popular Culture* 1, no. 1 (Summer 1967): 52–57, esp. 54.

62. *Tales and Sketches*, 149.

63. *Tales and Sketches*, 50.

64. For extended consideration of this problem, see Agnew, *Worlds Apart*, 37–38, 42–43.

65. Stories ending in a man-to-man struggle to the death include "Merry Terry" and "Brought to the Gangway" in *Naval Stories* and "A Watch in the Main-Top" in *Tales and Sketches*.

Stories ending with a wedding include "The Block-House" in *Tales of Glauber-Spa* and "The Steel Clasp," "The Rifle," "Near-Sighted," and "The Mistake" in *Tales and Sketches*.

66. *Tales and Sketches*, 16, 219, 91–92, 65, 141, 222, 21.

67. William Leggett, *Critic* 1, no. 3 (15 November 1828): 39. Thanks to Nancy O. Bryant for help in interpreting Leggett's portrait.

68. Procter, "Works of Leggett," 139, 152, 177; Ammon, "William Leggett," 29; *Critic* 2, no. 7 (20 June 1829): 89.

69. Taft, *Minor Knickerbockers*, xli; M. H. Abrams, *The Mirror and the Lamp: Romantic Theory and the Critical Tradition* (New York: Oxford University Press, 1953), 14; Gilmore, "Revolutionary and Early National Periods," 542–44.

70. *Critic* 1, no. 25A (26 April 1829): 396, 397.

71. On hostility to the theater during and after the American Revolution, see McConachie, "American Theatre," 127–29; Grimsted, *Melodrama Unveiled*, 22–45.

72. *Critic* 1, no. 4 (22 November 1828): 62.

73. *Critic* 1, no. 7 (13 December 1828): 107.

74. *Critic* 1, no. 4 (22 November 1828): 64, 63.

75. *Critic* 1, no. 3 (15 November 1828): 43.

76. *Critic* 1, no. 2 (8 November 1828): 25; *Critic* 1, no. 21 (28 March 1829): 332.

77. *Critic* 1, no. 2 (8 November 1828): 19–20.

78. *Critic* 1, no. 5 (29 November 1828): 65.

79. See Timothy A. Hickman, "'Mania Americana': Narcotic Addiction and Modernity in the United States, 1870–1920," *Journal of American History* 90, no. 4 (March 2004): 1269–94, esp. 1289–93.

80. *Critic* 1, no. 9 (27 December 1828): 138.

81. Allan Nevins, *The Evening Post: A Century of Journalism* (New York: Boni and Liveright, 1922), 141, 132.

82. See Gilmore, "Revolutionary and Early National Periods," 541–57.

83. F. Byrdsall, *The History of the Loco-Foco or Equal Rights Party: Its Movements, Conventions and Proceedings, with Short Characteristic Sketches of Its Prominent Men* (New York: Clement & Packard, 1842), 15.

84. David Reynolds, *Walt Whitman's America: A Cultural Biography* (New York: Alfred A. Knopf, 1995), 67, 100; Kenneth Cmiel, *Democratic Eloquence: The Fight over Popular Speech in Nineteenth-Century America* (New York: William Morrow and Co., 1990), 56–63; Theodore Sedgwick Jr., "Preface," in *A Collection of the Political Writings of William Leggett*, ed. Sedgwick, vol. 1 (New York: Taylor & Dodd, 1840), iii–xvii.

85. John G. Whittier, *Old Portraits and Modern Sketches* (Boston: Ticknor, Reed, and Fields, 1850), 218.

86. Garry Wills, *Lincoln at Gettysburg: The Words That Remade America* (New York: Simon & Schuster, 1992), 148–75.

87. Worton, "William Leggett," 47.

88. Cf. Worton, "William Leggett"; Lester Harvey Rifkin, "William Leggett: Journalist-Philosopher of Agrarian Democracy in New York," *New York History* 32, no. 1 (January 1951): 45–60.

89. *Plaindealer*, 3 December 1836, 1.

90. *Political Writings*, 1:257, 91–92, 103.

91. *Plaindealer*, 3 December 1836, 2.

92. *Political Writings*, 1:127–28, 303, 261–62, 94–95.

93. *Political Writings*, 1:21.

94. Leggett's line is the epigraph for Byrdsall, *Equal Rights Party*, n.p.

95. Bryant, "William Leggett," 19. See Richard Hofstadter, "William Leggett, Spokesman of Jacksonian Democracy," *Political Science Quarterly* 58 (1943): 581–94; Marvin Meyers, "A Free-Trade Version: William Leggett," in *The Jacksonian Persuasion: Politics and Belief* (Stanford, CA: Stanford University Press, 1957), 141–56; John Ashworth, *"Agrarians" and "Aristocrats": Party Political Ideology in the United States, 1837–1846* (London: Royal Historical Society, 1983), 94–97; Sean Wilentz, "Jacksonian Abolitionist: The Conversion of William Leggett," in *The Liberal Persuasion: Arthur Schlesinger Jr. and the Challenge of the American Past*, ed. John Patrick Diggins (Princeton, NJ: Princeton University Press, 1997), 84–106; Steven K. Beckner, "Leggett: Nineteenth-Century Libertarian," *Reason* 8, no. 10 (February 1977): 32–34; Lawrence H. White, "William Leggett: Jacksonian Editorialist as Classical Liberal Political Economist," *History of Political Economy* 18, no. 2 (1986): 307–24.

96. Pasley, *Tyranny of Printers*, 1–23. See also Carol Sue Humphrey, *The Press of the Young Republic, 1783–1833* (Westport, CT: Greenwood Press, 1996).

97. William Leggett, "Leading Publick Opinion," *Plaindealer* (21 January 1837): 113; William Leggett, "A Glimpse of Light in the Right Quarter," *Plaindealer* (24 December 1836): 53–54; cited in Worton, "William Leggett," 300, 304–5.

98. *Evening Post*, 17 December 1834; quoted in Worton, "William Leggett," 302.

99. Frank Luther Mott, *American Journalism: A History of Newspapers in the United States through 250 Years, 1690 to 1940* (New York: Macmillan Co., 1941), 215–16, 241–43; Michael Schudson, *Discovering the News: A Social History of American Newspapers* (New York: Basic Books, 1978), 12–60.

100. Humphrey, *Press of Young Republic*, xiv; Pasley, *Tyranny of Printers*, 2.

101. *Critic* 1, no. 22 (4 April 1829): 355 (emphasis in original).

102. Nevins, *New York Evening Post*, 135–36, 153, 166–67; Hugins, *Jacksonian Democracy*, 38; Arthur Schlesinger Jr., *The Age of Jackson* (Boston: Little, Brown and Co., 1945), 191; William Leggett to Robert Montgomery Bird, New York City, 8 November 1836, Robert Montgomery Bird Papers, Folder 84, University of Pennsylvania, Annenberg Rare Book and Manuscript Library, Special Collections, Van Pelt Library.

103. Alger, *Life of Forrest*, 1:373; William Leggett to Lewis Tappan, New Rochelle, New York, 22 November 1838, Rare Book, Manuscript, and Special Collections Library, Duke University, Call No. Sect. A.

104. *Plaindealer*, 4 February 1837, 149–50.

105. Meredith L. McGill, *American Literature and the Culture of Reprinting, 1834–1853* (Philadelphia: University of Pennsylvania Press, 2003).

106. *Political Writings*, 2:88–90.

107. *Plaindealer*, 10 December 1836, 19–20.

108. *Plaindealer*, 21 January 1837, 116–17; *Plaindealer*, 11 February 1837, 162–64; *Plaindealer*, 25 February 1837, 196–97.

109. Wilentz, *Chants Democratic*, 64–66, 76–77, 219–21; Sumner, "Citizenship," 177, 232–33, 275–75; Edward B. Mittelman, "Trade Unionism," in Commons et al., *History of Labour*, 381–82, 402–10; Dixon Ryan Fox, *The Decline of Aristocracy in the Politics of New York* (New York: Longmans, Green & Co., 1919), 391–93.

110. Byrdsall, *Equal Rights Party*, 26, 27, 46.

111. On the flour riot, see Byrdsall, *Equal Rights Party*, 99–107; *Plaindealer*, 18 February 1837, 190; Joshua R. Greenberg, *Advocating the Man: Masculinity, Organized Labor, and the House-*

hold in New York, 1800–1840 (New York: Columbia University Press, Project Gutenberg, 2006), "Conclusion—The Loco Foco Party"; Burrows and Wallace, *Gotham*, 609–11; J. T. Headley, *The Great Riots of New York, 1712 to 1873* (New York: E. B. Treat, 1873), 97–110.

112. *Plaindealer*, 25 February 1837, 194.

113. On Leggett's abolitionism, see Jonathan H. Earle, *Jacksonian Antislavery and the Politics of Free Soil, 1824–1854* (Chapel Hill: University of North Carolina Press, 2004), 17–26; J. David Greenstone, *The Liberal Persuasion: Remaking American Liberalism* (Princeton, NJ: Princeton University Press, 1993), 124–39; Wilentz, "Jacksonian Abolitionist."

114. Leonard L. Richards, *"Gentlemen of Property and Standing": Anti-Abolition Mobs in Jacksonian America* (New York: Oxford University Press, 1970), 7, 16, 48–52, 62–70, 72–73, 168.

115. *Political Writings*, 1:30, 207–9; *Political Writings*, 2:24, 33–34.

116. *Political Writings*, 2:14, 16. On Leggett's reaction to the abolitionist mails controversy and on his related advocacy of privatizing the postal service, see Richard R. John, *Spreading the News: The American Postal System from Franklin to Morse* (Cambridge, MA: Harvard University Press, 1995), 278, 252–55.

117. *Plaindealer*, 4 March 1837, 213.

118. *Plaindealer*, 24 December 1836, 54.

119. Wilentz, "Jacksonian Abolitionist."

120. *Colored American*, 15 June 1839.

121. *Political Writings*, 1:106.

122. *Plaindealer*, 14 January 1837, 100–101.

123. *Plaindealer*, 4 March 1837, 211.

124. *Political Writings*, 1:83–84, 106, 143; *Plaindealer*, 18 February 1837, 178–79.

125. *Political Writings*, 1:83–84, 106, 143; *Plaindealer*, 14 January 1837, 100–101; *Plaindealer*, 18 February 1837, 178–79; *Plaindealer*, 4 March 1837, 210–13.

126. *Political Writings*, 2:85–86, 87.

127. *Plaindealer*, 10 December 1836, 1.

128. Bray Hammond, *Banks and Politics in America: From the Revolution to the Civil War* (Princeton, NJ: Princeton University Press, 1957), 189.

129. Susan Hoffman, *Politics and Banking: Ideas, Public Policy, and the Creation of Financial Institutions* (Baltimore: Johns Hopkins University Press, 2001), 74–79.

130. *Political Writings*, 1:96, 99.

131. On the range of antibank politics, see Wilentz, *American Democracy*, 207–13, 288. On the pervasive fear of downward mobility among northern workers, see Laurie, "Spavined Ministers," 98–119.

132. *Political Writings*, 1:248; 2:86.

133. *Plaindealer*, 5 August 1837, 564.

134. *Political Writings*, 1:228.

135. *Political Writings*, 1:43.

136. *Political Writings*, 1:101; *Plaindealer*, 29 July 1837, 546.

137. *Plaindealer*, 12 August 1837, 579; *Political Writings*, 1:105.

138. See David Laidler, "Bullionist Controversy," in Eatwell, Milgate, and Newman, *New Palgrave*, 289–93; Lloyd W. Mints, *A History of Banking Theory in Great Britain and the United States* (Chicago: University of Chicago Press, 1945), 5, 9–10; Rogers, *Bills and Notes*, 228–32.

139. *Political Writings*, 1:21.

140. Fritz Redlich, *The Molding of American Banking: Men and Ideas*, part 1 (New York: Hafner Publishing Co., 1947), 10–11; Naomi R. Lamoreaux, *Insider Lending: Banks, Personal Connec-*

tions, and Economic Development in Industrial New England (Cambridge: Cambridge University Press, 1994), 2.

141. William M. Gouge, *A Short History of Paper Money and Banking in the United States* (New York: Augustus M. Kelley, 1968).

142. William Cullen Bryant to Frances F. Bryant, New York, 23 May 1836, in *The Letters of William Cullen Bryant*, vol. 2, ed. William Cullen Bryant II and Thomas G. Voss (New York: Fordham University Press, 1977), 23.

143. Gouge, *Short History*, 118, 41.

144. Gouge, *Short History*, 134.

145. Kellogg, *Labor and Other Capital*, 74.

146. Hugins, *Jacksonian Democracy*, 191.

147. Albert Gallatin, *Considerations on the Currency and Banking System of the United States*, reprinted in *The Writings of Albert Gallatin*, vol. 3, ed. Henry Adams (Philadelphia: J. B. Lippincott, 1879), 267–68.

148. See also Stephen Colwell, *The Ways and Means of Payment: A Full Analysis of the Credit System, with Its Various Modes of Adjustment*, 2nd ed. (Philadelphia: J. B. Lippincott, 1860).

149. On the oversights in the "real bills doctrine," see Laidler, "Bullionist Controversy"; Mints, *Banking Theory*, 30.

Chapter Four

1. Charles Dickens, *American Notes for General Circulation*, 2nd ed., vol. 1 (London: Chapman and Hall, 1842), 234–35, 237–38.

2. On Biddle as a pioneer of central banking, see Fritz Redlich, *The Molding of American Banking: Men and Ideas*, part 1 (New York: Hafner Publishing Co., 1947), 110–61; Richard H. Timberlake, *The Origins of Central Banking in the United States* (Cambridge, MA: Harvard University Press, 1978), 26–41; Bray Hammond, *Banks and Politics in America: From the Revolution to the Civil War* (Princeton, NJ: Princeton University Press, 1957), 286–450; Walter Buckingham Smith, *Economic Aspects of the Second Bank of the United States* (Cambridge, MA: Harvard University Press, 1953); Susan Hoffman, *Politics and Banking: Ideas, Public Policy, and the Creation of Financial Institutions* (Baltimore: Johns Hopkins University Press, 2001), 44–69.

3. Sidney George Fisher, *A Philadelphia Perspective: The Diary of Sidney George Fisher Covering the Years 1834–1871*, ed. Nicholas B. Wainwright (Philadelphia: Historical Society of Pennsylvania, 1967), 154. On the bank war, see Hammond, *Banks and Politics*, 369–450; John M. McFaul, *The Politics of Jacksonian Finance* (Ithaca, NY: Cornell University Press, 1972); Robert V. Remini, *Andrew Jackson and the Bank War: A Study in the Growth of Presidential Power* (New York: W. W. Norton & Co., 1967); Harry L. Watson, *Liberty and Power: The Politics of Jacksonian America* (New York: Hill & Wang, 1990), 132–71; Sean Wilentz, *The Rise of Jeffersonian Democracy: Jefferson to Lincoln* (New York: W. W. Norton & Co., 2005), 205–52, 360–402, 437–64; Daniel Walker Howe, *What Hath God Wrought: The Transformation of America, 1815–1848* (New York: Oxford University Press, 2007), 373–86.

4. Thomas Payne Govan, *Nicholas Biddle: Nationalist and Public Banker, 1786–1844* (Chicago: University of Chicago Press, 1959), 355.

5. *New York Evening Post*, 28 February 1844, in *The Letters of William Cullen Bryant*, vol. 2, *1836–1849*, ed. William Cullen Bryant II and Thomas G. Voss (New York: Fordham University Press, 1977), 214.

6. On Biddle's father, see Charles Biddle, *Autobiography of Charles Biddle, Vice-President*

of the Supreme Executive Council of Pennsylvania, 1745–1821, ed. James S. Biddle (Philadelphia: E. Claxton and Co., 1883). For admiring accounts of Biddle's career, see Govan, *Nicholas Biddle*; and Hammond, *Banks and Politics*, 286–325.

7. Hoffman, *Politics and Banking*, 45.

8. Nicholas Biddle to J. C. Spencer, 27 January 1819, Nicholas Biddle Papers, Library of Congress.

9. On the monetary provisions of the Constitution, see Hammond, *Banks and Politics*, 91–107; James Willard Hurst, *A Legal History of Money in the United States, 1774–1970* (Lincoln: University of Nebraska Press, 1973), 8–9.

10. Albert Gallatin, *Considerations on the Currency and Banking System of the United States*, reprinted in *The Writings of Albert Gallatin*, vol. 3, ed. Henry Adams (Philadelphia: J. B. Lippincott, 1879), 231, 236.

11. On the conflicts over the Bank of England during the so-called Restriction era, ca. 1797–1821, see David Laidler, "Bullionist Controversy," in *The New Palgrave: A Dictionary of Economics*, vol. 1, ed. John Eatwell, Murray Milgate, and Peter Newman (London: Macmillan, 1987), 289–93; Joseph A. Schumpeter, *History of Economic Analysis*, ed. Elizabeth Moody Schumpeter (New York: Oxford University Press, 1954), 688–711.

12. See David M. Henkin, *City Reading: Written Words and Public Spaces in Antebellum New York* (New York: Columbia University Press, 1998), 137–65; and Stephen Mihm, *A Nation of Counterfeiters: Capitalists, Con Men, and the Making of the United States* (Cambridge, MA: Harvard University Press, 2007).

13. Hoffman, *Politics and Banking*, 46.

14. Nicholas Biddle to W. B. Lewis, 15 November 1829, Biddle Papers.

15. Nicholas Biddle to J. C. Spencer, 2 February 1819, Biddle Papers.

16. C. Edward Skeen, *John Armstrong, Jr., 1758–1843: A Biography* (Syracuse, NY: Syracuse University Press, 1981), 8–17.

17. See George A. King, "The French Spoliation Claims," *American Journal of International Law* 6, no. 2 (April 1912): 359–80; Clifford L. Egan, *Neither Peace nor War: Franco-American Relations, 1803–1812* (Baton Rouge: Louisiana University Press, 1983).

18. William Maclure, *To the People of the United States* (Philadelphia: n.p., 1807), 15.

19. Nicholas Biddle to D. B. Warden, 30 June 1812, Biddle Papers.

20. Henry Bartholomew Cox, *The Parisian American: Fulwar Skipwith of Virginia* (Washington, DC: Mount Vernon Publishing Co., 1964), 148–53.

21. Peter Onuf and Nicholas Onuf, *Federal Union, Modern World: The Law of Nations in an Age of Revolutions, 1776–1814* (Madison, WI: Madison House, 1993); Gallatin, *Considerations on Currency*, 236; Eric Hobsbawm, *The Age of Revolution, 1789–1848* (New York: Vintage Books, 1996 [1962]), 109.

22. *Debate in the House of Representatives of Pennsylvania, on Mr. Holgate's Resolutions Relative to the Bank of the United States*, reported by W. Hamilton (Philadelphia: W. Hamilton, 1811), 34–35; Govan, *Nicholas Biddle*.

23. Nicholas Biddle, ed., *Commercial Regulations of the Foreign Countries with Which the United States Have Commercial Intercourse, Collected, Digested and Printed, under the Direction of the President of the United States, Conformably to a Resolution of the Senate, of the Third of March, 1817* (Washington, DC: Gales & Seaton, 1819).

24. Hoffman, *Politics and Banking*, 47. Cf. Timberlake, *Central Banking*, 28.

25. Hoffman, *Politics and Banking*, 50–52; Wilentz, *Rise of Democracy*, 206–7; Timberlake, *Central Banking*, 28.

26. On the economic influence of the bank, see Smith, *Economic Aspects*; and Peter Temin, *The Jacksonian Economy* (New York: W. W. Norton & Co., 1969).

27. Nicholas Biddle to Daniel Webster, 28 June 1831, Biddle Papers.

28. Edgar H. Adams, "Private Gold Coinage," *American Journal of Numismatics* 45 (1911): 129, 134 (emphasis mine).

29. Nicholas Biddle to John White, 3 March 1828, Biddle Papers.

30. Nicholas Biddle to Campbell P. White, 3 February 1823, Biddle Papers.

31. Nicholas Biddle to R. Campbell, president pro tem, Office of District and Department of Savannah, LCP McA MSS 012, Box 6, Folder 231, Bank of the United States Records, Library Company of Philadelphia.

32. Timblerlake, *Central Banking*, 39.

33. See, for example, Nicholas Biddle to J. C. Spencer, 27 January 1819, Biddle Papers.

34. Smith, *Economic Aspects*, 44, 46, 136; Hammond, *Banks and Politics*, 317, 538.

35. Nicholas Biddle to Robert Gilmore, 4 January 1826, Biddle Papers.

36. On the bank's dealings in domestic and foreign exchange, see Nicholas Biddle, *Report of the Proceedings of the Triennial Meeting of the Stockholders of the Bank of the United States* (Philadelphia: n.p., 1831), 13–18; Remini, *Andrew Jackson*, 37. On the bank's broader ties to southern cotton, see Roger G. Kennedy, *Architecture, Men, Women and Money in America, 1600–1860* (New York: Random House, 1985), 266; Smith, *Economic Aspects*, 33, 39–40, 136, 272. On the "financialization of American slavery," see Edward E. Baptist, "Toxic Debt, Collateralized and Securitized Human Beings, and the Panic of 1837," in *Capitalism Takes Command: The Social Transformation of Nineteenth-Century America*, ed. Michael Zakim and Gary J. Kornblith (Chicago: University of Chicago Press, 2012), 69–92, quoted passage at 71; Bonnie Martin, "Slavery's Invisible Engine: Mortgaging Human Property," *Journal of Southern History* 76, no. 4 (November 2010): 817–66.

37. Nicholas Biddle to Albert Gallatin, 29 July 1830, Biddle Papers.

38. Nicholas Biddle to Joseph Hemphill, 26 January 1830, Biddle Papers.

39. Biddle, *Meeting of Stockholders*.

40. Smith, *Economic Aspects*, 44–46.

41. Nicholas Biddle to Samuel Smith, 25 January 1830, Biddle Papers.

42. Nicholas Biddle, *Verses by Nicholas Biddle* (Philadelphia: n.p., 1889), 3, 5, 9. On Robert Bogle and the profession of public waiter, see W. E. B. DuBois, *The Philadelphia Negro: A Social Study* (Philadelphia: University of Pennsylvania Press, 1996 [1899]), 33–35.

43. Jean-Christophe Agnew, *Worlds Apart: The Market and the Theater in Anglo-American Thought, 1550–1750* (Cambridge: Cambridge University Press, 1986), 17–56.

44. Schumpeter, *Economic Analysis*, 277, 282; D. Foley, "Money in Economic Activity," in Eatwell, Newgate, and Milman, *New Palgrave*, 519–25.

45. Hanna Fenichel Pitkin, *The Concept of Representation* (Berkeley: University of California Press, 1967), 85, 35; Edmund S. Morgan, *Inventing the People: The Rise of Popular Sovereignty in England and America* (New York: W. W. Norton & Co., 1988), 39; J. R. Pole, *Political Representation in England and the Origins of the American Republic* (Berkeley: University of California Press, 1966), 4–5; Gaines Post, *Studies in Medieval Legal Thought: Public Law and the State, 1100–1322* (Princeton, NJ: Princeton University Press, 1964), 91–162.

46. See Aristotle's *Politics*, chaps. 9 and 10, but cf. his *Nichomachean Ethics*, chaps. 3–5, in *The Basic Works of Aristotle*, ed. Richard McKeon (New York: Random House, 1941).

47. On the rhetoric of corruption in Pennsylvania and the new nation more generally, see John M. Murrin, "Escaping Perfidious Albion: Federalism, Fear of Aristocracy, and the Democratization of Corruption in Postrevolutionary America," in *Virtue, Corruption and Self-Interest:*

Political Values in the Eighteenth Century, ed. Richard K. Matthews (London: Associated University Presses, 1994), 103–47. On the common concern with corruption on both sides of the bank war, see Major L. Wilson, "The 'Country' versus the 'Court': A Republican Consensus and Party Debate in the Bank War," *Journal of the Early Republic* 15 (Winter 1995): 619–47.

48. Robert E. Wright, *The First Wall Street: Chestnut Street, Philadelphia, and the Birth of American Finance* (Chicago: University of Chicago Press, 2005).

49. Louis Hartz, *Economic Policy and Democratic Thought: Pennsylvania, 1776–1860* (Cambridge, MA: Harvard University Press, 1948), 46.

50. James Willard Hurst, *The Legitimacy of the Business Corporation in the Law of the United States, 1780–1970* (Charlottesville: University Press of Virginia, 1970), 15–16; Hartz, *Economic Policy*, 46, 55, 82.

51. Scott R. Bowman, *The Modern Corporation and American Political Thought: Law, Power, and Ideology* (University Park: Pennsylvania State University Press, 1996), 43–46, 49.

52. Helen L. Sumner, "Citizenship," in John R. Commons et al., *History of Labour in the United States*, vol. 1 (New York: Macmillan Co., 1918), at 176; Wilentz, *Rise of Democracy*, 211–12; Michael Burrage, *Revolution and the Making of the Contemporary Legal Profession* (New York: Oxford University Press, 2006), 231.

53. Gary Nash, "The Philadelphia Bench and Bar, 1800–1861," *Comparative Studies in Society & History* 7, no. 2 (January 1965): 208, 214; Burrage, *Legal Profession*, 226–28, 231, 247–49, 252, 257.

54. Hartz, *Economic Policy*, 72–73.

55. Nicholas B. Wainwright, "Nicholas Biddle in Portraiture," *Antiques* 108 (November 1975): 956–64, quoted passages at 956; Fisher, *Philadelphia Perspective*, 154.

56. Biddle, untitled poem, in *Verses*, 11–14, at 12–13.

57. See Harold Milton Ellis, *Joseph Dennie and His Circle: A Study in American Literature From 1792 to 1812*, Bulletin of the University of Texas No. 40 (Austin: University of Texas, 1915); Ellis Paxson Oberholtzer, *The Literary History of Philadelphia* (Philadelphia: George W. Jacobs & Co., 1906), 168–88; Michael T. Gilmore, "The Literature of the Revolutionary and Early National Periods," in *The Cambridge History of American Literature*, vol. 1, *1590–1820*, ed. Sacvan Bercovitch and Cyrus R. K. Patell (Cambridge: Cambridge University Press, 1994), 539–694, at 558, 567–68.

58. [Biddle], untitled essay, *Port Folio* 4, no. 7 (18 February 1804): 1; [Biddle], untitled essay, *Port Folio* 4, no. 28 (14 July 1804): 1.

59. [Biddle], "Biographical Memoirs of the Late Captain Nicholas Biddle," *Port Folio* 2, no. 4 (October 1809): 285–93.

60. Nicholas Biddle, "On the study of the dead languages," undated essay, Nicholas Biddle Letters, vol. 1, Historical Society of Pennsylvania.

61. Nicholas Biddle, *Nicholas Biddle in Greece: The Journals and Letters*, ed. R. A. McNeal (University Park: Pennsylvania State University Press, 1993), 208, 50–51, 225, 60.

62. Sarah Tapper, "Maple over Mahogany: Nicholas Biddle's Taste in Empire Furniture, 1820–1844" (MA thesis, University of Delaware, 2001), 17–18.

63. Biddle, *Biddle in Greece*, 179.

64. Nicholas Biddle to Richard Rush, 13 October 1815, Biddle Papers; Marcus Tullius Cicero, *De Oratore*, trans. E. W. Sutton (Cambridge, MA: Harvard University Press, 1942), 104–5.

65. [Biddle], "To Readers and Correspondents," *Port Folio* 7, no. 2 (February 1812): 194–96; [Biddle], "To Readers and Correspondents," *Port Folio* 1, no. 6 (June 1813): 633–37.

66. "Philosophical statesman" is from Nicholas Biddle, *Eulogium on Thomas Jefferson* (de-

livered before the American Philosophical Society, 11 April 1827) (Philadelphia: Robert H. Small, 1827), 44.

67. Biddle, *Biddle in Greece*, 195.

68. See Wolf Lepenies, *Melancholy and Society*, trans. Jeremy Gaines and Doris Jones (Cambridge, MA: Harvard University Press, 1992), 31–39; Jennifer Radden, ed., *The Nature of Melancholy: From Aristotle to Kristeva* (New York: Oxford University Press, 2000), 12–13, 15.

69. Nicholas Biddle, *Oration* (delivered before the Pennsylvania State Society of Cincinnati, 4 July 1811) (Philadelphia: C. and A. Conrad and Co., 1811), 14.

70. Nicholas Biddle, *Address* (delivered before the Alumni Association of Nassau-Hall, 30 September 1835) (Princeton, NJ: R. Hornor, 1835), 7.

71. Thanks to David Schorr for his comments on the connections between Biddle and Cole.

72. Meriwether Lewis and William Clark, *History of the Expedition of Captains Lewis and Clark, 104-5-6*, ed. Nicholas Biddle (Chicago: A. C. McClurg & Co., 1902 [1814]), 1:255–56. On Biddle's contribution, see Gunther Barth, "Timeless Journals: Reading Lewis and Clark with Nicholas Biddle's Help," *Pacific Historical Review* 63, no. 4 (November 1994): 499–519; Kris Fresonke, "Introduction," in *Lewis and Clark: Legacies, Memories, and New Perspectives*, ed. Kris Fresonke and Mark Spence (Berkeley: University of California Press, 2004), 2–3; Edward C. Carter II, "Living with Lewis and Clark: The American Philosophical Society's Continuing Relationship with the Corps of Discovery from the Michaux Expedition to the Present," in Fresonke and Spence, *Lewis and Clark*, 26–27. On the literary and cultural significance of Biddle's history, see Bruce Greenfield, *Narrating Discovery: The Romantic Explorer in American Literature, 1790–1855* (New York: Columbia University Press, 1992), 71–81, 84–101; Robert E. Spiller et al., eds., *Literary History of the United States* (New York: Macmillan, 1948), 763.

73. Untitled essay, in Nicholas Biddle Letters, Historical Society of Pennsylvania, 1:36.

74. Biddle, *Oration*, 22.

75. Biddle, "The Address Pronounced on Laying the Corner Stone, July 4, 1833," in Thomas U. Walter, *A Description of the Girard College for Orphans* (contained in a final report of the Building Committee to the Select and Common Councils of Philadelphia) (Philadelphia: n.p., 1848), 21–37, at 21.

76. Stephen A. Larrabee, *Hellas Observed: The American Experience of Greece, 1775–1865* (New York: New York University Press, 1957), 18.

77. Michele Taillon Taylor, "Building for Democracy: Girard College, Political, Educational and Architectural Ideology" (PhD diss., University of Pennsylvania, 1997), 223; Kennedy, *Architecture in America*, 235.

78. On the design of Girard College, see Taylor, "Building for Democracy."

79. Roger G. Kennedy, *Greek Revival America* (New York: Stewart, Tabori and Chang, 1989), 11; Biddle, "Laying the Corner Stone," 27.

80. Taylor, "Building for Democracy," 231.

81. Kennedy, *Architecture in America*, 200, 235.

82. Dimitrios Gkamas, "Banking," in *Encyclopedia of Ancient Greece*, ed. Nigel Wison (New York: Routledge, 2006), 122–23.

83. Kennedy, *Architecture in America*, 20–23.

84. Lewis and Clark, *History of the Expedition*, 284. Not found in the original journals of Lewis and Clark, this phrase was evidently Biddle's.

85. [George Tucker], "On Architecture," *Port Folio* 4, no. 6 (December 1814): 559–69; [Tucker], "On Beauty," *Port Folio* 5, nos. 2–3 (February–March 1815): 148–62, 220–30; [Tucker],

"On Banks of Circulation," *Port Folio* 5, no. 5 (May 1815): 417–28; [Tucker], "On Simplicity in Ornament," *Port Folio* 6, no. 1 (July 1815): 82–91; [Tucker], "On Rhyme," *Port Folio* 6, no. 4 (October 1815): 371–76; [Tucker], "On National Debts," *Port Folio* 6, no. 6 (December 1815): 574–90. On the persona of the hermit in the political discourse of the early American republic, see Coby Dowdell, "The American Hermit and the British Castaway: Voluntary Retreat and Deliberative Democracy in Early American Culture," *Early American Literature* 46, no. 1 (2011): 121–56.

86. B. Henry Latrobe, *Anniversary Oration* (pronounced before the Society of Artists of the United States, 8 May 1811), addendum, *Port Folio 5, no. 6* (June 1811), 20, 17.

87. Bates Lowry, *Building a National Image: Architectural Drawings for the American Democracy, 1789–1912* (Washington, DC: National Building Museum, 1985), 39.

88. Hobsbawm, *Age of Revolution*, 110–11, 116, 140–42.

89. Kennedy, *Architecture and Money*, 224; Kennedy, *Greek Revival*, 3.

90. Caroline Winterer, *The Culture of Classicism: Ancient Greece and Rome in American Intellectual Life, 1780–1910* (Baltimore: Johns Hopkins University Press, 2002), 68–69; Larrabee, *Hellas Observed*, 3–26.

91. Kennedy, *Architecture in America*, 266. See William R. Taylor, *Cavalier and Yankee: The Old South and American National Character* (New York: G. Braziller, 1961).

92. Nicholas Biddle, *An Address Delivered before the Philadelphia Society for Promoting Agriculture*, supplement, *Niles Register* 22 (1822): 9.

93. Biddle, *Society for Promoting Agriculture*, 5.

94. Kennedy, *Architecture and Money*, 247–58.

95. Jeanne Boydston, *Home and Work: Housework, Wages, and the Ideology of Labor in the Early Republic* (New York: Oxford University Press, 1990), 142–63; Raymond Williams, *The Country and the City* (New York: Oxford University Press, 1973), 13–35.

96. See Jennifer Baker, *Securing the Commonwealth: Debt, Speculation, and Writing in the Making of Early America* (Baltimore: Johns Hopkins University Press, 2005); Mark G. Schmeller, *Invisible Sovereign: Imagining Public Opinion from the Revolution to Reconstruction* (Baltimore: Johns Hopkins University Press, 2016).

97. Biddle, *Nassau-Hall*, 10, 12.

98. Nicholas Biddle to John Quincy Adams, 10 December 1838, reprinted in *Poulson's American Daily Advertiser* [n.d.], in Nicholas Biddle Letters, Historical Society of Pennsylvania.

99. Nicholas Biddle to James Monroe, 8 October 1820, in *The Correspondence of Nicholas Biddle Dealing with National Affairs, 1807–1844*, ed. Reginald C. McGrane (Boston: Houghton Mifflin, 1919), 15.

100. Biddle, *Nassau-Hall*, 10.

101. Biddle, *Eulogium on Jefferson*, 47.

102. Biddle, *Nassau-Hall*, 16, 13, 14.

103. Biddle, *Eulogium on Jefferson*, 44.

104. Nicholas Biddle to Thomas Cooper, 8 May 1837, in McGrane, *Correspondence of Biddle*, 278.

105. Govan, *Nicholas Biddle*, 79, 83–84.

106. Nicholas Biddle [addressee missing], 29 October 1822, Biddle Papers.

107. Nicholas Biddle to Cadwallader Evans, 26 January 1830, Biddle Papers.

108. Nicholas Biddle to R. Smith, 5 February 1829, Houghton Library, Harvard University.

109. Nicholas Biddle to Samuel Smith, 29 December 29 1828, Biddle Papers.

110. Biddle to Gallatin, 29 July 1830, Biddle Papers.

111. Nicholas Biddle to Daniel Webster, 16 February 1826, Biddle Papers; Biddle, *Meeting of the Stockholders*, 16.

112. Nicholas Biddle [addressee missing], 29 October 1822, Biddle Papers; Nicholas Biddle to Isaac Laurence, 22 April 1825, Biddle Papers.

113. Nicholas Biddle to P. P. F. Degrand, 8 March 1831, Biddle Papers.

114. Biddle, *Holgate's Resolutions*, 28.

115. Biddle, *Verses*, 9.

116. Hammond, *Banks and Politics*, 440–41, 460–61, 467–68, 531.

117. Hammond, *Banks and Politics*, 502, 513, 518–19, 526; Tapper, "Maple over Mahogany," 10.

118. Fisher, *Philadelphia Perspective*, 154–55.

119. On the architecture of branch banking in recent years, see Mark Kendall, "When Banks Were Banks," *Los Angeles Times*, 11 August 2008.

Chapter Five

1. *Fort Worth Gazette*, 7 November 1883; Wayne Gard, "The Fence-Cutters," *Southwestern Historical Quarterly* 51, no. 1 (July 1947): 1–15; Robert C. McMath Jr., *Populist Vanguard: A History of the Southern Farmers' Alliance* (Chapel Hill: University of North Carolina Press, 1975), 10–11.

2. N. A. Dunning, ed., *The Farmers' Alliance History and Agricultural Digest* (Washington, DC: Alliance Publishing Co., 1891), 13–16; Lawrence Goodwyn, *Democratic Promise: The Populist Moment in America* (New York: Oxford University Press, 1976), 31–34.

3. On the Farmers' Alliance, see Goodwyn, *Democratic Promise*; McMath, *Populist Vanguard*; Donna A. Barnes, *Farmers in Rebellion: The Rise and Fall of the Southern Farmers Alliance and People's Party in Texas* (Austin: University of Texas Press, 1984); Theodore Mitchell, *Political Education in the Southern Farmers' Alliance, 1887–1900* (Madison: University of Wisconsin Press, 1987); Charles Postel, *The Populist Vision* (New York: Oxford University Press, 2007); Bruce Palmer, *"Man over Money": The Southern Populist Critique of American Capitalism* (Chapel Hill: University of North Carolina Press, 1980); Elizabeth Sanders, *Roots of Reform: Farmers, Workers, and the American State, 1877–1917* (Chicago: University of Chicago Press, 1999).

4. On Macune's life prior to joining the alliance, see Charles W. Macune Jr., "The Wellsprings of a Populist: Dr. C. W. Macune before 1886," *Southwestern Historical Quarterly* 90 (July 1986–April 1987), 139–58.

5. Sanders, *Roots of Reform*, 126.

6. McMath, *Populist Vanguard*, 146.

7. [C. W. Macune,] "Send the Story Abroad," *Burnet Bulletin* 3, no. 8 (27 February 1875): 2; Alwyn Barr, *Reconstruction to Reform: Texas Politics, 1876–1906* (Austin: University of Texas Press, 1971), 8–9, 244; Edmund Thornton Miller, "A Financial History of Texas," *Bulletin of the University of Texas* 37 (July 1916): 165–67.

8. Miller, "Financial History," 240–41; J. Mills Thornton III, "Fiscal Policy and the Failure of Radical Reconstruction in the Lower South," in *Region, Race, and Reconstruction: Essays in Honor of C. Vann Woodward*, ed. J. Morgan Kousser and James M. McPherson (New York: Oxford University Press, 1982), 349–94; C. Vann Woodward, *Origins of the New South, 1877–1913* (Baton Rouge: Louisiana State University Press and the Littlefield Fund for Southern History of the University of Texas, 1951), 58–60; Katherine S. Newman and Rourke O'Brien, *Taxing the Poor: Doing Damage to the Truly Disadvantaged* (Berkeley: University of California Press, 2011), 8–9; Alex Mathews Arnett, *The Populist Movement in Georgia: A View of the "Agrarian Crusade"*

in the Light of Solid-South Politics, Studies in History, Economics and Public Law No. 235 (New York: Columbia University, 1922), 72–74.

9. Macune Jr., "Wellsprings of a Populist," 145–49.

10. Macune Jr., "Wellsprings of a Populist," 149–50; Thomas D. Clark, *The Southern Country Editor* (Indianapolis: Bobbs-Merrill Co., 1948), 35.

11. C. W. Macune, "Salutory," *Burnet Bulletin* 2, no. 39 (26 September 1874): 2; *Burnet Bulletin* 2, no. 45 (7 November 1874): 2; *Burnet Bulletin* 2, no. 42 (17 October 1874): 2.

12. *Burnet Bulletin* 3, no. 5 (6 February 1875): 2. On the proslavery origins and regressive effects of "uniformity clauses" in southern tax codes, see Robin L. Einhorn, *American Taxation, American Slavery* (Chicago: University of Chicago Press, 2008), 202–10, 230–50.

13. *Burnet Bulletin* 2, no. 42 (17 October 1874): 2; *Burnet Bulletin* 3, no. 5 (6 February 1875): 2; *Burnet Bulletin* 2, no. 45 (7 November 1874): 2.

14. *Burnet Bulletin* 2, no. 41 (10 October 1874): 2; *Burnet Bulletin* 2, no. 45 (7 November 1874): 2–3.

15. *Burnet Bulletin* 3, no. 5 (6 February 1875): 2.

16. Hill's speech is excerpted at greater length in Edwin de Leon, "The New South: I. Its Agricultural Aspect," *Harper's New Monthly Magazine* (January 1874): 270–81, at 279. For his comments on "bondage to the negro," see E. Merton Coulter, "The New South: Benjamin H. Hill's Speech before the Alumni of the University of Georgia, 1871," *Georgia Historical Quarterly* 57, no. 2 (Summer 1973): 179–99, at 180.

17. De Leon, "New South," 279.

18. De Leon, "New South," 279; Sven Beckert, *Empire of Cotton: A Global History* (New York: Alfred A. Knopf, 2014), 274–311.

19. C. W. Macune, "The Farmers Alliance" (unpublished ms., University of Texas Library Archives, 1920), 7. "It was financialization, not proletarianization, that ushered American agriculture into the Age of Capital." Jonathan Levy, *Freaks of Fortune: The Emerging World of Capitalism and Risk in America* (Cambridge, MA: Harvard University Press, 2012), 158–59.

20. Bonnie Martin, "Slavery's Invisible Engine: Mortgaging Human Property," *Journal of Southern History* 76, no. 4 (2010): 817–66; Roger Ransom and Richard Sutch, "Capitalists without Capital: The Burden of Slavery and the Impact of Emancipation," in *Quantitative Studies in Agrarian History*, ed. Morton Rothstein and Daniel Field (Ames: Iowa State University Press, 1993), 130–57; Edward E. Baptist, "Toxic Debt, Collateralized and Securitized Human Beings, and the Panic of 1837," in *Capitalism Takes Command: The Social Transformation of Nineteenth-Century America*, ed. Michael Zakim and Gary Kornblith (Chicago: University of Chicago Press, 2012), 69–92.

21. Steven Hahn, *The Roots of Southern Populism: Yeoman Farmers and the Transformation of the Georgia Upcountry, 1850–1880* (New York: Oxford University Press, 1983), 190–91; Mitchell, *Political Education*, 27.

22. Harold D. Woodman, *King Cotton and His Retainers: Financing and Marketing the Cotton Crop of the South, 1800–1925* (Columbia: University of South Carolina Press, 1990 [1968]), 313, 346–56; Hahn, *Roots of Populism*, 192.

23. Roger L. Ransom and Richard Sutch, *One Kind of Freedom: The Economic Consequences of Emancipation*, 2nd ed. (Cambridge: Cambridge University Press, 2001), 106–62; Mitchell, *Political Education*, 28–29, 35–38.

24. Macune, "Farmers Alliance," 7.

25. C. W. Macune, Annual Address of the President of the Farmers' Alliance, Shreveport, Louisiana, October 1887, reprinted in Dunning, *Farmers' Alliance History*, 68.

26. Macune Jr., "Wellsprings of a Populist," 153–55.

27. "Farmer Philanthropy," *National Economist* 4, no. 5 (18 October 1890): 75; *National Economist* 3, no. 25 (6 September 1890): 401. Much of what was published in the *National Economist* did not bear an author's name. But as editor of the paper, Macune personally wrote or carefully reviewed and approved everything it printed.

28. *National Economist* 3, no. 12 (7 January 1890): 185.

29. *National Economist* 3, no. 25 (6 September 1890): 401.

30. "Diversify Industries," *National Economist* 2, no. 19 (25 January 1890): 297.

31. Ruth Allen, *Chapters in the History of Organized Labor in Texas* (Austin: University of Texas Publication No. 4143), 19–29; Goodwyn, *Democratic Promise*, 51–53; McMath, *Populist Vanguard*, 22–25.

32. Dunning, *Farmers' Alliance History*, 41–42.

33. "Message of the Acting President," in Dunning, *Farmers' Alliance History*, 49.

34. "Political Economy No. 4," *National Economist* 1, no. 5 (20 April 1889): 67; "Organization," *National Economist* 2, no. 20 (1 February 1890): 312.

35. Macune, "Farmers Alliance," 19.

36. "The Need of the Hour," *National Economist* 1, no. 16 (6 July 1889): 241.

37. Fred A. Shannon, "C. W. Macune and the Farmers' Alliance," *Current History* (June 1955): 330–35; McMath, *Populist Vanguard*, 3, 66–67; "Annual Address of Macune" (1889), 196.

38. Advertisement on one of the unnumbered first pages of the *National Economist Almanac 1890: National Farmers Alliance and Industrial Union Hand-Book* (Washington, DC: National Economist Publishing Co., 1890), n.p.

39. Address to the annual meeting of the Farmers' Alliance at Shreveport, Louisiana, October 1887, in Dunning, *Farmers' Alliance History*, 69–70 (emphasis added). See Ralph A. Smith, "'Macuneism,' or the Farmers of Texas in Business," *Journal of Southern History* 13, no. 2 (May 1947): 220–44.

40. See George Jacob Holyoake, *The History of the Rochdale Pioneers* (London: Swan Sonnenschein & Co., 1893).

41. Victoria Saker Woeste, *The Farmer's Benevolent Trust: Law and Agricultural Cooperation in Industrial America, 1865–1945* (Chapel Hill: University of North Carolina Press, 1998), 8.

42. Joseph G. Knapp, *The Rise of American Cooperative Enterprise: 1620–1920* (Danville, IL: Interstate Printers and Publishers, 1969), 47–49; Woeste, *Farmer's Benevolent Trust*, 21–22.

43. Macune, "Farmers Alliance," 9.

44. Barnes, *Farmers in Rebellion*, 57–59.

45. Stephen L. Piott, *American Reformers, 1870–1920* (Lanham, MD: Rowman & Littlefield, 2006), 48–49.

46. Mitchell, *Political Education*, 63–64; McMath, *Populist Vanguard*, 30–31; Macune, "Farmers Alliance," 24.

47. *Message of President C. W. Macune to the National Farmers Alliance and Co-Operative Union of America, Meridian, Mississippi, December 5th, 1888* (Dallas: Circular Letter Office, December 1888), 11, 13.

48. Barnes, *Farmers in Rebellion*, 81–91; Mitchell, *Political Education*, 64–66.

49. Macune, "Farmers Alliance," 34.

50. "Not That Kind of a Trust," *National Economist* 2, no. 3 (5 October 1889): 40.

51. "Annual Address by President C. W. Macune of the Farmers Alliance and Co-Operative Union of America," St. Louis, 4 December 1889, in *National Economist* 2, no. 13 (14 December 1889): 199.

52. Dunning, *Farmers' Alliance History*, 59.

53. C. W. Macune, "The Purposes of the Farmers' Alliance," in Dunning, *Farmers' Alliance History*, 257–61, at 260, 261.

54. On southern Methodism in the late nineteenth century, see Hunter Dickinson Farish, *The Circuit Rider Dismounts: A Social History of Southern Methodism, 1865–1900* (New York: Da Capo Press, 1969); Emery Stevens Bucke, ed., *The History of American Methodism*, vol. 2 (New York: Abingdon Press, 1964); William Warren Sweet, *Methodism in American History* (New York: Methodist Book Concern, 1933).

55. Postel, *Populist Vision*, 4. On the centrality of education to the alliance, see generally Mitchell, *Political Education*.

56. "History and Government," *National Economist* 2, no. 3 (5 October 1889): 34–36; "History and Government," *National Economist* 2, no. 4 (12 October 1889): 51–53.

57. *National Economist* 4, no. 11 (29 November 1890): 172.

58. "Alliance Education," *National Economist* 4, no. 15 (27 December 1890): 231.

59. *National Economist* 1, no. 1 (14 March 1889): 1.

60. *National Economist* 1, no. 1 (14 March 1889): 1.

61. Rosanne Currarino, *The Labor Question in America: Economic Democracy in the Gilded Age* (Urbana: University of Illinois Press, 2011), 13–15.

62. See Ellen Fitzpatrick, *History's Memory: Writing America's Past, 1880–1980* (Cambridge, MA: Harvard University Press, 2002), 13–50.

63. *National Economist* 1, no. 1 (14 March 1889): 1; "History and Government No. 4," *National Economist* 1, no. 4 (13 April 1889): 60; "History and Government," *National Economist* 2, no. 13 (14 December 1889): 195; *National Economist* 1, no. 12 (8 June 1889): 185.

64. "Political Economy," *National Economist* 1, no. 18 (20 July 1889): 274.

65. "Political Economy," *National Economist* 1, no. 18 (20 July 1889): 274; "Interest and Industry," *National Economist* 1, no. 14 (22 June 1889): 211; "Interest and Its Power," *National Economist* 1, no. 12 (8 June 1889): 188.

66. "Political Economy No. 10," *National Economist* 1, no. 19 (27 July 1889): 291. Cf. Rudolf Hilferding, *Finance Capital: A Study of the Latest Phase of Capitalist Development*, ed. Tom Bottomore, trans. Morris Watnick and Sam Gordon (London: Routledge & Kegan Paul, 1981 [1910]).

67. *National Economist* 1, no. 3 (6 April 1889): 41.

68. *National Economist Almanac*, 10.

69. On antimonopoly ideology among merchants and business owners, see Richard R. John, "Robber Barons Redux: Antimonopoly Reconsidered," *Enterprise and Society* 13 (March 2012): 1–38; Cory Davis, "A Commercial Republic: The National Board of Trade and Political Economy in the Nineteenth-Century U.S." (PhD diss., University of Illinois at Chicago, 2014).

70. See Gretchen Ritter, *Goldbugs and Greenbacks: The Antimonopoly Tradition and the Politics of Finance in America* (Cambridge: Cambridge University Press, 1997).

71. "Political Economy No. 4," *National Economist* 1, no. 20 (3 August 1889): 306; "The Origin and Results of Monopoly," *National Economist* 1, no. 5 (20 April 1889): 67.

72. "Combination," *National Economist* 1, no. 3 (6 April 1889): 33–34.

73. "The Sub-Treasury in the House: Address of Mr. Macune before the Committee on Ways and Means," *National Economist* 3, no. 10 (24 May 1890): 147.

74. "Political Economy No. 4," *National Economist* 1, no. 20 (3 August 1889): 306.

75. "The Key to the Present Policy," *National Economist* 2, no. 16 (4 January 1890): 241.

76. "Investment vs. Hoarding," *National Economist* 1, no. 19 (27 July 1889): 289; "The Money Mystery," *National Economist* 1, no. 8 (11 May 1889): 118.

77. Ritter, *Goldbugs and Greenbacks*, 1, 8, 78. See also Nicolas Barreyre, *Gold and Freedom: The Political Economy of Reconstruction*, trans. Arthur Goldhammer (Charlottesville: University of Virginia Press, 2015), chap. 2.

78. Edward Kellogg, *Labor and Other Capital: The Rights of Each Secured and the Wrongs of Both Eradicated; or, An Exposition of the Cause Why Few Are Wealthy and Many Poor, and the Delineation of a System, Which, without Infringing the Rights of Property, Will Give to Labor Its Just Reward* (New York: Edward Kellogg, 1849). See also Chester McArthur Destler, "The Influence of Edward Kellogg upon American Radicalism, 1865–96," *Journal of Political Economy* 40, no. 3 (June 1932): 338–65; Joseph Dorfman, *The Economic Mind in American Civilization, 1606–1865*, vol. 2 (New York: Viking Press, 1946), 678–80.

79. "History and Government No. 7," *National Economist* 1, no. 7 (4 May 1889): 102.

80. "Financial Reform Address of C. W. Macune, at Tomlinson Hall, Indianapolis, Ind., November 18, 1891," *National Economist* 6, no. 13 (12 December 1891): 198.

81. Henry C. Carey, *Principles of Social Science*, vol. 2 (Philadelphia: J. B. Lippincott Co., 1888 [1858–59]), 345, 343. On Carey's influence on postbellum financial reform, see A. D. H. Kaplan, *Henry Charles Carey: A Study in American Economic Thought* (Baltimore: Johns Hopkins University Press, 1931), 54–81; John Eric Wenzler, "Transcendental Economics: The Quest to Harmonize Economic and Moral Law in Nineteenth-Century American Social Thought" (PhD diss., University of Rochester, 1998), 143–99; Walter T. K. Nugent, *Money and American Society, 1865–1880* (New York: Free Press, 1968), 39–41.

82. Nugent, *Money and American Society*, 6–13; Irwin Unger, *The Greenback Era: A Social and Political History of American Finance, 1865–1879* (Princeton, NJ: Princeton University Press, 1964), 13–40.

83. "The Public Record: Financial Legislation," *National Economist* 5, no. 21 (8 August 1891): 325–26; "The Public Record," *National Economist* 5, no. 22 (15 August 1891): 341; "Investment vs. Hoarding," 289.

84. Alexander Campbell, *The True American System of Finance; the Rights of Labor and Capital, and the Common Sense Way of Doing Justice to the Soldiers and Their Families; No Banks: Greenbacks the Exclusive Currency* (Chicago: Evening Journal Book and Job Print, 1864).

85. "EUREKA! Key to the Solution of the Industrial Problem of the Age," *National Economist* 2, no. 15 (28 December 1889): 225–26.

86. "Sub-Treasury in the House," 147.

87. "EUREKA," 226.

88. "Address of C. W. Macune before the Committee on Agriculture and Forestry of the United States Senate," 22 April 1890 (Washington, DC: National Economist Publishing Co., 1890), 2–5, quoted passage at 4–5.

89. "Silver Coinage," *National Economist* 2, no. 22 (15 February 1890): 337.

90. Cf. Akinobu Kuroda, "What Is the Complementarity among Monies? An Introductory Note" and "Concurrent but Non Integrable Currency Circuits: Complementary Relationships among Monies in Modern China and Other Regions," *Financial History Review* 15, no. 1 (2008): 7–15, 17–36; Viviana Zelizer, "Making Multiple Monies," in Richard Swedberg, *Explorations in Economic Sociology* (New York: Russell Sage Foundation, 1993), 193–212.

91. "EUREKA," 227.

92. "Report of the Committee on the Monetary System," *National Economist* 2, no. 14 (21 December 1889): 216.

93. "Committee on Monetary System," 216; "Sub-Treasury in the House," 145–51.

94. "Committee on Agriculture and Forestry," 16.

95. On the commodity and cotton exchanges, see Beckert, *Empire of Cotton*, 320; Levy, *Freaks of Fortune*, 249–52; William Cronon, *Nature's Metropolis: Chicago and the Great West* (New York: W. W. Norton & Co., 1991), 120.

96. U.S. House of Representatives Committee on Agriculture, *Fictitious Dealings in Agricultural Products*, Hearings on H.R. Bills No. 392, 2699, and 3780 (Washington, DC: Government Printing Office, 1992), 252, 255.

97. "A Review of Modern Political Isms: Anarchism, Socialism, and Communism," *National Economist* 1, no. 11 (1 June 1889): 165–66.

98. P. J. Proudhon, *Proudhon's Solution of the Social Problem*, ed. Henry Cohen (New York: Vanguard Press, 1927), 46, 48, 49, 50–51, 60, 66, 67.

99. "History and Government," *National Economist* 2, no. 13 (14 December 1889): 194.

100. "The Financial Situation," *National Economist* 4, no. 15 (27 December 1890): 230.

101. Sanders, *Roots of Reform*, 173–75, 238–44, 256–59. On the Federal Reserve System and subsequent farm legislation in relation to Macuneite radicalism, see Goodwyn, *Democratic Promise*, 568–69; and Postel, *Populist Vision*, 280–81.

102. "Equivalence of Service," *National Economist* 2, no. 7 (2 November 1889): 97.

103. "Equivalence of Service," 97.

Chapter Six

1. U.S. Department of the Treasury, "History of 'In God We Trust,'" http://www.treasury.gov/about/education/Pages/in-god-we-trust.aspx.

2. See the entry for "fund" in the *Oxford English Dictionary*.

3. G. J. Smith, *History of the Town of Mont Vernon, New Hampshire* (Boston: Blanchard Printing Co., 1907); *The Boston Directory* (Boston: Samson, Davenport & Co., 1870), 167; Frederick Odell Conant, *A History and Genealogy of the Conant Family in England and America*, vol. 1 (Portland, ME: Portland, 1887), 108; John W. Leonard, ed., *Who's Who in New York City and State: A Biographical Dictionary of Contemporaries*, 4th ed., vol. 1 (New York: L. R. Hammersly & Co., 1909), 306; U.S. Federal Censuses for 1850, 1860, 1870, and 1880.

4. "Charles A. Conant," *Bankers' Magazine* 77, no. 6 (December 1908): 886–88, quoted passage at 886.

5. Jane Addams, "The Subjective Necessity for Social Settlements," in Addams, *Twenty Years at Hull-House, with Autobiographical Notes* (New York: Macmillan Co., 1910), 120, 116, 117, 115, 121, 126.

6. Cf. Van Wyck Brooks, *America's Coming-of-Age* (New York: B. W. Huebsch, 1915).

7. Frederick J. Turner, "The Significance of the Frontier in American History," in *Annual Report of the American Historical Association* (1894): 119–227.

8. Thorstein Veblen, *The Theory of the Leisure Class: An Economic Study in the Evolution of Institutions* (New York: Macmillan Co., 1899); Theodore Roosevelt, *The Strenuous Life: Essays and Addresses* (New York: Century Co., 1902), 1–24. On broader turn-of-the-century efforts to overcome the perils of "overcivilization," see T. J. Jackson Lears, *No Place of Grace: Antimodernism and the Transformation of American Culture, 1880–1920* (New York: Pantheon Books, 1981).

9. Reinhart Koselleck, "Crisis," trans. Michaela W. Richter, *Journal of the History of Ideas* 67, no. 2 (April 2006): 357–400.

10. Carroll D. Wright, *Industrial Depressions: The First Annual Report of the U.S. Commissioner of Labor* (Washington, DC: General Printing Office, 1886), 256–57, quoted in Carl Parrini, "Theories of Imperialism," in *Redefining the Past: Essays in Diplomatic History in Honor of Wil-*

liam Appleman Williams, ed. Lloyd C. Gardner (Corvallis: Oregon State University Press, 1986), 65–83, at 67–68; Henry George, *Progress and Poverty: An Inquiry into the Cause of Industrial Depressions and of Increase of Want with Increase of Wealth . . . The Remedy* (New York: Robert Schalkenbach Foundation, 1962 [1879]), 10, 6.

11. See Carl P. Parrini and Martin J. Sklar, "New Thinking about the Market, 1896–1904: Some American Economists on Investment and the Theory of Surplus Capital," *Journal of Economic History* 43, no. 3 (September 1983): 559–78; Martin J. Sklar, *The Corporate Reconstruction of American Capitalism, 1890–1916: The Market, the Law, and Politics* (Cambridge: Cambridge University Press, 1988), 53–57, 64.

12. Conant, "The Economic Basis of Imperialism" [originally published in *North American Review*, (September 1898)], in Conant, *The United States in the Orient: The Nature of the Economic Problem* (Boston: Houghton, Mifflin and Co., 1900), 8; Conant, *A History of Modern Banks of Issue: With an Account of the Economic Crises of the Present Century*, 2nd ed. (New York: G. P. Putnam's Sons, 1896), 461.

13. Conant, *History of Modern Banks*, 460.

14. Conant, "Economic Basis of Imperialism," 3–4, quoted passage at 23–24; Conant, "The Struggle for Commercial Empire" [originally published in *The Forum* (June 1899)], in Conant, *United States in the Orient*, 62; Conant, "Can New Openings Be Found for Capital" [originally published in *Atlantic Monthly* (November 1899)], in Conant, *United States in the Orient*, 92–93; Charles A. Conant, "The Future of Undigested Securities," in Conant, *Wall Street and the Country: A Study of Recent Financial Tendencies* (New York: Greenwood Press, 1968 [1904]), 4–5.

15. Conant, "Struggle for Empire," 62; Conant, "Economic Basis," 19, 16; Conant, "New Openings," 95–96; Conant, *History of Modern Banks*, 464; H. R. Chamberlain, "Farmers' Alliance and Other Political Parties," *Chautauquan: A Monthly Magazine* 13 (April 1891–September 1891): 338–42, quoted passage at 338.

16. Conant, "New Openings," 92–93; Conant, *History of Modern Banks*, 463–64; Conant, "Economic Basis," 9–10.

17. On the related rise of "investmentality" in the nineteenth-century United States, see Eli Cook, *The Pricing of Progress: Economic Indicators and the Capitalization of American Life* (Cambridge, MA: Harvard University Press, 2017).

18. Andrew Carnegie, "The Bugaboo of Trusts," *North American Review* 148, no. 387 (February 1889): 141–50, quoted passages at 141, 142, 150.

19. Andrew Carnegie, "Wealth," *North American Review* 148, no. 391 (June 1889): 653–64, quoted passages at 653, 654, 657, 661–62, 664.

20. Carnegie, "Wealth," 664; Olivier Zunz, *Philanthropy in America: A History* (Princeton, NJ: Princeton University Press, 2011), 8–17; Paul L. Krause, "Patronage and Philanthropy in Industrial America: Andrew Carnegie and the Free Library in Braddock, Pa.," *Western Pennsylvania Historical Magazine* 71, no. 2 (April 1988): 127–45.

21. F. W. Maitland, "Trust and Corporation" (originally published in German in 1904), in Maitland, *State, Trust and Corporation*, ed. David Runciman and Magnus Ryan (Cambridge: Cambridge University Press, 2003), 94; Maitland, "The Unincorporate Body" (originally published in 1911, written between 1901 and 1903), in Maitland, *State, Trust and Corporation*, 52. On the publication history, see the editors' bibliographical notes in Maitland, *State, Trust and Corporation*, xxxv.

22. F. W. Maitland, *Equity, Also the Forms of Action at Common Law: Two Courses of Lectures* (Cambridge: Cambridge University Press, 1909), 23.

23. Peter Charles Hoffer, *The Law's Conscience: Equitable Constitutionalism in America*

(Chapel Hill: University of North Carolina Press, 1990), 8–12, 16; Nancy Buenger, "Extraordinary Remedies: The Court of Chancery and Equitable Justice in Chicago" (PhD diss., University of Chicago, 2009), 1–2, 17–19.

24. Maitland, "Trust and Corporation," 84; Maitland, "Unicorporate Body," 56; James G. Smith, *The Development of Trust Companies in the United States* (New York: Henry Holt and Co., 1928), 214–21. On women's property rights, see also Peggy A. Rabkin, *Fathers to Daughters: The Legal Foundations of Female Emancipation* (Westport, CT: Greenwood Press, 1980); Marylynn Salmon, *Women and the Law of Property in Early America* (Chapel Hill: University of North Carolina Press, 1986).

25. Charles Dickens, *Bleak House* (London: J. M. Dent & Sons, 1907 [1852–53]), 4.

26. Elizabeth Blackmar, "Inheriting Property and Debt: From Family Security to Corporate Accumulation," in *Capitalism Takes Command: The Social Transformation of Nineteenth-Century America*, ed. Michael Zakim and Gary Kornblith (Chicago: University of Chicago Press, 2012), 93–117, quoted passage at 100.

27. Donald Holbrook, *The Boston Trustee* (Boston: Marshall Jones Co., 1937), 5, 9; Peter Dobkin Hall, "What the Merchants Did with Their Money: Charitable and Testamentary Trusts in Massachusetts, 1780–1880," in *Entrepreneurs: The Boston Business Community, 1700–1850*, ed. Conrad Edick Wright and Katheryn P. Viens (Boston: Massachusetts Historical Society, 1997), 365–421, esp. 372–83. See also Noam Maggor, *Brahmin Capitalism: Frontiers of Wealth and Populism in America's First Gilded Age* (Cambridge, MA: Harvard University Press, 2017).

28. Hall, "What Merchants Did," 366; Lawrence M. Friedman, "The Dynastic Trust," *Yale Law Journal* 73, no. 4 (March 1964): 547–92; John H. Langbein, "The Contractarian Basis of the Law of Trusts," *Yale Law Journal* 105 (1995): 625–75, at 629, 637–44.

29. Hall, "What Merchants Did," 383–85; Holbrook, *Boston Trustee*, 5; Emily S. Rosenberg, *Financial Missionaries to the World: The Politics and Culture of Dollar Diplomacy, 1900–1930* (Cambridge, MA: Harvard University Press, 1999).

30. Eliot Jones, *The Trust Problem in the United States* (New York: Macmillan Co., 1926), 1, 4, 19–23. On the problem of "producing scarcity" in the modern oil industry, see Timothy Mitchell, *Carbon Democracy: Political Power in the Age of Oil* (London: Verso, 2011), 39–42.

31. "The New 'Trusts' and the Courts," *Chicago Daily Tribune*, 25 October 1887, 4; Sklar, *Corporate Reconstruction*, 98–104.

32. Jones, *Trust Problem*, 27–28, 44; Sklar, *Corporate Reconstruction*, 49–50; Blackmar, "Inheriting Property," 94–95.

33. "In the eyes of contemporary commentators, . . . the key development in the financial sector during the huge merger movement of 1898–1902 was the rapid rise of the trust companies." Larry Neal, "Trust Companies and Financial Innovation, 1897–1914," *Business History Review* 45, no. 1 (Spring 1971): 35–51, quoted passage at 36–37.

34. George Cator, "Trust Companies in the United States," *Johns Hopkins University Studies in Historical and Political Science*, ser. 20, nos. 5–6 (Baltimore: Johns Hopkins University Press, May–June 1902), 9, 14, 62; Clay Herrick, *Trust Companies: Their Organization, Growth, and Management* (New York: Bankers Publishing Co., 1909), 2, 31, 33, 48; Neal, "Trust Companies," 37–39; Smith, *Trust Companies*, 4, 238.

35. Conant, "Trust Companies," 215, 220–21, 223–24. See also Charles A. Conant, "The Existing Mechanism of the New York Money Market," *Bankers' Magazine* 75, no. 1 (July 1907): 18–28.

36. Charles A. Conant, "The Concentration of Capital in New York, and Those Who Manage It," *Bankers' Magazine* 75, no. 5 (November 1907): 659–66, quoted passage at 659.

37. Ridgely quoted in F. B. Kirkbride and J. E. Sterrett, *The Modern Trust Company: Its Functions and Organization* (New York: Macmillan Co., 1905), v.

38. Herrick, *Trust Companies*, 32.

39. Charles A. Conant, "The New Economic Problems" [originally published as "Recent Economic Tendencies" in *Atlantic Monthly* (June 1900)], in Conant, *United States in the Orient*, 153.

40. Ellen Meiksins Wood, *The Origin of Capitalism* (New York: Monthly Review Press, 1999), 80–86.

41. Ritu Birla, *Stages of Capital: Law, Culture, and Market Governance in Late Colonial India* (Durham, NC: Duke University Press, 2009), 71. See also Julia C. Ott, *When Wall Street Met Main Street: The Quest for an Investors' Democracy* (Cambridge, MA: Harvard University Press, 2011).

42. Conant, "The Trusts and the Public," in Conant, *Wall Street*, 63–64.

43. Conant, "Concentration of Capital," 666.

44. Charles A. Conant, *Principles of Money and Banking*, vol. 2 (New York: Harper & Bros., 1905), 213, 214, 217.

45. Conant, *Principles of Banking*, 2:118.

46. Conant, "Concentration of Capital," 659.

47. Conant, "Undigested Securities," 4.

48. "The theory which attributes crises to conditions of credit and banking inverts cause and effect." Conant, *Principles of Banking*, 2:402.

49. James Livingston, *Origins of the Federal Reserve System: Money, Class, and Corporate Capitalism, 1890–1913* (Ithaca, NY: Cornell University Press, 1986), 72–73.

50. Cf. David Laidler, "Bullionist Controversy," in *The New Palgrave: A Dictionary of Economics*, ed. John Eatwell, Murray Milgate, and Peter Newman (London: Macmillan, 1987), 289–93.

51. Conant, *Principles of Banking*, 1:v.

52. See the distinguished endorsements of Conant's candidacy in an advertisement in the *Cambridge Tribune* (3 November 1894), 1C; coverage of the campaign in "Political Gossip," *Washington Post* (13 October 1894), 4; and "Only One Out of Thirteen: Massachusetts Democrats Not Hopeful of Success," *New York Times* (29 October 1894), 9; and local election results in *Boston Daily Advertiser* (29 November 1894), 2. On the "Gold Democrats" and the Republican landslide of 1894, see Richard Franklin Bensel, *The Political Economy of American Industrialization, 1877–1900* (Cambridge: Cambridge University Press, 2000), 419.

53. Conant, *History of Modern Banks*, v.

54. Charles A. Conant, "The Battle for Currency Reform," *Bankers' Magazine* (March 1908): 326–32; Charles A. Conant, *The Plans for Currency Reform* (New York: Bankers Publishing Co., 1906).

55. Conant, *Principles of Banking*, 2:134–35, 119; Conant, *History of Modern Banks*, 568, 566.

56. Conant, *History of Modern Banks*, 568.

57. Conant, *History of Modern Banks*, 7.

58. Conant, *History of Modern Banks*, 564, ix, 565–66, 572.

59. Conant, *History of Modern Banks*, 7–8, 12, 15; Conant, *Principles of Banking*, 2:20–21, 33.

60. Conant, *Principles of Banking*, 2:187, 197; 1:215.

61. Charles A. Conant, "The Battle for Currency Reform," *Bankers' Magazine* (March 1908): 326–32; Conant, *Plans for Currency Reform*.

62. Conant, *History of Modern Banks*, 13.

63. Conant, *Principles of Banking*, 2:278, 284–85, 290–91; Conant, "Concentration of Capital."

64. Conant, *Principles of Banking*, 2:232–33.

65. Conant, "Battle for Currency Reform"; Livingston, *Origins of the Federal Reserve*, 172–73.

66. [Conant,] "A Central Bank of Issue," *Wall Street Journal*, 22 September 1909, 9 October 1909, 16 October 1909, and 23 October 1909, 1. (Each article in the series begins on the front page.)

67. Livingston, *Origins of the Federal Reserve*, 228. See also Elizabeth Sanders, *Roots of Reform: Farmers, Workers, and the American State, 1877–1917* (Chicago: University of Chicago Press, 1999), 238, 257, 266.

68. Conant, "The Functions of Centralized Banking," *Bankers' Magazine* 89 (October 1914): 388–90, quoted passage at 388.

69. Parrini and Sklar, "New Thinking," 571; Conant, *Principles of Banking*, 1:192–93.

70. Keynes, *Treatise on Money*, 2:292.

71. *American Ideals: Address of Charles A. Conant, of Boston, at Winchester, Mass., on Memorial Day, May 30, 1900* (Washington, DC: Gibson Bros., 1900), 7, 8, 12.

72. Sklar, *Corporate Reconstruction*, 79–81; Rosenberg, *Financial Missionaries*, 24–25, 27.

73. Conant, *United States in the Orient*, v.

74. Maitland, "Trust and Corporation," 127.

75. Buenger, "Extraordinary Remedies," 138–47.

76. Conant, "New Openings for Capital," 114.

77. Conant, "Commercial Empire," 73; Conant, "Economic Basis of Imperialism," 25–26.

78. Conant, "Economic Basis of Imperialism," 27–28; Conant, "New Openings for Capital," 97–98; Conant, "Commercial Empire," 79; Conant, "The United States as a World Power—Nature of the Economic and Political Problem" [originally published in *The Forum*, (July 1900)], in *United States in the Orient*, 172–73; Conant, *Principles of Banking*, 2:181–82; Conant, "The Economic Benefits of Investments Abroad," *Bankers' Magazine* 74, no. 5 (May 1907): 699–705, quoted passage at 699.

79. Conant, "New Openings for Capital," 112.

80. Charles A. Conant, *Coinage and Banking in the Philippine Islands: A Special Report Made to the Secretary of War* (Washington, DC: Government Printing Office, 1901), 64.

81. Charles A. Conant, "The Way to Attain and Maintain Monetary Reform in Latin-America," *Annals of the American Academy of Political and Social Science* 37, no. 3 (1 January 1911): 40–49, quoted passage at 40.

82. Rosenberg, *Financial Missionaries*, 15; Parrini, "Theories of Imperialism," 72. See also Carl Parrini, "Charles A. Conant, Economic Crises and Foreign Policy, 1896–1903," in *Behind the Throne: Servants of Power to Imperial Presidents, 1898–1968*, ed. Thomas J. McCormick and Walter LaFeber (Madison: University of Wisconsin Press, 1993), 35–59.

83. "His almost visionary faith in the gold-exchange standard as the magic key to an integrated progressive order gave his work a decidedly nineteenth-century cast." Rosenberg, *Financial Missionaries*, 24.

84. Conant, "Monetary Reform in Latin-America," 41; Charles A. Conant, "The Gold Exchange Standard in the Light of Experience," *Economic Journal* 19, no. 74 (June 1909): 190–200, quoted passages at 190, 200. On the gold-exchange system in India, see John Maynard Keynes's first book, *Indian Currency and Finance* (London: Macmillan, 1913), 15–36. The University of Chicago economist J. Laurence Laughlin proposed essentially the same system for the Dominican Republic in the 1890s. See Cyrus Veeser, *A World Safe for Capitalism: Dollar Diplomacy and America's Rise to Global Power* (New York: Columbia University Press, 2002), 70–72, 194.

85. Charles A. Conant, *The Future of the Limping Standard* (Boston: Ginn & Co., 1903), 216.

86. Thomas J. Sargent and François R. Velde, *The Big Problem of Small Change* (Princeton, NJ: Princeton University Press, 2002), 4.

87. Karl Polanyi, *The Great Transformation* (New York: Rinehart & Co. 1944), 25.

88. Barry Eichengreen and Marc Flandreau, "Introduction," in *The Gold Standard in Theory and History*, ed. Eichengreen and Flandreau, 2nd ed. (New York: Routledge, 1997), 3–7; Jeffry A. Frieden, "The Dynamics of International Monetary Systems: International and Domestic Factors in the Rise, Reign, and Demise of the Classical Gold Standard," in Eichengreen and Flandreau, *Gold Standard*, 207–27, at 214–18.

89. Conant, *Limping Standard*, 216; Léon Walras, *Théorie de la Monnaie* (Lausanne: Corbaz & Co., 1886); *Report of the Monetary Commission of the Indianapolis Convention of Boards of Trade, Chambers of Commerce, Commercial Clubs, and Other Similar Bodies of the United States* (Chicago: University of Chicago Press, 1898), 113; Sargent and Velde, *Small Change*, 3–5, 308–9; Carlo M. Cipolla, *Money, Prices, and Civilization in the Mediterranean World: Fifth to Seventeenth Century* (Princeton, NJ: Princeton University Press, 1956), 27.

90. See Dennis O. Flynn and Arturo Giráldez, "Born with a 'Silver Spoon': The Origins of World Trade in 1571," *Journal of World History* 6, no. 2 (1995): 201–21.

91. Willem G. Wolters, "From Silver Currency to the Gold Standard in the Philippine Islands," *Philippine Studies* 51, no. 3 (2003): 375–404, at 378–80.

92. Charles A. Conant, "Putting China on the Gold Standard," in Conant, *Wall Street*, 201–2.

93. Conant, *Coinage and Banking*, 16; Conant, "Putting China on Gold," 201.

94. Allan E. S. Lumba, "Imperial Standards: Colonial Currencies, Racial Capacities, and Economic Knowledge during the Philippine-American War," *Diplomatic History* 39, no. 4 (September 2015): 603–28; Rosenberg, *Financial Missionaries*, 15; Wolters, "From Silver to Gold," 382, 394–95.

95. Charles A. Conant, "The Currency of the Philippine Islands," *Annals of the American Academy of Political and Social Science* 20, no. 3 (November 1902): 44–59, quoted passage at 44.

96. Conant, *Coinage and Banking*, 10.

97. Conant, "Limping Standard," 232–33; Conant, "Gold in Light of Experience," 200.

98. Conant, *Coinage and Banking*, 5–6, 25–27; Conant, "Monetary Reform in Latin-America," 42, 45.

99. Conant, *Coinage and Banking*, 20; Conant, "Limping Standard," 216.

100. Lumba, "Imperial Standards," 15.

101. "Charles A. Conant Dies in Havana," *New York Times*, 7 July 1915, 11.

102. Thomas L. Haskell, "Capitalism and the Origins of the Humanitarian Sensibility," in *The Antislavery Debate: Capitalism and Abolitionism as a Problem in Historical Interpretation*, ed. Thomas Bender (Berkeley: University of California Press, 1992), 144 (first presented at the Institute for Advanced Study in 1979); Stephen Mihm, *A Nation of Counterfeiters: Capitalists, Con Men, and the Making of the United States* (Cambridge, MA: Harvard University Press, 2007), 10–11.

103. "The Giant Pool of Money," from *This American Life* (episode 355; 9 May 2008); http://www.thisamericanlife.org/radio-archives/episode/355/the-giant-pool-of-money. On the proliferation of investment trusts, see John H. Langbein, "The Secret Life of the Trust: The Trust as an Instrument of Commerce," *Yale Law Journal* 107 (1997–98): 165–89, at 189; Herbert B. Chermside Jr., "Annotation: Modern Status of the Massachusetts or Business Trust," *American Law Reports*, 3rd ser., 88 (1978): 704–88.

Conclusion

1. Herman Melville, *Moby-Dick*, ed. Hershel Parker and Harrison Hayford, 2nd ed. (New York: W. W. Norton & Co., 2002), 103, 332. First mentioned in chapter 36, "The Quarter-Deck," the coin forms the centerpiece of chapter 99, "The Doubloon."

2. Melville, *Moby-Dick*, 332, 333, 335, 139.

3. Hershel Parker, "Damned by Dollars: *Moby-Dick* and the Price of Genius," in Melville, *Moby-Dick*, 713–24, quoted passage at 713.

4. See chapter 89, "Fast-Fish and Loose-Fish."

5. Melville, *Moby-Dick*, 335.

6. R. G. Collingwood, *Essay on Metaphysics*, rev. ed. (Oxford: Oxford University Press, 1998 [1940]), 21–33, definition at 27.

7. *A Letter to An Eminent Clergy-Man in the Massachusetts Bay. Containing some Just Remarks, and necessary Cautions, relating to Publick Affairs in that Province* (Boston: n.p., 1720), 5.

8. *Letter to Clergy-Man*, 5.

9. William Douglass, *A Second Letter to —— Merchant in London, Concerning a late Combination in the* Massachusetts-Bay *in* New-England, *to impose or force a private Currency, called* Land Bank Money (Boston, n.p., 1741), 9–10.

10. Louis Demblitz Brandeis, *Other People's Money: And How the Bankers Use It* (New York: F. A. Stokes, 1914); Franklin D. Roosevelt, Acceptance Speech for Renomination, June 27, 1936, in *The Most Important Speeches of America's Presidents, from George Washington to Barack Obama*, ed. Michael Waldman (Naperville, IL: Sourcebooks, 2010), 106.

11. Elizabeth Sanders, *Roots of Reform: Farmers, Workers, and the American State, 1877–1917* (Chicago: University of Chicago Press, 1999), 259.

12. Steve Fraser, "The Labor Question," in *The Rise and Fall of the New Deal Order, 1930–1980*, ed. Steve Fraser and Gary Gerstle (Princeton, NJ: Princeton University Press, 1989), 57.

13. Angela Redish, "Anchors Aweigh: The Transition from Commodity Money to Fiat Money in Western Economies," *Canadian Journal of Economics* 26, no. 4 (November 1993): 777–95.

14. See Jeffrey Sklansky, "Marxism in the Age of Financial Crises: Why Conventional Economics Can't Explain the Great Recession," *New Labor Forum* 21, no. 3 (Fall 2012): 49–56; John Bellamy Foster and Fred Magdoff, *The Great Financial Crisis: Causes and Consequences* (New York: Monthly Review Press, 2009).

15. Paul Vigna and Michael J. Casey, *The Age of Cryptocurrency: How Bitcoin and the Blockchain Are Challenging the Global Economic Order* (New York: St. Martin's Press, 2015), 99–102; Nigel Dodd, *The Social Life of Money* (Princeton, NJ: Princeton University Press, 2014), 378–79.

16. Peter North, *Money and Liberation: The Micropolitics of Alternative Currency Movements* (Minneapolis: University of Minnesota Press, 2007); Katie Gilbert, "Why Local Currencies Could Be on the Rise in the U.S.—and Why It Matters," *Forbes* (22 September 2014), http://onforb.es/1B1Gu5L.

17. Dodd, *Social Life*, 314–16.

18. Vigna and Casey, *Age of Cryptocurrency*, 278, 5.

19. North, *Money and Liberation*, xiv.

20. Mary Mellor, *Debt or Democracy: Public Money for Sustainability and Social Justice* (London: Pluto Press, 2016), 12, 193.

21. Jerome Roos, "In Each Other We Trust: Coining Alternatives to Capitalism," *ROAR Magazine* (31 March 2014), https://roarmag.org/essays/money lab-conference-alternative-currencies/.

22. Randy Martin, *Financialization of Daily Life* (Philadelphia: Temple University Press, 2002); Maurizio Lazzarato, *The Making of the Indebted Man: An Essay on the Neoliberal Condition* (Amsterdam: Semiotext(e), 2012); Keith Hart, *Money in an Unequal World: Keith Hart and His Memory Bank* (London: Texere, 2000), 4. See also David Birch, *Identity is the New Money* (London: London Publishing Partnership, 2014).

23. Amicus Patriæ [John Wise], *A Word of Comfort to a Melancholy Country. Or the Bank of Credit Erected in the Massachusetts-Bay, Fairly Defended by a Discovery of the Great Benefit, accruing by it to the Whole PROVINCE; With a Remedy for Recovering a Civil State when Sinking under Desperation by Defeat on their Bank of Credit* (Boston, 1721), 54–55.

24. William M. Gouge, *A Short History of Paper Money and Banking in the United States* (New York: Augustus M. Kelley, 1968), 134.

25. Nicholas Biddle to James Monroe, 8 October 1820, in Reginald C. McGrane, ed., *The Correspondence of Nicholas Biddle Dealing with National Affairs, 1807–1844* (Boston: Houghton Mifflin, 1919), 15; Meriwether Lewis and William Clark, *History of the Expedition of Captains Lewis and Clark, 104-5-6*, ed. Nicholas Biddle (Chicago: A. C. McClurg & Co., 1902 [1814]), 284.

26. "Address of C. W. Macune before the Committee on Agriculture and Forestry of the United States Senate," 22 April 1890 (Washington, DC: National Economist Publishing Co., 1890), 16.

27. On the "dangerous fantasy of apolitical money," see Yanis Varoufakis, *And the Weak Suffer What They Must? Europe's Crisis and America's Economic Future* (New York: Nation Books, 2016), 91.

Index